THE TRUMAN PRESIDENCY:
THE ORIGINS OF THE
IMPERIAL PRESIDENCY AND THE
NATIONAL SECURITY STATE

Other Titles on U.S. Presidents:

THE TRUMAN PRESIDENCY:

THE ORIGINS OF THE IMPERIAL PRESIDENCY AND THE NATIONAL SECURITY STATE

Edited with Commentary
and Introduction by

Athan G. Theoharis

Professor of History, Marquette University

Earl M. Coleman Enterprises, Inc., Publishers
Stanfordville, New York • 1979

Library of Congress Cataloging in Publication Data

Theoharis, Athan G.
  The Truman presidency.

  Includes index.
    1. Internal security—United States.   2. Executive
privilege (Government information)—United States.
3. United States—National security.   4. United
States—Politics and government—1945-1953.
5. Truman, Harry S., Pres. U.S., 1884-1972.
I. Title.
JK734.T53   353.03′2   79-4073
ISBN 0-930576-12-8

To my father,
an unassimilated Greek shepherd,
who tolerated neither cant nor indifference to principle

TABLE OF CONTENTS

for presidential commission, White
House consideration of rescission of
1946 directive, McGrath's 1952
directive.

Custodial Detention and Security Index,
the Department's Portfolio of 1948, the
Internal Security Act of 1950, Administration efforts to amend the 1950 Act
and decision to ignore its provisions.

The Justice Department's internal security proposals of 1947 and 1949, the
Justice Department's alien detention
bill, a White House attempt to control
the Justice Department, the Justice Department's legislative program of 1950-
1952 - immunity, wiretapping, denial of
bail, official secrets.

FBI political reports to the White House,
FBI leaks to the media, FBI leaks to the
Congress - the FBI/HUAC (Nixon) rela-
tionship.

Herbert Hoover, Dennis v. U.S.

Internal Security Act of 1950, H.R. 3899

List of Documents by Title

INTRODUCTION

In the aftermath of the Watergate Affair of 1972-1973 and the subsequent congressional disclosures of the federal intelligence agencies' abuses of power during 1975-1976, there occurred a parallel public response aptly described by *Time* magazine as "Trumania in the '70's." Reacting emotionally to Richard Nixon's secretive presidency, his arrogant conceptions of Presidential powers and his attendant disdain for the press and democratic politics, Americans discovered a "folk hero" in Harry Truman. Merle Miller's frankly partisan interviews with Truman, *Plain Speaking*, sold 2½ million copies while thousands queued up outside playhouses for the opportunity to view the even more partisan theatrical play on Truman's career, *Give 'Em Hell Harry* - soon adapted for television. "Vote Truman in '48" campaign buttons sold for $150 at antique stores; t-shirts were printed carrying the message "America Needs You Harry Truman"; and the incumbent Republican President Gerald Ford sought to capitalize on this Trumania by publicly praising Truman's presidency, attempting to portray his own presidency in Trumanesque terms (projecting an image of accessibility and simplicity to the extent of allowing photographers to capture the President making his own breakfast), and encouraging the media to report and photograph the fact that he maintained a bust of Truman in the Oval Office.

This Truman nostalgia, ironically, bore little relationship to the contemporary image of Truman's presidency and leadership abilities. Acceding to the presidency on April 12, 1945 with the sudden, and unexpected death of the popular Franklin Roosevelt. Truman conceded his inadequacies to deal with the complex and overwhelming responsibilities of the office. Commenting to reporters that he thought that the "heaven and the earth" had fallen on him, asking the public for their prayers and support, an ill-prepared but personally appealing Harry Truman in early 1945 commanded widespread sympathy. Conservatives hoped that this conventional politician from Missouri would abandon the New Deal and Roosevelt's activist style of presidential leadership while liberals hoped he would be a more adequate and liberal president than they had reason to expect on the basis of his record. More important, this was a time of crisis - the war had yet to be won, a peace forged, and a myriad of decisions had yet to be made to convert to a peacetime economy and at the same time avert an expected depression.

This sympathy and these hopes quickly dissipated. Truman's initial months in office proved disastrous and successfully alienated groups across the political spectrum. Vacillating only to act and then to reverse himself as suddenly, Truman conveyed an image which Republican politicians capitalized upon during the 1946 congressional elections - "To Err is Truman." Exploiting this antipathy to Truman's inept leadership, Republican campaign literature appealed to Americans to repudiate the Democratic Party of Harry Truman through such slogans as "Had Enough? Vote Republican" or "Under Truman, Two Families in Every Garage."

As a partial consequence of Truman's ineptness and unpopularity, Republican candidates swept the 1946 congressional elections to gain control of both houses of Congress for the first time since 1930 (commanding majorities of 245-188 in the House and 51-45 in the Senate). Those elected for the first time in 1946 included Congressman Richard Nixon and Senator Joseph McCarthy. The Republican congressional leadership, however, interpreted the 1946 election results not as a repudiation of Truman's indecisive and incompetent leadership but as a popular mandate to repeal the New Deal. This erroneous assessment, and the Republican 80th Congress resultant legislative actions, provided the basis for the temporary recovery in Truman's political fortunes. Adopting the mantle of liberalism, exercising the presidential veto either to repulse this conservative Republican assault on New Deal policies or in an effort to influence public opinion and the postwar debate, Truman succeeded in making the record of the Republican 80th Congress (as he described it the "do nothing," "reactionary" 80th Congress) the issue in the 1948 presidential campaign and to execute one of the most stunning political upsets in American political history, winning the presidency in his own right in 1948.

Despite this dramatic victory, Truman's political fortunes soon plummeted again, reaching the low point of popularity in November, 1951 when only 23% of the public expressed a favorable rating of his presidential leadership. (This 23% rating has since become the benchmark used by columnists and pollsters to assess presidential unpopularity - even the discredited Richard Nixon left the presidency, perhaps barely in time, with a slightly higher approval rating.) Contributing to this decline in public esteem were a host of issues other than the vacillating and temporizing leadership of Truman's early presidency. After 1948, a series of scandals surfaced to raise public doubts about Truman's abilities. On the one hand, the press and Congress highlighted those cases wherein Justice Department, Reconstruction Finance Corporation (RFC), Internal Revenue Service, and White House staff officials had used their official positions for personal gain. The most controversial of these involved White House aide Harry Vaughan's role in securing a deep freeze for the President (and other prominent Administration officials) and the 5% scandals involving the RFC (in one case, the wife of an RFC official received

a mink coat from a company executive in return for favorable action on a RFC loan request). "Deep freezes" and "mink coats" -
these became important political symbols effectively exploited by
Republican candidates during the 1952 national elections when cam-
paigning on the theme of "Time for a Change."

A far more powerful issue than corruption, however, was that
of national security policy. Concerns about the adequacy of the
Truman Administration's conduct of foreign affairs and internal
security contributed significantly to the plummet in Truman's popularity and the prevalent conception in the early 1950s of Truman's
incompetence. Dramatically raised by Senator Joseph McCarthy in
his now-infamous Wheeling (West Virginia) speech of February, 1950
and adopted enthusiastically by Republican partisans thereafter,
the charge of "Communists in the State Department," and in 1952
"Twenty Years of Treason," became the issue dominating the national political debate of the 1950s. McCarthy, and the McCarthyites,
offered a simplistic explanation for the international crisis confronting American society in the 1950s and the frustration of
postwar hopes for a permanent and just peace: the Administration's "softness toward communism" abroad and at home had made
possible the expansion of Soviet power and influence and the resultant Cold War. According to this scenario, because Communists
or Communist sympathizers had secured high positions in the federal bureaucracy, they were able to influence crucial Administration decisions which undermined American interest whether the
"sell-out" and "betrayal" of Eastern Europe and China at the
Tehran, Yalta, and Potsdam conferences; the shackling of the FBI
and the stymieing of a needed congressional inquiry into federal
loyalty procedures; or the disastrous "limited war" strategy for
waging the Korean War and resultant dismissal in April, 1951 of
the military hero General Douglas MacArthur (who alone promised
a strategy of victory).

The point to be emphasized is not that contemporary and recent
Americans judged Harry Truman differently or that one judgment
was fairer or more appropriate. The resurgency of Truman's popularity in the 1970s was not based on more scholarly or objective
analyses of Truman's presidency. Rather, Truman's new popularity
derived from his more attractive personality - his forthright manner, simplicity, lack of pretense and accessibility. These
qualities contrasted favorably with Richard Nixon's contrary
style. To a public personally betrayed by Richard Nixon's lies
but yet committed to the concept of strong, dynamic leadership,
the apparent decisiveness of Truman's presidency (captured by the
plaque on his desk "the buck stops here"), and Truman's willingness
to hold regular press conferences and not hide in the Oval Office
or simply refuse to hold press conferences, made his a particularly attractive presidency.

Ironically, however, the very issues which had surfaced to
undermine Nixon's credibility and which ultimately led to his
resignation in disgrace, thus providing the basis in the 1970s
for this ambivalent reaction of anti-Nixon revulsion yet continued
quest for principled and dynamic leadership, had their antecedents
in the Truman years. This is not to say that the Truman presidency either paved the way for Richard Nixon's abuses of power or
that we can trace the "road to Watergate" back to Truman's presidency. Rather, the institutional developments transforming the

office of the presidency and the role of the intelligence bureaucracy (defined loosely as the "Imperial Presidency" and the "National Security State"*) which combined to make possible the
Watergate Affair of 1972-1974 and the earlier, more serious
abuses of power of the federal intelligence agenices, publicized
by the Church and Pike Committees in 1975-1976, had their origins during the Truman years. There is, indeed, a striking
parallel between the Nixon and the Truman presidencies ranging
from the political uses of the intelligence agencies, the authorization of illegal programs and investigative activities, claims
of inherent powers and executive privilege to a globalist inter-
ventionst foreign policy based on a domino theory rationale and
initiated unilaterally and secretively by the White House, the
radical expansion of the intelligence agencies' power and authority, impoundment, and even opposition to the principles that the
official papers of the nation's leaders are and ought to be public
property and that the Congress has the responsibility to investigate and disclose abuses of power by executive officials. For
those having a detailed knowledge of the Nixon years, the documents reprinted in this volume on the Truman presidency will undoubtedly elicit a sense of *déjà vu*.

Thus, although the term was formally coined only during
Eisenhower's Administration, "executive privilege" claims originated during Truman's presidency. As Raoul Berger convincingly
demonstrates in his magisterial study *Executive Privilege: A
Constitutional Myth*, the presidential claim to an "uncontrolled
discretion" to withhold information from the Congress lacked
either a constitutional basis or pre-nineteenth century precedent.
Berger locates the specific origin of the "myth" during Eisenhower's presidency; in fact, however, the first such expansive
and unprecedented claims originated during Truman's presidency
(see Section IIA). Although more restrained in practice than was
the case under Eisenhower, Truman and his legal advisers fran-
tically sought to create a historical precedent for a quest for
secrecy which was based on distinct political criteria: to preclude a searching and potentially effective congressional scrutiny of executive politics. (Ironically, Truman's first such
claimed right, refusing a 1948 request for the loyalty files of
Bureau of Standards Director Edward Condon, was assailed by then
Congressman Richard Nixon as effectively immunizing federal officials and thereby making possible abuses of power or political
corruption.) More important than the mere claim, Truman's transformation of the office of the presidency to centralize power in
the White House [whether the Bureau of the Budget's legislative

---

*These terms - Imperial Presidency and National Security
State - were popularized during the early 1970s by historians
Arthur Schlesinger, Jr. and Daniel Yergin. In his study, aptly
titled *The Imperial Presidency*, Schlesinger chronicles the expansion of presidential powers reaching imperial dimensions during
Nixon's tenure in office. In contrast, Yergin's study *Shattered
Peace* charts the expansion of the powers of the "national security" bureaucracy as the direct product of the onset of the Cold
War. Involved here were radical institutional changes and an
equally radical change in popular attitudes toward centralized
power.

clearance role (see Section IA) or the White House staff's and
the National Security Council's assumption of those policy-
formulation and advisory roles formerly the province of Cabinet
officials (see Sections IA and IB)], had made "executive privilege"
claims an effective means to check congressional oversight.
Cabinet officials might still be required to testify before congressional committees - having been confirmed and their departments having been created by the Congress. This potential leverage of the Congress, carrying with it the risk of exposure, was
significantly undermined when executive decisions were increasingly determined by presidential appointees - whether the NSC Executive Secretary, the Special Counsel to the President, or the
Bureau of the Budget's legislative clearance staff.

As importantly, and in instances contrary to provisions of
law, the role and authority of the federal intelligence agencies
expanded drastically during the Truman years (see Sections IIIA2
and IIIB). Whether because of their elitist conviction that the
public and the Congress lacked the expertise and/or foresight essential to making a judgment on policy or their alarmist fears of
Soviet objectives and subversion, increasingly Truman Administration officials turned to the intelligence bureaucracy to formulate and implement "national security" policy. In time, then,
the role of the CIA altered from an agency which collected and
coordinated intelligence to one which conducted psychological
warfare, covert operations, and even initiated an illegal mail
program in New York City (see Section III A 2). A disdain for the
law similarly led to the authorization of an illegal international
interception program by the ASA and its successor the NSA (see
Section III A 2). The NSC's role evolved equally dramatically,
to the point wherein it displaced the Department of State as the
principal advisory and policy-planning institution in the foreign
policy area - in the process minimizing an earlier reliance on
diplomacy and maximizing the importance of military strength and
technology (see Section I B). The most dramatic and fearful
change, however, involved the role and authority of the FBI.
During the Truman years, the FBI's authority expanded radically,
often without careful review and direction from the President, to
the point where the Bureau under its ambitious director J. Edgar
Hoover had become an independent secret police force. By 1952
FBI officials effectively determined the Bureau's authority and
guidelines (see Sections IIIB1, 2, 3, and 4). FBI investigations, moreover, had become highly politicized to the point where
FBI officials, through carefully orchestrated leaks, actively
sought to shape congressional and public opinion (see Section
IIIB6). At times voluntarily and at times in response to White
House requests, the FBI also served the partisan interests of the
incumbent Administration.

The Truman years, then, witnessed two fundamental developments
warranting the description of Truman's as a formative presidency
- the evolution of an Imperial Presidency and of a National Security State. No longer were presidents and intelligence bureaucrats accountable to the Congress and the public; their authority,
moreover, derived not from the law, but from independently-
reached judgments about the president's "constitutional" powers,
and was based on the conviction that the "national security" required immediate and effective action. Former FBI Assistant

Director William Sullivan's executive session testimony of November, 1975 before the Senate Select Committee on Intelligence Activities graphically captures this mind-set:

> During the ten years that I was on the U.S. Intelligence Board, . . . never once did I hear anybody, including myself, raise the question: "Is this course of action which we have agreed upon lawful, is it legal, is it ethical or moral?" We never gave any thought to this realm of questioning, because we were just naturally pragmatists. The one thing we were concerned about was this: will this course of action work will it get us what we want, will we reach the objective we desire to reach.

The legacies of Truman's Administration, accordingly, continue to shape national politics and society today, and constitute the basis for what came to be recognized only in the 1970s as a serious constitutional crisis. A secretive, quasi-independent presidency, indifferent to the law or the limitations imposed by the Constitution, had been able to employ "national security" and "executive privilege" claims to further essentially conservative policy goals. This success determined how subsequent administrations operated tactically. That Richard Nixon overplayed his hand* and thereby created a political dynamic resulting in his loss of public confidence and pending impeachment does not mean that this crisis has been resolved. The underlying institutional framework and value changes remain and constitute the dilemma confronting American society in the 1970s and beyond. The issue before the Congress today, when specifically assessing the two central policy issues of the nature of legislative charters for the intelligence agencies and the proper presidential role in the national security area, can be succinctly captured by the question: Can the balance between liberty and security be reached within the framework of the Constitution? Harry Truman's presidency suggests that this balance is difficult to achieve at best and further that even a slight tilt can have portentous consequences. Not nostalgia, then, but a search for answers to the problems of the present justify renewed study of the Truman years.

The majority of the documents reprinted in this collection (and particularly those involving the intelligence agencies) have only recently been declassified. These recently-declassified documents were made available either as the result of the investigation of the intelligence community conducted by the Senate Select Committee on Intelligence Activities (the so-called Church

---

*Richard Nixon's crude political uses of "national security" are starkly recorded in his taped March 21, 1973 conversation with White House aides John Dean and H. R. Haldeman. When responding to Nixon's query as to what could be done should it be revealed that the White House plumbers had been involved in engineering the break-in to the office of Dr. Lewis Fielding, Dean glibly asserted, "You might put it on a national security basis." Haldeman and Nixon concurred, the President adding that should other revelations occur the proper response should be "The whole thing was national security." Dean then predicted "I think we could get by on that."

Committee), in response to requests brought under provisions of the Freedom of Information Act of 1966 (as amended in November 1974), or under established declassification procedures of the executive agencies and departments.

These declassified documents reveal that earlier scholarly research had been strikingly limited and, more importantly, that before the 1970s we knew very little about crucial executive branch international and internal security policy decisions. Thus, rather than viewing the most serious threat to civil liberties of the Truman years as emanating from the McCarthyites in the Congress, we now recognize that the greatest threat emanated from the actions of high-level officials in the intelligence agencies. Similarly, and without minimizing the importance of policy decisions such as the Truman Doctrine, the Marshall Plan, or the Korean War, we now recognize that the developments of more enduring significance involved the expansion of the role and authority of the National Security Council and the Central Intelligence Agency. In short, the recently-declassified documents do not merely add detail: collectively they call for a radical reassessment of the conventional wisdom concerning the Truman Presidency.

In conclusion, I should outline the criteria employed in reprinting and editing the particular documents included in this collection. Because of the scope of the changes occurring during Truman's presidency, no one-volume work could attain comprehensiveness even when this volume focused exclusively on the themes of the "Imperial Presidency" and the "National Security State." Accordingly, when selecting documents, I aimed to insure that the documents would at least survey all of the important issues and changes. This meant that an in-depth documentary record of decisions from proposal to execution could not be assured. Thus, for example, I included President Truman's speech to the joint session of Congress enunciating what became the Truman Doctrine but not the legislation enacted by Congress concerning that request. These legislative provisions were not as important as the speech in defining policy and in highlighting Administration priorities. Moreover, I did not include documents pertaining either to the congressional investigations or court rulings involving the series of major internal security cases of this period - whether the Alger Hiss, William Remington, Judith Coplon, Julius and Ethel Rosenberg, or Smith Act cases. The sole citations to documents involving these cases (Coplon and Hiss) involved policy matters or highlighted the FBI's separate filing procedures or political activities when leaking derogatory information to conservative congressmen or reporters. Nonetheless, I maintain that this collection does not sacrifice comprehensiveness of treatment and the major policy and institutional developments have been adequately covered. My editing of the documents was also based upon the objective of insuring as complete a survey of important policy developments as is possible within the limitations of a one-volume work. Accordingly, those sections of speeches or memorandums that did not pertain to the themes of this collection - the expansion of presidential powers and the role of the intelligence agencies - were not reprinted. Sections of speeches and memorandums were not reprinted if they were either merely rhetorical or were intended to provide additional justification for a controversial policy. The source citation, moreover, enables the reader

to locate the unedited documents. Indirectly, the editorial decisions highlight the major thesis of this work as to the formative and radical impact of the Truman Presidency on American
politics and society.

I. THE EMERGENCE OF THE PRESIDENTIAL BUREAUCRACY

A. The Executive Office of the President

Under Franklin Roosevelt's direction, the office of the President came to be radically transformed with the creation of a limited presidential bureaucracy. Exploiting the authority provided under the Reorganization Act of 1939, on September 8, 1939, Roosevelt issued Executive Order 8248 creating the Executive Office of the President. Roosevelt's order provided for the creation of a White House staff and physically transferred the Bureau of the Budget from the Treasury Department to the newly-created Executive Office, thereby forging a bureaucracy that presidents could employ to permit tighter control over the Cabinet and which increased the president's sources of information. Roosevelt's successor, Harry Truman, built upon these institutional changes. Under Truman, a more specialized and more tightly organized White House staff emerged - providing the basis for a greater degree of presidential independence. The White House staff provided Truman independent advice and legwork; not coincidentally this encouraged the increasing resort to "executive privilege" claims. In addition, the Bureau of the Budget was assigned responsibility to review and clear the various executive agencies' and departments' legislative recommendations, and this legislative clearance role maximized presidential direction and thereby enhanced presidential powers. Concurrently, those emergency powers created by U.S. involvement in World War II remained despite the fact that military conflict had been terminated. And, when the imminent conclusion of peace treaties threatened to undercut this authority, President Truman successfully pressed for legislation extending presidential war power authority. In combination, then, the institutional changes in the office of the president and the emergency powers justified by the needs of World War II and the Cold War contributed to a more centralized and efficient presidency.

(1) <u>MESSAGE TO CONGRESS, PRESIDENT TRUMAN</u>, May 24, 1945 [Extract]

Source: *Public Papers of the Presidents: Harry S. Truman, 1945.*
Washington: U.S. Government Printing Office, 1961, pp. 69-72.

. . . I wish to draw the attention of the Congress . . . to
the conversion of the Executive Branch of the Government.

Immediately after the declaration of war the Congress, in
Title I of the First War Powers Act, 1941, empowered the President to make necessary adjustments in the organization of the
Executive Branch with respect to those matters which relate to
the conduct of the present war. . . . It is difficult to conceive
how the executive agencies could have been kept continuously attuned to the needs of the war without legislation of this type.

The First War Powers Act expires by its own terms six months
after the termination of the present war. Pending that time,
Title I will be of very substantial further value in enabling the
President to make such additional temporary improvements in the
organization of the Government as are currently required for the
more effective conduct of the war.

However, further legislative action is required in the near
future, because the First War Powers Act is temporary, and because, as matters now stand, every step taken under Title I will
automatically revert, upon the termination of the Title, to the
pre-existing status.

Such automatic reversion is not workable. . . . In some instances it will be necessary to delay reversion beyond the period
now provided by law, or to stay it permanently. In other instances it will be necessary to modify actions heretofore taken
under Title I and to continue the resulting arrangement beyond
the date of expiration of the Title. . . .

Quite aside from the disposition of the war organization of
the Government, other adjustments need to be made currently and
continuously in the Government establishment. . . . by and large,
the Congress cannot deal effectively with numerous organizational
problems on an individual item basis. . . . Yet it is imperative
that these matters be dealt with continuously if the Government
structure is to be reasonably wieldy and manageable, and be responsive to proper direction by the Congress and the President on
behalf of the people of this country. The question is one that

goes directly to the adequacy and effectiveness of our Government as an instrument of democracy.

Suitable reshaping of those parts of the Executive Branch of the Government which require it from time to time is necessary and desirable from every point of view. A well organized Executive Branch will be more efficient than a poorly organized one. It will help materially in making manageable the Government of this great nation. . . .

Experience has demonstrated that if substantial progress is to be made in these regards, it must be done through action initiated or taken by the President. The results achieved under the Economy Act (1932), as amended, the Reorganization Act of 1939, and Title I of the First War Powers Act, 1941, testify to the value of Presidential initiative in this field.

Congressional criticisms are heard, not infrequently, concerning deficiencies in the Executive Branch of the Government. I should be less than frank if I failed to point out that the Congress cannot consistently advance such criticisms and at the same time deny the President the means of removing the causes at the root of such criticisms.

Accordingly, I ask the Congress to enact legislation which will make it possible to do what we all know needs to be done continuously and expeditiously with respect to improving the organization of the Executive Branch of the Government. In order that the purposes which I have in mind may be understood, the following features are suggested: (a) the legislation should be generally similar to the Reorganization Act of 1939, and part 2 or Title I of that Act should be utilized intact, (b) the legislation should be of permanent duration, (c) no agency of the Executive Branch should be exempted from the scope of the legislation, and (d) the legislation should be sufficiently broad and flexible to permit of any form of organizational adjustment, large or small, for which necessity may arise.

It is scarcely necessary to point out that under the foregoing arrangement (a) necessary action is facilitated because initiative is placed in the hands of the President, and (b) necessary control is reserved to the Congress since it may, by simple majority vote of the two Houses, nullify any action of the President which does not meet with its approval. . . .

(2) SPECIAL MESSAGE TO CONGRESS, PRESIDENT TRUMAN, September 6, 1945 [Extract]

Source: *Public Papers of the Presidents: Harry S. Truman, 1945.* Washington: U.S. Government Printing Office, 1961, pp. 275-279.

. . . I should like to bring to the attention of the Congress the legal difficulties that will arise unless care is taken in the drafting of legislation terminating wartime controls and wartime agencies. . . .

. . . in the opinion of the Attorney General . . . the broad basis of governmental power on which the existing emergency and wartime statutes rest has not been terminated by the unconditional surrender of our enemies.

Certain of the wartime statutes which have been made effective "in time of war," "during the present war," or "for the duration of the war" continue to be effective until a formal state of peace has been restored, or until some earlier termination date is made applicable by appropriate governmental action. Another group of statutes which by their provisions terminate "upon the cessation of hostilities" or "upon termination of the war," will in fact and in law terminate only by a formal proclamation to that effect by the President or by appropriate congressional action.

From time to time action will be taken with respect to these agencies, with the general objective of streamlining the Government into a peacetime organization as quickly as possible.

The time has not yet arrived, however, for the proclamation of the cessation of hostilities, much less the termination of the war. . . .

It has been necessary during the course of the war to make numerous important redistributions of functions among executive agencies.

This has been accomplished by the President under the authority of Title I of the First War Powers Act. This act expires six months after the termination of the war, or at such earlier time as may be designated by appropriate governmental action.

If the Congress or the President were formally to declare the present war terminated, it would automatically cause all the steps taken under the First War Powers Act with respect to the war agencies to expire, and would have the Government revert automatically to its preexisting status six months after the declaration.

If this were to occur, it would cause great confusion and chaos in the Government.

It is the policy of this administration not to exercise wartime powers beyond the point at which it is necessary to exercise them.

Similarly, the wartime agencies of the Government will not be allowed to continue to perform functions not required by present conditions.

Those functions of the wartime agencies which must be retained during part or all of the period of reconversion should be transferred as promptly as practicable to the permanent departments and agencies of the Government. The remaining functions, appropriate only to the crisis through which we have passed, should be terminated in an orderly, systematic fashion as soon as possible.

A program of winding up wartime agencies and distributing their functions on a peacetime basis is now being pursued under the powers vested in the President by Title I of the First War Powers Act.

Therefore, I urge that the Congress do [sic] not yet adopt a resolution proclaiming the termination of the war or the termination of the emergency or the cessation of hostilities. Such a resolution would automatically cause the death of many war powers and wartime agencies before we are ready.

At the same time I recognize that the Congress may wish to repeal certain specific wartime statutes. If this is to be done, the repeal should be on a selective basis, through the adoption of specific statutes dealing with each wartime power which the Congress decides should be terminated.

. . . my message dated May 24, 1945 . . . recommended that permanent legislation be enacted which would authorize the President to submit to the Congress, from time to time, plans providing for the reorganization of executive agencies, each such plan to become effective unless the Congress should reject it by concurrent resolution.

This type of joint action by the Congress and the President has produced, and will produce, far better results than can be achieved by the usual legislative process in the field of executive reorganization. If proper progress is to be made, it is necessary to permit the President to lay out the machinery for carrying out his responsibility for the conduct of the executive branch, subject to rejection by the two Houses of Congress. Executive initiative, subject to congressional veto, is an effective approach to governmental reorganization.

The responsibility of conducting the executive branch rests upon the President. It is fair and efficient to permit him to lay out the machinery for carrying out that responsibility. . . .

Considerable progress was made in efficiency of government under this Reorganization Act of 1939. I recommend that such powers be made of permanent duration and that the legislation be sufficiently flexible to permit any kind of adjustment for which necessity may arise. . . .

Our Government has never been as efficient as we should like to see it. To some degree this may be charged to the size of some of the tasks assigned to it. To some extent, it is also due to the lack of trained Government personnel and the low salaries paid to Government officials.

There is no question that the war has taught us a great deal about Government administration. There is still, however, much room for improvement.

I have undertaken directly through the members of the Cabinet and also through the Directors of the Office of War Mobilization and Reconversion and the Bureau of the Budget to emphasize the need for more efficient operation in all the executive branches of the Government. I have requested them to examine adminstrative procedures, and to speed up and simplify their operations to the maximum practical degree.

I have also requested the Bureau of the Budget to examine closely with each department and agency head, the actual needs of his office following the surrender of Japan. They have been asked to reduce budgets promptly and fully wherever cuts are indicated. The Bureau of the Budget is now completing studies which will result in reductions of millions of dollars in the expense of operating our Government.

We must continue relentlessly this program for increased Government efficiency. The Congress can depend upon the Executive to push this program with the utmost vigor. . . .

(3) LETTER, PRESIDENT TRUMAN TO SPEAKER OF HOUSE SAM RAYBURN,
February 19, 1952 [Extract]

Source: *Public Papers of the Presidents: Harry S. Truman, 1952-53.*
Washington: U.S. Government Printing Office, 1966, pp. 160-161.

I transmit herewith a draft Emergency Powers Continuation
Act, . . . and I recommend immediate and favorable consideration
of it by the Congress.

The purpose of this draft bill is to insure the continuation
of certain specific powers which the Government is exercising for
the preservation of the national security. Under the language
used in the statutes conferring these powers they exist now only
because we are still technically in a state of war. The only
state of war still existing between this country and others
is the state of war with Japan. Accordingly, unless the Congress
acts to continue these powers they will end when that state of war
ends or, in some cases, within a fixed period thereafter. The
consideration of this measure is a matter of urgency since the
Treaty of Peace with Japan has now been favorably acted on by the
Senate Committee on Foreign Relations. It will come into force,
after ratification by the United States, when four countries
among a group named in the Treaty ratify, in addition to Japan and
the United Kingdom, which have already ratified.

This bill continues only the specific acts or parts of acts
cited in it, some sixty in number, . . . They deal with such
widely varying subjects as those covered by provisions under
which: (1) the President, in time of war, may assume control over
the railroads; (2) the Government may reduce the royalties to be
paid by it on articles used in the defense programs; (3) Reserve
officers may be appointed without peacetime limitations; and (4)
members of the Armed Forces may vote for Federal officials notwithstanding absence from home. . . .

The bill is based on an intensive study of Federal law, which
took account of legislation enacted up to the close of the last
session of Congress and even during the present session. But a
limited purpose has guided the drafting. . . [to deal] only with
such of the war-dependent authorizations now existing as should
be continued in the interest of national security during a period
when disturbance in world affairs makes it necessary to exercise
unusual powers. Consequently the powers specifically dealt with
in the bill - and only these - are continued only for the duration
of the national emergency proclaimed on December 16, 1950 and six
months thereafter, with a provision that any or all of them may
be terminated at earlier times by concurrent resolution of the
Congress or by the President. The bill does not alter these
powers except in one particular section 1(a)(27). It continues
them as they are, and it does not deal at all with powers which
existed at one time during the war but have now lapsed or been
repealed. . . .

To insure a full presentation of the issues to the Congress
and to eliminate any legal uncertainty or litigation which might
arise if it were not made perfectly clear which statutes are in
force and which have been allowed to lapse, it has been assumed
for the purpose of the bill that the conflict now going on in
Korea does not constitute a state of war within the meaning of

the statutes dealt with. It has also been assumed that the termination of the state of war with Japan would terminate the national emergencies proclaimed by the President in 1939 and 1941. It is my intention, in order to eliminate any doubt on this latter point, that the proclamation of the Treaty of Peace with Japan, after its coming into force, shall expressly terminate those emergencies. . . .

I hope that the Congress will enact this measure promptly so that the coming into force of the Treaty of Peace with Japan will not deprive the Government of powers necessary for the national security.

(4) <u>LUNCHEON MEETING OF CABINET OFFICIALS</u>, August 16, 1946 [Extract]

Source: James Webb Papers, Harry S. Truman Library.

[Secretary of Agriculture Clinton Anderson suggested:]

1. That members of Congress in charge of specific bills be contacted before taking a position that a bill is not a part of the President's program.

Mr. Anderson's view is that frequently such members have commitments from the Congressional leaders and from the President and are frequently embarrassed if the Bureau [of the Budget] takes the contrary position. He cited one instance in his own experience where the President specifically authorized him to sponsor certain legislation, approved the particular language and had it incorporated in notes made by [Presidential Secretary Matthew] Connelly of the conference. However, the Budget Director would never clear the legislation.

2. That inasmuch as some of the members of the Cabinet who were least inclined to be team players were now out of the picture, and that the Cabinet is working together as a team better than at any time recently, the Budget Director should integrate his activities with this team and keep this viewpoint in mind in his consideration of various matters. . . .

The Attorney General [Tom Clark] questioned the procedure under which the Bureau advises that a proposed bill is not in accordance with the President's program but still permitted the department or agency report to be transmitted to Congress. His view was that with the present teamwork most measures which were not cleared in the President's program should not be submitted to Congress. [Bureau of Budget Director Harold Smith] explained to him that the Bureau did not desire to draw a barrier between departments or agencies and Congress, but felt that in many cases direct contact on matters even though not within the President's program was desirable. Secretary Anderson immediately agreed with this view.

(5) BUDGET AND ACCOUNTING PROCEDURES ACT, 1950 [Extract]

Source: 6 U.S. Code 31, §65-§66; 64 Statute 834-837 (1950).

§65. Congressional declaration of policy. It is the policy of the Congress in enacting this chapter that –

(a) The accounting of the Government provides full disclosure of the results of financial operations, adequate financial information needed in the management of operations and the formulation and execution of the Budget, and effective control over income, expenditures, funds, property, and other assets. . . .

(c) The maintenance of accounting systems and the producing of financial reports with respect to the operations of executive agencies, including central facilities for bringing together and disclosing information on the results of the financial operations of the Government as a whole, be the responsibility of the executive branch. . . .

(e) Emphasis be placed on effecting orderly improvements resulting in simplified and more effective accounting, financial reporting, budgeting, and auditing requirements and procedures and on the elimination of those which involved duplication or which do not serve a purpose commensurate with the costs involved.

(f) The Comptroller General of the United States, the Secretary of the Treasury, and the Director of the Bureau of the Budget conduct a continuous program for the improvement of accounting and financial reporting to the Government. . . .

§66. . . . The head of each executive agency shall establish and maintain systems of accounting and internal control designed to provide –

(1) full disclosure of the financial results of the agency's activities;

(2) adequate financial information needed for the agency's management purposes;

(3) effective control over and accountability for all funds, property, and other assets for which the agency is responsible, including appropriate internal audit;

(4) reliable accounting results to serve as the basis for preparation and support of the agency's budget requests for controlling the execution of its budget, and for providing financial information required by the Bureau of the Budget. . . .

(5) suitable integration of the accounting of the agency with the accounting of the Treasury Department in connection with the central accounting and reporting responsibilities imposed on the Secretary of the Treasury . . .

The Secretary of the Treasury shall prepare such reports for the information of the President, the Congress, and the public and will present the results of the financial operations of the Government: Provided, That there shall be included such financial data as the Director of the Bureau of the Budget may require in connection with the preparation of the Budget or for other purposes of the Bureau. Each executive agency shall furnish the Secretary of the Treasury such reports and information relating

to its financial condition and operations as the Secretary, by
rules and regulations, may require for the effective performance
of his responsibilities. . . .

B. _The National Security Bureaucracy and the Presidency_

Problems pertaining to the coordination and implementation of foreign and military policy during the World War II period impelled President Truman and other high-level Administration officials to advocate rationalizing decision-making. As part of this effort, President Truman in 1946 issued an executive order and then in 1947 recommended specific legislation (which became the National Security Act of 1947) to create institutions (the National Security Council and the Central Intelligence Agency) which could provide the means for better coordinating and refining foreign policy decision-making and which could insure the needed intelligence upon which policy could be based. At the time, in 1947 that is, Truman's legislative recommendation was understood as providing such limited benefits - the NSC would ensure improved coordination among the various military and diplomatic departments while the CIA would coordinate various intelligence estimates and reports prepared by existing agencies involved in intelligence collection thereby providing the President with a more comprehensive intelligence product. Both the NSC and the CIA were to be service agencies, neither independent collectors of intelligence nor policy-making bodies. Despite the President's limited intent (as conveyed to the Congress in support of the specific legislative recommendations), a radically different, because more independent and secretive, bureaucracy evolved.

As one result, presidential powers were enhanced insofar as crucial decisions were insulated from external scrutiny and presidential dependence on external sources of information and support assistance was reduced. At the same time, the NSC and the CIA themselves (owing to the quest for secrecy and perceptions of a serious national security threat) assumed a direct policy-making role verging on independence. Thus, if the National Security Act of 1947 had been justified and understood as a legislative measure whose principal purpose was to ensure unification of the armed services, it nonetheless provided the legislative foundation for what evolved into a fundamentally radical institutional development. The 1949 amendments to this Act, most notably those exempting the CIA from normal budgetary accounting requirements, only further centralized power in the executive branch. In time, as the documents reprinted in this section and in Section IIIA2 confirm, the NSC's and the CIA's roles evolved to the point where they became the agencies which either shaped or set foreign policy. Two consequences resulted from this institutional change. First, the Department of State no longer determined foreign policy priorities and objectives. Second, the role and influence of military considerations on national policy increased. No less importantly, the CIA almost immediately abandoned its proposed role of intelligence analysis and became directly involved in covert activities. The exigencies of waging the Cold War, combined with the seductive appeal of the Agency's secrecy, encouraged the President and his national security advisers to employ the CIA in this different capacity. This aspect is covered in greater detail in Section IIIA2.

(6) <u>SPECIAL MESSAGE TO CONGRESS, PRESIDENT TRUMAN</u>, December 19,
1945 [Extract]

Source: *Public Papers of the Presidents: Harry S. Truman, 1945*.
Washington: U.S. Government Printing Office, 1961, pp. 547-560.

   . . . Today, again in the interest of national security and
world peace, I make this further recommendation to you. I recommend that the Congress adopt legislation combining the War and
Navy Departments into one single Department of National Defense.
Such unification is another essential step - along with universal
training - in the development of a comprehensive and continuous
program for our future safety and for the peace and security of
the world.

   I urge this as the best means of keeping the peace.

   No nation now doubts the good will of the United States for
the maintenance of a lasting peace in the world. Our purpose is
shown by our efforts to establish an effective United Nations
Organization. But all nations - and particularly those unfortunate nations which have felt the heel of the Nazis, the Fascists
or the Japs - know that desire for peace is futile unless there
is also enough strength ready and willing to enforce that desire
in any emergency. Among the things that have encouraged aggression and the spread of war in the past have been the unwillingness of the United States realistically to face this fact, and
her refusal to fortify her aims of peace before the forces of
aggression could gather in strength. . . .

   Whether we like it or not, we must all recognize that the
victory which we have won has placed upon the American people the
continuing burden of responsibility for world leadership. The
future peace of the world will depend in large part upon whether
or not the United States shows that it is really determined to
continue in its role as a leader among nations. It will depend
upon whether or not the United States is willing to maintain the
physical strength necessary to act as a safeguard against any
future aggressor. Together with the other United Nations, we
must be willing to make the sacrifices necessary . . . to maintain in constant and immediate readiness sufficient military
strength to convince any future potential aggressor that this
Nation, in its determination for a lasting peace, means business.

We would be taking a grave risk with the national security if we did not move now to overcome permanently the present imperfections in our defense organization. However great was the need for coordination and unified command in World War II, it is sure to be greater if there is any future aggression against world peace. Technological developments have made the Armed Services much more dependent upon each other than ever before. . . .

We must assume, further, that another war would strike much more suddenly than the last, and that it would strike directly at the United States. . . . True preparedness now means preparedness not alone in armaments and numbers of men, but preparedness in organization also. It means establishing in peacetime the kind of military organization which will be able to meet the test of sudden attack quickly and without having to improvise radical readjustment in structure and habits.

The basic question is what organization will provide the most effective employment of our military resources in time of war and the most effective means for maintaining peace. The manner in which we make this transition in the size, composition, and organization of the armed forces will determine the efficiency and cost of our national defense for many years to come. . . .

. . . To me the most important reasons for combining the two existing Departments are these:

I. We should have integrated strategic plans and a unified military program and budget.

With the coming of peace, it is clear that we must not only continue, but strengthen, our present facilities for integrated planning. We cannot have the sea, land, and air members of our defense team working at what may turn out to be cross purposes, planning their programs on different assumptions as to the nature of the military establishment we need, and engaging in an open competition for funds.

Strategy, program, and budget are all aspects of the same basic decisions. Using the advice of our scientists and our intelligence officers, we must make the wisest estimate as to the probable nature of any future attack upon us, determine accordingly how to organize and deploy our military forces, and allocate the available manpower, material, and financial resources in a manner consistent with the overall plan. . . .

[World War II] has demonstrated completely that the resources of this nation in manpower and in raw materials are not unlimited. To realize this is to comprehend the urgent need for finding a way to allocate these resources intelligently among the competing services. This means designing a balanced military structure reflecting a considered apportionment of responsibility among the services for the performance of a joint mission.

From experience as a member of the Congress, I know the great difficulty of appraising properly the over-all security needs of the nation from piecemeal presentations by separate departments appearing before separate congressional committees at different times. It is only by combining the armed forces into a single department that the Congress can have the advantage of considering a single coordinated and comprehensive security program.

2. We should realize the economies that can be achieved through unified control of supply and service functions. . . .

3. We should adopt the organizational structure best suited to fostering coordination between the military and the remainder of the Government.

Our military policy and program are only a part of a total national program aimed at achieving our national objectives of security and peace. . . .

Our military policy, for example, should be completely consistent with our foreign policy. It should be designed to support and reflect our commitments to the United Nations Organization. It should be adjusted according to the success or lack of success of our diplomacy. It should reflect our fullest knowledge of the capabilities and intentions of other powers. Likewise, our foreign policy should take into account our military capabilities and the strategic power of our Armed Forces.

A total security program has still other major aspects. A military program, standing alone, is useless. It must be supported in peacetime by planning for industrial mobilization and for development of industrial and raw material resources where these are insufficient. Programs of scientific research must be developed for military purposes, and their results woven into the defense program. The findings of our intelligence service must be applied to all of these.

Formulation and execution of a comprehensive and consistent national program embracing all these activities are extremely difficult tasks. They are made more difficult the greater the number of departments and agencies whose policies and programs have to be coordinated at the top level of the Executive Branch. . . .

The consolidation of the War and Navy Departments would greatly facilitate the ease and speed with which the Armed Forces and the other departments could exchange views and come to agreement on matters of common concern. It would minimize the extent to which inter-service differences have to be discussed and settled by the civilian leaders whose main concern should be the more fundamental job of building over-all national policy.

4. We should provide the strongest means for civilian control of the military.

Civilian control of the military establishment - one of the most fundamental of our democratic concepts - must be strengthened if the President and the Congress had but one Cabinet member with clear and primary responsibility for the exercise of that control. When the military establishment is divided between two civilian Secretaries, each is limited necessarily to a restricted view of the military establishment. Consequently, on many fundamental issues where the civilian point of view should be controlling, the Secretaries of the two Departments are cast in the role of partisans of their respective Services, and real civilian control can be exercised by no one except the President or the Congress.

During and since the war, the need for joint action by the Services and for objective recommendations on military matters has led inevitably to increasing the authority of the only joint

organization and the most nearly objective organization that
exists - the Joint Chiefs of Staff. But the Joint Chiefs of Staff
are a strictly military body. Responsibility for civilian control should be clearly fixed in a single full-time civilian below
the President. This requires a Secretary for the entire military
establishment, aided by a strong staff of civilian assistants.

There is no basis for the fear that such an organization
would lodge too much power in a single individual - that the concentration of so much military power would lead to militarism.
There is no basis for such fear as long as the traditional policy
of the United States is followed that a civilian, subject to the
President, the Congress and the will of the people, be placed at
the head of this Department. . . .

7. We should allocate systematically our limited resources
for scientific research.

No aspect of military preparedness is more important than
scientific research. Given the limited amount of scientific talent that will be available for military purposes, we must systematically apply that talent to research in the most promising
lines and on the weapons with the greatest potentiality, regardless of the Service in which these weapons will be used. We cannot afford to waste any of our scientific resources in duplication
of effort.

This does not mean that all Army and Navy laboratories would
be immediately or even ultimately consolidated. The objective
should be to preserve initiative and enterprise while eliminating
duplication and misdirected effort. This can be accomplished
only, if we have an organizational structure which will permit
fixing responsibility at the top for coordination among the Services. . . .

****

I recommend that . . . :

(1) There should be a single Department of National Defense.
This Department should be charged with the full responsibility
for armed national security. It should consist of the armed and
civilian forces that are now included within the War and Navy
Departments.

(2) The head of this department should be a civilian, a member of the President's cabinet, to be designated as the Secretary
of National Defense. Under him there should be a civilian Under
Secretary and several civilian Assistant Secretaries.

(3) There should be three coordinated branches of the Department of National Defense: one for the land forces, one for the
naval forces, and one for the air forces, each under an Assistant
Secretary. . . .

(5) The President and the Secretary should be provided with
ample authority to establish central coordinating and service
organizations, both military and civilian, where these are found
to be necessary. Some of these might be placed under Assistant
Secretaries, some might be organized as central service organizations, and some might be organized in a top military staff to
integrate the military leadership of the department. I do not

believe that we can specify at this time the exact nature of these organizations. They must be developed over a period of time by the President and the Secretary as a normal part of their executive responsibilities. Sufficient strength in these department-wide elements of the department, as opposed to the separate Service elements, will insure that real unification is ultimately obtained. The President and the Secretary should not be limited in their authority to establish department-wide coordinating and service organizations.

(6) There should be a Chief of Staff of the Department of National Defense. There should also be a commander for each of the three component branches - Army, Navy, and Air.

(7) The Chief of Staff and the commanders of the three coordinate branches of the Department should together constitute an advisory body to the Secretary of National Defense and to the President. There should be nothing to prevent the President, the Secretary, and other civilian authorities from communicating with the commanders of any of the components of the Department on such vital matters as basic military strategy and policy and the division of the budget. Furthermore, the key staff positions in the Department should be filled with officers drawn from all the services, so that the thinking of the Department would not be dominated by any one or two of the services.

As an additional precaution, it would be wise if the post of Chief of Staff were rotated among the several services, whenever practicable and advisable, at least during the period of evolution of the new unified Department. The tenure of the individual officer designated to serve as Chief of Staff should be relatively short - two or three years - and should not, except in time of a war emergency declared by the Congress, be extended beyond that period.

Unification of the services must be looked upon as a long-term job. We all recognize that there will be many complications and difficulties. Legislation of the character outlined will provide us with the objective, and with the initial means whereby forward-looking leadership in the Department, both military and civilian, can bring real unification into being. . . .

Once a unified department has been established, other steps necessary to the formulation of a comprehensive national security program can be taken with greater ease. Much more than a beginning has already been made in achieving consistent political and military policy through the establishment of the State-War-Navy Coordinating Committee. With respect to military research, I have in a previous message to the Congress proposed the establishment of a federal research agency, among whose responsibilities should be the promotion and coordination of fundamental research pertaining to the defense and security of the Nation. The development of a coordinated, government-wide intelligence system is in process. As the advisability of additional action to insure a broad and coordinated program of national security becomes clear, I shall make appropriate recommendations or take the necessary action to that end. . . .

(7) LETTER, PRESIDENT TRUMAN TO SECRETARY OF STATE JAMES BYRNES, September 20, 1945

Source: *Public Papers of the Presidents: Harry S. Truman, 1945.* Washington: U.S. Government Printing Office, 1961, p. 331.

I have today signed an Executive order which provides for the transfer to the State Department of the functions, personnel, and other resources of the Research and Analysis Branch and the Presentation Branch of the Office of Strategic Services. The order also transfers the remaining activities of the Office of Strategic Services to the War Department and abolishes that Office. These changes become effective October 1, 1945.

The above transfer to the State Department will provide you with resources which we agreed you will need to aid in the development of our foreign policy, and will assure that pertinent experience accumulated during the war will be preserved and used in meeting the problems of the peace. Those readjustments and reductions which are required in order to gear the transferred activities and resources into State Department operations should be made as soon as practicable.

I particularly desire that you take the lead in developing a comprehensive and coordinated foreign intelligence program for all Federal agencies concerned with that type of activity. This should be done through the creation of an interdepartmental group, heading up under the State Department, which would formulate plans for my approval. This procedure will permit the planning of complete coverage of the foreign intelligence field and the assigning and controlling of operations in such manner that the needs of both the individual agencies and the Government as a whole will be met with maximum effectiveness.

(8) MEMO, SECRETARY OF STATE JAMES BYRNES TO SECRETARIES OF WAR AND NAVY, December 3, 1945 [Extract]

Source: Clark Clifford Papers, National Intelligence Authority, Harry S. Truman Library.

. . . Attached is a Plan for carrying out the President's directive [of September 20, 1945]. . . . I now recommend it for your favorable consideration.

Attention is invited especially to the following points:

a. The Plan sets up a National Intelligence Authority consisting of the Secretary of State as Chairman and the Secretaries of War and Navy, but authorizes the Chairman to call in the heads of other Departments and agencies on matters of special interest to them.

b. The Plan is designed to make fullest use of the intelligence resources of all agencies of the Government, by coordinating their efforts under a comprehensive, Government-wide program. The proposed machinery is an interdepartmental organization under the Authority, with personnel drawn from existing agencies, rather than an independent agency with a separate budget. This is considered advantageous because it tends (1) to avoid publicity and (2) to reduce competition and duplication between the central agency and the intelligency organizations of existing departments and agencies.

c. Executive direction of the central agency is put in the hands of an official of the Department of State, but it is provided that the Secretaries of War and Navy must approve the person selected. In that manner the coordinating responsibility of the State Department for matters involving foreign affairs is recognized, but the executive is made a representative of the Authority as a whole, and not merely of a single Department.

d. The central Secretariat is envisaged as a working staff of personnel contributed primarily by the State, War and Navy Departments.

e. The Plan does not preclude any centralized intelligence operations (either under the central agency or outside of it) which may prove feasible and desirable as the program of the Authority is developed. It provides planning mechanisms that may well lead to centralization of intelligence responsibilities in many of the specialized fields, either (1) by vesting responsibility for a particular field in a single existing agency or (2) by bringing together the working units of several agencies on a subject into a joint unit under direction of the Authority.

f. With respect to clandestine activities ("secret intelligence" and "counter-espionage") I understand the prevailing opinion to be that such operations, if they are to be conducted, might well be under a central agency; and the Plan sets up machinery for study of the problem in detail and for development of specific operating plans in those fields.

The central agency is conceived in the first instance as a coordinating and planning mechanism, whose mission is to develop the comprehensive program envisaged by the President; to determine foreign intelligence requirements on a Government-wide basis, and to recommend means and methods for meeting those requirements, making use of all the intelligence resources of the Government. Many agencies, in addition to the State, War and Navy Departments, are engaged in collection and analysis of foreign information, including the Treasury, the Departments of Agriculture, Commerce and Labor, the Tariff and Maritime Commissions, the Federal Reserve Board and numerous others. Such agencies can make important contributions to foreign intelligence if they work under a coordinated program, so that, within their special fields, they may serve the needs of other Government agencies as well as their own.

Under the Plan as proposed, the primary coordinating mechanism is a group of interdepartmental Committees for the various fields of intelligence, which, in addition to their planning functions, will "Serve as a continuing group responsible for maintaining a coordinated program and for reviewing the adequacy and efficiency of all operations involved in the carrying out of such a program."
. . .

(9) MEMO, CLARK CLIFFCRD (WHITE HCUSE COUNSEL) TO SAMUEL
ROSENMAN (WHITE HOUSE AIDE), December 13, 1945 [Extract]
Source: Samuel Rosenman Papers, Harry S. Truman Library.

I have read the second draft of the Message on Unification of
the Armed Services and present herewith my comments. . . .

. . . I am not in accord with the basic approach presented by
the draft nor with the general tone.

The following will serve as illustrations:

1. War is emphasized to an unusual degree. . . . I believe
that the President should approach the problem from the standpoint of recommending the most effective organization for
keeping the peace. There will be some who will attach the
wrong implication and connotation to the President recommending a certain "war-making organization." Stress should be
placed upon the fact that the President's proposal is presented in the hope of preventing war.

2. Considerable attention is devoted to the saving of money
which will be effected by a unification of the War and Navy
Departments in case of another war. I believe that the question of economy should be treated differently. . . .

I submit that it would be most effective if the President
took the approach that unification of the Services is necessary because it would place this country in a better position
to integrate its foreign, military and economic policies, and
that such integration is our greatest hope in preventing our
participation in another war. Such an approach appears to me
to be better calculated to win Congressional and public support.

I believe it is advisable for the Message to discuss the
question of national security in a much broader scope than
simply the merger of the War and Navy Departments. . . .
The question of the form of organization of our military
forces must be viewed in its proper perspective as only one
of many important elements, military and civilian, which contribute to our security. Our needs cannot be met by one
single administrative change such as unification of the War
and Navy Departments. Our needs require integration of the
whole organizational structure of the government. This proposal for unification of the two Departments falls short of
our present requirements on two counts. It does not provide
for the needed comprehensive relationship between the military
services and the State Department, or for the relationship
between the military services and the civilian economy.
These form the foundation of our national security. . . .

One of the most vital recommendations . . . is the creation of a National Security Council. This Council would
provide a permanent organization for maintaining a close and
continuous contact between the departments and agencies of
the government responsible for our foreign and military policies. The Council would be charged with the duty of formulating and coordinating overall policies in the political and
military fields, of assessing and appraising our foreign

objectives and commitments, and keeping these commitments in balance with our military power. The National Security Council would be a policy-forming and advisory body. The Council would have under its jurisdiction a Central Intelligence Agency which would serve all departments of the government, not just the Armed Forces.

I also believe that there is definite merit to the recommendation that there be established a National Security Resources Board. The major task of such a Board would be to provide the country with an existing organization that could, upon short notice, mobilize industry and civilians in event of an emergency. It would maintain a skeleton organization to formulate plans and their implementation for the prompt and effective translation of military needs into industrial and civilian activity. . . .

(10) PRESIDENTIAL DIRECTIVE ON COORDINATION OF FOREIGN INTELLI-GENCE ACTIVITIES TO SECRETARY OF STATE JAMES BYRNES, SECRETARY OF WAR ROBERT PATTERSON, AND SECRETARY OF THE NAVY JAMES FORRESTAL, January 22, 1946

Source: *Public Papers of the Presidents: Harry S. Truman, 1946.* Washington: U.S. Government Printing Office, 1962, pp. 88-89.

1. . . . I hereby direct, that all Federal foreign intelligence activities be planned, developed and coordinated so as to assure the most effective accomplishment of the intelligence mission related to the national security. I hereby designate you, together with another person to be named by me as my personal representative, as the National Intelligence Authority to accomplish this purpose.

2. Within the limits of available appropriations, you shall each from time to time assign persons and facilities from your respective Departments, which persons shall collectively form a Central Intelligence Group and shall, under the direction of a Director of Central Intelligence, assist the National Intelligence Authority. The Director of Central Intelligence shall be designated by me, shall be responsible to the National Intelligence Authority, and shall sit as a non-voting member thereof.

3. Subject to the existing law, and to the direction and control of the National Intelligence Authority, the Director of Central Intelligence shall:

a. Accomplish the correlation and evaluation of intelligence relating to the national security, and the appropriate dissemination within the Government of the resulting strategic and national policy intelligence. In so doing, full use shall be made of the staff and facilities of the intelligence agencies of your Departments.

b. Plan for the coordination of such of the activities of the intelligence agencies of your Departments as relate to the national security and recommend to the National Intelligence Authority the establishment of such over-all policies and objectives as will assure the most effective accomplishment of the national intelligence mission.

c. Perform, for the benefit of said intelligence agencies, such services of common concern as the National Intelligence Authority determines can be more efficiently accomplished centrally.

d. Perform such other functions and duties related to intelligence affecting the national security as the President and the National Intelligence Authority may from time to time direct.

4. No police, law enforcement or internal security function shall be exercised under this directive.

5. Such intelligence received by the intelligence agencies of your Departments as may be designated by the National Intelligence Authority shall be freely available to the Director of Central Intelligence for correlation, evaluation or dissemination. To the extent approved by the National Intelligence Authority, the operations of said intelligence agencies shall be open to inspection by the Director of Central Intelligence in connection with planning functions.

6. The existing intelligence agencies of your Departments shall continue to collect, evaluate, correlate and disseminate departmental intelligence.

7. The Director of Central Intelligence shall be advised by an Intelligence Advisory Board consisting of the heads (or their representatives) of the principal military and civilian intelligence agencies of the Government having functions related to national security, as determined by the National Intelligence Authority.

8. Within the scope of existing law and Presidential directives, other departments and agencies of the executive branch of the Federal Government shall furnish such intelligence information relating to the national security as is in their possession, and as the Director of Central Intelligence may from time to time request pursuant to regulations of the National Intelligence Authority.

9. Nothing herein shall be construed to authorize the making of investigations inside the continental limits of the United States and its possessions, except as provided by law and Presidential directives.

10. In the conduct of their activities the National Intelligence Authority and the Director of Central Intelligence shall be responsible for fully protecting intelligence sources and methods.

(11) LETTER, PRESIDENT TRUMAN TO CHAIRMEN CONGRESSIONAL COMMITTEES ON MILITARY AND NAVAL AFFAIRS, June 15, 1946 [Extract]

Source: *Public Papers of the Presidents: Harry S. Truman, 1946.* Washington: U.S. Government Printing Office, 1962, pp. 303-305.

One of the most important problems confronting our country today is the establishment of a definite military policy.

In the solution of this problem, I consider it vital that we have a unified armed force for our national defense. . . .

. . . there are now presented twelve basic principles upon which the unification of the services can be based.

They are as follows:

1. Single military department.

There should be one Department of National Defense. It would be under the control of a civilian who would be a member of the cabinet. Each of the services would be headed by a civilian with the title of "Secretary." These secretaries would be charged with the internal administration within their own services. They would not be members of the cabinet. Each service would retain its autonomy, subject of course to the authority and overall control by the Secretary of National Defense. It is recognized that the services have different functions and different organizations and for these reasons the integrity of each service should be retained. The civilian secretaries of the services would be members of the Council of Common Defense and in this capacity they would have the further opportunity to represent their respective services to the fullest extent.

2. Three coordinate services.

There should be three coordinate services - the Army, Navy and Air Force. The three services should be on a parity and should operate in a common purpose toward overall efficiency of the National Defense under the control and supervision of the Secretary of National Defense. . . .

5. Council of National Defense.

To integrate our foreign and military policies and to enable the military services and other agencies of government to cooperate more effectively in matters involving our national security. The membership of this council should consist of the Secretary of State, the civilian head of the military establishment, the civilian heads of the military services, and the Chairman of the National Security Resources Board, referred to below.

6. National Security Resources Board.

To establish, and keep up to date, policies and programs for the maximum use of the Nation's resources in support of our national security. It should operate under the Council and be composed of representatives of the military services and of other appropriate agencies.

7. The Joint Chiefs of Staff.

To formulate strategic plans, to assign logistic responsibilities to the services in support thereof, to integrate the military programs, to make recommendations for integration of the military budget, and to provide for the strategic direction of the United States military forces. . . .

9. Central Intelligence Agency.

To compile, analyze, and evaluate information gathered by various government agencies, including the military, and to furnish such information to the National Defense Council and to other government agencies entitled thereto. It should operate under the Council. An organization along these lines, established by Executive Order, already exists. . . .

(12) MEMO, CLARK CLIFFORD (SPECIAL COUNSEL TO THE PRESIDENT) TO
GENERAL HOYT VANDENBERG (DIRECTOR, CENTRAL INTELLIGENCE GROUP),
July 12, 1946 [Extract]

Source: Clark Clifford Papers, National Intelligence Authority,
Harry S. Truman Library.

In compliance with your request I submit herewith suggestions
concerning the proposed bill [an earlier draft of the National
Security Act of 1947].

In several places the language seems difficult to follow and
unnecessarily repetitious. I believe that a more serious objection than that of language, however, is the failure of the bill
to define in clear terms the sense in which the word "intelligence" is used. For example, "intelligence," "foreign intelligence," "intelligence relating to the national security," "strategic and national policy intelligence," "the national intelligence
mission," and "intelligence affecting the national security," are
used indiscriminately as though they were synonymous.

The failure to distinguish between "intelligence" and "foreign
intelligence" will raise a serious question in many minds as to
whether the real intent of the bill is actually the same as that
stated in the "Purpose of the Act." The "declared policy" in
section I(a) refers only to "foreign intelligence" and section
I(b) states that it is the purpose of the Act to carry out that
"declared policy." However, the same section, I(b), provides for
several programs which embrace all existing intelligence activities of the Federal Government, both foreign and domestic. I fear
that this will lead to the suspicion that the "National Intelligence Authority" and the "Central Intelligence Agency" will attempt to control, with the powers granted to them in this bill,
the F.B.I. and other intelligence activities.

I fear that there are some serious omissions in the bill.
For example, the functions and duties of the National Intelligence
Authority are not specific. . . . nowhere is the purpose or the
reason for its existence set forth. Although section 2(a)(1)
states that the bill provides for a Director of Central Intelligence, the bill does not provide for such an officer. . . .

In some respects I consider that the proposed bill is self-
contradictory. Section 2(d) states that "the responsibility and
authority of the Departments and other Agencies of the Government"
with respect to intelligence shall not be affected by the establishment of the Central Intelligence Agency. The next paragraph,
2(e), is in direct contradiction to 2(d) in stating that the
other intelligence agencies of the government are "directed" to
make their facilities and services available to the Central Intelligence Agency. It is obvious that both the responsibility and
the authority of existing government agencies are affected when
they are "directed" to make their facilities available to the
Central Intelligence Agency. . . .

I have a number of comments on specific minor points. I
shall not burden this memorandum with them all, but the following are illustrative:

    (3) Page 1, Line 7: "foreign intelligence"
          Query: Is "foreign intelligence" or "intelligence"
          meant here? . . .

    (5) Page 1, Line 11: "intelligence"
          Query: Is "intelligence" or "foreign intelligence"
          meant here?

    (6) Page 1, Lines 15 & 16: "processing, analysis and dissem-
          ination of foreign intelligence"
          Comment: This seems unnecessarily difficult. Would
          not "acquisition and analysis" be a satis-
          factory substitute? . . .

    (10) Page 1, Lines 25 & 26: Suggestion: Rewrite this sentence
          to read: "A program for the analysis and evaluation
          of foreign intelligence."

    (11) Page 2, Lines 1 - 3: Suggestion: Rewrite to read: "A
          program for distribution of intelligence material to
          appropriate Government officials."

    (12) Page 2, Lines 4 - 7: Suggestion: Rewrite to read: "A
          program to procure all available foreign intelligence
          and to take such other measures in the field of for-
          eign intelligence as will best ensure the national
          defense." . . .

(13) MEMO, GEORGE ELSEY FOR THE FILE, July 17, 1946

Source: George Elsey Papers, Central Intelligence, Harry S.
Truman Library.

On 16 July [Clark] Clifford met Mr. [Lawrence] Huston [sic, Houston] and Mr. [James] Lay from the Central Intelligence Group, in his office and discussed with them a proposed bill for the establishment of the Central Intelligence Agency. [George] Elsey was also present.

The basis of the discussion was the draft bill which had been submitted by [CIG Director] General [Hoyt] Vandenberg to Mr. Clifford for comment, and Mr. Clifford's memorandum in reply of 12 July 1946.

Mr. Clifford pointed out that it was not the President's ori- ginal intention that a new agency be created and he remarked that it appeared that the proposed bill was departing from the Presi- dent's intention by establishing a separate and sizeable govern- ment agency. Mr. Clifford also remarked that the President had intended that his letter of 22 January 1946 would provide a work- able plan for the Central Intelligence Group. Mr. Clifford then asked if experience had shown that the plan outlined in the President's letter was not workable.

Mr. Huston [sic] and Mr. Lay discussed at some length the ad- ministrative difficulties which the Central Intelligence Group has had due to its being a step-child of three separate depart- ments. They stated that experience showed that enabling legisla- tion was necessary in order that the Central Intelligence Group could operate as an integrated organization. They also informed Mr. Clifford that experience had shown that the Central Intelligence Group should become an operating agency with a large staff of Intelligence experts.

After lengthy discussion, it was agreed by all present that the original concept of the Central Intelligence Group should now be altered; experience had shown that it would be ineffective if it remained only a small planning staff and that it must now become a legally established, fairly sizeable, operating agency. Mr. Clifford stated that he would discuss this new concept with [presidential aide] Admiral [William] Leahy and the President.

There followed a detailed examination of the draft bill in light of the comments and criticisms made in Mr. Clifford's memorandum of 12 July. Mr. Huston [sic] and Mr. Lay agreed that all of Mr. Clifford's points were well taken and they agreed to rewrite the bill incorporating his suggestions.

It was apparent during this part of the discussion that neither Mr. Huston [sic] nor Mr. Lay had given much thought to the words which they had used in drafting the bill. Both stated that large parts of it had been extracted from other proposed legislation or other documents relating to Intelligence. In their hasty preparation of the draft in this scissors-and-paste method, they had failed to grasp the essential point that the National Intelligence Authority should be a planning group and the Central Intelligence Agency an operating group.

Mr. Clifford pointed out to them the probable opposition which a proposed bill would arouse if great care and thought were not given to the choice of words used.

Mr. Huston [sic] and Mr. Lay will prepare a new bill and send it to Mr. Clifford for comment.

(14) MEMO, WALTER PFORZHEIMER (CHIEF, LEGISLATIVE LIAISON BRANCH, CENTRAL INTELLIGENCE GROUP) TO DIRECTOR OF CENTRAL INTELLIGENCE HOYT VANDENBERG, November 26, 1946 [Extract]

Source: Clark Clifford Papers, National Intelligence Authority, Harry S. Truman Library.

. . . [Clark Clifford's July 12, 1946] memorandum points out the indiscriminate use of such undefined terms as "Intelligence," "Foreign Intelligence," and "Strategic and National Policy Intelligence," which appeared to be confusing. The Current Draft has eliminated these phrases and restricted itself to the use of the terms "Foreign Intelligence" and "Foreign Intelligence Information," both of which terms have been completely defined in Section 2 of the Current Draft, in accordance with the accepted C.I.G. [Central Intelligence Group] terminology. In addition the terms "national intelligence" and "national intelligence mission" have been used. The national intelligence mission is set forth in Section 1(a) of the Current Draft.

3. [Clifford's] memorandum refers to the failure to distinguish between "Intelligence," and "Foreign Intelligence" with the possible result that suspicions could be aroused that the Central Intelligence Agency might attempt to control the F.B.I. and other intelligence activities not originally contemplated. As pointed out in paragraph 3 above, this objection has been met by the

strict use of the terms "Foreign Intelligence" and "Foreign Intelligence Information."

4. [Clifford's] memorandum indicates that the functions and duties of the N.I.A. [National Intelligence Authority] were not specified. These functions and duties are set forth in detail in Sections 3(a)(6), (7), and (8) of Current Draft. . . .

8. [Clifford's] memorandum suggests in connection with Section 1(b) the use of the phrase "A program for the analysis and evaluation of foreign intelligence." Section 1(b)(4) of Current Draft reads: "A program of evaluation, correlation, and interpretation of the foreign intelligence information collected, . . . " In view of the fact that the term "evaluation, correlation, and interpretation" is defined in Section 2 of the Current Draft as the component parts of research, it is felt that the present phraseology is more complete, and therefore preferable to that suggested in reference memorandum.

9. [Clifford's] memorandum suggests in connection with Section 1(b) the use of the phrase "A program for distribution of intelligence material to appropriate Government officials." In Section 1(b)(5) of the Current Draft the phrase "A program for dissemination to the President and the appropriate departments and agencies of the Federal Government of the intelligence produced" is used. It is felt that the word "dissemination" is preferable to "distribution" in view of the fact that dissemination is the term widely and most generally used in connection with intelligence. It is further felt that the use of the phrase "appropriate departments and agencies" is preferable in this instance to "appropriate Government officials."

10. [Clifford's] memorandum suggests that there should be included "A program to procure all available foreign intelligence and to take such other measures in the field of foreign intelligence as will best ensure the national defense." It is felt that Section 1(b)(3) of Current Draft now sets forth the collection program, and that the other Sub-sections of Section 1(b) include phraseology similar to that desired. . . .

(15) <u>NATIONAL SECURITY ACT OF 1947</u> [Extract]

Source: 61 Statute 495 (1947).

. . . Sec. 2. In enacting this legislation, it is the intent of Congress to provide a comprehensive program for the future security of the United States; to provide for the establishment of integrated policies and procedures for the departments, agencies, and functions of the Government relating to the national security; to provide three military departments for the operation and administration of the Army, the Navy (including naval aviation and the United States Marine Corps), and the Air Force, with their assigned combat and service components; to provide for their authoritative coordination and unified direction under civilian control but not to merge them; to provide for the effective strategic direction of the armed forces and for their operation under unified control and for their integration into an efficient team of land, naval, and air forces. . . .

National Security Council

Sec. 101. (a) There is hereby established a council to be known as the National Security Council . . .

The function of the Council shall be to advise the President with respect to the integration of domestic, foreign, and military policies relating to the national security so as to enable the military services and the other departments and agencies of the Government to cooperate more effectively in matters involving the national security.

****

(b) In addition to performing such other functions as the President may direct, for the purpose of more effectively coordinating the policies and functions of the departments and agencies of the Government relating to the national security, it shall, subject to the direction of the President, be the duty of the Council -

> (1) to assess and appraise the objectives, commitments, and risks of the United States in relation to our actual and potential military power, in the interest of national security, for the purpose of making recommendations to the President in connection therewith; and

> (2) to consider policies on matters of common interest to the departments and agencies of the Government concerned with the national security, and to make recommendations to the President in connection therewith. . . .

(d) The Council shall, from time to time, make such recommendations, and such other reports to the President as it deems appropriate or as the President may require.

Central Intelligence Agency

Sec. 102. (a) There is hereby established under the National Security Council a Central Intelligence Agency with a Director of Central Intelligence, who shall be the head thereof. The Director shall be appointed by the President, by and with the advice and consent of the Senate, from among the commissioned officers of the armed services or from among individuals in civilian life. . . .

(d) For the purpose of coordinating the intelligence activities of the several Government departments and agencies in the interest of national security, it shall be the duty of the Agency, under the direction of the National Security Council -

> (1) to advise the National Security Council in matters concerning such intelligence activities of the Government departments and agencies as relate to national security.

> (2) to make recommendations to the National Security Council for the coordination of such intelligence activities of the departments and agencies of the Government as relate to the national security;

(3) to correlate and evaluate intelligence relating to the national security, and provide for
the appropriate dissemination of such intelligence
within the Government using where appropriate existing agencies and facilities: <u>Provided</u>, That the
Agency shall have no police, subpoena, law-
enforcement powers, or internal-security functions:
<u>Provided further</u>, That the departments and other
agencies of the Government shall continue to collect,
evaluate, correlate, and disseminate departmental
intelligence: <u>And provided further</u>, That the Director of Central Intelligence shall be responsible
for protecting intelligence sources and methods
from unauthorized disclosure;

(4) to perform, for the benefit of the existing
intelligence agencies, such additional services of
common concern as the National Security Council
determines can be more efficiently accomplished
centrally;

(5) to perform such other functions and duties
related to intelligence affecting the national
security as the National Security Council may from
time to time direct.

(e) To the extent recommended by the National Security Council and approved by the President, such intelligence of
the departments and agencies of the Government, except as hereinafter provided, relating to the national security shall be open
to the inspection of the Director of Central Intelligence, and
such intelligence as relates to the national security and is
possessed by such departments and other agencies of the Government, except as hereinafter provided, shall be made available to
the Director of Central Intelligence for correlation, evaluation,
and dissemination: <u>Provided</u>, <u>however</u>, That upon the written request of the Director of Central Intelligence, the Director of
the Federal Bureau of Investigation shall make available to the
Director of Central Intelligence such information for correlation,
evaluation, and dissemination as may be essential to the national
security.

****

(16) <u>FINAL REPORT, SENATE SELECT COMMITTEE ON INTELLIGENCE</u>
<u>ACTIVITIES, THE CIA</u>, 1945-1953 [Extract]

Source: U.S. Senate, Select Committee to Study Governmental Opera-
tions with respect to Intelligence Activities, *Final Report,*
Supplementary Detailed Staff Reports on Foreign and Military
Intelligence, Book IV, 94th Congress., 2d session, 1976, pp.12-40.

The CIG [Central Intelligence Group] had been established to
rectify the duplication among the military intelligence services
and to compensate for their biased analyses. The rather vaguely
conceived notion was that a small staff would assemble and review
the raw data collected by the departmental intelligence services
and produce objective estimates for the use of senior American
policymakers. Although in theory the concept was reasonable and

derived from real informational needs, institutional resistance
made implementation virtually impossible. The military intelligence services jealously guarded both their information and what
they believed were their prerogatives in providing policy guidance
to the President, making CIG's primary mission an exercise in
futility. . . .

In January 1946, [Sidney] Souers assumed direction over a
feeble organization [CIG]. Its personnel had to be assigned from
other agencies, and its budget was allocated from other departments. Clearly, the Departments [of State, War, and Navy] were
not inclined to relinquish manpower and money to a separate organization, even if that organization was little more than an ad-
junct of their own. Postwar personnel and budget cuts further
limited the support which the Departments were willing to provide.
. . .

. . . The Departments' failure to provide personnel to CIG
was only the first indication of the resistance which they posed
on every level.

The military particularly resented having to provide a civilian agency with military intelligence data. The services regarded this as a breach of professionalism, and more importantly,
believed that civilians could not understand, let alone analyze,
military intelligence data. The intensity of the military's
feelings on the issue of civilian access is indicated by the fact
that CIG could not receive information on the capabilities and
intentions of U.S. armed forces.

Almost immediately the State Department challenged CIG on the
issue of access to the President. Truman had requested that CIG
provide him with a daily intelligence summary from the Army, Navy,
and State Departments. However, Secretary of States Byrnes asserted his Department's prerogative in providing the President
with foreign policy analyses. While CIG did its summary, the
State Department continued to prepare its own daily digest.
Truman received both. . . .

In the spring of 1946 the NIA [National Intelligence Author-
ity], probably at the request of [CIG Director Hoyt] Vandenberg,
authorized CIG to carry out independent research and analysis "not
being presently performed" by the other Departments. The authorization led to a rapid increase in the size and functions of
CIG's intelligence staff. In August 1946, DCI Vandenberg established the Office of Research and Evaluation (ORE) to replace the
Central Reports Staff, which had been responsible for correlation.
ORE's functions were manifold - the production of national current
intelligence, scientific, technical, and economic intelligence,
as well as interagency coordination for national estimates. At
the same time, CIG was granted more money and personnel, and
Vandenberg took full advantage of the opportunity to hire large
numbers of people. . . .

With its own research and analysis capability, CIG could
carry out an independent intelligence function without having to
rely on the Departments for guidelines or for data. In effect,
it made CIG an intelligence producer, while still assuming the
continuation of its role in the production of coordinated national
estimates. Yet acquisition of an independent intelligence role

meant that production would outstrip coordinated analysis as a primary mission. . . .

The same 1946 directive which provided the CIG with an independent research and analysis capability also granted the CIG a clandestine collection capability. Since the end of the war, the remnant of the OSS [Office of Strategic Services] clandestine collection capability rested with the Strategic Services Unit (SSU), then in the War Department. In the postwar dismantling of OSS, SSU was never intended to be more than a temporary body. In the spring of 1946, an interdepartmental committee, whose members had been chosen by the President, recommended that CIG absorb SSU's functions.

The amalgamation of SSU constituted a major change in the size, structure, and mission of CIG. . . .

The transfer resulted in the establishment of the Office of Special Operations (OSO). OSO was responsible for espionage and counter-espionage. Through SSU, the CIG acquired an infusion of former OSS personnel, who were experienced in both areas. . . .

The nature and extent of the requests made to ORE [Office of Reports and Estimates of the CIG] contributed to its failure to fulfill its intended role in national intelligence estimates. President Truman expected and liked to receive CIG's daily summary of international events. His known preference meant that work on the Daily, as it was called, assumed priority attention - every day. . . . Although CIG had been created to minimize the duplicative efforts of the Departments, its acquisition of an independent intelligence production capability was now contributing to the problem.

The pressures of current events and the consequent demand for information within the government generated a constant stream of official requests to ORE. Most were concerned with events of the moment rather than with national intelligence, strictly defined. ORE, in turn, tended to accept any and all external requests - from State, from the JCS [Joint Chiefs of Staff], from the NSC [National Security Council]. As ORE attempted to satisfy the wide-ranging demands of many clients, its intelligence became directed to a working level audience rather than to senior policy-makers. . . . Gradually, ORE built up a series of commitments which made it less likely and less able to direct its efforts to estimate production.

****

The passage of the National Security Act in July 1947 legislated the changes in the Executive branch that had been under discussion since 1945. The Act established an independent Air Force; provided for coordination by a committee of service chiefs, the Joint Chiefs of Staff (JCS), and a Secretary of Defense; and created the National Security Council (NSC). The CIG became an independent department and was renamed the Central Intelligence Agency.

Under the Act, the CIA's mission was only loosely defined, since efforts to thrash out the CIA's duties in specific terms would have contributed to the tension surrounding the unification of the services. The five general tasks assigned to the Agency

were (1) to advise the NSC on matters related to national security; (2) to make recommendations to the NSC regarding the coordination of intelligence activities of the Departments; (3) to correlate and evaluate intelligence and provide for its appropriate
dissemination; (4) to carry out "service of common concern" and
(5) "to perform such other functions and duties related to intelligence affecting the national security as the NSC will from time
to time direct. . . . " The Act did not alter the functions of
the CIG. Clandestine collection, overt collection, production of
national current intelligence, and interagency coordination for
national estimates continued, and the personnel and internal structure remained the same.

As the CIA evolved between 1947 and 1950, it never fulfilled
its estimates function, but continued to expand its independent
intelligence production. . . . incentives existed within ORE for
the production of current rather than national coordinated intelligence. . . . Since the President's daily summary quickly became
ORE's main priority, contributions to the summary were visible
evidence of good work. . . . To have undertaken a longer-term
project would have meant depriving oneself of a series of opportunities for quick recognition. . . .

The drive for individuals in the branches to have their material printed and the role of the staffs in reviewing, editing and
often rejecting material for publication caused antagonism between the two groups. The branches regarded themselves as experts in their given fields and resented the staff's claims to
editorial authority. . . .

A July 1949 study conducted by a senior ORE analyst stated
that ORE's emphasis in production had shifted "from the broad
long-term type of problem to a narrowly defined short-term type
and from the predictive to the non-predictive type." The same
year a National Security Council-sponsored study concluded that
"the principle of the authoritative NIE [National Intelligence
Estimate] does not yet have established acceptance in the government. Each department still depends more or less on its own
intelligence estimates and establishes its plans and policies
accordingly." . . .

By the time Walter Bedell Smith became DCI [in October 1950],
it was clear that the CIA's record in providing national intelligence estimates had fallen far short of expectation. The obstacles presented by the departmental intelligence components,
the CIA's acquisition of authority to carry out independent research and analysis, demands from throughout the government for
CIA analyses, and internal organizational incentives had contributed to the failure of the coordinated national estimates function and to ORE's current intelligence orientation. In 1950 ORE
did little more than produce its own analyses and reports. . . .

These problems appeared more stark following the outbreak of
the Korean War in June 1950. Officials in the Executive branch
and members of Congress criticized the Agency for its failure to
predict more specifically the timing of the North Korean invasion
of South Korea. . . .

The immediacy of the war and the influence of William H.
Jackson who served with [Smith] as Deputy Director for Central

Intelligence (DDCI), convinced Smith of the necessity for changes.
After taking office, Smith and Jackson defined three major problems in the execution of the CIA's intelligence mission: the
need to ensure consistent, systematic production of estimates;
the need to strengthen the position of the DCI relative to the
departmental intelligence components; and the need to delineate
more clearly CIA's research and analysis function. Within three
months the two men had redefined the position of the DCI; had
established the Office of National Estimates, whose sole task was
the production of coordinated "national estimates"; and had
limited the Agency's independent research and analysis to economic
research on the "Soviet Bloc" nations. . . .

In an August 1950 memorandum to Smith, CIA General Counsel
Lawrence R. Houston stressed that the Intelligence Advisory Committee had assumed an advisory role to the NSC and functioned as
a supervisory body for the DCI - contrary to the initial intention. The IAC's inflated role had diminished the DCI's ability
to demand departmental cooperation for the CIA's national estimates responsibility. Houston advised that the DCI would have to
exert more specific direction over the departmental agencies, if
coordinated national intelligence production was to be achieved.
Smith acted on Houston's advice and informed the members of the
IAC that he would not submit to their direction. At the same
time, Smith encouraged their participation in the discussion and
approval of intelligence estimates. . . .

Smith's real attempt to establish an ongoing process for the
production of national estimates focused on the Office of National
Estimates (ONE). . . .

As organized in 1950, the Office of National Estimates had
two components, a group of staff members who drafted the estimates
and a senior body, known as the Board, who reviewed the estimates
and coordinated the intelligence judgments of the several Departments. Jackson envisioned the Board members as "men of affairs,"
experienced in government and international relations who could
make sage, pragmatic contributions to the work of the analysts.
At first all staff members were generalists, expected to write on
any subject, but gradually the staff broke down into generalists,
who wrote the estimates and regional specialists, who provided
expert assistance. . . .

As ONE was conceived in 1950, it was to be entirely dependent
on departmental contributions for research support. . . . However,
as a result of the CIA's gradual development of its own independent research capabilities over the next twenty years, ONE increasingly relied on CIA resources. The shift in ONE's sources
meant that the initial draft estimates - the estimates over which
the Departments negotiated - became more CIA products than interdepartmental products. . . .

ONE's link to policymakers existed through the NSC, where
meetings opened with a briefing by the DCI. Bedell Smith's regular attendance and his personal stature meant that the Agency was
at least listened to when briefings were presented. . . . The
precise way in which [the CIA's] NIEs [National Intelligence
Estimates] were used is unclear. . . .

The estimates problem was only symptomatic of the Agency's broader difficulties in intelligence production. By 1950 ORE had become a directionless service organization, attempting to answer requirements levied by all agencies related to all manner of subjects - politics, economics, science, technology. ORE's publications took the form of "backgrounders," country studies, surveys, and an occasional estimate. In attempting to do everything, it was contributing almost nothing. . . .

The issue of responsibility for political research had been a source of contention between ORE and State, which objected to the Agency's use of its data to publish "Agency" summations on subjects which State believed were appropriately its own and which were covered in State's own publications. . . .

There were three components of ORR [Office of Research and Reports]: the Basic Intelligence Division and Map Division, both of which were maintained intact from ORE, and the newly created Economic Research Area (ERA). Basic Intelligence had no research function. It consisted of a coordinating and editing staff in charge of the production of National Intelligence Surveys, compendia of descriptive information on nearly every country in the world, which were of primary interest to war planning agencies. The Map Division consisted of geographers and cartographers, most of whom were veterans of OSS. As the only foreign map specialists in the government, the division provided government-wide services.

The Economic Research Area became the focus of the Agency's research and analysis effort, and the Agency's development of this capability had a major impact on military and strategic analysis of the Soviet Union in the decade of the 1950's. . . .

. . . In July 1951, ORR personnel numbered 461, including the Map and Basic Intelligence Divisions and some ORE personnel who had been retained. By January 1952, . . . ORR's strength had increased to 654, with all of that growth in ERA. ORR continued to grow, and in February 1953, it employed 766 persons.

This remarkable and perhaps excessive escalation was a result of the redefinition of the Agency's research and analysis mission and the immediate pressures of the Korean War. Although the Agency was limited to economic research, its intelligence had to service virtually all levels of consumers. Unlike ONE, ORR's intelligence was never intended to be directed to senior policy-makers alone. Instead, ORR was to respond to the requests of senior and middle-level officials throughout the government, as well as serving a coordinating function. The breadth of ORR's clientele practically insured its size. In addition, the fact that ORR was created at the height of the Korean War, when the pressure for information was at a consistent peak, and when budgetary constraints were minimal, meant that personnel increases could be justified as essential to meet the intelligence needs of the war. After the war there was no effort to reduce the personnel strength.

Despite ORR's agreement with State regarding jurisdiction for political and economic intelligence, there remained in 1951 twenty-four government departments and agencies producing economic intelligence. Part of ORR's charge was to coordinate production on the "Soviet Bloc." . . .

The Agency's assumption of the economic research function and the subsequent creation of the EIC [Economic Intelligence Committee, a subcommittee of IAC] is a prime example of the ill-founded attempts to exert control over the departmental intelligence components. While the Agency was given primary responsibility for economic research on the "Soviet Bloc," other departments still retained their own intelligence capabilities to meet what they regarded as their specific needs. Senior officials, particularly the military, continued to rely on their departmental staffs to provide them with information. The EIC thus served primarily as a publication body. . . .

Completely contrary to its intended functions, ORE had developed into a current intelligence producer. . . .

Internal demands soon developed for the Agency to engage in current political research. Immediately following the disbandment of CIA's current political intelligence functions, the Agency's clandestine components insisted on CIA-originated research support. They feared that the security of their operations would be jeopardized by having to rely on the State Department. As a result of their requests, OCI [Office of Current Intelligence] developed into an independent political research organization. Although OCI began by providing research support only to the Agency's clandestine components, it gradually extended its intelligence function to service the requests of other Departments. . . .

The Office of Scientific Intelligence (OSI) had been created in 1949, and like other CIA components, had confronted military resistance to the execution of its coordination role. OSI's real conflict with the military lay with the division of responsibility for the production of scientific and technical intelligence. The chief issue was the distinction between intelligence relating to weapons and means of warfare already reduced to known prototypes and intelligence at the pilot-plant stage, anterior to prototypes. . . .

In August 1952 the military succeeded in making the distinction . . . that the services would have primary responsibility for the production of intelligence on all weapons, weapons systems, military equipment and techniques in addition to intelligence on research and development leading to new military material and techniques. OSI assumed primary responsibility for research in the basic sciences, scientific resources and medicine. . . Ultimately, the agreement imposed few restraints on OSI. With technological advances in the ensuing years, OSI developed its own capability for intelligence on weapons systems technology and continued to challenge the military on the issue of basic science-technology research. . . .

In January 1952, CIA's intelligence functions were grouped under the Directorate for Intelligence (DDI). In addition to ONE, the DDI's intelligence production components included: the Office of Research and Reports (ORR), the Office of Scientific Intelligence (OSI), and the Office of Current Intelligence (OCI). Collection of overt information was the responsibility of the Office of Operations (OO). The Office of Collection and Dissemination (OCD) engaged in the distribution of intelligence as well as storage and retrieval of unevaluated intelligence.

The immediate pressures for information generated by the Korean War resulted in continued escalation in size and intelligence production. Government-wide demands for the Agency to provide information on Communist intentions in the Far East and around the world justified the increases. By the end of 1953 DDI personnel numbered 3,338. Despite the sweeping changes, the fundamental problem of duplication among the Agency and the Departments remained. . . .

Apart from their role in the production of coordinated national estimates CIG and the CIA were intended to exercise some direction over the intelligence activities of the State Department and the military – determining which collection and production functions would most appropriately and most efficiently be conducted by which Departments to avoid duplication. . . .

A major problem related to the coordination of departmental activities was the role of the Director of Central Intelligence, specifically his relationship to the military intelligence chiefs. Thus, he could not exert any real pressure on behalf of the Agency and its objectives. Confronted with objections or a challenge from the Army G-2 chief, for example, the Director had no basis on which to press his arguments or references except in terms of the Agency's overall mission. . . .

By the end of his term Vandenberg had become convinced that the only means by which CIG could accomplish its coordination mission was through control of the departmental intelligence agencies. Approaching the Intelligence Advisory Board [IAB], Vandenberg asked that they grant the DCI authority to act as "executive agent" for the departmental secretaries in matters related to intelligence. In effect, the DCI was to be given authority for supervision of the departmental intelligence components. The IAB approved Vandenberg's request and drafted an agreement providing for the DCI's increased authority. However, [CIG Director] Hillenkoetter [Vandenberg's successor] preferred not to press for its enactment and instead, hoped to rely on day-to-day cooperation. By failing to act on Vandenberg's initative, Hillenkoetter undermined the position of the DCI in relation to the Departments.

Consideration of the 1947 National Security Act by the Congress was accompanied by active deliberation in the Executive about the newly constituted Central Intelligence Agency. The DCI's relationship to the departmental intelligence components, the Departments' authority over the Agency, and the Departments' roles in the production of national intelligence continued to be sources of contention. The fundamental issue remained one of control and jurisdiction: how much would the CIA gain and how much would the Departments be willing to concede?

As the bill took shape, the Departments resented the DCI's stated role as intelligence advisor to the NSC, thereby responsible to the President. The military intelligence chiefs, [Thomas] Inglis of the Navy and [S.J.] Chamberlin of the Army, favored continuation of the Intelligence Advisory Board. They advocated providing it with authority to grant approval or dissent for recommendations before they reached the NSC. If enacted, this arrangement would have given the Departments veto power over the Agency and, in effect, would have made the IAB the advisory body to the NSC.

Robert Lovett, Acting Secretary of State, made a similar recommendation. He proposed an advisory board to insure "prior consideration by the chiefs of the intelligence services" for matters scheduled to go before the NSC. The positions of both Lovett and the military reflected the reluctance of the Departments to give the CIA the primary intelligence advisory role for senior policymakers.

More specifically, the Departments themselves resisted conceding a direct relationship between the President and the DCI. Such an arrangement was perceived as limiting and threatening the Secretaries' own advisory relationships to the President.

Between 1946 and 1947, in an effort to curb the independence of the DCI, the military considered successive pieces of legislation restricting the Director's position to military careerists. Whether the attempted legislation was prompted by the concern over civilian access to military intelligence or by a desire to gain control of the Agency is unknown. In either case, the Departments were tenaciously protecting what they perceived to be their best interests.

In spite of continued resistance by the Departments the National Security Act affirmed the CIA's role in coordinating the intelligence activities of the State Department and the military. In 1947 the Intelligence Advisory Committee (IAC) was created to serve as a coordinating body in establishing intelligence requirements among the Departments. Chaired by the DCI, the IAC included representatives from the Department of State, Army, Air Force, the Joint Chiefs of Staff, and the Atomic Energy Commission. Although the DCI was to "establish priorities" for intelligence collection and analysis, he did not have the budgetary or administrative authority to control the departmental components. Moreover, no Department was willing to compromise what it perceived as its own intelligence needs to meet the collective needs of policymakers as defined by the DCI.

V. Clandestine Activities

A. Origins of Covert Action

The concept of a central intelligence agency developed out of a concern for the quality of intelligence analysis available to policymakers. The 1945 discussion which surrounded the creation of CIG focused on the problem of intelligence coordination. Two years later debates on the CIA in the Congress and the Executive assumed only the coordination role along with intelligence collection (both overt and clandestine) and analysis for the newly constituted Agency.

Yet, within one year of the passage of the National Security Act, the CIA was charged with the conduct of covert psychological, political, paramilitary, and economic activities. The acquisition of this mission had a profound impact on the direction of the Agency and on its relative stature within the government.

The precedent for covert activities existed in OSS. The clandestine collection capability had been preserved through the Strategic Services Unit, whose responsibilities CIG absorbed in

June 1946. The maintenance of that capability and its presence in CIA contributed to the Agency's ultimate assumption of a covert operational role.

. . . initiation of covert operations is usually associated with the 1948 Western European elections. . . .this was the first officially recorded evidence of U.S. covert political intervention abroad. However, American policymakers had formulated plans for covert action - at first covert psychological action - much earlier. Decisions regarding U.S. sponsorship of clandestine activities were gradual but consistent, spurred on by the growing concern over Soviet intentions.

By late 1946, cabinet officials were preoccupied with the Soviet threat, and over the next year their fears intensified. For U.S. policymakers, international events seemed to be a sequence of Soviet incursions. In March 1946, the Soviet Union refused to withdraw its troops from the Iranian province of Azerbaijan; two months later civil war involving Communist rebel forces erupted in Greece. By 1947, Communists had assumed power in Poland, Hungary, and Rumania; and in the Philippines the government was under attack by the Hukbalahaps, a communist-led guerrilla group.

For U.S. officials, the perception of the Soviet Union as a global threat demanded new modes of conduct in foreign policy to supplement the traditional alternatives of diplomacy and war. Massive economic aid represented one new method of achieving U.S. foreign policy objectives. . . . By insuring economic stability, U.S. officials hoped to limit Soviet encroachments. Covert operations represented another, more activist departure in the conduct of U.S. peacetime foreign policy. Covert action was an option that was something more than diplomacy but still short of war. As such, it held the promise of frustrating Soviet ambitions without provoking open conflict.

The suggestion for the initiation of covert operations did not originate in CIG. Sometime in late 1946, Secretary of War Robert Patterson suggested to Forrestal that military and civilian personnel study this form of war for future use. . . . from Patterson's suggestions policymakers proceeded to consider the lines of authority for the conduct of psychological operations. Discussion took place in the State-War-Navy Coordinating Committee (SWNCC), whose members included the Secretaries of the three Departments, Byrnes, Patterson and Forrestal. In December 1946, a SWNCC subcommittee formulated guidelines for the conduct of psychological warfare in peacetime and wartime. The full SWNCC adopted the recommendation later that month.

Discussion continued within the Executive in the spring and summer of 1947. From all indications, only senior-level officials were involved, and the discussions were closely held. From establishing guidelines for the possibility of psychological warfare, policymakers proceeded to contingency planning. On April 30, 1947, a SWNCC subcommittee was organized to consider and actually plan for a U.S. psychological warfare effort. On June 5, 1947, the subcommittee was accorded a degree of permanency and renamed the Special Studies and Evaluations Subcommittee. By this time, the fact that the U.S. would engage in covert operations was a given; what remained were decisions about the organizational arrangements and actual implementation.

In the fall of 1947 policymakers engaged in a series of discussions on the assignment of responsibility for the conduct of covert operations. There was no ready consensus and a variety of opinions emerged. . . . Sometime in October 1947 [DCI Roscoe Hillenkoetter] recommended "vitally needed psychological operations - again in general terms without reference to specific countries or groups - but believed that such activities were military rather than intelligence functions and therefore belonged in an organization responsible to the JCS. Hillenkoetter also believed congressional authorization would be necessary both for the initiation of psychological warfare and for the expenditure of funds for that purpose. . . . Hillenkoetter's . . . opinions were undoubtedly influenced by the difficulties he had experienced in dealing with the Departments. It is likely that he feared CIA's acquisition of an operational capability would precipitate similar problems of departmental claims on the Agency's operational functions. Hillenkoetter's stated preferences had no apparent impact on the outcome of the psychological warfare debate.

Within a few weeks of Hillenkoetter's statement, [Secretary of Defense James] Forrestal, the Secretaries of the Army, Navy, and Air Force, along with the JCS, advanced their recommendations regarding the appropriate organization to conduct covert psychological warfare. In a proposal dated November 4, they held that propaganda of all kinds was a function of the State Department and that an Assistant Secretary of State in consultation with the DCI and a military representative should be responsible for the operations.

On November 24, President Truman approved the November 4 recommendation, assigning psychological warfare coordination to the Secretary of State. Within three weeks, the decision was reversed. Despite the weight of numbers favoring State Department control, the objections of Secretary of State George Marshall eliminated the option advanced by the other Secretaries. Marshall opposed State Department responsibility for covert action. . . . and believed that such activities, if exposed as State Department actions, would embarrass the Department and discredit American foreign policy both short-term and long-term. . . .

. . . It was out of concern for the success and credibility of the United States' recently articulated economic program that Marshall objected to State Department conduct of covert action. Marshall favored placing covert activities outside the Department, but still subject to guidance from the Secretary of State.

Marshall's objections prevailed, and on December 14 the National Security Council adopted NSC 4/A, a directive which gave the CIA responsibility for covert psychological operations. The DCI was charged with ensuring that psychological operations were consistent with U.S. foreign policy and overt foreign information activities. On December 22 the Special Procedures Group was established within the CIA's Office of Special Operations to carry out psychological operations. . . .

State and the military wanted to maintain control over covert psychological operations, but they did not want to assume operational responsibility. The sensitive nature of the operations made the Departments fear exposure of their association with the activities. The CIA offered advantages as the organization to execute covert operations. Indeed, in 1947 one-third of the CIA's personnel had served with OSS. The presence of former OSS personnel, who had experience in wartime operations, provided the Agency with a group of individuals who could quickly develop and implement programs. This, coupled with its overseas logistical apparatus, gave the Agency a ready capability. In addition, the Agency also possessed a system of unvouchered funds for its clandestine collection mission, which meant that there was no need to approach Congress for separate appropriations. With the Departments unwilling to assume the risks involved in covert activities, the CIA provided a convenient mechanism.

During the next six months psychological operations were initiated in Central and Eastern Europe. The activities were both limited and amateur and consisted of unattributed publications, radio broadcasts, and blackmail. By 1948 the Special Procedures Group had acquired a radio transmitter for broadcasting behind the Iron Curtain, had established a secret propaganda printing plant in Germany, and had begun assembling a fleet of balloons to drop propaganda materials into Eastern European countries.

Both internally and externally the pressure continued for an expansion in the scope of U.S. covert activity. The initial definition of covert action had been limited to covert psychological warfare. In May 1948, George F. Kennan, Director of the State Department's Policy Planning Staff, advocated the development of a covert political action capability. The distinction at that time was an important and real one. Political action meant direct intervention in the electoral processes of foreign governments rather than attempts to influence public opinion through media activities.

International events gave force to Kennan's proposal. In February 1948, Communists staged a successful coup in Czechoslovakia. At the same time, France and Italy were beleaguered by a wave of Communist-inspired strikes. In March 1948, near hysteria gripped the U.S. Government with the so-called "war scare." . . .

The war scare launched a series of interdepartmental intelligence estimates on the likelihood of a Soviet attack on Western Europe and the United States. Although the estimates concluded that there was no evidence that the U.S.S.R. would start a war, [General Lucius] Clay's [Commander in Chief, European Command] cable had articulated the degree of suspicion and outright fear of the Soviet Union that was shared by policymakers at this time. Kennan proposed that State, specifically the Policy Planning Staff, have a "directorate" for overt and covert political warfare. The director of the Special Studies Group, as Kennan named it, would be under State Department control, but not formally associated with the Department. Instead, he would have concealed funds and personnel elsewhere, and his small staff of eight people would be comprised of representatives from State and Defense.

Kennan's concept and statement of function were endorsed by the NSC. In June 1948, . . . the NSC adopted NSC 10/2 . . . authorizing a dramatic increase in the range of covert operations directed against the Soviet Union, including political warfare, economic warfare, and paramilitary activities.

While authorizing a sweeping expansion in covert activities, NSC 10/2 established the Office of Special Projects, soon renamed the Office of Policy Coordination (OPC), within the CIA to replace the Special Procedures Group. As a CIA component OPC was an anomaly. OPC's budget and personnel were appropriated within CIA allocations, but the DCI had little authority in determining OPC's activities. Responsibility for the direction of OPC rested with the Office's director, designated by the Secretary of State. Policy guidance - decisions on the need for specific activities - came to the OPC director from State and Defense, bypassing the DCI.

The organizational arrangements established in 1948 for the conduct of covert operations reflected both the concept of covert action as defined by U.S. officials and the perception of the CIA as an institution. Both the activities and the institution were regarded as extensions of State and the military services. The Departments (essentially the NSC) defined U.S. policy objectives; covert action represented one means of attaining those objections; and the CIA executed the operations.

In a conversation on August 12, 1948, Hillenkoetter, Kennan, and [NSC Executive Secretary] Sidney Souers discussed the implementation of NSC 10/2. The summary of the conversation reveals policymakers firm expectation that covert political action would serve strictly as a support function for U.S. foreign and military policy and that State and the services would define the scope of covert activities in specific terms. . . .

Clearly, in recommending the development of a covert action capability in 1948, policymakers intended to make available a small contingency force that could mount operations on a limited basis. Senior officials did not plan to develop large scale continuing covert operations. Instead, they hoped to establish a small capability that could be activated at their discretion.

B. The Office of Policy Coordination, 1948-1952.

OPC developed into a far different organization from that envisioned by Forrestal, Marshall, and Kennan in August 1948. By 1952, when it merged with the Agency's clandestine collection component, the Office of Special Operations, OPC had expanded its activities to include worldwide covert operations, and it had achieved an institutional independence that was unimaginable at the time of its inception.

The outbreak of the Korean War in the summer of 1950 had a significant effect on OPC. Following the North Korean invasion of South Korea, the State Department as well as the Joint Chiefs of Staff recommended the initiation of paramilitary activities in Korea and China. OPC's participation in the war effort contributed to its transformation from an organization that was to provide the capability for a limited number of ad hoc operations to an organization that conducted continuing, ongoing activities on a massive scale. . . . In 1949 OPC's total personnel strength was 302; in 1952 it was 2,812 plus 3,142 overseas contract personnel. In 1949 OPC's budget figure was $4,700,000; in 1952 it was $82,000,000. In 1949 OPC had personnel assigned to seven overseas stations; in 1952 OPC had personnel at forty-seven stations.

Apart from the impetus provided by the Korean War several other factors converged to alter the nature and scale of OPC's activities. First, policy direction took the form of condoning and fostering activity without providing scrutiny and control. Officials throughout the government regarded the Soviet Union as an aggressive force, and OPC's activities were initiated and justified on the basis of this shared perception. The series of NSC directives which authorized covert operations laid out broad objectives and stated in bold terms the necessity for meeting the Soviet challenge head on. After the first 1948 directive authorizing covert action, subsequent directives in 1950 and 1951 called for an intensification of these activities without establishing firm guidelines for approval. . . .

On October 21, 1951 NSC 10/5 replaced NSC 10/2 as the governing directive for covert action. It once again called for an intensification of covert action and reaffirmed the responsibility of the DCI in the conduct of covert operations. Each of these policy directives provided the broadest justification for large-scale covert activity.

Second, OPC operations had to meet the very different policy needs of the State and Defense Departments. The State Department encouraged political action and propaganda activities to support its diplomatic objectives, while the Defense Department requested paramilitary activities to support the Korean War effort and to counter communist-associated guerrillas. These distinct missions required OPC to develop and maintain different capabilities, including manpower and support material.

The third factor contributing to OPC's expansion was the organizational arrangements that created an internal demand for projects. The decision to undertake covert political action and to lodge that responsibility in a group distinct from the Departments required the creation of a permanent structure. OPC required regular funding to train and pay personnel, . . . [and] had to be budgeted for in advance. With budgeting came the need for ongoing activities to justify future allocations – rather than leaving the flexibility of responding to specific requirements.

To fulfill the different State and Defense requirements OPC adopted a "project" system rather than a programmed financial system. This meant that operations were organized around projects – individual activities, e.g. funding to a political candidate – rather than general programs or policy objectives, and the OPC budgeted in terms of anticipated numbers of projects. . . . The result was competition among individuals and among the OPC divisions to generate the maximum number of projects. . . .

A reorganization in 1950 attempted to rectify the problem by assigning responsibility for planning single-country operations to the appropriate geographical division. This meant that the divisions assumed real operational control. . . . staffs seized on their authority over multiple country activities to maintain an operational role in such areas as labor operations. . . .

The relationship between Washington and the field was subject to pressures similar to those that influenced the interaction between the divisions and the staffs. Predictably, field personnel began to develop their own perspective on suitable operations and

their mode of conduct. . . . Gradually, as the number of overseas
personnel grew and as the number of stations increased, the stations assumed the initiative in project development. . . .

C.   Policy Guidance

Responsibility for coordination with the State and Defense
Departments rested with Frank G. Wisner, appointed Assistant Director for Policy Coordination (ADPC) on September 1, 1948. . . .
Wisner possessed the operational instincts, the activist temper-
ament, and the sheer physical energy required to develop and
establish OPC as an organization. . . .

Although the stipulation of NSC 10/1 that the Secretary of
State designate the ADPC was intended to insure the ADPC's primary
identification with State, that did not occur. . . .

The guidance that State and Defense provided OPC became very
general and allowed the maximum opportunity for project development. . . .

With the broad objectives laid out in NSC 10/2, the means of
implementation were left to OPC. The representatives were not an
approval body, and there was no formal mechanism whereby individual projects had to be brought before them for discussion. Because it was assumed that covert action would be exceptional,
strict provisions for specific project authorization were not considered necessary. With minimal supervision for State and Defense
and with a shared agreement on the nature of the OPC mission,
individuals in OPC could take the initiative in conceiving and
implementing projects. In this context, operational tasks, personnel, money and material tended to grow in relation to one
another with little outside oversight.

In 1951, DCI Walter Bedell Smith took the initiative in requesting more specific high-level policy direction. In May of
that year, . . . Smith called for NSC restatement or redetermina-
tion of the several responsibilities and authorities involved in
U.S. covert operations. More importantly, Smith proposed that
the the newly created Pscyhological Strategy Board provide CIA
guidance on the conduct of covert operations.

The NSC adopted Smith's proposal making the Psychological
Strategy Board the approval body for covert action. . . .

D.   OPC Activities

At the outset OPC activities were directed toward four principal operational areas: refugee programs, labor activities,
media development, and political action. Geographically, the area
of concentration was Western Europe. . . . Western Europe was the
area deemed most vulnerable to Communist encroachment; . . . until
1950 both CIA (OSO) and OPC were excluded from the Far East by
General Douglas MacArthur, who refused to concede any jurisdiction to the civilian intelligence agency in the Pacific theater.
. . .

The national elections in Europe in 1948 had been a primary
motivation in the establishment of OPC. By channeling funds to
center parties and developing media assets, OPC attempted to influence election results - with considerable success.   These

activities formed the basis for covert political action for the next twenty years. . . .

Until 1950 OPC's paramilitary activities . . . were limited to plans and preparations for stay-behind nets in the event of future war. Requested by the Joint Chiefs of Staff, these projected OPC operations focused, once again, on Western Europe and were designed to support NATO forces against Soviet attack.

The outbreak of the Korean War significantly altered the nature of OPC's paramilitary activities as well as the organization's overall size and capability. Between fiscal year 1950 and fiscal year 1951, OPC's personnel strength jumped from 584 to 1531. Most of that growth took place in paramilitary activities in the Far East. In the summer of 1950, following the North Korean invasion of South Korea, the State Department requested the initiation of paramilitary and psychological operations on the Chinese mainland. Whatever MacArthur's preferences, the JCS were also eager for support activities in the Far East. This marked the beginning of OPC's active paramilitary engagement. The Korean War established OPC's and CIA's jurisdiction in the Far East and created the basic paramilitary capability that the Agency employed for twenty years. . . .

E. OPC Integration and the OPC-OSO Merger

. . . OPC's anomalous position in the Agency revealed the difficulty of maintining two separate organizations for the execution of varying but overlapping clandestine activities. The close "tradecraft" relationship between clandestine collection and covert action, and the frequent necessity for one to support the other was totally distorted with the separation of functions in OSO and OPC. Organizational rivalry rather than interchange dominated the relationship between the two components.

On the operating level the conflicts were intense. Each component had representatives conducting separate operations at each station. Given the related missions of the two, OPC and OSO personnel were often competing for the same agents and, not infrequently, attempting to wrest agents from each other. . . .

F. Congressional Review

The CIA was conceived and organized as an agent of the Executive branch. Traditionally, Congress' only formal relationship to the Agency was through the appropriations process. The concept of Congressional oversight in the sense of scrutinizing and being fully informed of Agency activities did not exist. The international atmosphere, Congress' relationship to the Executive branch and the Congressional committee structure determined the pattern of interaction between the Agency and members of the legislature. Acceptance of the need for clandestine activities and of the need for secrecy to protect those activities contributed to Congress' relatively unquestioning and uncritical attitude regarding the CIA, as did the Executive branch's ascendancy in foreign policy for nearly two decades following World War II. The strong committee system which accorded enormous power to committee chairmen and limited the participation of less senior members in committee business resulted in informal arrangements whereby selected members were kept informed of Agency activities primarily through one-to-one exchanges with the DCI. . . .

For nearly twenty years a small group of ranking members dominated [congressional] relationships with the Agency. As Chairman of the House Armed Services Committee, Representative Carl Vinson, a Democrat from Georgia, presided over CIA matters from 1949 to 1953 and from 1955 to 1965. Clarence Cannon served as chairman of the House Appropriations Committee from 1949 to 1963 and chaired the Defense Subcommittee which had supervising authority over CIA appropriations. Cannon organized a special group of five members to meet informally on CIA appropriations. In the Senate between 1947 and 1954 chairmanship of the Armed Services Committee was held by Chan Gurney, Millard Tydings, Richard Russell and Leverett Saltonstall. . . .

Because the committee chairmen maintained their positions for extended periods of time, they established continuing relationships with DCIs and preserved an exclusivity in their knowledge of Agency activities. They were also able to develop relationships of mutual trust and understanding with the DCIs which allowed informal exchanges to prevail over formal votes and close supervision.

Within the Congress procedures governing the Agency's budget assured maximum secrecy. The DCI presented his estimate of the budget for the coming fiscal year broken down into general functional categories. Certification by the subcommittee chairmen constituted approval. Exempt from floor debate and from public disclosure, CIA appropriations were and are concealed in the Department of Defense budget. In accordance with the 1949 Act the DCI has only to certify that the money as appropriated has been spent. He does not have to account publicly for specific expenditures, . . .

To allow greater flexibility for operational expenditures the Contingency Reserve Fund was created in 1952. The Fund provided a sum independent of the regular budget to be used for unanticipated large projects. . . . The most common use of the Fund was for covert operations.

Budgetary matters rather than the specific nature of CIA activities were the concern of Congressional members, and given the perception of the need for action against the Soviet Union, approval was routine. . . .

Limited information sharing rather than rigorous oversight characterized Congress' relationship to the Agency. Acceptance of the need for secrecy and Congressional procedures would perpetuate what amounted to mutual accommodation.

****

By 1953 the Agency had achieved the basic structure and scale it retained for the next twenty years. The Korean War, United States foreign policy objectives, and the Agency's internal organizational arrangements had combined to produce an enormous impetus for growth. The CIA was six times the size it had been in 1947.

(17) <u>SPECIAL MESSAGE TO CONGRESS, PRESIDENT TRUMAN</u>, March 5, 1949 [Extract]

Source: *Public Papers of the Presidents: Harry S. Truman, 1949.* Washington: U.S. Government Printing Office, 1964, pp. 164-165.

. . . [The National Security] Act [of 1947] has provided a practical and workable basis for beginning the unification of the military services and for coordinating military policy with foreign and economic policy. . . .

The efficiency of military purchasing has steadily increased until today more than 75 percent of the material of the armed services is procured under coordinated purchasing arrangements. . . .

The coordination of military policy with foreign and economic policies has been greatly improved, principally through the efforts of the National Security Council and the National Security Resources Board.

The past eighteen months have dispelled any doubt that unification of the armed forces can yield great advantages to the Nation. No one advocates a return to the outmoded organization of the days preceeding the National Security Act. On the contrary, the issue today is not whether we should have unification, but how we can make it more effective.

We have now had sufficient experience under the Act to be able to identify and correct its weaknesses, . . . we should now proceed to make the needed improvements in the Act.

The duties and responsibilities of the Secretary of Defense as now set forth in the Act are of too limited a character, and are restricted to specified items. For example, the Act expressly provides that all duties not specifically conferred upon the Secretary of Defense are to remain vested in the Secretaries of the Army, the Navy and the Air Force. While the Secretary of Defense, as the head of the National Military Establishment, ought to be ultimately accountable, under the President, for its administration, he is specifically limited by this Act in the degree to which he may hold the military departments responsible to him. The departmental Secretaries are specifically authorized to deal directly with higher authority. Furthermore, many of the key responsibilities of the Secretary of Defense have been assigned by this statute, not to the Secretary, but to Boards and agencies which derive much of their authority from the military departments themselves.

In short, the Act fails to provide for a fully responsible official with authority adequate to meet his responsibility, whom the President and the Congress can hold accountable. The Act fails to provide the basis for an organization and a staff adequate to achieve the most efficient and economical defense program and to attain effective and informed civilian control.

I, therefore, recommend that the National Security Act be amended to accomplish two basic purposes: first, to convert the National Military Establishment into an Executive Department of the Government, to be known as the Department of Defense; and, second, to provide the Secretary of Defense with appropriate responsibility and authority, and with civilian and military assistance adequate to fulfill his enlarged responsibility.

Within the new Department of Defense, I recommend that the Departments of the Army, the Navy and the Air Force be designated as military departments. The responsibility of the Secretary of Defense for exercising direction, authority, and control over the affairs of the Department of Defense should be made clear. Furthermore, the present limitations and restrictions which are inappropriate to his status as head of an Executive Department should be removed. The Secretary of Defense should be the sole representative of the Department of Defense on the National Security Council. . . .

(18) <u>STATEMENT, PRESIDENT TRUMAN</u>, August 10, 1949 [Extract]

Source: *Public Papers of the Presidents: Harry S. Truman, 1949.* Washington: U.S. Government Printing Office, 1964, pp. 417-418.

I have today signed H.R. 5632, the National Security Act Amendments of 1949.

This legislation represents a major step toward more responsible and efficient administration of the military affairs of the Nation. It converts the National Military Establishment into a new executive Department of Defense, within which the former executive departments of the Army, Navy, and Air Force are included as military departments. It gives the Secretary of Defense, under the direction of the President, direction, authority and control over the Department of Defense, appropriate to his responsibility as head of that Department. It provides for a Deputy Secretary and three Assistant Secretaries of Defense, and for a Chairman of the Joint Chiefs of Staff, to assist the Secretary in carrying out his responsibilities. It provides for better financial management of the Department by requiring a "performance-type" budget, allowing greater flexibility in the control and use of funds, and establishing a Comptroller in the Department of Defense and in each of the military departments.

These provisions afford [a] sound basis for further progress toward the unification of our Armed Forces and the unified management of our military affairs. . . .

It is unfortunate that in this generally progressive legislation at least one provision represents a backward step. New and cumbersome restrictions are placed on the membership of the National Security Council - whereas the desirable course would be to follow the recommendation of the Commission on Organization of the Executive Branch and remove the statutory restrictions on the Council's membership.

This legislation as a whole represents a great advance. Action will be taken under it, both immediately and in the long run, to achieve increased efficiency and economy and greater coordination of our military forces. I believe that this act will permit us to make real progress toward building a balanced and effective national defense.

(19) <u>MESSAGE TO CONGRESS, PRESIDENT TRUMAN</u>, June 20, 1949
[Extract]

Source: *Public Papers of the Presidents: Harry S. Truman, 1949.*
Washington: U.S. Government Printing Office, 1964, pp. 316-317.

I transmit herewith Reorganization Plan No. 4 of 1949, prepared in accordance with the provisions of the Reorganization Act
of 1949. The plan transfers the National Security Council and
the National Security Resources Board to the Executive Office of
the President. . . .

The growth of the executive branch and the increasingly complex nature of the problems with which it must deal have greatly
intensified the necessity of strong and well-coordinated staff
facilities to enable the President to meet his responsibilities
for the effective administration of the executive branch of the
Government. Ten years ago several of the staff agencies of the
executive branch were brought together in the Executive Office of
the President under the immediate direction of the President.
The wisdom of this step has been demonstrated by greatly improved
staff assistance to the President, which has contributed importantly to the management of the Government during the trying
years of war and of post-war adjustment.

Since the creation of the Executive Office of the President,
however, the Congress has further recognized the need for more
adequate central staff and created two new important staff agencies to assist the President - the National Security Council and
the National Security Resources Board. The primary function of
the first of these agencies as defined by statute, is "to advise
the President with respect to the integration of domestic, foreign, and military policies relating to the national security."
The function of the second is "to advise the President concerning
the coordination of military, industrial, and civilian mobilization."

Within their respective fields these agencies assist the
President in developing plans and policies which extend beyond
the responsibility of any single department of the Government.
In this they play a role similar in character to that of the
various units of the Executive Office of the President. In fact,
many of the problems with which they deal require close collaboration with the agencies of the Executive Office.

Since the principal purpose of the National Security Council
and the National Security Resources Board is to advise and assist
the President and their work needs to be coordinated to the fullest degree with that of other staff arms of the President, such
as the Bureau of the Budget and the Council of Economic Advisers,
it is highly desirable that they be incorporated in the Executive
Office of the President. . . .

Because of the necessity of coordination with other staff
agencies, the National Security Council and the National Security
Resources Board are physically located within the Executive Office
of the President and I have taken steps to assure close working
relations between them and the agencies of the Executive Office.
This plan, therefore, will bring their legal status into accord
with existing administrative practice. It is not probable that

the reorganization included in the plan will immediately result in reduced expenditures. They will, however, provide a firm foundation for maintaining and furthering the efficient administrative relationships already established, and for assuring that we have provided permanent arrangements vitally necessary to the national security.

(20) RECORD, UNDER SECRETARY OF STATE'S STAFF MEETING, April 15, 1949

Source: *Foreign Relations of the United States: 1949 Vol. I National Security Affairs, Foreign Economic Policy*. Washington: U.S. Government Printing Office, 1976, p. 284.

. . . (6) [Here, as in other recent instances, the Staff reflected the uncertainty of the purpose and use of the National Security Council. However, Mr. Webb threw in an interesting point, that he felt it necessary for the Department to work with (NSC executive secretary Sidney) Souers in order that the State Department could give direction to the use which the President would make of the NSC. . . .] . . . *

(21) MEMORANDUM, UNDER SECRETARY OF STATE JAMES WEBB, May 4, 1949 [Extract]

Source: *Foreign Relations of the United States: 1949 Vol. I National Security Affairs, Foreign Economic Policy*. Washington: U.S. Government Printing Office, 1976, pp. 296-298.

I arranged a meeting with [NSC Executive Secretary Sidney] Souers and George Kennan [Director, State Department's Planning Staff] in order that we might have a discussion on the Department's participation in the NSC. I opened the discussion by saying that the State Department was interested in reaching an agreement on how we could best furnish the President with what he needed to carry out his duties relating to the National security. Mr. Souers agreed that we all had the same objective (i.e., giving the President what he needs) and that we only needed to agree on the procedures by which we could accomplish this. I stated that I would like to discuss four subjects regarding Council procedure on which I felt that agreement was essential to achieve our common objectives. . . .

1. Consideration by the Council of Measures to Implement Policies.

I stated that the State Department has been concerned because of the tendency of the Military Establishment to agitate for specific "measures" papers designed to implement broad policies. I stated that it was the State Department's belief that "measures" papers generally should not be considered in the NSC. I cited the cases of the "measures" paper designed to implement NSC 20/4 (US Objectives Toward the USSR) which was drafted over State protests. I asked Admiral Souers if we could not have that paper

---

*Paraphrase taken directly from the original source document. (Editor).

removed from the agenda. Admiral Souers agreed with our position as to consideration of "measures" papers by the NSC. He said that he would take appropriate action to remove the paper in question from the agenda.

2. Role of the NSC Staff.

I informed Admiral Souers that the Department had some doubts as to the desirability of continuing the NSC contributed staff in its present role (each member agency contributes one staff member and the State Department supplies an additional officer known as the Staff Coordinator). I pointed out that the role of the Staff had never been clearly defined and that we doubted that it served a useful purpose. Admiral Souers agreed that the accomplishments of the staff had not been impressive but stated that he believed it would be a worthwhile unit if it were used as a forum for analysis of problems and a bringing together of military and political views to be taken into consideration by State in its drafting papers. He agreed that the staff should not generally attempt to draft papers and that State should not have to submit its papers to the Council through the Staff. Admiral Souers then explained [Director of the Joint Staff, Joint Chiefs of Staff] General [Alfred] Gruenther's role as set up by Secretary [of Defense Louis] Johnson in handling NSC business. Contrary to the former arrangement when the Secretary of Defense was not represented on the working levels in the Council, General Gruenther will have responsibility for the Secretary of Defense for all working level participation by the National Military Establishment.

Admiral Souers agreed with our suggestion that State needed only one man on the Staff and not two. He agreed that if we placed one good man in this role he could serve as Staff member and coordinator. I asked [Director, Policy Planning Staff George] Kennan, [Executive Secretary of the Policy Planning Staff George] Butler and [Assistant to the Director of the Executive Secretariat, Department of State William] McWilliams to give their attention to finding a suitable officer for this role. They are to consult with [Deputy Under Secretary of State John] Peurifoy and forward recommendations to me.

Mr. Kennan and I agreed that Admiral Souers' conception of the role of the Staff seemed to have merit and stated that we would be willing to give the suggestion a thorough trial.

3. Implementation of NSC Papers.

I stated that the State Department was concerned that whereas we were required to submit reports of progress of our implementation of NSC papers, no action was taken when we reported failure of other agencies to carry out their assigned responsibilities. The case in point is NSC 13/2 (US Policy Toward Japan) on which State has reported failure by the Military Establishment and General MacArthur in carrying out the provisions of the paper. I asked Admiral Souers how he thought this should be taken care of. Admiral Souers said he had not been aware of this problem but thought that there were several ways in which it might be handled. We agreed that [NSC Assistant Executive Secretary James] Lay and Mr. McWilliams would get together and prepare a paper suggesting ways of handling this issue.

4. Objectives

I stated that we were aware of the President's need in having an overall summary of our objectives in the field of foreign relations to help him with the many decisions he has to make. We recognize the need of the Military to have an estimate of our objectives so that they can plan their budget; of the Budget Director so that he can plan an overall budget; of all the other government agencies so that their programs can be tied in to our foreign program. I asked Mr. Kennan to outline what we planned in this regard.

Mr. Kennan said that the Policy Planning Staff planned to draw up annually a review of our Foreign Policy to cover where we have been and where we are going. The paper, which would be an estimate, would attempt to forecast the areas and projects to which we should give primary attention. It would attempt to give some broad dollar estimates in needs for specific programs such as European Recovery Program. It will attempt to present a framework within which all government agencies could make plans for the following twelve months. Mr. Kennan said that his staff was starting preliminary work on this project and estimated that it would take two or three months to complete. Admiral Souers thought this was an excellent idea and believed that it would be a great help to the President. . . .

(22) MEMORANDUM, ACTING SECRETARY OF STATE JAMES WEBB TO SIDNEY SOUERS (EXECUTIVE SECRETARY, NATIONAL SECURITY COUNCIL), May 24, 1949

Source: *Foreign Relations of the United States: 1949 Vol. I National Security Affairs, Foreign Economic Policy.* Washington: U.S. Government Printing Office, 1976, pp. 313-314.

Pursuant to NSC Action No. 88-b, the NSC Staff has prepared a draft report on measures required to achieve the US objectives with respect to the USSR, as stated in NSC 20/4, which is now before the NSC Consultants for concurrence.

Examination of this draft report within the Department of State has confirmed the Department's previous feeling that this project is not a proper function of the National Security Council. The statutory function of the NSC is clearly stated to be the integration of policies relating to the national security, rather than the determination of the measures required to implement those policies. Under established procedures such measures are left to the determination of the responsible Departments and Agencies under the coordination of the Department or Agency having primary responsibility in each case as designated by the President. Use of the NSC for the determination of these measures would be contrary to the principles under which the Executive Branch of the Government operates, and would limit the flexibility in the conduct of operations which is essential in the rapidly changing world situation.

It is recognized that the NSC will from time to time be called upon to advise the President as to specific measures which are of such major significance to the national security as to require his personal consideration. Such instances, however, should be considered the exception rather than the rule, and should not be interpreted as changing the basic concept of the NSC as an advisory body on policies.

On the other hand, the Department of State appreciates the fact that it has the responsibility for furnishing guidance as to US foreign policies to the other Executive Departments and Agencies to assist them in the conduct of their operations, including the formulation of programs and the preparation of budgets therefor. The Department of State therefor intends to prepare, about September of each year, for the information of the other Executive Departments and Agencies, a paper which will furnish such guidance for the following fiscal year.

It is therefore recommended that the National Security Council:

   a. Cancel the directive to the NSC Staff contained in NSC Action No. 88-b.

   b. Note that the Department of State will transmit to the members of the NSC and other appropriate Executive Departments and Agencies, about September of each year, a review of the existing trends of international life, in their relation to US foreign policy, with a corresponding estimate of their projection into the future and with an indication of our probable national requirements in the foreign affairs field for the next fiscal year.

(23) LETTER, PRESIDENT TRUMAN TO SIDNEY SOUERS (EXECUTIVE SECRETARY NSC), July 26, 1949 [Extract]

Source: *Foreign Relations of the United States: 1949 Vol. I National Security Affairs, Foreign Economic Policy.* Washington: U.S. Government Printing Office, 1976, pp. 501-503.

On April 8, 1949, . . . I approved a joint recommendation by the National Military Establishment and the Atomic Energy Commission with respect to the level of the Commission's program for the production of fissionable materials and atomic weapons. At that time, I was informed that new objectives were under study by the Joint Chiefs of Staff looking toward accelerated production schedules and increased weapon requirements.

It has been brought to my attention recently that the National Military Establishment will soon come forward with new proposals which, if approved, would increase very substantially the presently-approved program of the Commission and would entail major expenditures over the next three years by the Commission for which no provision has been made in the budget. . .

The National Security Council is now reviewing the national defense and international programs, including the program of the Atomic Energy Commission, at my request. I regard it as essential that the revised objectives and requirements for the fissionable materials and atomic weapons program, as formulated by the National Military Establishment, be thoroughly studied and evaluated against the Council's perspective of our total defense requirements. It is equally important that the proposed sharp acceleration of this program be considered from the standpoint of its relationship to the foreign policy of the United States.

To assist me in reaching a judgment with respect to the forthcoming proposals, I desire advice as to the necessity for expansion of the Commission's program along the lines to be recommended
by the National Military Establishment. For this purpose I am
designating the Secretary of State, the Secretary of Defense, and
the Chairman of the Atomic Energy Commission as a special committee within the framework of the Council to prepare a recommendation upon this matter. I suggest that they should each furnish
appropriate staff from their respective agencies to work under
your direction in the preparation of the necessary staff studies.
. . . I would particularly value its opinions on . . .

1. The adequacy of the present program for production of
fissionable materials and weapons to safeguard our national security through January, 1956.

2. The relative gain in terms of national security to be derived from the proposed increased expenditure versus the degree
of security resulting from a continuation of the program at its
present level (including development of improved atomic bombs and
applications in the field of guided missiles).

3. The soundness of the timing of the proposed acceleration,
from the standpoint of (a) the stringency of the over-all budgetary situation, (b) the status of the Commission's research and
development looking toward a smaller and lighter atomic bomb
which might significantly improve existing deliverability consid
erations, and (c) the effect upon the international situation of
so great an acceleration of visible effort in this area of our
national defense program.

4. The effect of making offsetting reductions in other areas
of the national defense program to permit the proposed acceleration in the atomic weapons area without a net increase in the
budget.

Other factors to be considered by the committee in arriving
at a judgment are (a) the calculations underlying the National
Military Establishment's revised estimates of requirements for
fissionable materials and weapon production levels, and (b) the
prospects of an adequate supply of basic raw materials to support
the production rates deemed desirable by the National Military
Establishment. . . .

I assume that it will be necessary for the committee to inform
itself upon a number of matters which heretofore have been reserved, for reasons of the highest security, to a limited number
of persons. It is very important, of course, that this number
continue to be held to a minimum in connection with the committee's study. However, in order that the committee may have the
benefit of full and complete information as its study proceeds,
it is my desire that both the Atomic Energy Commission and the
National Military Establishment afford the committee all the assistance which it requires. . . .

I desire to be kept informed of the progress which the Council
makes on this assignment and will anticipate its recommendations
at the conclusion of its study.

(24) MEMORANDUM, DEPUTY UNDER SECRETARY OF STATE FOR ADMINISTRA-
TION, JOHN PEURIFOY, November 17, 1949 [Extract]

Source: *Foreign Relations of the United States: 1949 Vol. I
National Security Affairs, Foreign Economic Policy.* Washington:
U.S. Government Printing Office, 1976, pp. 409-411.

With the completion of the organization within the Department
for high-level politico-military liaison, it is now possible to
provide clarification of the respective responsibilities of
[Deputy Under Secretary of State Dean] Rusk, [Special Assistant
to the Secretary of State William] Sheppard and [State Department
representative to the NSC Staff Max] Bishop.

Before describing these politico-military duties, I should
like to point out that . . . liaison between the State Department
and the Defense Department should be conducted at all levels and
by all offices charged with politico-military responsibilities.
Moreover, the Department and its officers should make every effort
to cultivate friendly and cooperative relations with the Defense
Department on an informal as well as formal basis. . . .

Nothing that follows in this memorandum should be construed
to place limitations upon the responsibilities of Assistant Secretaries and their subordinates in conducting liaison with the Defense Department, on matters within their functional areas. . . .
In short, the basic State-Defense liaison channel is between the
Department's action office and the Defense Department. Other
liaison arrangements exist to assist and to supplement the action
offices and to handle matters on which action cannot be confined
to one office. . . .

. . . Dean Rusk, Deputy Under Secretary, has been designated the
Department's NSC consultant. He has also been delegated responsibility for State-Defense relationships on important matters of
broad policy requiring high-level consultation and for maintaining these relationships on a sound and cooperative basis. . . .

Mr. Max Bishop has been designated the Department's representative on the NSC Staff in which capacity he acts as coordinator
of the NSC Staff. He also is the Department's NSC Staff member
and is responsible for coordinating within the Department NSC
papers at the Staff level. In addition, to his NSC Staff member
function, he assists Mr. Rusk in the discharge of the latter's
NSC function. . . .

William Sheppard, Special Assistant to the Secretary, is
responsible for continuing review of the coordination and participation of the Department in the US national security organization,
including the NSC, CIA, the NSRB [National Security Resources
Board], the Defense Department and its components, and for recommending action to improve the Department's coordination and participation in this field. In this capacity, Mr. Sheppard is
available to help in any relationships with these agencies which
present special problems, or which have become chronically difficult. He will also make special studies relating to these functions for the Secretary and Under Secretary.

In order to provide him access to the flow of communications
relating to the national security organization, Mr. Sheppard
serves as a member of the executive Secretariat, particularly on

matters affecting S/P [Policy Planning Staff] and R [Office of the Special Assistant for Intelligence, Department of State] within the Department and the agencies outside the Department listed above. . . .

(25) MEMORANDUM, ACTING SECRETARY OF STATE JAMES WEBB, October 1, 1949 [Extract]

Source: *Foreign Relations of the United States: 1949 Vol. I National Security Affairs, Foreign Economic Policy.* Washington: U.S. Government Printing Office, 1976, p. 543.

[Director of the Policy Planning Office George] Kennan gave the President [on September 26, 1949] a report on the progress being made in the atomic energy discussions with the British and Canadians and indicated that he believed it might be possible to arrive at an understanding which would be satisfactory to this country. The President was very interested in this report and also in [Deputy U.S. Representative at the UN Ernst] Gross' Memorandum of Conversation with [Republican] Senator [Arthur] Vandenberg. . . . The President approved taking soundings with the Joint Committee on Atomic Energy to determine whether an agreement of the type which it appears possible to obtain would be endorsed and supported by the Committee.

Note: At the Cabinet luncheon immediately following, the President requested me to inform the Cabinet of the status of the atomic energy talks. . . . The President stated quite frankly to the Cabinet that he believed he had full authority under the law to enter into proper arrangements with the British and Canadians, but that there was a difference of opinion as to the interpretation of the law. For his own part, the President indicated that he thought the provision of the law restricting or limiting his powers in this field was unconstitutional. Both the Vice President [Alben Barkley] and the Attorney General [J. Howard McGrath] indicated that they thought it would be unwise to proceed without consultation and approval of the Joint Committee at this time. They doubted the feasibility of obtaining any constructive legislation at this session, given the temper and partisan nature of some of the members of the Committee. The President agreed that this was the best procedure and reiterated his instructions to feel out the Committee to see what could be done before reaching any decision.

(26) LETTER, PRESIDENT TRUMAN TO SIDNEY SOUERS (EXECUTIVE SECRETARY, NSC), November 19, 1949

Source: *Foreign Relations of the United States: 1949 Vol. I National Security Affaris, Foreign Economic Policy.* Washington: U.S. Government Printing Office, 1976. pp. 587-588.

I have recently received a report* by the Chairman of the Atomic Energy Commission [David Lilienthal] which raises the

---

*The report is reprinted in Section IIIA1 of this volume dealing with the decision to develop thermonuclear weapons. See page 172 (Editor).

question as to whether the United States should proceed with the construction of "super" atomic weapons. This question involves consideration not only of the factors presented by the Atomic Energy Commission in its report but also political and military factors of concern to the Departments of State and Defense.

To assist me in reaching a decision with respect to this vital question, I am therefore designating the Secretary of State, the Secretary of Defense and the Chairman of the Atomic Energy Commission as a special committee of the National Security Council to advise me on this problem. I suggest that each member of the committee provide from his agency appropriate staff officers to prepare under your supervision the necessary studies. I desire that the committee analyze all phases of the question including particularly the technical, military and political factors, and make recommendations as to whether and in what manner the United States should undertake the development and possible production of "super" atomic weapons. Included in these recommendations, I should like the advice of the Council as to whether and when any publicity should be given to this matter.

In the meantime, pending the completion of this project and my final decision with respect thereto, it is my considered judgment that any publicity regarding this question in the absence of the development of all the facts involved, would be seriously prejudicial to the national interest and security. I therefore desire that the knowledge of and participation in this study be restricted so far as practicable and that this question be neither mentioned nor discussed except among the participants.

(27) <u>MEMORANDUM, SIDNEY SOUERS (EXECUTIVE SECRETARY, NSC) TO NATIONAL SECURITY COUNCIL</u>, December 20, 1949

Source: *Foreign Relations of the United States: 1949 Vol. I National Security Affairs, Foreign Economic Policy.* Washington: U.S. Government Printing Office, 1976, pp. 416-418.

The National Security Act of 1947, as amended, specifies that the first duty of the National Security Council, subject to the direction of the President, shall be "to assess and appraise the objectives, commitments and risks of the United States in relation to our actual and potential military power, in the interest of national security, for the purpose of making recommendations to the President in connection therewith."

At its first meeting, the National Security Council directed that the preparation of such a study for consideration by the Council should be a basic responsibility of the Executive Secretary and a permanent assignment to the Council staff, which should utilize for this purpose the advice and assistance of all appropriate departments and agencies of the Government.

Recognizing that such a study could not be undertaken as a single project without a background of approved policies on the specific problems which directly affect our national security, the NSC staff during the two years of its existence has carried out this directive by the preparation of specific recommendations as to current policies regarding the principal areas, countries and subjects that are significant from the viewpoint of national security. . . . The outstanding project of this nature has been the formulation of "U.S. Objectives with Respect to the USSR to Counter Soviet Threats to U.S. Security" (NSC 20/4), which states not only our general objectives with respect to Russia both in peace or war, but also supplementary aims to achieve those objectives by methods short of war on the one hand or in the event of war on the other.

These reports prepared by the NSC staff to date, taken in their entirety, are believed to present a very comprehensive set of politico-economic policies in the field of national security. There can be no certainty, however, that such an accumulation of separate policy statements adequately meets the requirements of our national security without an integrated assessment and appraisal, particularly in relation to our actual and potential military power and the manner in which it can best be employed. Such an assessment and appraisal should therefore consider not only our current objectives, commitments and risks, but also indicate what they would be (a) under a continuation of present conditions, or (b) in the event of war in the near future.

By submitting to the President an over-all assessment and appraisal of this type, there can be no question that the National Security Council has performed the first of its statutory duties.

Accordingly, it is recommended that the Council now direct the NSC staff, with the advice and assistance of all appropriate executive departments and agencies, to prepare a report for Council consideration [this became NSC 68] assessing and appraising the objectives, commitments and risks of the United States under a continuation of present conditions or in the event of war in the near future, in relation to our actual and potential military power, in the interest of national security, including any recommendations which should be made to the President in connection therewith.

(28) **LETTER, PRESIDENT TRUMAN TO NSC EXECUTIVE SECRETARY JAMES LAY**, April 12, 1950

Source: *Foreign Relations of the United States: 1950 Vol. I National Security Affairs; Foreign Economic Policy*. Washington: U.S. Government Printing Office, 1977, pp. 234-235.

After consideration of the Report [NSC 68] by the Secretaries of State and Defense, dated April 7, 1950, re-examining our objectives in peace and war and the effect of these objectives on our strategic plans, I have decided to refer that Report to the National Security Council for consideration, with the request that the National Security Council provide me with further information on the implications of the Conclusions contained therein. I am particularly anxious that the Council give me a clearer indication of the programs which are envisaged in the Report, including estimates of the probable cost of such programs.

Because of the effect of these Conclusions upon the budgetary and economic situation, it is my desire that the Economic Cooperation Administrator, the Director of the Bureau of the Budget, and the Chairman, Council of Economic Advisers, participate in

the consideration of this Report by the Council, in addition to
the regular participation of the Secretary of the Treasury.

Pending the urgent completion of this study, I am concerned
that action on existing programs should not be postponed or delayed. In addition, it is my desire that no publicity be given
to this Report or its contents without my approval.

(29) LETTER, PRESIDENT TRUMAN TO SECRETARY OF STATE ACHESON,
July 19, 1950

Source: *Foreign Relations of the United States: 1950 Vol. I
National Security Affairs; Foreign Economic Policy*. Washington:
U.S. Government Printing Office, 1977, p. 348.

I have been considering the steps which are now necessary to
make the National Security Council of maximum value in advising
me as to the major policies required in the interest of our national security as a result of the present international situation. It is my desire that all such policies should be recommended to me through the Council in order that I may readily have the
benefit of the collective views of the officials of the Government primarily concerned with the national security. This result
can be achieved only if there are frequent Council meetings at
which the responsible officials may freely discuss specific recommendations on which there has previously been coordinated staff
work.

Attendance at recent meetings of the Council has been so
large that I feel it has discouraged free discussion. I therefore
direct that the Council meet regularly every Thursday with the
Secretary of State presiding in my absence and additional attendance confined to the Secretary of the Treasury, Mr. [W. Averell]
Harriman [head, Mutual Security Agency], Mr. Sidney Souers
[National Security Adviser to the President], the Chairman of the
Joint Chiefs of Staff, the Director of Central Intelligence, and
the Executive Secretary of the Council. Participation by other
officials will be only with my specific approval.

To be effective these meetings should be preceded by carefully
coordinated staff work by the best qualified individuals who can
be made available for this task. I would therefore like the Secretary of State, the Secretary of Defense, the Chairman of the
National Security Resources Board, the Secretary of the Treasury,
the Joint Chiefs of Staff, and the Director of Central Intelligence, each to nominate for my consideration one individual to
be a member of a senior NSC staff group which will be designated
by me as Chairman of the Council and which will be headed by the
Executive Secretary of the Council. . . .

II. EXECUTIVE PRIVILEGE AND INHERENT POWERS

A. *Executive Privilege*

Although presidents in the nineteenth and twentieth centuries had refused to honor all congressional requests for infomation, what could be termed an "executive privilege" claim (namely, an "uncontrolled discretion" to determine whether information should be released to the Congress) was not enunciated until Truman's administration. Truman's claim to "executive privilege," however, resulted not from a conscious decision based on a careful review of presidential constitutional powers and prerogatives. Instead, Truman's first refusal to comply with a congressional request was in reaction to a particular congressional request for certain files and was principally motivated by a concern over the political uses which the Truman Administration's conservative congressional critics might make of the requested information. The specific occasion for Truman's March 13, 1948, executive order was a request of the House Committee on Un-American Activities (HUAC) for the FBI's file on Bureau of Standards Director Edward Condon. (HUAC had had access to this file on Condon earlier but Committee staff had not taken full notes on all the derogatory, and unsubstantiated, information contained therein.) Significantly, in March 1948, Truman's rationale for this decision was the need to further the national security - requiring that the confidentiality of FBI sources and methods be preserved - and to protect innocent individuals from unfounded allegations. Truman reaffirmed this rationale in 1950, in response then to requests for the loyalty files of those individuals whom Senator Joseph McCarthy charged were "known Communists" employed by the Department of State. In time, Truman also justified this claim as a constitutional prerogative founded in the separation of powers. Although limited to certain classified reports, and deriving support from an adverse reaction to the methods and charges of Senator McCarthy and the McCarthyites, Truman's "executive privilege" claims and the increasingly more important policy role assumed by advisers to the President (whether members of the White House, NSC, or Bureau of the Budget staffs) in effect isolated executive decisions from congressional scrutiny and reduced the effectiveness of congressional oversight. Only when a presidential claim was vulnerable for political reasons, as in the case of Truman's initial response to the inquiry into the Justice Department's political favoritism instituted by Congressman Frank Chelf, did presidents hereafter honor congressional requests.

(30) MEMO, V. L. ALMOND (BUREAU OF BUDGET OFFICIAL) TO BUREAU OF BUDGET ASSISTANT DIRECTOR ELMER STAATS, March 3, 1948 [Extract]

Source: Bureau of the Budget Files, Record Group No. 51, National Archives.

The joint resolution [H.J. Res. 289] would authorize and direct the [Civil Service] Commission "to make available to, permit examination of, and furnish to the House Committee on Expenditures in the Executive Departments" records and information which disclose the acts, opinions, or policies of Members of Congress, and individuals who are not Federal employees and not applicants for positions in the Federal Government, when such records and information may be deemed necessary by the Committee in connection with any investigation held by it to ascertain the manner in which the [Civil Service] Commission is expending its funds, compiling or holding in its possession the information above referred to . . .

Section 2 of the joint resolution would authorize and direct the Commission to permit the Committee or a representative thereof to examine the so-called "Investigators' leads file," and all duplications thereof, . . .

The records of the Commission contain information of a highly confidential nature, much of which was secured by the Commission under a pledge of confidence to the informants that their views about applicants would not be made public. That pledge and the policy of adhering to it have been observed by the Commission since its creation in 1883. Indeed, that practice antedates the Civil Service System as it is now known.

Both the Department of Justice and the Civil Service Commission are opposed to the enactment of this measure.

(31) EXECUTIVE DIRECTIVE, March 13, 1948

Source: *Public Papers of the Presidents: Harry S. Truman, 1948*. Washington: U.S. Government Printing Office, 1964, pp. 181-182.

The efficient and just administration of the Employee Loyalty Program, under Executive Order No. 9835 of March 21, 1947, requires that reports, records, and files relative to the program be preserved in strict confidence. This is necessary in the interest of our national security and welfare, to preserve the confidential character and sources of information furnished, and to protect Government personnel against the dissemination of unfounded or disproved allegations. It is necessary also in order to insure the fair and just disposition of loyalty cases.

For these reasons, and in accordance with the long-established policy that reports rendered by the Federal Bureau of Investigation and other investigative agencies of the executive branch are to be regarded as confidential, all reports, records, and files relative to the loyalty of employees or prospective employees (including reports of such investigative agencies), shall be maintained in confidence, and shall not be transmitted or disclosed except as required in the efficient conduct of business.

Any subpena or demand or request for information, reports, or files of the nature described, received from sources other than those persons in the executive branch of the Government who are entitled thereto by reason of their official duties, shall be respectfully declined, on the basis of this directive, and the subpoena or demand or other request shall be referred to the Office of the President for such response as the President may determine to be in the public interest in the particular case. There shall be no relaxation of the provisions of this directive except with my express authority.

(32) ORDER, ATTORNEY GENERAL TOM CLARK TO ALL AGENCY AND DEPART-
MENT HEADS, April 23, 1948
Source: Harry S. Truman Papers, Official File 252-K, Harry S. Truman Library.

As you are aware, the Federal Bureau of Investigation from time to time makes available to Government departments, agencies and commissions information gathered by the Federal Bureau of Investigation which is of interest to such departments, agencies or commissions. These reports and communications are confidential. All such reports and communications are the property of the Federal Bureau of Investigation and are subject at all times to its control and to all privileges which the Attorney General has as to the use or disclosure of documents of the Department of Justice. Any department, agency or commission receiving such reports or communications is merely a custodian thereof for the Federal Bureau of Investigation, and the documents or communications are subject to recall at any time.

Neither the reports and communications nor their contents may be disclosed to any outside person or source without specific prior approval of the Attorney General or of the Assistant to the Attorney General or an Assistant Attorney General acting for the Attorney General.

Should any attempt be made, whether by request or subpoena or motion for subpoena or court order, or otherwise, to obtain access to or disclosure of any such report or communication, either separately or as part of the files and records of a Government department, agency or commission, the reports and communications involved should be immediately returned to the Federal Bureau of Investigation in order that a decision can be reached by me or by my designated representative in each individual instance as to the action which should be taken.

(33) <u>VETO MESSAGE, PRESIDENT TRUMAN</u>, May 15, 1948 [Extract]

Source: *Public Papers of the Presidents: Harry S. Truman, 1948.*
Washington: U.S. Government Printing Office, 1964, pp. 262-263.

I return herewith, without my approval, the enrolled bill
(S. 1004) . . .

. . . [which] would amend section 15(e) of the Atomic Energy
Act of 1946 . . . [authorizing] the Senate members of the Joint
Committee to direct the Federal Bureau of Investigation to investigate the character, associations, and loyalty of any person
appointed by the President under the Act, whose appointment requires the advice and consent of the Senate, and would require
the Director of the Federal Bureau of Investigation to report to
the Senate Committee in writing, setting forth the information
developed by such investigation. . . .

S. 1004 . . . would permit an unwarranted encroachment of the
Legislative upon the Executive branch. Five Senators would be
authorized to direct the Federal Bureau of Investigation . . . to
make investigations for them. The complete independence of the
Executive branch renders it imperative that the Executive have
sole authority over the officers whom he appoints. . . .

Aside from the question of constitutionality, which I am
advised is serious, I believe the bill is wholly unnecessary and
unwise. It would authorize the Senate members of the Joint Committee to utilize a bureau of an Executive department and direct
its head to perform functions for the Legislative branch, at the
same time that he was performing similar functions as part of the
Executive branch, with the possibility of confusion and misunderstanding as to which branch controlled.

I fully recognize my obligation in exercising my constitutional duty of appointment to obtain the facts about any person nom-
inated to serve as a member of the Atomic Energy Commission.
Every facility of the Executive branch, including the Federal
Bureau of Investigation, will be used to obtain those facts.
am entitled to have placed before me all relevant information,
including material which in the public interest should be maintained on a highly confidential basis.

The measure, furthermore, appears impractical because . . .
investigations conducted by the Federal Bureau of Investigation
after the nomination of an individual has been publicly announced
are not and cannot be as productive as those which are conducted
on a confidential basis prior to an announcement. . . . The most
reliable information is that which is obtained by the Executive
branch prior to nomination. This information is frequently of a
category which cannot be made public without damage to the national interest. Although I have no desire to keep from Congress
information which it should properly have, I must emphasize that
the provisions of this bill are completely incompatible with the
necessities of the operation of our Government and with the National security. . . .

(34) PRESENT CONFERENCE, PRESIDENT TRUMAN, August 5, 1948 [Extract]

Source: *Public Papers of the Presidents: Harry S. Truman, 1948.*
Washington: U.S. Government Printing Office, 1964, pp. 432-434.

Question: Mr. President, do you think that the Capitol Hill spy scare is a "red herring" to divert public attention from inflation?

THE PRESIDENT: Yes, I do, and I will read you another statement on that, since you brought it up.

"In response to written requests from congressional groups for information relating to the employment of individuals, the department or agency may forward to the committee all unclassified routine papers, such as Civil Service Form 57, records of promotion, efficiency ratings, letters of recommendation, etc.

"No information of any sort relating to the employee's loyalty, and no investigative data of any type, whether relating to loyalty or other aspects of the individual's record, shall be included in the material submitted to a congressional committee. If there is doubt as to whether a certain document or group of documents should be supplied, the matter should be referred to the White House. . . .

"The public hearings [conducted by HUAC and by a Senate Subcommittee on Expenditures in the Executive Departments] now under way are serving no useful purpose. On the contrary, they are doing irreparable harm to certain people, seriously impairing the morale of Federal employees, and undermining public confidence in the Government."

And they are simply a "red herring" to keep from doing what they ought to do.

Question: Don't you think the American public is entitled to this information?

THE PRESIDENT: What information?

Question: That has been brought out in these investigations?

THE PRESIDENT: What useful purpose is it serving when we are having this matter before a grand jury where action has to take place, no matter what this committee [HUAC] does? They haven't revealed anything that everybody hasn't known all along, or hasn't been presented to the grand jury. That is where it has to be taken, in the first place, if you are going to do anything about it. They are slandering a lot of people that don't deserve it.
. . .

Question: Mr. President, the reports of the hearings [by the Senate Subcommittee then investigating the federal employee loyalty program] yesterday indicated that [Secretary of the Navy] John Sullivan might ask you with respect to [Commerce Department employee William] Remington -

THE PRESIDENT: That is the answer for John Sullivan.

Question: What?

THE PRESIDENT: That is the answer for John Sullivan, right there.

Question: Does that mean they won't get the information on Remington?

THE PRESIDENT: They will get all the information that they are entitled to on Remington. They will not get any confidential information on him. . . .

Question: You mean, Mr. President, you think that both Senate and House [HUAC] committees ought to call a halt on these investigations now?

THE PRESIDENT: Well, that is up to Congress. I have said it as plainly as I can. . . .

Question: Mr. President, would you bracket the Senate and House committees in this statement you just made on Congress?

THE PRESIDENT: Yes.

Question: Mr. President, Mr. [Karl] Mundt, the acting chairman of the Un-American Committee, says today that there is now a Communist spy ring operating in the Capital?

THE PRESIDENT: It's in his mind, I think.

Question: If there wasn't ever anything to it, why did the FBI start the investigation?

THE PRESIDENT: To be on the safe side, of course. They got a lot of indictments on these people in New York, on those that got indicted. That was the reason for it. Everything has been presented to the grand jury that they wanted to know about, and if it was possible to indict these people, they would have been indicted. . . .

(35) MEMO, ATTORNEY GENERAL J. HOWARD McGRATH TO PRESIDENT TRUMAN, March 17, 1950 [Extract]

Source: Harry S. Truman Papers, Official File 419-K, Harry S. Truman Library.

It is my understanding that the Department of State has asked you for permission to reveal to the Subcommittee of the Senate Foreign Relations Committee [the so-called Tydings Committee] . . . the contents of the investigative files concerning those [81] persons against whom Senator [Joseph] McCarthy has preferred charges before the Subcommittee.

As you know, there is no question as to your authority to withhold these files from the Subcommittee. The only question is whether, as a matter of policy, you deem it advisable to make them available. I strongly urge that you withhold permission to make the files available to the Subcommittee. Your directive of March 13, 1948, to all officers and employees in the executive branch of the Government pointed out that the efficient and just operation of the Employee Loyalty Program required that all reports, records, and files in connection with the program be preserved in strict confidence. . . . Unless there are special reasons . . . existing at the present time which compel a different practice, I suggest that the confidential nature of these loyalty files be maintained and preserved. . . . any deviation from this policy, even under the conditions outlined by the Department of

State, would create an unfortunate precedent and would do much more harm than good. . . .

Disclosure of the documents here in question would . . . seriously impair the effectiveness of the Employee Loyalty Program. It would make it extremely difficult, if not impossible, for the Federal Bureau of Investigation to perform its investigative duties under the program. And it would also subject the persons in question to a type of double jeopardy which is contrary to sound concepts of good government, fairness, and justice.

In this connection I should like to point out to you the views of the Director of the Federal Bureau of Investigation which he submitted to me in a recent report:

1. The public disclosure of FBI reports will reveal investigative procedures and techniques. If publicized, criminals, foreign agents, subversives, and others would thus be forewarned and seek ways and means to carry out their activities, thus avoiding detection and hampering the efficiency of an investigative agency. The underground operations of criminals and subversives already are most difficult of detection and I do not believe the security of the nation would be furthered by applying any additional shackles to the FBI.

2. For the past 25 years, the FBI has represented to the American public that the FBI would maintain their confidences. To make public FBI reports would be to break confidences and persons interviewed in the future might be even more reluctant to furnish information. . . .

3. A public disclosure of FBI reports would reveal the identity of sources of information and in some cases at least, would place in jeopardy the lives of confidential sources of information.

4. Disclosure of information contained in FBI reports might result in an injustice to innocent individuals, who find themselves entwined in a web of suspicious circumstances, which can be explained only by further investigation, and disclosures might be made under circumstances which would deny the aggrieved to publicly state their positions.

5. A public disclosure could warn persons whose names appear in FBI reports of the investigation and serve as an effective means of enabling them to avoid detection, to approach witnesses, to bring about the destruction of evidence, or permit them to flee the country.

6. Public disclosure of FBI reports could contribute to blackmail of persons investigated or could result in degrading persons who have made a mistake or fallen prey to false propaganda.

7. Disclosures might reveal highly restricted information vital to the national security and of considerable value to a foreign power.

8. A complete and thorough investigation in certain types of cases, of necessity must reveal administrative procedures, trade practices, and manufacturing operations, which, if publicized, would enable persons with a subversive or ulterior motive to misuse information.

9. FBI reports are prepared for official usage only and in setting forth full details secured from a witness, if publicized, could be subject to misinterpretation, quoting out of context, or used to thwart truth, distort half truths, and misrepresent facts.

As an alternative to permitting the Subcommittee to inspect the files, it is my suggestion that you might, in the interest of making it clear to the public that you do not wish to withhold the information in question, transmit the files to the Loyalty Review Board, as to whose competence and impartiality in these matters there can be no question, and request the Board to review the files and report its findings, with respect to each person against whom Senator McCarthy has brought charges, in the light of the factual evidence adduced before the Subcommittee. . . . There could then be no charge that the people being investigated were the very people making the decisions as to the merits of the charges, and turning the files over to the Board would be in keeping with the existing procedures, which are intended to safeguard both the integrity of the Loyalty Program and of investigative procedures and the rights of individuals.

(36) LETTER, PRESIDENT TRUMAN TO SENATOR MILLARD TYDINGS, March 28, 1950 [Extract]

Source: *Public Papers of the Presidents: Harry S. Truman, 1950.* Washington: U.S. Government Printing Office, 1965, pp. 229-231.

This is in reply to your letter of March 22, 1950, in which you have asked for the production before your Subcommittee of the investigative files relating to Government employees who are to have been employed in the Department of State and against whom charges of disloyalty have been made before your Subcommittee by Senator McCarthy. . . .

In March of 1948, I issued a Directive to all officers and employees in the Executive Branch of the Government, directing that all reports, records, and files relating to the employee loyalty program be kept in strict confidence, even in instances where subpoenas were received. . . . this Directive was clearly within the power of the President, and I issued it only . . . after I had satisfied myself beyond any doubt that any other decision would have resulted in the collapse of the loyalty program.

At that time, . . . I pointed out the long-standing precedents regarding the production of confidential files and the reasons for my decision. . . .

. . . three elements - the serious prejudice to the effectiveness of the Federal Bureau of Investigation as an investigative agency, the resulting embarrassment and danger to confidential informants, and injustice and unfairness to innocent individuals - led me to the inescapable conclusion that the single most important element in an effective and at the same time just and fair loyalty program was the preservation of all files in connection therewith in the strictest confidence.

During the last month, I have been re-examining with utmost care this entire problem, and in this connection I have asked the Attorney General [J. Howard McGrath], the Director of the Federal Bureau of Investigation [J. Edgar Hoover], and Mr. Seth Richardson, Chairman of the Loyalty Review Board, to give their careful consideration to this matter. They have unanimously advised me that disclosure of loyalty files would be contrary to the public interest, and would do much more harm than good. The Director of the Federal Bureau of Investigation in a report to the Attorney General has outlined the very serious consequences that would result from any such disclosure.

It is my desire, however, that the charges of disloyalty made before your Subcommittee be given the most thorough and complete investigation, and it is my purpose to cooperate with your Subcommittee to the greatest extent possible, bearing in mind at all times my responsibility to take care that the investigative activities and efficiency of the Federal Bureau of Investigation and other investigative agencies remain unimpaired, that innocent people - both those under investigation and those who have provided information - not be unnecessarily injured, and that the effectiveness of the employee loyalty program as a whole not be interfered with.

I am, therefore, asking Mr. Seth Richardson, Chairman of the Loyalty Review Board, to have the Board arrange for a complete and detailed review, as soon as possible, of the cases in which charges of disloyalty have been made before your Subcommittee (including cases heretofore reviewed by the Board), and am asking him to give me a full and complete report after review. . . .

Upon receipt of Mr. Richardson's report, I will advise your Subcommittee further. . . .

(37) LETTER, PRESIDENT TRUMAN TO SENATOR MILLARD TYDINGS, April 3, 1950 [Extract]

Source: *Public Papers of the Presidents: Harry S. Truman, 1950.* Washington: U.S. Government Printing Office, 1965, pp. 240-241.

The Secretary of State, the Attorney General, and the Chairman of the Civil Service Commission have referred to me the matter of the subpoenas which have been served on them, directing them to appear on April 4, 1950, before the Subcommittee . . . and to produce various documents and papers relating to a number of persons whose names appear on a confidential list attached to each subpoena.

The disclosure of these files would seriously prejudice the future effectiveness and usefulness of the Federal Bureau of Investigation as an investigative agency; the embarrassment, and even danger, to those who have given confidential information cannot be overemphasized. Disclosure would not only deprive the Federal Bureau of Investigation and other investigative agencies of the Government of the availability of those confidential informants in the future, but would also gravely impair their ability to gather confidential information from other sources as well.

The employee loyalty program depends upon the investigative services of the Federal Bureau of Investigation. The disclosure of the files would, therefore, result in serious harm to that program. Such disclosure, instead of helping to keep disloyal people out of the Government service, would impair the very effective means we now have for accomplishing that purpose.

The investigative files of the Federal Bureau of Investigation do not contain proven information alone. They include many unverified charges and allegations, leads and suspicions. Disclosure of the files would, therefore, result in serious injustice to, and damage to the reputations of, many innocent persons.

The authority of the President in this regard has been recognized since the beginnings of our Government. Our first President and his Cabinet, in considering the first request made by a House of Congress for executive papers, concluded that while the Congress might call for papers generally, the Executive ought to communicate only such papers as the public good would permit, and ought to refuse those the disclosure of which would be contrary to the public interest.

No President has ever complied with an order of the Legislative Branch directing the Executive Branch to produce confidential documents, the disclosure of which was considered by the President to be contrary to the public interest. The Presidents who have had to meet that issue are numerous, and they have uniformly rejected such encroachments on the Constitutional power of the President. . . . Attorneys General serving in the Cabinets of Presidents Theodore Roosevelt, Taft, Wilson, Coolidge and Franklin D. Roosevelt, have [also] re-stated the responsibility of the Executive Branch to maintain the integrity of confidential information when its disclosure would be contrary to the public interest. . . .

I have felt obliged, therefore, to direct the Secretary of State, the Attorney General and the Chairman of the Civil Service Commission not to comply with your subpoenas.

(38) MEMO, ASSISTANT ATTORNEY GENERAL ABRAHAM HARRIS TO DEPUTY ATTORNEY GENERAL PEYTON FORD, June 2, 1950 [Extract]
Source: J. Howard McGrath Papers, Harry S. Truman Library.

In a memorandum to you dated May 8, 1950, the Director of the Federal Bureau of Investigation called your attention to the fact that several former agents of the Bureau had been questioned by representatives of the Subcommittee of the Senate Foreign Affairs Committee the so-called Tydings Committee concerning their

knowledge of the Amerasia* case [of 1945]. These former agents
have advised the Bureau that they furnished no information at
these interviews. They indicated, however, that they might be
subpoenaed to testify before the Subcommittee and requested advice
as to what they should do in that event, in view of the fact that
the information obtained by them in the course of their official
duties with the Bureau was confidential information and they had
taken oaths to retain such information in confidence. The Director has asked "your suggestions as to any advice the Department
may desire to make available to these former Special Agents and
any others in like position who may make inquiry of the Bureau."

. . . Assistant Attorney General [James] McInerney pointed
out [in a May 11, 1950 memorandum] that there is no existing Federal statute which prohibits former agents from testifying before
Congressional committees with respect to information obtained by
them in the course of their official duties with the FBI, and
suggested that "former agents be advised that they may not refuse
the committee's request to testify, and if questioned by the committee, they should, to the best of their recollection, answer
all pertinent questions because refusal to do otherwise, in the
absence of legal justification, may very well result in contempt
proceedings." . . .

I have carefully considered Mr. McInerney's memorandum and I
agree that there is no existing Federal statute prohibiting former
FBI agents from testifying before Congressional committees. . . .

I know of no existing statute which prohibits agents presently
employed by the Bureau from testifying before Congressional committees, but I am certain that the Department would not advise
those agents to testify before a Congressional committee with
respect to confidential matters obtained in the course of their
official duties. . . . presently employed agents who testify notwithstanding instructions from the Department to the contrary can
be discharged and that in the case of former agents there can be
no discharge. But this distinction seems immaterial in my judgment. I cannot believe that information which can be kept in
confidence today should be disclosed tomorrow simply because an
agent having knowledge of the information resigns from his position this evening. The right of the Department of Justice to
maintain certain information of the FBI in confidence is, it seems
to me, more substantial than that.

The Bureau in hiring its agents obviously did not intend that
those agents be permitted to disclose information they had gained
in the course of their official duties after they had left the
Bureau. Indeed, the exact opposite was intended. . . .

. . . the mere fact that [a non-disclosure] oath is required
and [an FBI] regulation exists is clear evidence that the Bureau

---

*This case resulted from the discovery of hundreds of classi-
fied documents in the offices and homes of individuals associated
with Amerasia, a journal of Far Eastern affairs. Because information leading to the indictment of the individuals arrested for transmitting or receiving these government documents had been illegally
obtained (including wiretaps and break-ins), the Justice Department
eventually decided not to prosecute these individuals. (Editor).

intended that the confidential nature of information received by an agent in the course of his official duties be maintained after the employment of the agent has ceased.

It is unnecessary to discuss in detail at this time the right of the President and the heads of the executive departments to maintain in confidence information the disclosure of which would, in the opinion of the executive branch of the Government, be contrary to the public interest. Suffice it to say that such a right has been asserted by the executive branch since the founding of the Government, is well recognized today, and applies even with respect to demands for information from Congressional committees.

While there may be differences of opinion as to the kinds of information which may properly be kept in confidence, I believe that no differences can, or should be, drawn which are based on the status of a person as a former FBI agent rather than one presently employed by the Bureau. If this were not so, the privilege of the executive branch would be largely illusory because a former agent would then be free to disclose the very information which the Department desired and had the right to keep in confidence.

The privilege of keeping in confidence information of the kind here involved is not a privilege personal to the person who may be called upon to divulge it, . . . [but] is a privilege which belongs to the executive branch of the Government, to be withdrawn only by the head of the executive department or by the President himself. . . .

It is [also] well settled that one of the implied terms of a contract of employment is that the employee will not disclose trade secrets or other confidential information acquired in the course of his employment. This implied obligation continues after termination of the employment and will in many cases be enforced by injunction. In the situation here under discussion, the requirement of secrecy has been made an express term of employment. . . .

I am of the opinion that, as a matter of policy, the Department should take the position that former agents of the Bureau may not be compelled, without prior approval of the Department, to testify before Congressional committees with respect to confidential information obtained by them in the course of their official duties. And I am of the further opinion that such a position may reasonably be supported legally by an argument along the lines above suggested. It is by no means certain that such a position would be sustained in the courts, but the position is far from frivolous in my judgment and, in view of the policy considerations, should be asserted. . . . former agents should be advised to bring to the attention of the Director any requests or subpenas for testimony before Congressional committees, so that a decision may be made in each case whether the agent shou d be permitted to testify. . . . in taking this position, the Department should be prepared to render legal assistance to the former agents, which assistance would include not only appearing with the agents before the committees but also defending them in any contempt proceedings in which they might become involved with respect to this matter. . . .

(39) PRESS CONFERENCE, PRESIDENT TRUMAN, January 25, 1951 [Extract]

Source: *Public Papers of the Presidents: Harry S. Truman, 1951*
Washington: U.S. Government Printing Office, 1965, p. 126.

****

Question: Mr. President, about that preceding question on the loyalty files, you made some files available to the Tydings subcommittee [a special subcommittee of the Senate Foreign Relations Committee established in February 1950 to investigate Senator McCarthey's charges about Communists in the State Department]. Is it your intention to make files available to the [recently established presidential] commission [on internal security and individual rights] on the same basis?

THE PRESIDENT: On exactly the same basis.

Question: Well, Mr. President, what is the basis? As I remember it, the Tydings committee had to examine the files at the White House, is that right?

THE PRESIDENT: That's right.

Question: Is that the basis you speak of?

THE PRESIDENT: That is it exactly.

Question: Mr. President, in other words, this new commission when they want to look into a file which there is some security, they will have to come here to the White House?

THE PRESIDENT: They will ask me about it, and I will give them permission to see it.

Question: Mr. President, did you make the files available in the Anna Rosenberg [a Defense Department employee] case to the Senate committee?

THE PRESIDENT: I don't remember whether I did or not. . . . I would have, if they had asked for it. I can't remember whether I did or not.

Question: Whether there is a distinction between one or the other?

THE PRESIDENT: I don't think there is any.

Question: They sent the full files in the Rosenberg case and did not in the other committees?

THE PRESIDENT: Oh, yes they did. They had all the full files they asked for in the Tydings investigation, and in several other instances, they have had the same privilege. But they have had to ask me for them, and I have to authorize them to see them. That is the formality they have to go through.

Question: This committee . . . come[s] to you, and you give them the permission -

THE PRESIDENT: That's right.

Question: . . . in individual cases?

THE PRESIDENT: That's right. . . .

(40) REMARKS, PRESIDENT TRUMAN, February 12, 1951 [Extract]

Source: *Public Papers of the Presidents: Harry S. Truman, 1951.*
Washington: U.S. Government Printing Office, 1965, p. 152.

. . . the Government's loyalty program, I think, has worked
well. The [Presidential] Commission [on internal security and
individual rights] will probably find ways in which it can be
improved, and should try to find ways in which that loyalty program can be improved.

It must be kept in mind fundamentally, however, that the Bill
of Rights . . . is still the principal part of the Constitution
of the United States so far as the individual in this country is
concerned. And we must find a balance where we can be sure that
the employees of the Government are loyal to the Government, and
are really interested in the welfare of the United States of
America, and at the same time see that the rights of individuals
are amply protected so that there will be no one who feels that
he has been persecuted because he will have to answer questions
before this commission.

You have the authority to administer oaths and they must answer the questions that you ask. They must give you a fair and
straightforward statement when you ask for it.

You have access to the loyalty files of the FBI, just as the
loyalty boards have had directly. You will not have to come to
me for that authorization, because it is already implied, . . .
So that you will have access to whatever papers are necessary to
find out the facts, and by obtaining them in that way, nobody can
say that the files have been rifled, as we were charged with doing
when we furnished files to the Tydings committee. We were charged
here in the White House that the files had been picked and rifled
so that they couldn't use them. There wasn't a word of truth to
that. . . .

(41) PRESS CONFERENCE, PRESIDENT TRUMAN, May 17, 1951 [Extract]

Source: *Public Papers of the Presidents: Harry S. Truman, 1951.*
Washington: U.S. Government Printing Office, 1965, pp. 289-291.

****

Question: Mr. President, the [Joint] Senate Committee [Armed
Forces and Foreign Relations] today sustained the right of General
[Omar] Bradley to treat as confidential his coversations with
you on April 6th meeting [1951, at which General MacArthur's dismissal was discussed], a position which you had taken.

THE PRESIDENT: They did exactly right, and I am happy that
they did.

Question: Now, of course, there are certain charges and as-
sertions being made that this adds a lot of mystery to what happened on April 6.

THE PRESIDENT: Who is making those charges? The Republicans
that are trying to overthrow the foreign policy of the United
States? I don't think anybody who understands the Government of
the United States is making any such charges.

Question: Quite apart, sir, from any right to demand from you information on what happened on April 6th, would you care to say anything voluntarily about what happened on April 6th?

THE PRESIDENT: All the information in connection with the thing is taken by the actions and decisions which I make. The conversations with my advisers and my private staff before decisions are made is my business and mine alone. . . .

Question: Sir, you are a careful student of American history, would you care to comment upon some historical precedents for this keeping of Presidential conversations confidential?

THE PRESIDENT: Well, nearly every President has had the same experience. You can just pick up the life of any President you choose, and you will find experiences just like this in the lives of nearly every one of them.

Question: Could you name any?

THE PRESIDENT: Well, I don't recall any specific instances. Grover Cleveland had the same trouble, so did Abraham Lincoln. And Andrew Jackson was quite active in that line. Andrew Jackson, I think, had the worst experience of any of them, but if you go on down the the line you will find that nearly every president has had the same experience. It is nothing new. . . .

(42) LETTER, PRESIDENT TRUMAN TO CONGRESSMAN FRANK CHELF (CHAIR-
MAN, SPECIAL SUBCOMMITTEE OF THE HOUSE COMMITTEE ON THE JUDICIARY),
March 7, 1952

Source: *Public Papers of the Presidents: Harry S. Truman, 1952-53.*
Washington: U.S Government Printing Office, 1966, pp. 199-200.

It has come to my attention that you have requested a number of departments and agencies in the Executive Branch to furnish the following information:

A list of all cases referred to the Department of Justice or U.S. Attorneys for either criminal or civil action by any governmental department or agency within the last six years, in which:

    a. Action was declined by the Department of Justice, including in each such case the reason or reasons assigned by said Department for such refusal to act.

    b. Said cases were returned by the Department of Justice to the governmental Department or agency concerned for further information or investigation. In such cases, a statement of all subsequent action taken by the Department of Justice should be included.

    c. Said cases have been referred to the Department of Justice and have been pending in the Department for a period of more than one year and are not included in b. above.

In my view, it would be impractical and unwise for the departments and agencies to endeavor to comply with that request.

I want to make it clear that I have no wish to obstruct your subcommittee in any legitimate inquiry it may wish to make. . . .

However, this request of yours is so broad and sweeping in scope that it would seriously interfere with the conduct of the Government's business if the departments and agencies should undertake to comply with it. I am advised that it would require the examination of hundreds of thousands of files, that it would take hundreds of employees away from their regular duties for an extensive period of time, and that it would cost the Government millions of dollars. All this would be done, not for the purpose of investigating specific complaints, not for the purpose of evaluating credible evidence of wrongdoing, but on the basis of a dragnet approach to examining the administration of the laws.

I do not believe such a procedure to be compatible with those provisions of the Constitution which vest the executive power in the President and impose upon him the duty to see that the laws are faithfully executed. I believe that the investigative functions of the Congress have an important place in our Constitutional system, and I believe that they can be and should be used to help reform and strengthen the laws to be administered by the Executive. However, I believe just as strongly that this Congressional power should be exerted only in a fashion that is consistent with the proper discharge of the Constitutional responsibilities of the Executive Branch. I feel sure that you agree with these propositions as a general matter, and I am confident that we can agree upon their practical application with respect to the work of your subcommittee.

However, in the light of the considerations set forth above, I am advising the departments and agencies that they should not undertake to comply with this particular request.

(43) MEMORANDUM, PRESIDENT TRUMAN TO ALL EXECUTIVE AGENCY HEADS, April 12, 1952

Source: *Public Papers of the Presidents: Harry S. Truman, 1952-53.* Washington: U.S. Government Printing Office, 1966, p. 263.

The House Judiciary Committee . . . [recently] established a special subcommittee [chaired by Congressman Chelf] to conduct an inquiry of specific allegations and complaints, based upon credible evidence determined by the subcommittee, with reference to the administration of the Department of Justice and the Office of the Attorney General of the United States. It is my desire that the Executive branch of the Government cooperate with the committee to the end that a fair, impartial, and thorough investigation may be made.

Accordingly, I have today issued an Executive Order empowering the committee to inspect tax returns under appropriate limitations, and I now request that all departments and agencies, to the fullest extent consistent with the proper performance of their work and duties, cooperate with Chairman Frank L. Chelf and his subcommittee for the purpose of such an investigation.

(44) LETTER, PRESIDENT TRUMAN TO SECRETARY OF STATE DEAN ACHESON, April 3, 1952 [Extract]

Source: *Public Papers of the Presidents: Harry S. Truman, 1952-53.* Washington: U.S. Government Printing Office, 1965, pp. 235-236.

On March 28 you sought my guidance regarding the response which the Department of State should make to the requests of members of the Senate Appropriations Subcommittee for detailed information on administration of the Department's loyalty-security program. I understand . . . that the information requested falls generally into four categories . . .

1. The complete files in specified loyalty-security cases, detailed information concerning the substance of investigative reports in certain additional cases, and the procedural steps and actions taken in the handling of various individual cases.

2. The names of all present and former State Department employees who have been investigated under the Federal Employees Loyalty Program or the Department's security program, together with the status or the disposition of their respective cases.

3. The names of all employees who resigned or retired from the Department while under investigation or during processing of their loyalty-security cases.

4. The names of State Department officers who sat as members of the Loyalty Security Board on a particular case, and the way each officer voted.

The information sought by the Appropriations Subcommittee cannot be considered solely from the standpoint of the Subcommittee or from the standpoint of the Department of State. If one Department is required or permitted to supply information of the character requested, all other agencies of the Government would have to respond to similar demands from other sources. If all Executive agencies were to release information of this nature, I am convinced that the over-all result would be to wreck the Federal Employees Loyalty Program. In the process, the reputations of hundreds of loyal Government employees would be pilloried and the entire civil service would be severely demoralized. Accordingly, I must advise you not to furnish the information requested by the Subcommittee, for to do so would be clearly contrary to the public interest.

Much of the information wanted by the Subcommittee falls within the letter or the spirit of my memoranda of March 13 and August 5, 1948, in which I stated that the efficient and just administration of the Employee Loyalty Program requires that reports, records, files and investigative data relative to the program be preserved in strict confidence. That is necessary in the interest of our national security, to preserve the confidential character and sources of information, to protect Government personnel against the dissemination of unfounded or disproved allegations, and to insure the fair and just disposition of loyalty cases. The need for these directives is just as compelling today as it was in 1948.

It would be a great mistake to release the names of State Department and other Federal personnel who have been subjected to loyalty investigations, and to divulge the specific steps and actions taken in the processing of individual loyalty-security cases. The FBI, which checks all Government employees, institutes full field investigations upon the basis of derogatory allegations, whether or not true, and questionable affiliations or associations, however innocent in fact they may prove to be. In the overwhelming majority of loyalty cases, thorough FBI investigation and careful loyalty board inquiry establishes the employee's loyalty. To divulge the names of these loyal employees, and the specific steps taken in adjudicating their cases, would serve no useful purpose. In the hands of unscrupulous persons, however, this information could be distorted and used to subject the employees and their families to untold embarrassment and distress. My apprehension in this regard is not based upon idle fancy, as you well know.

Nor would the public interest be served by releasing the names of individuals determined to be security risks. Persons discharged as security risks are in a distinctly different category from persons discharged on loyalty grounds. They usually are employees who cannot be trusted with classified information because they have questionable associates, talk too much, are careless, or may be unduly susceptible to outside influences. In enacting Public Law 733 . . . providing for suspension of employees in the interest of national security, the Congress [in 1950] clearly recognized that a security risk may be a useful and suitable employee in nonsensitive Government positions not involving access to classified information. Similarly, he may be an entirely loyal citizen who will render excellent service in private employment. The reputations of these persons should not be besmirched unnecessarily by making their names public.

Many Federal employees leave the service while under routine investigations or prior to the completion of their loyalty-security processing. . . . To protect the innocent from groundless accusations and unwarranted inferences, therefore, it is clear that these names should not be released in response to blanket requests. All of the names, of course, are flagged for attention in case the individuals should seek to re-enter Government service.

There is no objection to making available the names of all members of an agency loyalty board, but it is entirely improper to divulge how individual board members voted in particular cases or to divulge the members who sat on particular cases. If this type of information were divulged freely, the danger of intimidation would be great, and the objectivity, fairness and impartiality of board members would be seriously prejudiced.

Hereafter, no information regarding individual loyalty or security cases shall be provided in response to inquiries from outside the Executive branch unless such inquiries are made in writing. Where proper inquiries are made in writing, replies will be confined to . . . (1) If an employee has been separated on loyalty grounds, advice to that effect may be given in response to a specific request for information concerning the particular individual; and (2) if an employee has been separated as a security risk, replies to requests for information about that individual may state only that he was separated for reasons relating to suitability for employment in the particular agency. No information shall be supplied as to any specific intermediate steps, proceedings, transcripts of hearings, or actions taken in processing an individual under loyalty or security programs.

No exceptions shall be made to the above stated policy unless the agency head determines that it would be clearly in the public interest to make specified information available, . . . In all such cases, the requested information shall be released only after obtaining the approval of my office. . . .

B. *Executive Secrecy and Classification*

   *Executive classification orders might not have been
founded on specific statutory authority; nonethless, they
commanded support within the Congress and the informed
public because of the recognized need to safeguard sensitive
security information. The rather nebulous standards, and
lack of intensive scrutiny, concerning documents stamped
"restricted," "confidential," "secret," and "top secret,"
however, meant that executive officials were encouraged to
overclassify. Truman Administration officials' obsession
with "national security" threats soon led to a decision to
extend classification restriction. These extensions not only
reached non-military agencies, as in the President's September 1951 order, but reports produced by agencies such as the
Federal Trade Commission and the records and papers of prominent federal officials. (See also Official Secrets section,
pp. 370-373.)*

(45)   PRESS CONFERENCE, PRESIDENT TRUMAN, February 2, 1950
[Extract]

Source: *Public Papers of the Presidents: Harry S. Truman, 1950.*
Washington: U.S. Government Printing Office, 1950, p. 141.

****

Question: Mr. President, yesterday you issued an Executive
order on the dissemination of information, and in it, . . . you
include military documents and reports which have been marked
"Confidential" and "Restricted" . . . That classification "Restricted" is one of the most general I have ever seen.

THE PRESIDENT: It is exactly a copy of the order that has
been in effect all the time, and the only reason that order was
issued was that it conforms with the new Defense Act [of 1949].
There isn't any difference with this order and the one that has
been in effect . . . it's an order to conform with the Unification Act.   That's all there is to it.   That order has been in
effect ever since I have been President.

Question: Is there any way to get a definition of "Restricted," so that the Army officers would know what it means?
In some places it refers to clippings.

THE PRESIDENT: I can't answer the question.   You will have
to talk to somebody that uses "Restricted."   I don't use it.
(Laughter)

Question: Well, every office boy seems to stamp "Restricted"
or "Confidential," and I have seen many "Confidential" and "Restricted" documents which had no reason whatever to be . . .

THE PRESIDENT: You never saw one come out with <u>my</u> signature
on it.   (Laughter)   You talk to them, now.   That's their business
not mine.   Those "Restricted" documents are mostly military. . . .

(46)   BULLETIN NO. 51-6, BUREAU OF THE BUDGET DIRECTOR FREDERICK
LAWTON TO ALL AGENCY AND DEPARTMENT HEADS, November 24, 1950
[Extract]

Source: Frederick Lawton Papers, Harry S. Truman Library.

The attached copy of a letter from the President requests
the Director of the Bureau of the Budget to maintain a surveil-

lance of the publication of statistics, and to restrict publication whenever, in any instance, release of the information might endanger the national security. Pending further instructions to be issued by the Bureau of the Budget, I request that you submit to the Bureau of the Budget for approval any proposal for the publication of statistical information that in your opinion may possibly involve questions of national security. . . .

(47) LETTER, PRESIDENT TRUMAN TO BUREAU OF BUDGET DIRECTOR LAWTON, November 17, 1950 [Extract]

Source: Frederick Lawton Papers, Harry S. Truman Library.

The international situation at this time requires that we be prepared once more to impose such restrictions on the publication and dissemination of statistical information by agencies of the government as may be necessary in the interests of national security. . . .

Necessary as control over publication may be, we must also remember that it is in the national interest to keep such restrictions to a minimum. Statistical information needed by the Government and its citizens should be made available to the general public to the fullest extent compatible with national security. . . . the restrictions imposed [must also] be uniform and consistent in order to be effective. Statistical series published by different agencies, each of which might be harmless in itself, might be combined to produce information harmful to the national security. Centralization of this control in one agency is therefore essential.

This responsibility belongs appropriately in the Bureau of the Budget in accordance with its existing responsibilities for the improvement, development and coordination of Federal statistical services. . . . until further notice you maintain a continuous surveillance of the publication of statistical information by executive agencies of the Federal Government, and advise them in any instance whether or not such publication would be compatible with national security. If, in your opinion, the publication of the information would endanger the national security, it is to be withheld. . . .

You are also requested to take steps . . . to insure that statistical information ordinarily released to the public, but withheld from general publication because of security considerations, will be released to authorized users, in such manner as you may prescribe. Decisions on whether such release can be made must not be contrary to law or the regulations of the agencies possessing the data. . . .

(48) PRESS CONFERENCE, PRESIDENT TRUMAN, May 3, 1951 [Extract]

Source: *Public Papers of the Presidents: Harry S. Truman, 1951.*
Washington: U.S. Government Printing Office, 1965, pp. 262-263.

****

Question: Mr. President, General [Douglas] MacArthur has expressed an opinion on the question of whether or not Russia might intervene [in the Korean War]?

THE PRESIDENT: He is entitled to that opinion - he is entitled to any opinion he chooses.

Question: You have the benefit of the information gathered by the Central Intelligence Agency . . .

THE PRESIDENT: . . . which he didn't have because he wouldn't let the Central Intelligence Agency work in Japan until just recently. . . .

Question: Mr. President, . . . even though he wouldn't let the CIA work there, I think that he said that the CIA last November [1950] had given the opinion that the Chinese Communists wouldn't come in?

THE PRESIDENT: I didn't know that. The CIA usually reports to me. If they made any such report to him, they didn't make it to me.

Question: Isn't it true, sir, that they made a report to you on November 21?

THE PRESIDENT: They make a report to me every day, so they must have made a report to me on November 21, but I don't know what was in it. That has been quite a while ago.

Question: It was my idea that it was quite contrary to what he said today.

THE PRESIDENT: If it's a secret document, I don't know how you found out about it.

Question: Mr. President, when was the CIA . . .

THE PRESIDENT: I don't remember the exact date. If you will talk to [CIA Director] Gen. Bedell Smith, he can tell you.

Question: I am not sure he [Smith] will, Mr. President.

THE PRESIDENT: What?

Question: I am not sure he will.

THE PRESIDENT: He's the right kind of an intelligence man, isn't he! (Laughter)

Question: Not unless you were to call him up and say he could.

THE PRESIDENT: Well, I won't do that, but I am telling you the truth and the facts. . . .

(49) <u>STATEMENT, PRESIDENT TRUMAN</u>, September 25, 1951 [Extract]

Source: *Public Papers of the Presidents: Harry S. Truman, 1951.*
Washington: U.S. Government Printing Office, 1965, pp. 535-536.

I have today signed an Executive order to strengthen our safeguards against divulging to potential enemies information harmful
to the security of the United States.

This order provides, for the first time, uniform standards
for classifying and protecting security information throughout
the executive branch of the Government. At the same time, the
order prohibits the classification of any information by any
agency unless it can show affirmatively that disclosure of the
information would harm the national security. . . .

The necessity for this order arises from the fact that security information occasionally involves, and must be handled by,
agencies which normally do not handle security matters. The order
requires them to protect security matters in the same manner as
they would be protected in one of the key defense agencies which
have traditional classification systems. On the other hand, the
order prohibits any agency from classifying nonsecurity matters.

The American people have a fundamental right to information
about their Government, and there is no element of censorship,
either direct or implied, in this order. The order applies only
to officials and employees of the executive branch of the Government. The public is requested to cooperate, but is under no com-
pulsion or threat of penalty to do so as a result of this order.
Furthermore, I have directed every agency to keep constant watch
over its classification activities for the purpose of reducing or
eliminating classifications wherever and whenever conditions permit. I expect each department head or his designated subordinate
to investigate promptly and carefully any alleged instance of
unjustified use of security classifications. As the result of
these policies, and as the result of the clear segregation of
security from nonsecurity information, I hope that the American
people will receive more, rather than less, information about
their Government as a result of this Executive order.

Under the order, any agency which originates an item of security information is directed to mark it with the words "security
information" plus one of the four following classifications: "top
secret," "secret," "confidential," or "restricted." The Order
specifies the precautions then to be taken in accordance with
these classifications, ranging from the most stringent precautions
for "top secret" to the minimum precautions for "restricted."
The four classifications are the standard marking used by the
Departments of Defense and State and no new security classifications are authorized.

. . . I have also directed the National Security Council,
through its Interdepartmental Committee on Internal Security, to
maintain a continuing review of classification activities in all
agencies with a view to achieving uniform compliance with this
order, both as to safeguarding security information and to prevent
the classification procedure from being used to withhold information which can be divulged without harm to the national security.

(50) ASSOCIATED PRESS MANAGING EDITORS' ASSOCIATION, RESOLUTION,
September 29, 1951 [Extract]
Source: Associated Press Managing Editors' Association.

The Associated Press Managing Editors' association opposes as
a dangerous instrument of the news suppression the President's
executive order of September 25, 1951, extending the cloak of
military secrecy to the civilian establishments of the Government.

Free people have the right to the fullest information about
conduct of their own Government. They can safely consent to its
abridgment only on the plainest demonstration of national peril.
Even then, any curtailment of this right to which they do consent
must be so plainly prescribed and so narrowly limited that safety
from external aggression is not bought at the internal risk of
secret government.

That this is a time of national peril none would dispute. It
is, however, a peril that can be met as it was met in World War II,
without the sacrifice of essential freedom. Information useful
to the enemy can be withheld without depriving the American people
of the information about their Government that they must have to
preserve intact the democratic process.

The [President's] September 25 [order] . . . whatever motive
may have inspired it, is not drawn with sufficient precision to
avoid risks of secrecy to which no free government ought to expose
its people. Among deficiencies instantly apparent are these:

1. The order purposes to set up standards of security to the
civilian agencies of Government, but it fails to define closely
the classification terms that it employs and it furnishes to
untrained Government personnel, to which it entrusts the largest
responsibility, no clear guide by which they may govern their
official acts.

2. Agencies, according to the President's statement, must "show
affirmatively" that disclosure of the information would harm national security, but no authority to which this showing must be
made, in advance of classification, is prescribed.

3. The National Security Council is given broad review powers,
but the machinery and method by which this review is to be accomplished is not prescribed and no means is set forth by which an
immediate review of classification decisions can be obtained.

4. Citizens are enjoined to support the classifications decided
upon. They do not participate directly, or through any representatives, in the making of the initial classifications. They have
no authority to which they can appeal but the authority which
made the classification in the first place. They have no means
of discovering for themselves or through proper representative
agencies, what information is being withheld or if decisions to
withhold information have been wisely made. At no stage in the
operation of the classification system is there provision by which
a hearing may be given to those who desire to have the interests
of information weighed against the interests of security.

5. Heads of the civilian departments, agencies and bureaus are
given the broadest powers to delegate a classification authority

that frequently has been [confined to] the most experienced and competent personnel.

6. The Government of the United States, during World War II, found it inadvisable to entrust any such power to civilian or military agencies, without the safeguard and the check of the Office of War Information and of the Office of Censorship, established directly under the President to protect the people against concealment or news suppression.

Whatever respect now exists for the top secret, secret, confidential and restricted classifications used by the Departments of Defense and State will not long survive the indiscriminate use of these labels by civilian departments. Security as a result will be endangered, rather than safeguarded.

This executive order has been issued without any showing of necessity.

It has been promulgated without the careful public discussion and honest debate that ought to precede any departure from democratic methods.

It has been drawn without regard for the lessons of World War II when the Government achieved a workable compromise of the sometimes conflicting claims of complete information and absolute security.

This executive order should be rescinded. If the need for some system of classification can be demonstrated, there should be a re-examination of the whole problem of achieving in the civilian departments a system of security consistent with the right of the people to be informed fully about their government.

The president of this association is authorized to appoint a committee to make these views known to the President of the United States.

(51) PRESS CONFERENCE, PRESIDENT TRUMAN, October 4, 1951 [Extract]

Source: *Public Papers of the Presidents: Harry S. Truman, 1951.* Washington: U.S. Government Printing Office, 1965, pp. 554-560.

. . . "There has been considerable misrepresentation and misunderstanding of the Executive order issued on September 24, 1951, relating to the handling of information which has been classified, in order to protect the national security."

"And right here I want to stop and tell you that Central Intelligence had Yale University make a survey, and that survey found . . . that 95 percent of all our information was public property.

"This executive order represented an honest effort to find the best approach to a problem that is important to the survival of the United States of America. I issued the order with great reluctance, and only when I was convinced, after lengthy consideration, that it was necessary to protect the United States against its potential enemies. . . .

"In its simplest terms, the problem is what we should do to keep military and related secrets from falling into the hands of the enemies of the United States. I do not believe that anyone could seriously contend that military secrets should be published in the newspapers, or that anyone has a right or a duty to see that military secrets are published. . . .

"Whether it be treason or not, it does the United States just as much harm for military secrets to be made known to potential enemies through open publication, as it does for military secrets to be given to an enemy through the clandestine operations of spies. . . .

"On the other hand, I do not believe that protection of military secrets should be made a cloak or a cover for withholding from the people information about their Government which should be made known to them. . . .

"It is easy to agree on these two objectives, but it was difficult to establish the means for accomplishing both of them.

"In those agencies of the Government primarily concerned with national security matters, . . . we have had for a number of years a system of classifying information to prevent its disclosure to unauthorized persons when it would be dangerous to the national security. This system . . . has not in all instances prevented the publication of information which aided our enemies against the United States, and in other cases it has been used to classify information which actually has no particular relationship to national security. . . .

"In the present defense mobilization period, it has become necessary in an increasing number of cases to make military secrets available to executive agencies other than the military departments, in order that these other agencies might effectively perform their functions that are necessary in supporting the defense effort. It is also necessary for some of these civilian agencies - such as the Central Intelligence Agency, the Federal Bureau of Investigation, for example - to originate and protect some information vital to our defense.

"It should be readily apparent that military secrets in the hands of these other agencies should be protected just as much as when they are in the hands of the military departments. . . .

" . . . the purpose of this executive order . . . is to provide that information affecting the national security shall continue to be protected when it gets out of the hands of the military departments and into the hands of other agencies. . . .

"Another purpose of the order . . . is to provide that information shall not be classified and withheld from the public on the ground that it affects the national security, unless it is in fact actually necessary to protect such information in the interest of national security. . . .

"I think this Executive order represents a reasonable approach to a very difficult problem. I think it will work in the public interest, and I expect to watch it closely, to see that it is not used as an excuse for withholding information to which the public is entitled.

"It may well be that experience under the order will indicate that it should be changed. In that case, I will be glad to change it - and . . . to give consideration to reasonable suggestions for changes that are advanced in good faith.

"I would like to suggest to those who are seriously and honestly concerned about this matter, that they consider it objectively and with the interests of the United States uppermost in their minds. I would like to suggest that they consider how we can best accomplish objectives which all of us should be able to agree upon. I do not believe that the best solution can be reached by adopting an approach based on the theory that everyone has a right to know our military secrets and related information affecting the national security."

" . . . remember that 95 percent of our secret information has been revealed by newspapers and slick magazines, and that is what I am trying to stop.

Question: Mr. President, can you give us some example of what caused this order?

THE PRESIDENT: Yes. The most outstanding example was the publication in *Fortune* magazine of all the locations and the maps of our atomic energy plants. And then, . . . in every town in the country - were published air maps of Washington, New York, Chicago, San Francisco, Seattle, and other of our great cities, with arrows pointing to the key points in those towns.

Question: I think that information was given out by the departments. . . .

THE PRESIDENT: Well, I don't care who gave it out. The publishers had no business to use it, if they had the welfare of the United States at heart.

Question: I don't know if the miliary or atomic energy . . .

THE PRESIDENT: I don't care who gave it out. The publisher should be just as patriotic as I am, and I wouldn't give it out.

Question: The story was over the wire . . .

THE PRESIDENT: Well, I don't care about that. . . .

Question: . . . attributed to a military agency . . .

THE PRESIDENT: Yes, and if the military agency gives you that, and an atomic bomb falls on you on account of that, at the right place, who is to blame? . . . they were air pictures of the great cities. And it's terrible. I wish I had them of Russia and their manufacturing plants. I could use them.

Question: Mr. President, when was the Yale survey made, sir?

THE PRESIDENT: Oh, just a short time ago - just a short time ago.

Question: May I ask, Mr. President, right along the line of your effort to safeguard military and security information, what safeguards are there that the security officer will not be overzealous? As I recall, the first action taken under your Executive order was the statement by the security officer of the OPS [Office of Personnel Security] who said that security information is anything which is embarrassing to OPS?

THE PRESIDENT: And he had the carpet pulled out from under him, if you remember!

Question: You are the one man to watch everything, except no one human being can watch everything.

THE PRESIDENT: No - that is correct - that is correct. And I hate censorship just as badly as you do, and I will protect you against that as far as I can. But the safety and welfare of the United States of America comes first with me.

Question: As a corollary question, there was a suggestion on Capitol Hill, I believe by Senator [William] Benton [Democrat, Connecticut] - although I am not sure - that each department which has a security officer also have a man who fights for release of information?

THE PRESIDENT: Well, I don't know about that. I don't know about that. . . .

Question: Mr. President, have you weighed the importance of the free press in relation to military security. . . .

THE PRESIDENT: Yes. . . .

Question: . . . as both important to this country?

THE PRESIDENT: Yes, yes. A free press is just as important as the Bill of Rights, and that is what is contained in the Bill of Rights.

Question: Yes, sir. But do you not think you are giving dangerous power to civilian agencies to say what shall be given to the people?

THE PRESIDENT: I am not so sure. We will have to wait and find out. If that is the case, why we will change it, . . .

Question: Do you not think that censorship is always abused to a degree?

THE PRESIDENT: I don't know. I have had no experience.

Question: I have, sir, and I find that it always is, even by the military.

THE PRESIDENT: Well, where is Elmer Davis? He can tell us about that.

Mr. Davis: Is there any program giving training in uniform standards for the security officers?

THE PRESIDENT: I hope there will - I hope there will be.

Joseph H. Short (Secretary to the President): Mr. President, that was provided, sir. There is training in uniform standards by the ICIS [Interdepartment Conference on Internal Security, a subcommittee of the NSC] and ICIS is going to review all of these classifications.

Question: Didn't hear what Joe said, Mr. President?

THE PRESIDENT: He said that there was provided in the order a training program for these men, and for uniform standards, and that that training would be carefully supervised.

Question: Did I understand you to say, sir, that 95 percent of our secret information has been revealed?

THE PRESIDENT: Yes. Ninety-five percent of all our information has been revealed in the press in one way or another. . . .

Question: Mr. President, on this question of the maps, I wonder if we could recapitulate that just a little? Do we understand correctly that in event that a newspaper or magazine gets some information from, say, the Defense Department, do you think, sir, that the primary responsibility on whether that is published is on the publisher and not on the originating agency?

THE PRESIDENT: There is no question about that, because they are very careful not to publish a lot of things that I say. . . .

Question: Mr. President, I would like to clear up this 95 percent. You say secret information has been disclosed. You would not have had that 95 percent disclosed that has already been disclosed?

THE PRESIDENT: No. There's a lot of it I wouldn't disclose, but 95 percent of it has been made public.

Question: Well, I know that the Central Intelligence [Agency] and the others say that 95 percent of their information comes from magazines.

THE PRESIDENT: That is correct.

Question: Yes.

THE PRESIDENT: That is absolutely correct.

Question: As I understood the statement, that . . .

THE PRESIDENT: Ninety-five percent of our secret information has been disclosed.

Question: I think we are talking about two different things.

THE PRESIDENT: Well, maybe . . .

Question: . . . But this 95 percent of our secret information which you want to keep secret has been disclosed?

THE PRESIDENT: That is the information I have from Central Intelligence.

Question: Well, Mr. President, who classified that 95 percent as secret?

THE PRESIDENT: The military.

Question: The military? Thank you.

THE PRESIDENT: Military and State.

Question: Mr. President, could you say what is the unit of information? Is it 95 percent of the facts, or 95 percent of the documents or maps? How is the 95 percent figure arrived at?

THE PRESIDENT: It takes into consideration all the things you mentioned.

Question: Mr. President, I am a little confused. Was that the Yale survey. . . .

THE PRESIDENT: That's right.

Question: . . . that you are thinking about, that said that 95 percent of the secret information has been revealed?

THE PRESIDENT: That's correct.

Question: Mr. President, I would like to raise a case in point and get your reaction to it. Yesterday, Mr. Short announced on your behalf, another atomic bomb had been exploded. . . .

THE PRESIDENT: That's right.

Question: . . . and said that further details would not be given, because it would adversely affect our national security. Right after that, the Associated Press came through with a story quoting an unidentified, authoritative source as saying that there had been two explosions, one of them a fizzle, and then quoting still later a Congressman - also unidentified - as saying that the explosions had taken place in the last 3 or 4 days. Now, would you give me some reaction to that, as a specific example of information over and above that which was released by the White House?

THE PRESIDENT: I think that is an example.

Question: What was that, Mr. President?

THE PRESIDENT: I said I think that is an example.

Question: Of what, sir?

THE PRESIDENT: Of disclosing information that should not be disclosed.

Question: Well, Mr. President, don't you think the Russians knew it? I mean . . .

THE PRESIDENT: They exploded it. Of course they knew it! (Laughter)

Question: Yes, sir, so why would it hurt our national defense?

THE PRESIDENT: Because we have got to find out what they are doing, so we will know what to do.

Question: I didn't get the last part? Disclosure of our means of detecting . . .

THE PRESIDENT: That's right - that's right. That's right, that is exactly right.

Question: Mr. President, how far did this Yale survey figure in the decision to put out this order?

THE PRESIDENT: I didn't sign the order until I got it.

Question: Mr. President, some of this information comes out from Congress. Now the Executive order doesn't apply to that. What about the responsibility of the publisher on information released by Congressmen?

THE PRESIDENT: I can't answer that.

Question: Mr. President, this may be - I may be simple-minded about this . . .

THE PRESIDENT: No you're not, Smitty [Merriman Smith of AP].

Question: . . . But how did Yale know? . . . How did they get all this secret information?

THE PRESIDENT: They made a survey and supplied it to Central Intelligence. That is how it came about.

Question: I just wonder what Yale was doing with that information?

THE PRESIDENT: They got it out of the newspapers and magazines and sent it down here, and Central Intelligence came to the conclusion that they knew that 95 percent of it was disclosed.

Question: Mr. President, did the CIA recognize and agree with the Yale survey that 95 percent . . .

THE PRESIDENT: Yes. Yes.

Question: They agreed with it?

THE PRESIDENT: Yes. They made the report to me.

Question: The CIA reported to you?

THE PRESIDENT: Yes.

Question: Mr. President, recently the Defense Department gave out certain information about the Matador, also on these guided missiles, and so forth. That was published probably in every paper in the land. Was that the publishers' responsibility not to publish it?

THE PRESIDENT: I think so, if they want to protect the country.

Question: Wouldn't it be better to tighten up over at Defense?

THE PRESIDENT: That is what we are doing. I say, that is what we are doing, and that is what you are fussing about.

Question: Do you think publishers - if the publishers wanted to protect the country, they shouldn't have printed the pictures. . . .

THE PRESIDENT: They ought to think about the welfare of the country, just the same as I do, and I think most of them would, if they would stop and think about it.

Question: Mr. President, . . . these maps were used as part of the civilian defense program, to make the people alert to the dangers of atomic bombs.

THE PRESIDENT: I agree, but then I don't think that it should have been made available to the Russians. . . .

Question: Mr. President, . . . Are you suggesting that perhaps - that the editors and publishers that we supply our news stories to, should ask some agency in the Government . . .

THE PRESIDENT: No, I am not.

Question: . . . whether a thing should be published or not?

THE PRESIDENT: No, I am not. I am asking the editors and the publishers to take the same viewpoint of the safety of the United States that I take, and I am not asking them to ask anybody to help them do it. They ought to know.

Question: I know that many times we receive statements from Members of Congress, for instance, and we go ahead and write stories about those statements. Perhaps many times a reporter feels that that information might be of a security nature, but if it is on the record up there on the Hill, there is nothing we can really do except to go ahead and put it out.

THE PRESIDENT: That is up to you. The safety of the country is in your hands just the same as it is in mine.

Question: Mr. President, do you think everyone in Washington talks too much?

THE PRESIDENT: I wouldn't say that. . . .

(52) STATEMENT, PRESIDENTIAL PRESS SECRETARY JOSEPH SHORT, October 4, 1951

Source: *Public Papers of the Presidents: Harry S. Truman, 1951.* Washington: U.S. Government Printing Office, 1965, p. 563.

The President has directed me to clarify his views on security information as follows:

1. Every citizen - including officials and publishers has a duty to protect our country.

2. Citizens who receive military information for publication from responsible officials qualified to judge the relationship of such information to the national security may rightfully assume that it is safe to publish the information.

3. Citizens who receive military information from sources not having the necessary responsibilities, and qualifications to evaluate such information should, as loyal Americans, exercise the most careful judgment in determining the safety of publishing such information.

4. The recent Executive order on classified information does not in any way alter the right of citizens to publish anything.

(53) LETTER, PRESIDENT TRUMAN TO HERBERT CORN (PRESIDENT, ASSOCIATED PRESS MANAGING EDITORS ASSOCIATION), December 17, 1951 [Extract]

Source: *Public Papers of the Presidents: Harry S. Truman, 1951.* Washington: U.S. Government Printing Office, 1965, pp. 648-649.

I am unable to reconcile your letter of December fourth with statements made to me by members of the special committee of the Associated Press Managing Editors Association on October seventeenth.

The committee, which included you, made the following statements to me:

(1) The Associated Press Managing Editors were as interested as I am in protecting secrets from the enemy.

(2) That you were sure I had acted in good faith in signing the order and that I was sincere in the letter of transmittal to Departments and Agencies in admonishing all officials of the Executive Branch to guard against abuse of the order.

(3) You (the committee) told me that the order was imperfectly drawn and, at the conclusion of our conversation, you as a group informed me that you would suggest changes therein.

You may recall that, as we sat down together, M. J. Russell Wiggins, Chairman of the Committee, assured me that the committee has constructive criticisms to make and I replied that I wished to hear them. The burden of your criticism, as I recall it, was against "definitions" and you went out of my office promising to write better ones.

Your concern over definitions seemed to arise from a fear that some agencies, particularly civilian agencies, might classify non-security information, something I had explicitly prohibited in my memorandum to all Department and Agency heads. I said, "To put the matter bluntly, these regulations are designed to keep security information away from potential enemies and must not be used to cover up mistakes made by any official or employee of the Government." Although I thought your fears were groundless, nevertheless, I was glad to have you offer suggestions so that every effort could be made to reinforce my policy of confining the order to matters genuinely involving the safety of our country. . . .

My attitude has not changed. I still feel that way. But your letter would indicate that the Associated Press Managing Editors, after indicating otherwise, intend to stand on the outside and carp and criticize without being at all helpful.

I would like to remind you that . . . I did not single out your Association for the role of re-drafting the order. At their meeting with me, members of the committee suggested that improvements could be made in the order. Then when I countered that I would be glad to improve the order, you said that your committee would make a try.

I thought that, because your group espouses freedom of information, it might be willing to join me in reinforcing that principle. I still cannot understand why you editors reversed yourselves and passed up this opportunity to serve the cause of freedom of information in the dangerous days ahead when the safety of our country and the freedoms for which it stands are in peril.

I also want to refer again to the matter of protecting secrets from the enemy and to say: This is your country as well as mine. We can only win in the present world struggle if we all work together.

(54) PRESS CONFERENCE, PRESIDENT TRUMAN, July 3, 1952 [Extract]

Source: *Public Papers of the Presidents: Harry S. Truman 1952-53.* Washington: U.S. Government Printing Office, 1966, pp. 468-469,

****

Question: It seems that the Federal Trade Commission has a report on an alleged oil cartel. Could you tell us when that will be made public, or what disposition will be made of it?

THE PRESIDENT: It is a document that is not for publication at the present time. It has been - the committee which is headed by Senator [Thomas] Hennings has had access to it.

Question: Mr. President, is the reason that it will not be made public at this time one of national security, or other considerations?

THE PRESIDENT: There are other considerations. . . .

Question: Mr. President, to return to the Federal Trade Commission oil cartel report: There has been a considerable amount of speculation that the reason for its nondisclosure - that it has not been disclosed on the grounds that it affected national security - is that there were other less justifiable reasons for holding it back?

THE PRESIDENT: It was classified in the first place by the Federal Trade Commission itself, for national security reasons, but there are other reasons why it should be classified at this time.

Question: But can you explain what they are?

THE PRESIDENT: No.

Question: Can you say whether . . .

THE PRESIDENT: I have no further comment on it at all.

(55) LETTER, ATTORNEY GENERAL McGRATH TO SENATOR PAT McCARRAN, copy undated but in 1952 [Extract.]

Source: J. Howard McGrath Papers, Harry S. Truman Library.

This is in response to your request for the views of the Department of Justice relative to the bill (S. 2255) "To provide that records made by public officers and employees shall be the property of the people and making unlawful failure or refusal to open such records to the public and the American press."

The bill would add a new section . . . which section would make it a felony for any officer or employee of the United States, or any other person whose compensation is in any part paid from the Treasury of the United States, to willfully fail or refuse to open to the public or to the American press any records made in his official capacity or in connection with his official duties, except as Congress shall have otherwise specifically provided by law. . . .

Enactment of this measure would authorize undue interference with the conduct of the routine business of Government, jeopardize the conduct of the foreign affairs and international relations of the country, and threaten its national security.

The Government must unquestionably be responsible and responsive to the American people. But . . . the machinery with which the routine operation of its affairs is conducted must not be so fettered and interfered with by those without a legitimate particular interest as to impede the affairs of state.

Moreover, . . . the measure makes no particular provision for maintaining inviolate the many items of highly classified information gathered and prepared daily by various agencies of Government. Troop movements, military strategy, the state of preparedness for world conflict, information relative to persons known to be subversives or other dangerous criminals, plans for United States action on delicate questions before the United Nations, and other equally confidential and secret information, would be available without limitation to "the public or to the American press." Informers, from whom is obtained a great deal of information vital to the security of the country, could no longer be protected against having their identities disclosed, and could not, therefore, be expected to be as cooperative. The confidential nature of executive sessions of the Congress, the deliberations of the justices of the Supreme Court, the recommendations made to the President by his close advisers, all of the Government's evidence in criminal prosecutions, and many other instances wherein information obviously should be kept confidential, may be cited as indicating the inadvisability of this enactment.

The Department of Justice recognizes that a successful democracy is to a large measure dependent upon an informed public. However, how to furnish the public a maximum of information without unnecessarily interfering with the operations of the Government and without threatening its security is a problem most difficult of solution. It is clear that a solution is not to be found in a bill such as this.

The Director of the Bureau of the Budget has advised that there is no objection to the submission of this report.

C. Inherent Powers

The nature of the Cold War, and the Truman Administration's particular conceptions of the Soviet threat, combined to enhance presidential powers. Nonetheless, it was not until June 25, 1950, when North Korean troops invaded South Korea, that a significantly far-reaching development occurred: the enunciation of a claimed presidential power to commit U.S. troops anywhere in the world under the president's "Commander-in-Chief" powers without a formal congressional declaration of war. President Truman's initial decision to commit U.S. troops to Korea had not been based on a conscious assessment of presidential powers; the rationale was offered after the fact. Truman's Korean action, moreover, was unprecedented; earlier instances wherein presidents had unilaterally authorized military action were either more limited or were clearly defensive. None actually involved the nation in an ongoing war, particularly one which threatened to escalate into a major atomic confrontation. Even President Franklin Roosevelt, who had stretched presidential powers during the 1940-1941 period (whether in his September 1940 "destroyer-bases" deal with Great Britain or in his September 1941 "shoot on sight" order following the Greer incident) recognized the Congress' exclusive right to involve the nation in war. As Arthur Schlesinger has argued, Truman's Korean action provided the precedent relied upon by subsequent presidents (most notably by President Lyndon Johnson during 1964-1968) to commit U.S. troops to war. A January 17, 1962 Justice Department memorandum succinctly captures this presidential arrogance:

> Just as "the power to wage war is the power to wage war successfully," so the power of the President to conduct foreign relations should be deemed to be the power to conduct foreign relations successfully, by any means necessary to combat the measures taken by the Communist bloc, including both open and covert measures.

President Truman did not, moreover, confine his actions to sending U.S. troops to Korea. In the aftermath of an intensive policy review concerning the need to strengthen the NATO military alliance, on September 9, 1950, Truman announced his decision to assign four U.S. divisions to Western Europe and subsequently to appoint Dwight Eisenhower as commander-in-chief of NATO forces. Responding to this unilateral initiative and alarmed by the Korean precedent, conservatives in Congress, led by Republican Senator Kenneth Wherry, challenged Truman's claimed authority. Introducing Senate Resolution 8 on January 8, 1951 (which stipulated "That it is the sense of the Senate that no ground forces of the United States should be assigned to duty in the Korean area for the purposes of the North Atlantic Treaty pending the formulation of a policy with respect thereto by the Congress"), Senator Wherry precipitated the so-called "Great Debate" of 1951. To undercut the appeal of Wherry's resolution, the Democratic Senate leadership supported another resolution, S. Res. 99, which eventually passed on April 4, 1951. Under this resolu-

*tion, the Senate approved the President's decision to assign
the four divisions to Western Europe but insisted on its
right to prior consultation should the President conclude
additional troops were needed. Responding to political realities, Truman modified his position tactically. Throughout
the debate, nonetheless, he claimed as a presidential power
the right to assign troops anywhere in the world on his own
authority.*

(56) <u>STATEMENT, PRESIDENT TRUMAN</u>, June 27, 1950 [Extract]

Source: *Public Papers of the Presidents: Harry S. Truman, 1950.* Washington: U.S. Government Printing Office, 1965, p. 492.

In Korea the Government forces, which were armed to prevent border raids and to preserve internal security, were attacked by invading forces from North Korea. The Security Council of the United Nations called upon the invading troops to cease hostilities and to withdraw to the 38th parallel. This they have not done, . . . The Security Council called upon all members of the United Nations to render every assistance to the United Nations in the execution of this resolution. In these circumstances I have ordered United States air and sea forces to give the Korean Government troops cover and support.

The attack upon Korea makes it plain beyond all doubt that communism has passed beyond the use of subversion to conquer independent nations and will now use armed invasion and war. It has defied the orders of the Security Council of the United Nations issued to preserve international peace and security. In these circumstances the occupation of Formosa by Communist forces would be a direct threat to the security of the Pacific area and to United States forces performing their lawful and necessary functions in that area.

Accordingly I have ordered the 7th Fleet to prevent any attack on Formosa. As a corollary of this action I am calling upon the Chinese Government on Formosa to cease all air and sea operations against the mainland. . . . The determination of the future status of Formosa must await the restoration of security in the Pacific, a peace settlement with Japan, or consideration by the United Nations.

I have also directed that United States Forces in the Philippines be strengthened and that military assistance to the Philippine Government be accelerated.

I have similarly directed acceleration in the furnishing of military assistance to the forces of France and the Associated States in Indochina and the dispatch of a military mission to provide close working relations with those forces. . . .

(57) SPEECH, SENATOR ROBERT TAFT, June 28, 1950 [Extract]

Source: U.S. Congress, *Congressional Record*, 81st Congress, 2d
session, pp. 9319-9323.

. . . Early on Sunday morning, June 25, the Communist-
dominated Republic of North Korea launched an unprovoked aggressive military attack on the Republic of Korea, . . .

The attack did not cease, and on Tuesday, June 27, the President issued a statement announcing that he had "ordered United
States air and sea forces to give the Korean Government troops
cover and support." . . . that he had ordered the Seventh Fleet
to prevent any attack on Formosa, and that he had directed that
United States forces in the Philippines be strengthened, and that
military assistance to the Philippine Government and the forces
of France and the associated states in Indochina be accelerated.
. . .

No one can deny that a serious crisis exists. The attack was
as much a surprise to the public as the attack at Pearl Harbor,
although, apparently, the possibility was foreseen by all our
intelligence forces, and should have been foreseen by the administration. We are now actually engaged in a de facto war with the
northern Korean Communists. That in itself is serious, but nothing compared to the possibility that it might lead to war with
Soviet Russia. It is entirely possible that Soviet Russia might
move in to help the North Koreans and that the present limited
field of conflict might cover the entire civilized world. . . .
The attack in all probability was instigated by Soviet Russia.
We can only hope that the leaders of that country have sufficient
judgment to know that a world war will result in their own destruction, and will therefore refrain from such acts as might
bring about such a tragic conflict.

. . . Korea itself is not vitally important to the United
States. It is hard to defend. We have another instance of communism picking out a soft spot where the Communists feel that they
can make a substantial advance and can obtain a moral victory
without risking war. From the past philosophy and declarations of
our leaders, it was not unreasonable for the North Koreans to
suppose that they could get away with it and that we would do
nothing about it.

The President's statement of policy represents a complete
change in the programs and policies heretofore proclaimed by the
administration. I have heretofore urged a much more determined
attitude against communism in the Far East, and the President's
new policy moves in that direction. It seems to me that the time
had to come, sooner or later, when we would give definite notice
to the Communists that a move beyond a declared line would result
in war. . . .

It seems to me that the new policy is adopted at an unfortunate time, and involves the attempt to defend Korea, which is a
very difficult military operation indeed. . . . In any event, I
believe the general principle of the policy is right, and I see
no choice except to back up wholeheartedly and with every available resource the men in our Armed Forces who have been moved
into Korea.

If we are going to defend Korea, it seems to me that we should have retained our Armed Forces there and should have given, a year ago, the notice which the President has given today. With such a policy, there never would have been such an attack by the North Koreans. In short, this entirely unfortunate crisis has been produced first, by the outrageous, aggressive attitude of Soviet Russia, and second, by the bungling and inconsistent foreign policy of the administration.

I think it is important to point out, Mr. President, that there has been no pretense of any bipartisan foreign policy about this action. The leaders of the Republican Party in Congress have never been consulted on . . . Chinese policy or Formosa or Korea or Indochina. . . .

Furthermore, it should be noted that there has been no pretense of consulting the Congress. No resolution has ever been introduced asking for the approval of Congress for the use of American forces in Korea. I shall discuss later the question of whether the President is usurping his powers as Commander in Chief. My own opinion is that he is doing so; that there is no legal authority for what he has done. But I may say that if a joint resolution were introduced asking for approval of the use of our Armed Forces already sent to Korea and fully support of them in their present venture, I would vote in favor of it. . . .

. . . we should long ago have declared a definite policy. In certain areas we may have to undertake an actual defense with American troops. In other areas we can perhaps undertake only to furnish arms. . . .

I welcome the indication of a more definite policy, and I strongly hope that having adopted it the President may maintain it intact.

. . . since I approve of the changes now made in our foreign policy, I approve of the general policies outlined in the President's statement. I feel that we must back up our troops, where they have been sent by the President, with unstinted support. Whether the President chose the right time for his new policy, or right place, can be discussed in the future. I suggest, however, that any Secretary of State [then Dean Acheson] who has been so reversed by his superiors and whose policies have precipitated the danger of war, had better resign and let someone else administer the program to which he was, and perhaps still is, so violently opposed.

(58) SPECIAL MESSAGE TO CONGRESS, PRESIDENT TRUMAN, July 19, 1950 [Extract]

Source: *Public Papers of the Presidents: Harry S. Truman, 1950.* Washington: U.S. Government Printing Office, 1965, pp. 527-536.

I am reporting to the Congress on the situation which has been created in Korea, . . . [and] my views concerning the significance of these events for this Nation and the world, and certain recommendations for legislative action . . .

[The North Korean invasion] created a real and present danger
to the security of every nation. This attack was, in addition, a
demonstration of contempt for the United Nations, since it was an
attempt to settle, by military aggression, a question which the
United Nations had been working to settle by peaceful means.

The attack on the Republic of Korea, therefore, was a clear
challenge to the basic principles of the United Nations Charter
. . . If this challenge had not been met squarely, the effectiveness of the United Nations would have been all but ended, and the
hope of mankind that the United Nations would develop into an
institution of world order would have been shattered.

Prompt action was imperative. The Security Council of the
United Nations met [on June 25 and] . . . passed a resolution
which called for the immediate cessation of hostilities and for
the withdrawal of the invading troops to the thirty-eighth parallel, and which requested the members of the United Nations to refrain from giving aid to the northern aggressors and to assist in
the execution of this resolution. . . .

Throughout Monday, June 26th, the invaders continued their
attack with no heed to the resolution of the Security Council of
the United Nations. Accordingly, in order to support the resolution, and on the unanimous advice of our civil and military authorities, I ordered United States air and sea forces to give the
Korean Government troops cover and support.

On Tuesday, June 27th, . . . the United Nations Security
Council met again and passed a second resolution recommending
that members of the United Nations furnish to the Republic of
Korea such aid as might be necessary to repel the attack and to
restore international peace and security in the area. . . .

The vigorous and unhesitating actions of the United Nations
and the United States in the face of this aggression met with an
immediate and overwhelming response throughout the free world.
The first blow of aggression had brought dismay and anxiety to the
hearts of men the world over. The fateful events of the 1930's,
when aggression unopposed bred more aggression and eventually war,
were fresh in our memory.

But the free nations had learned the lesson of history. Their
determined and united actions uplifted the spirit of free men
everywhere. As a result, where there had been dismay there is
hope; where there had been anxiety there is firm determination.
. . .

All the members of the United Nations who have endorsed the
action of the Security Council realize the significance of the
step that has been taken. This united and resolute action to put
down lawless aggression is a milestone toward the establishment of
a rule of law among nations.

Only a few countries have failed to support the common action
to restore the peace. The most important of these is the Soviet
Union.

Since the Soviet representative had refused to participate in
the meetings of the Security Council which took action regarding
Korea, the United States brought the matter directly to the attention of the Soviet Government in Moscow. On June 27th, we re-

quested the Soviet Government, in view of its known close relations with the north Korean regime, to use its influence to have
the invaders withdraw at once.

The Soviet Government, in its reply on June 29th, and in subsequent statements, has taken the position that the attack
launched by the north Korean forces was provoked by the Republic
of Korea, and that the actions of the United Nations Security
Council were illegal.

These Soviet claims are flatly disproved by the facts. . . .

As the situation has developed, I have authorized a number of
measures to be taken. . . . General MacArthur was authorized to
use United States Army troops in Korea, and to use United States
aircraft of the Air Force and the Navy to conduct missions against
specific military targets in Korea north of the thirty-eighth
parallel, where necessary to carry out the United Nations resolution. General MacArthur was also directed to blockade the Korean
coast. . . .

It should be made perfectly clear that the [U.S.] action was
undertaken as a matter of basic moral principle. The United
States was going to the aid of a nation established and supported
by the United Nations and unjustifiably attacked by an aggressor
force. . . .

. . . our assistance to the Republic of Korea has prevented
the invaders from crushing that nation in a few days — as they
had evidently expected to do. We are determined to support the
United Nations in its effort to restore peace and security to
Korea, and its effort to assure the people of Korea an opportunity
to their own form of government free from coercion, . . .

. . . the outbreak of aggression [in Korea] requires us to consider its implications for peace throughout the world. The attack
upon the Republic of Korea makes it plain beyond all doubt that
the international communist movement is prepared to use armed invasion to conquer independent nations. We must therefore recognize the possibility that armed aggression may take place in other
areas.

In view of this, I have already directed that United States
forces in support of the Philippines be strengthened, and that
military assistance be speeded up to the Philippine Government
and to the Associated States of Indo-China and to the forces of
France in Indo-China. I have also ordered the United States
Seventh Fleet to prevent any attack upon Formosa, and I have requested the Chinese government on Formosa to cease all air and
sea operations against the mainland. . . .

The outbreak of aggression in the Far East does not, of
course, lessen, but instead increases, the importance of the common strength of the free nations in other parts of the world.
The attack on the Republic of Korea gives added urgency to the
efforts of the free nations to increase and to unify their common
strength, in order to deter a potential aggressor.

. . . the free nations must maintain a sufficient defensive
military strength in being, and, even more important, a solid
basis of economic strength, capable of rapid mobilization in the
event of emergency.

The strong cooperative efforts that have been made by the United States and other free nations, since the end of World War II, to restore economic vitality to Europe and other parts of the world, and the cooperative efforts we have begun in order to increase the productive capacity of under-developed areas, are extremely important contributions to the growing economic strength of all the free nations, and will be of even greater importance in the future. . . .

Under all the circumstances, it is apparent that the United States is required to increase its military strength and preparedness not only to deal with the aggression in Korea but also to increase our common defense, with other free nations, against further aggression.

The increased strength which is needed falls into three categories.

In the first place, . . . we shall need to send additional men, equipment and supplies to General MacArthur's command [in Korea] as rapidly as possible.

In the second place, . . . we [must] increase substantially the size and materiel support of our armed forces, over and above the increases which are needed in Korea.

In the third place, we must assist the free nations associated with us in common defense to augment their military strength. . . . .

. . . I have authorized the Secretary of Defense to exceed the budgeted strength of military personnel for the Army, Navy, and Air Force, and to use the Selective Service system to such extent as may be required in order to obtain the increased strength which we must have. I have also authorized the Secretary of Defense to meet the need for military manpower by calling into active Federal service as many National Guard units and as many units and individuals of the Reserve forces of the Army, Navy, and Air Forces as may be required.

I have directed the Secretary of Defense and the Joint Chiefs of Staff to keep our military manpower needs under constant study, in order that further increases may be made as required. There are now statutory limits on the sizes of the armed forces, and since we may need to exceed these limits, I recommend that they be removed.

To increase the level of our military strength will also require additional supplies and equipment. Procurement of many items has already been accelerated, in some cases for use in Korea, in others to replace reserve stocks which are now being sent to Korea, and in still others to add to our general level of preparedness. Further increases in procurement, resulting in a higher rate of production of military equipment and supplies, will be necessary.

The increases in the size of the armed forces, and the additional supplies and equipment which will be needed, will require additional appropriations. . . . of approximately ten billion dollars. . . .

The authorization bill for the Mutual Defense Assistance Program for 1951, now before the House of Representatives, is an important immediate step toward the strengthening of our collective security. It should be enacted without delay.

. . . the free nations of the world must step up their common security program. The other nations associated with us in the Mutual Defense Assistance Program, like ourselves, will need to divert additional economic resources to defense purposes. In order to enable the nations associated with us to make their maximum contribution to our common defense, further assistance on our part will be required. Additional assistance may also be needed to increase the strength of certain other free nations whose security is vital to our own. . . .

The steps which we must take to support the United Nations action in Korea, and to increase our own strength and the common defense of the free world, will necessarily have repercussions upon our domestic economy. . . .

We must continue to recognize that our strength is not to be measured in military terms alone. Our power to join in a common defense of peace rests fundamentally on the productive capacity and energies of our people. . . . we must make sure that the economic strength which is at the base of our security is not impaired, but continues to grow.

Our economy has tremendous productive power. Our total output of goods and services is now running at an annual rate of nearly 270 billion dollars - over 100 billion dollars higher than in 1939. . . . The index of industrial production, now at 197, is 12 percent higher than the average for last year, and 81 percent higher than in 1939.

We now have . . . 16 million more people in productive jobs than there were in 1939. We are now producing 11 million more tons of steel a year than in the peak war year 1944. Electric power output has risen from 128 billion kilowatt hours in 1939, to 228 billion hours in 1944, to 317 billion hours now. Food production is about a third higher than it ever was before the war, and is practically as high as it was during the war years, when we were sending far more food abroad than we are now.

The potential productive power of our economy is even greater. We can achieve some immediate increase in production by employing men and facilities not now fully utilized. . . .

With this enormous economic strength, the new and necessary programs I am now recommending can be undertaken with confidence in the ability of our economy to bear the strains involved. Nevertheless, the magnitude of the demands for military purposes that are now foreseeable, in an economy which is already operating at a very high level, will require substantial redirection of economic resources.

Under the program for increasing military strength which I have outlined above, military and related procurement will need to be expanded at a more rapid rate than total production can be expanded. Some materials were in short supply even before the Korean situation developed. . . .

The substantial speed-up of military procurement will intensify these shortages. Action must be taken to insure that these
shortages do not interfere with or delay the materials and the
supplies needed for the national defense.

Further, the dollars spent now for military purposes will have
a magnified effect upon the economy as a whole, since they will
be added to the high level of current civilian demand. These
increased pressures, if neglected, could drive us into a general
inflationary situation. The best evidence of this is the recent
price advances in many raw materials and in the cost of living,
even upon the mere expectancy of increased military outlays.

In these circumstances, we must take action to insure that
the increased national defense needs will be met, and that in the
process we do not bring on an inflation, with its resulting hardship for every family.

At the same time, we must recognize that it will be necessary
for a number of years to support continuing defense expenditures,
including assistance to other nations, at a higher level than we
had previously planned. Therefore, the economic measures we take
now must be planned and used in such a manner as to develop and
maintain our economic strength for the long run as well as the
short run.

I am recommending [prompt enactment of] certain legislative
measures to help achieve these objectives. . . .

First, . . . Congress [should] now enact legislation authorizing the Government to establish priorities and allocate materials as necessary to promote the national security; to limit the
use of materials for non-essential purposes; to prevent inventory
hoarding; and to requisition supplies and materials needed for
the national defense, particularly excessive and unnecessary in-
ventories.

Second, . . . I am directing all executive agencies to conduct
a detailed review of Government programs, for the purpose of modi-
fying them wherever practicable to lessen the demand upon services, commodities, raw materials, manpower, and facilities which
are in competition with those needed for national defense. The
Government, as well as the public, must exercise great restraint
in the use of those goods and services which are needed for our
increased defense efforts.

Nevertheless, the increased appropriations . . . will mean
sharply increased Federal expenditures. For this reason, we
should increase Federal revenues more sharply than I have previously recommended, in order to reduce the inflationary effect of
the Government deficit. . . .

At an appropriate time, . . . I shall present to the Congress
a program . . . to assure the financing of our needs in a manner
which will be fair to all our citizens, which will help prevent
inflation, and which will maintain the fiscal position of the
Nation in the soundest possible condition.

As a further important safeguard against inflation, . . . I
recommend that the Congress now authorize the control of consumer
credit and credit used for commodity speculation. In the housing
field, . . . I have directed that certain available credit re-

straints be applied, and I recommend that further controls be authorized, particularly to restrain expansion of privately-financed real estate credit. . . .

Third, we must take steps to accelerate and increase the production of essential materials, products, and services. I recommend, therefore, that the Congress authorize, for national defense purposes, production loan guarantees and loans to increase production. I also recommend that the Congress authorize the making of long-term contracts and other means to encourage the production of certain materials in short supply. . . .

The hard facts of the present situation require relentless determination and firm action. The course of the fighting thus far in Korea shows that we can expect no easy solution to the conflict there. We are confronted in Korea with well-supplied well-led forces which have been long trained for aggressive action. We and the other members of the United Nations who have joined in the effort to restore peace in Korea must expect a hard and costly military operation.

We must also prepare ourselves better to fulfill our responsibilities toward the preservation of international peace and security against possible further aggression. . . .

The free world has made it clear, through the United Nations, that lawless aggression will be met with force. This is the significance of Korea - and it is a significance whose importance cannot be over-estimated.

I shall not attempt to predict the course of events. But I am sure that those who have it in their power to unleash or withhold acts of armed aggression must realize that new recourse to aggression in the world today might well strain to the breaking point the fabric of world peace. . . .

(59) PRESS CONFERENCE, PRESIDENT TRUMAN, September 29, 1950 [Extract]

Source: *Public Papers of the Presidents: Harry S. Truman, 1950.* Washington: U.S. Government Printing Office, 1956, p. 661.

****

Question: Mr. President, in relation to what you just said about enforcing the law, do you draw a distinction between enforcing a law and spending money that Congress has given you to spend?

THE PRESIDENT: Well, what do you mean by that, Miss May [Craig]?

Question: I was thinking particularly of the air groups last year. You didn't spend all the money they gave you.

THE PRESIDENT: It wasn't necessary. It was not necessary.

Question: But you do draw a distinction between spending and appropriation . . .

THE PRESIDENT: I certainly do. That is the discretionary power of the President. If he doesn't feel like the money should be spent, I don't think he can be forced to spend it. How would you go about making him spend it, Miss May? (Laughter)

Question: Oh, I believe in Congress being paramount.

THE PRESIDENT: Of course you do, I don't. (More laughter). I think they are equal - I think they are equal. The Congress' job is to make the laws, and the President's job is to carry them out and enforce them, and he does just that.

Question: But not spend the money?

THE PRESIDENT: That's right - that's right. . . .

(60) STATEMENT, PRESIDENT TRUMAN, September 9, 1950 [Extract]

Source: *Public Papers of the Presidents: Harry S. Truman, 1950.* Washington: U.S. Printing Office, 1965, p. 626.

. . . I have today approved substantial increases in the strength of United States forces to be stationed in Western Europe in the interest of the defense of that area. The extent of these increases and the timing thereof will be worked out in close co-ordination with our North Atlantic Treaty partners. . . . Firm programs for the development of their forces will be expected to keep full step with the dispatch of additional United States forces to Europe. Our plans are based on the sincere expectation that our efforts will be met with similar action on their part. The purpose of this measure is to increase the effectiveness of our collective defense efforts and thereby insure the maintenance of peace.

(61) PRESS CONFERENCE, PRESIDENT TRUMAN, December 19, 1950 [Extract]

Source: *Public Papers of the Presidents: Harry S. Truman, 1950.* Washington: U.S. Government Printing Office, 1965, pp. 754-755.

****

Question: Mr. President, do I understand that you as of today have designated General Eisenhower as commander in chief?

THE PRESIDENT: As commander in chief of Allied forces in Europe, he has exactly the same position in Europe that MacArthur has in Asia.

Question: Mr. President, is it your intention to designate American forces in the near future to be a part of that army?

THE PRESIDENT: Yes.

Question: Additional American forces?

THE PRESIDENT: Yes.

Question: Could you say how many?

THE PRESIDENT: No I can't do that. If I knew I wouldn't tell you.

Question: Or how soon, sir?

THE PRESIDENT: Just as soon as it is possible to get ready. That is the reason for this emergency I have just declared.

Question: Mr. President, how soon does General Eisenhower expect to go, do you know?

THE PRESIDENT: I talked to him last night on the telephone, and he is coming to see me, and then he is going to Europe as promptly as possible. . . .

Question: Mr. President, can you say how soon American divisions will be moving . . .

THE PRESIDENT: No, I can't - no, I can't.   As I said, if I could I wouldn't tell you.   You fellows ought to have some ideas of security the same as I have.

Question: Well, perhaps this question doesn't violate security?

THE PRESIDENT: All right.

Question: Will it be a National Guard division?

THE PRESIDENT: I can't answer that . . .

(62)   PRESS CONFERENCE, PRESIDENT TRUMAN, January 4, 1951
[Extract]

Source: *Public Papers of the Presidents: Harry S. Truman, 1951.* Washington: U.S. Government Printing Office, 1965, p. 2.

****

Question: Mr. President, . . . At what point do you have to consult Congress on its constitutional right to declare war?

THE PRESIDENT: I will take care of that, May [Craig], when the time comes.   It isn't here yet.

Question: You know that resolution by [Republican Congressman Frederick] Coudert of New York . . .

THE PRESIDENT: I read something about it in the paper.   I have not received any official notice of it. . . . proper action would be taken on that when the time came, and the time is not here yet.   I hope it will never come. . . .

Question: Sir, do you consider that my question was confusing?

THE PRESIDENT: Yes.   Intended for that purpose, May, I think.

Question: No, sir, it is being discussed at the Capitol a good deal, that we are at war and that Congress has not declared war.

THE PRESIDENT: I have no comment to make on that, May.

Question: Yes, sir.

Question: Well, Mr. President, the Nation is not formally at war [in Korea], isn't that so?

THE PRESIDENT: No - that is correct.   We are carrying out an obligation for the United Nations.

Question: I beg your pardon, sir?

THE PRESIDENT: Carrying out an obligation for the United Nations, one which was assumed when we signed the charter. . . .

(63) PRESS CONFERENCE, PRESIDENT TRUMAN, January 11, 1951 [Extract]

Source: *Public Papers of the Presidents: Harry S. Truman, 1951.* Washington: U.S. Government Printing Office, 1965, pp. 18-22.

****

Question: Mr. President, Senator Connally made a speech on the floor today and said, "As for the future, I am confident that the executive branch will consult Congress on troop commitments to the integrated European defense forces now being mobilized." Is that an accurate reflection of your position?

THE PRESIDENT: . . . "Under the President's constitutional powers as Commander in Chief of the Armed Forces he has the authority to send troops anywhere in the world. That power has been recognized repeatedly by the Congress and the courts.

"This Government will continue to live up to its obligations under the United Nations, and its other treaty obligations, and we will continue to send troops wherever it is necessary to uphold these obligations."

Now, Dean Acheson in his testimony before the [Senate] Foreign Relations Committee [in 1949] made it perfectly plain that the Atlantic Treaty did not require that troops be sent, but that each country itself should make up its own mind as to what was necessary for the defense of the Atlantic Treaty countries. . . .

Question: Well, Mr. President, Senator Connally did not dispute your right to do so, he defended it; but he said that he understood you would consult with Congress before you would do it, and continuing: "It is my understanding that administration leaders plan to do so."

THE PRESIDENT: We always do that, May [Craig]. We never make any moves in foreign affairs or on any domestic affairs, or any other affairs, that we do not very considerably consult with the committees that are interested in it. We have always done that, and there has been no change in that policy, and won't be. And any Senator who wants to talk to the President can always get a date to do it.

Question: Mr. President, have you made any commitments, verbal or written, to the Atlantic Pact countries, on how many divisions we will send to Europe?

THE PRESIDENT: No. Can't make a commitment like that because we don't know how many people we are going to have.

Question: Well, Mr. President, just to make it explicit, you make no distinction, then, in the exercise of your constitutional powers to send troops, say, for reinforcement of our garrison in Germany, or later, perhaps in sending troops for a North Atlantic army. Do you feel you have as much of a right to do one as the other?

THE PRESIDENT: I do. But, of course, in the latter case, the Congress would be consulted before we do it, as we always do. . . .

Question: Mr. President, please let me get this straight. You said that you had the authority by court and Constitution to send them anywhere in the world. Did those opinions given by the courts say that you had to consult Congress?

THE PRESIDENT: No it did not . . . and I do not have to unless I want to. But of course I am polite, and I usually always consult them. (Laughter)

Question: Mr. President, you wouldn't be bound - necessarily bound by any opinion . . .

THE PRESIDENT: Well . . .

Question: . . . consulting is one thing . . .

THE PRESIDENT: . . . the opinions are all in favor of the President's exercise of the Presidential power when in his judgment is it necessary. . . . The opinions don't have any bearing on what the President intended, because they are all on his side.

Question: No, I don't have reference to policy opinions - congressional opinions - I mean you said that you would consult, and I said that wouldn't necessarily mean that you would be bound by . . .

THE PRESIDENT: No, no. That's correct.

Question: Mr. President, . . . then you will consult Congress before we send any troops to Western Europe, is that correct?

THE PRESIDENT: No, I didn't say that. I said in case of necessity for the defense of the Atlantic Charter countries - treaty countries - of course I would consult the Congress. It may be necessary to use troops in Germany in an emergency. You can't tell.

Question: Mr. President, would you be more explicit about the form that consultation would take? Would it be with the Senate Foreign Relations Committee? Would the whole Congress . . .

THE PRESIDENT: No - it would be with the Senate Foreign Relations and Armed Services Committees, which we always consult on every subject that has to do with foreign relations and with defense. I want to make that perfectly plain.

Question: Mr. President, . . . In this particular case, with the debate raging in Congress over whether you do or do not have the authority to send troops to Europe - and [former President Herbert] Hoover said not another man or another dollar should be sent - the debate has been quite general. Do I understand that you will ask Congress for permission . . .

THE PRESIDENT: No.

Question: . . . before sending troops. . . .

THE PRESIDENT: No, you do not want to take that view of the thing. I said that - in case of necessity and it became necessary, for the defense of the Atlantic Treaty countries, that Congress would be consulted before troops were sent. I don't ask their permission, I just consult them.

Question: Well, Mr. President, do you - when you say "if it became necessary for the defense of the Atlantic Treaty countries," you seem to be presuming hostilities, and things of that sort, taking place at that time, or would that include increasing forces in Germany or France now?

THE PRESIDENT: Yes - well, the latter.

Question: The latter?

THE PRESIDENT: The latter.

Question: In other words, Mr. President, no further United States troops - no troops aside from the occupation forces in Germany itself - would be sent to, say, England, France, Belgium, or Holland without consultation with the Congress?

THE PRESIDENT: Of course the Armed Services and Foreign Relations Committees would be consulted and told about it. . . .

Question: Mr. President, there is one thought I was not getting on the question of consultation. You don't need their permission, but as a matter of courtesy you would consult them?

THE PRESIDENT: Certainly. You must always bear in mind, in the background, that it is necessary for the Congress to appropriate the money for the Government to be carried on. . . .

Question: Mr. President, what will be the effect, sir, of an attempt on the part of Congress to restrict, through the appropriations bill, the use of forces . . .

THE PRESIDENT: That is up to the Congress, if they want to go to the country with that - and I'll go with them. And I licked them once.

Question: As I understand it, sir, the decision already has been made to send our forces to Europe. . . .

THE PRESIDENT: Those that are necessary, yes.

Question: Now just - what will you consult these committees about, if the decision has been made?

THE PRESIDENT: Well, we will have to wait and see what General Eisenhower's report is before we make any definite plans.

Question: About size, and so forth?

THE PRESIDENT: That's right.

(64) PRESS CONFERENCE, PRESIDENT TRUMAN, January 18, 1951
[Extract]

Source: *Public Papers of the Presidents: Harry S. Truman, 1951.*
Washington: U.S. Government Printing Office, 1965, p. 112.

****

Question: Mr. President, the Democratic leadership of the Senate is preparing a resolution, in which it will say that if it is necessary, it will be desirable to send troops to Europe at this time. Was that move taken with your consent?

THE PRESIDENT: I know nothing about it. If the Democratic majority in the Senate takes an action like that, I shall appreciate it very highly.

Question: Would you abide by the - or is that beside the point - by the outcome of the vote?

THE PRESIDENT: What's that?

Question: Would you abide by the outcome of the vote, or have you . . .

THE PRESIDENT: I shall do whatever is necessary to meet the situation as it comes up.

Question: Mr. President, I would like to get that clear. You would like to see the Senate approve . . .

THE PRESIDENT: I would appreciate it very highly.

Question: If they would affirmatively approve the sending of troops. . . .

THE PRESIDENT: Why certainly - certainly. Of course I would appreciate it, but I will do whatever is necessary to meet the situation when it comes up.

Question: Mr. President, you don't intend to request that as an administration . . .

THE PRESIDENT: No. I am making no request. I think I was told that it was the Democratic majority in the Senate that was working on it, and I am happy that they are.

Question: That is the resolution which would express approval of your . . .

THE PRESIDENT: That is correct.

Question: . . . existing authority?

THE PRESIDENT: That is right - which is constitutional, by the way. . . .

(65) <u>PRESS CONFERENCE, PRESIDENT TRUMAN</u>, March 1, 1951 [Extract]

Source: *Public Papers of the Presidents: Harry S. Truman, 1951.* Washington: U.S. Government Printing Office, 1965, p. 176.

Question: In a statement on the powers of the President, which was sent to the Capitol from the executive departments, it says that the use of congressional power to declare war has fallen into abeyance because wars are no longer declared in advance. How would you fill the gap between the constitutional declaration of war by Congress and the Executive actions?

THE PRESIDENT: Well now, I would advise you to read the history of 1941 - December 7. I think that will answer your question.

Question: Well, couldn't you tell me how you propose to do it?

THE PRESIDENT: No, I cannot, because I am not faced with any such condition.

Question: Well, may I ask you one other question . . . in relation to the same document? It says that debates over the prerogatives and powers of Congress and the President are essentially sterile, if not dangerous, to the success of the foreign policy?

THE PRESIDENT: That is correct.

Question: Do you mean that Congress ought not even to debate foreign policy?

THE PRESIDENT: Oh, no. I don't mind their talking about anything they want to. This is a free country. They can make any number of speeches they want, on any subject they want to, but that does not mean that it helps the relations with the rest of the world.

Question: Do you think then, that congressional participation in the declaration of war is completely out?

THE PRESIDENT: No, I didn't say that. . . .

(66) <u>PRESS CONFERENCE, PRESIDENT TRUMAN</u>, March 15, 1951 [Extract]

Source: *Public Papers of the Presidents: Harry S. Truman, 1951.* Washington: U.S. Government Printing Office, 1965, p. 189.

****

Question: Mr. President, would you like to say anything . . . at this time about the move in Congress lately to place some restraints upon your constitutional powers - that you will send troops to Europe . . .

THE PRESIDENT: . . . do you think that the Constitution can be amended by a Senate and House resolution?

Question: No sir, I don't.

THE PRESIDENT: All right.

Question: I thought maybe . . .

THE PRESIDENT: I don't either.

Question: You might go further along the line of the whole - the impact of that whole movement in Congress on people abroad. . . .

THE PRESIDENT: Oh, no. I don't have anything to do with the actions of the Congress. They are a free, elective body. They are elected to carry out all the legislative provisions of the Constitution of the United States. I am elected to carry out the Executive powers in that same Constitution, and we usually get along all right in the end.

Question: You will go ahead, sir, with the . . .

THE PRESIDENT: We are going to do whatever is necessary to meet the present emergency under the Constitution of the United States. That is what I am sworn to uphold and defend, and I propose to do just that.

Question: Sir, do you see any harm in any such restrictions, that is, limiting 4 million on the . . .

THE PRESIDENT: You want to get me into a discussion of a legislative matter which is not before me, and I don't intend to do that.

Question: Well, your spokesmen have opposed any such limitations on the Hill, haven't they?

THE PRESIDENT: I don't know that I have any special spokesmen. There are lots of Democrats and Republicans down there who are doing everything they can to support the foreign policy of the United States.

Question: Doing what to it, sir?

THE PRESIDENT: To support it. A number of Democratic and Republican Senators and Congressmen who are doing everything they possibly can to support the foreign policy of the United States.

Question: Excuse me - support?

THE PRESIDENT: Support the bipartisan foreign policy of the United States.

Question: That would include, also, your fixing of the limits on the number of divisions that General Eisenhower . . .

THE PRESIDENT: I won't go into that. . . .

(67) SENATE RESOLUTION 99, April 4, 1951 [Extract]

Source: U.S. *Congressional Record*, 82nd Congress, 2d session, p. 3282.

1. The Senate approved the action of the President of the United States in cooperating in the common defensive effort of the North Atlantic Treaty nations by designating, at their unanimous request, General of the Army Dwight D. Eisenhower as Supreme Allied Commander, Europe, and in placing Armed Forces of the United States in Europe under his command;

2. It is the belief of the Senate that the threat to the security of the United States and our North Atlantic Treaty partners makes it necessary for the United States to station abroad such units of our Armed Forces as may be necessary and appropriate to contribute our fair share of the forces needed for the joint defense of the North Atlantic area;

3. It is the sense of the Senate that the President of the United States as Commander in Chief of the Armed Forces, before taking action to send units of ground troops to Europe under article 3 of the North Atlantic Treaty, should consult the Secretary of Defense and the Joint Chiefs of Staff, the Committee on Foreign Relations of the Senate, the Committee on Foreign Affairs of the House of Representatives, and the Armed Services Committees of the Senate and the House of Representatives, and that he should likewise consult the Supreme Allied Commander, Europe;

4. It is the sense of the Senate that before sending units of ground troops to Europe under article 3 of the North Atlantic Treaty, the Joint Chiefs of Staff shall certify to the Secretary Defense that in their opinion the parties to the North Atlantic Treaty are giving, and have agreed to give full, realistic force

and effect to the requirement of article 3 of said treaty that
"by means of continuous and effective self-help and mutual aid"
they will "maintain and develop their individual and collective
capacity to resist armed attack," specifically insofar as the
creation of combat units is concerned;

5.   The Senate herewith approves the understanding that the
major contribution to the ground forces under General Eisenhower's
command should be made by the European members of the North Atlantic Treaty, and that such units of United States ground forces as
may be assigned to the above command shall be so assigned only
after the Joint Chiefs of Staff certify to the Secretary of Defense that in their opinion such assignment is a necessary step
in strengthening the security of the United States; and the cer-
tified opinions referred to in paragraphs 4 and 5 shall be transmitted by the Secretary of Defense to the President of the United
States, and to the Senate Committees on Foreign Relations and
Armed Services, and to the House Committees on Foreign Affairs
and Armed Services as soon as they are received;

6.   It is the sense of the Senate that, in the interests of
sound constitutional processes, and of national unity and understanding, congressional approval should be obtained of any policy
requiring the assignment of American troops abroad when such assignment is in implementation of article 3 of the North Atlantic
Treaty; and the Senate hereby approves the present plans of the
President and the Joint Chiefs of Staff to send four additional
divisions of ground forces to Western Europe, but it is the sense
of the Senate that no ground troops in addition to such four divisions should be sent to Western Europe in implementation of
article 3 of the North Atlantic Treaty without further congressional approval;

7.   It is the sense of the Senate that the President should
submit to the Congress at intervals of not more than 6 months
reports on the implementation of the North Atlantic Treaty, including such information as may be made available for this purpose
by the Supreme Allied Commander, Europe; . . .

(68) STATEMENT, PRESIDENT TRUMAN, April 5, 1951

Source: *Public Papers of the Presidents: Harry S. Truman, 1951.*
Washington: U.S. Government Printing Office, 1965, pp. 217-218.

The adoption by the Senate of Senate Resolution 99 is further
evidence that the country stands firm in its support of the North
Atlantic Treaty. It reaffirms the basic principle of our foreign
policy - that the security of the United States is intimately
bound up with the security of other free nations.

The clear endorsement of the appointment of General Eisenhower
and the plans to assign troops to his command shows that there
has never been any real question but that this country would do
its part in helping to create an integrated European defense
force.

Our main task now is to get on with the job of building our
own strength and help to build the strength of the free world - a
job which we all agree should continue to be carried out through

collaboration by the executive and the legislative branches of the Government.

(69) PRESS CONFERENCE, PRESIDENT TRUMAN, April 5, 1951 [Extract]

Source: *Public Papers of the Presidents: Harry S. Truman, 1951.* Washington: U.S. Government Printing Office, 1965, pp. 214-215

****

Question: I just have a very simple question. What is Resolution 99?

THE PRESIDENT: It's the resolution that has to do with the sending of troops to Europe.

Question: I just wonder if the Senate's action will alter your policy in any way regarding sending troops to Europe?

THE PRESIDENT: The only thing under consideration in that resolution is the sending of four divisions, which was approved.

Question: Mr. President, how do you feel about the section in which they say that it is essential that you not send more without their approval?

THE PRESIDENT: Well, the situation will develop as we go along. The Senate and the House have always been consulted in any major policy, and that situation will develop in the usual manner. Every part of our foreign policy has been carried out after careful consideration and consultation with both Houses of the Congress from the beginning, since I have been President on April 12, 1945. The policy had been carried out by President Roosevelt, and I continued the policy.

President Truman's claimed "inherent" presidential powers did not go unchallenged. On the one hand, on February 7, 1952, conservative Republican Senator John Bricker introduced S.J. Res. 130 "proposing an amendment to the Constitution of the United States relative to the making of treaties and making of executive agreements." Bricker's proposed constitutional amendment was endorsed by 44 Republican and 12 Democratic Senators. (Companion resolutions were introduced in the House on February 11 and 14, 1952.) Earlier, on January 21, 1952, conservative Democratic Senator Pat McCarran had introduced S.J. Res. 122 "to impose limitations with regard to executive agreements." A number of resolutions similar to McCarran's were also introduced in the House on February 11 and 14, 1952. Following President Truman's secret meeting with British Prime Minister Winston Churchill in January 1952, moreover, conservative Democratic Congressman John Rankin introduced a resolution demanding that the Congress be fully informed on possible commitments and conclusions resulting from the Truman-Churchill talks. Rankin's resolution passed the House, by a vote of 189-143, but was never acted upon by the Senate. In response to both developments, Truman Administration officials denied that Congress had the right to insist upon full disclosure and further sought to preclude congressional approval of the so-called Bricker Amendment.

(70) <u>MEMO, PRESIDENT TRUMAN TO ALL AGENCY AND DEPARTMENT HEADS</u>,
May 23, 1952 [Extract]

Source: *Public Papers of the Presidents: Harry S. Truman, 1952.*
Washington: U.S. Government Printing Office, 1966, pp. 367-368.

The two Senate joint resolutions [S.J. Res. 122 and S.J. Res.
130 proposing to limit presidential uses of executive agreements]
have been called to my attention. These resolutions concern matters which directly affect the activities and responsibilities of
almost every department and agency of the executive branch.

A sub-committee of the Senate Committee on Judiciary began
hearings on S.J. Res. 130 on May 21. . . . In a matter of such
fundamental importance it is vital that the Congress know the
views of the executive branch. Accordingly, I request the head
of each department and agency to examine the effects which these
joint resolutions would have on matters coming under the jurisdiction of his department or agency, and to prepare an official
statement of views concerning them. I also request the head of
each department and agency to ask the Committee promptly for an
opportunity to appear and testify at the earliest practicable
date. . . .

Any agency which believes that it is not affected directly
enough by the resolutions to warrant presentation of its views
with respect to them, is requested to send me . . . its reasons
for not seeking to testify.

The importance of the issues raised cannot be overestimated.
The constitutional amendment proposed in S.J. Res. 130 is not
routine, and it is not limited in its affect to the imposition of
restraints upon the President or agencies of the executive branch.
This proposed amendment and the provisions of S.J. Res. 122 vitally affect the powers of the Federal Government as a whole and
have a bearing on the welfare of every State and every person in
our country. . . .

The executive branch has a responsibility to see to it that
it does not default on its responsibilities as a part of the
Federal structure which was created by all of the States at the
time our Constitution was adopted.

*In the final analysis, though, neither the Bricker Amendment
nor the McCarran/Rankin-type resolutions were enacted by the Congress. The criticisms of Truman's claimed prerogatives and conduct of policy might have had major political consequences, and
partially explain the Republicans' electoral successes in 1952.
These criticisms, however, did not affect Truman's claimed powers
and exercise of these powers. The President's speech of April 8,
1952 and the resultant Executive Order 10340 announcing his decision to seize the steel industry highlight the extent of this
claim. Truman's steel seizure order was challenged in the courts
and was eventually struck down as being unconstitutional by the
U.S. Supreme Court on June 2, 1952. The Supreme Court's decision
might have ruled that there were limits to presidential powers to
seize private property and denied that "emergencies" create powers.
However, the Court had not, and did not in the future, address
the broader question of "inherent" presidential "national security"*

powers. When confronting this challenge again in 1974 involving President Nixon's claim to an unreviewable "executive privilege," the Supreme Court in U.S. v. Nixon *limited its ruling to denying that a president was the final and exclusive authority on an "executive privilege" claim and left unresolved whether the standard for an adverse ruling against such a claim would have to be confined to the possible involvement of White House aides in criminal activities.*

(71) <u>RADIO AND TV ADDRESS, PRESIDENT TRUMAN</u>, April 8, 1952 [Extract]

Source: *Public Papers of the Presidents: Harry S. Truman, 1952-53.* Washington: U.S. Government Printing Office, 1966, pp. 246-274, 249-250.

Tonight, our country faces a grave danger. We are faced by the possibility that at midnight tonight the steel industry will be shut down. . . .

Steel is our key industry. It is vital to the defense effort. It is vital to peace. . . .

If steel production stops, we will have to stop making the shells and bombs that are going directly to our soldiers at the front in Korea. If steel production stops, we will have to cut down and delay the atomic energy program. If steel production stops, it won't be long before we have to stop making engines for the Air Force planes.

. . . A prolonged shutdown would bring defense production to a halt and throw our domestic economy into chaos.

These are not normal times. These are times of crisis. We have been working and fighting to prevent the outbreak of world war. So far we have succeeded. The most important element in this successful struggle has been our defense program. If that is stopped, the situation can change overnight.

All around the world, we face the threat of military action by the forces of aggression. Our growing strength is holding these forces in check. If our strength fails, these forces may break out in renewed violence and bloodshed.

Our national security and our chances for peace depend on our defense production. Our defense production depends on steel. . . .

With American troops facing the enemy on the field of battle, I would not be living up to my oath of office if I failed to do whatever is required to provide them with the weapons and ammunitions they need for their survival.

Therefore, I am taking two actions tonight.

First, I am directing the Secretary of Commerce [Charles Sawyer] to take possession of the steel mills, and to keep them operating.

Second, I am directing the Acting Director of Defense Mobilization to get the representatives of the steel companies and the steelworkers down here to Washington at the earliest possible date in a renewed effort to get them to settle their dispute.

I am taking these measures because it is the only way to prevent a shutdown and to keep steel production rolling. It is also my hope that they will help bring about a quick settlement of the dispute. . . .

In normal times - if we were not in a national emergency - this dispute might not have arisen. In normal times, unions are entitled to whatever wages they can get by bargaining, and companies are entitled to whatever prices they can get in a competitive market.

But today, this is different. There are limitations on what wages employees can get, and there are limitations on what prices employers can charge.

We must have these limitations to prevent a wage-price spiral that would send prices through the roof, and wreck our economy and our defense program.

For more than a year we have prevented any such runaway inflation. We have done it by having rules that are fair to everyone - that require everyone to sacrifice some of his own interests to the national interest. These rules have been laid down under laws enacted by Congress, and they are applied by fair, impartial Government boards and agencies.

These rules have been applied in this steel case. They have been applied to the union, and they have been applied to the companies. The union has accepted these rules. The companies have not accepted them. The companies insist that they must have price increases that are out of line with the stabilization rules. The companies have said that unless they can get those increases they will not settle with the union. The companies have said, in short, that unless they can have what they want, the steel industry will shut down. . . .

If we gave in to the steel companies on this issue [of price control], you could say goodbye to stabilization. If we knuckled under to the steel industry, the lid would be off. Prices would start jumping up all around us - not just prices of things using steel, but prices of many other things we buy, . . .

If we granted the outrageous prices the steel industry wants, we would scuttle our whole price control program. And that comes pretty close to home for everybody in the country. . . .

As President of the United States it is my plain duty to keep this from happening. And that is the reason for the measures I have taken tonight.

At midnight the Government will take over the steel plants. Both management and labor will then be working for the Government. And they will have a clear duty to heat up their furnaces again and go on making steel.

When management and labor meet down here in Washington they will have a chance to go back to bargaining and settle their dispute. As soon as they do that, we can turn the steel plants back to their private owners with the assurance that production will continue. . . .

A lot of people have been saying I ought to rely on the procedures of the Taft-Hartley Act to deal with this emergency.

This has not been done because the so-called emergency provisions of the Taft-Hartley Act would be of no help in meeting the situation that confronts us tonight. . . .

(72) EXECUTIVE ORDER 10340, April 8, 1952 [Extract]

Source: *3 Code of Federal Regulations, 1949-1953 Comp.*, p. 861.

Whereas on December 16, 1950, I proclaimed the existence of a national emergency . . . ; and

Whereas American fighting men . . . are now engaged in deadly combat with the forces of aggression in Korea, and forces of the United States are stationed elsewhere overseas for the purpose of participating in the defense of the Atlantic Community against aggression; and

Whereas the weapons and other materials needed by our armed forces . . . are produced to a great extent in this country, and steel is an indispensable component of substantially all such weapons and materials; and

Whereas steel is likewise indispensable to the carrying out of programs of the Atomic Energy Commission of vital importance to our defense efforts; and

Whereas a continuing and uninterrupted supply of steel is also indispensable to the maintenance of the economy of the United States, upon which our military strength depends; and

Whereas a controversy has arisen between certain [steel] companies . . . and certain of their workers . . . ; and

Whereas the controversy has not been settled through the processes of collective bargaining . . . , and a strike has been called for 12:01 A.M., April 9, 1952; and

Whereas a work stoppage would immediately jeopardize and imperil our national defense . . . , and would add to the continuing danger of our soldiers, sailors, and airmen engaged in combat in the field; and

Whereas in order to assure the continued availability of steel and steel products during the existing emergency, it is necessary that the United States take possession of and operate the plants, facilities, and other property of the said companies as hereinafter provided;

Now, therefore, by virtue of the authority vested in me by the Constitution and laws of the United States, and as President of the United States and Commander in Chief of the armed forces of the United States, it is hereby ordered as follows: . . .

****

(73) <u>YOUNGSTOWN SHEET & TUBE COMPANY ET AL. V. CHARLES SAWYER</u>,
June 2, 1952 [Extract]

Source: 343 U.S. 579 (1952).

Opinion of Justice Hugo Black (Felix Frankfurter, William Douglas,
Robert Jackson, and Harold Burton concurring but filing separate
opinions)

We are asked to decide whether the President was acting within
his constitutional power when he issued an order directing the
Secretary of Commerce to take possession of and operate most
of the nation's steel mills. . . .

The President's power, if any, to issue the order must stem
either from an act of Congress or from the Constitution itself. There is no statute that expressly authorizes the
President to take possession of property as he did here. Nor
is there any act of Congress to which our attention has been
directed from which such a power can fairly be implied. . . .

Moreover, the use of the seizure technique to solve labor
disputes in order to prevent work stoppages was not only unauthorized by any congressional enactment, prior to this controversy, Congress had refused to adopt that method of settling
work disputes. . . .

It is clear that if the President had authority to issue the
order he did, it must be found in some provision of the Constitution. . . . The contention is that presidential power
should be implied from the aggregate of his powers under the
Constitution. Particular reliance is placed on provisions in
Article II which say that "The executive Power shall be vested
in a President . . . "; that "he shall take Care that the Laws
be faithfully executed"; and that he "shall be Commander in
Chief of the Army and Navy of the United States."

The order cannot properly be sustained as an exercise of the
President's military power as Commander in Chief of the Armed
Forces. . . . Even though "theater of war" be an expanding
concept, we cannot with faithfulness to our constitutional
system hold that the Commander in Chief of the Armed Forces
has the ultimate power as such to take possession of private
property in order to keep labor disputes from stopping production. That is a job for the Nation's lawmakers, not for its
military authorities. Nor can the seizure only be sustained
because of the several constitutional provisions that grant
executive power to the President. In the framework of our
Constitution, the President's power to see that the laws are
faithfully executed refutes the idea that he is to be a law-
maker. The Constitution limits his functions in the lawmaking
process to the recommending of laws he thinks wise and the
vetoing of laws he thinks bad. . . .

The President's order does not direct that a congressional
policy be executed in a manner prescribed by Congress - it
directs that a presidential policy be executed in a manner
prescribed by the President. . . .

The Founders of this Nation entrusted the lawmaking power to
the Congress alone in both good and bad times. It would do

no good to recall the historical events, the fears of power
and the hopes for freedom that lay behind their choice. Such
a review would but confirm our holding that this seizure order
cannot stand.

III. NATIONAL SECURITY

A. _International Security_

1. Evolution of Foreign Policy Decisions

The death of Franklin Roosevelt on April 12, 1945 elevated an unprepared Harry Truman to the presidency at a time when crucial decisions relating to postwar diplomacy had not been made final. To reassure the nation and the world of his commitment to Roosevelt's policies, Truman pledged to support these goals. A crucial part of Rooseveltian public diplomacy, and one which embodied the popular conviction that international collaboration was essential to preserving the peace and averting future wars, involved the planned conference at San Francisco to draft a charter for the United Nations. In his radio address of April 25, 1945, President Truman affirmed his commitment to the proposed United Nations Organization and the importance he then ascribed to diplomacy and international cooperation to preserve the peace and further U.S. interests.

(74) RADIO ADDRESS, PRESIDENT TRUMAN TO SAN FRANCISCO (UNITED
NATIONS) CONFERENCE, April 25, 1945 [Extract]

Source: *Public Papers of the Presidents: Harry S. Truman, 1945*.
Washington: U.S. Government Printing Office, 1961, pp. 20-23.

    . . . The world has experienced a revival of an old faith in
the everlasting moral force of justice. At no time in history
has there been a more important conference, nor a more necessary
meeting, than this one in San Francisco, which you are opening
today. . . .

    You members of this Conference are to be the architects of
the better world. In your hands rests our future. By your labors
at this Conference, we shall know if suffering humanity is to
achieve a just and lasting peace. . . .

    We hold a powerful mandate from our people. They believe we
will fulfill this obligation. We must prevent . . . the repeti-
tion of the disaster from which the entire world will suffer for
years to come.

    If we should pay merely lip service to inspiring ideals, and
later do violence to simple justice, we would draw down upon us
the bitter wrath of generations yet unborn.

    We must not continue to sacrifice the flower of our youth
merely to check madmen, those who in every age plan world domination. The sacrifices of our youth today must lead, through your
efforts, to the building for tomorrow of a mighty combination of
nations founded upon justice for peace.

    Justice remains the greatest power on earth. . . .

    We must, once and for all, reverse the order, and prove by
our acts conclusively that Right Has Might.

    If we do not want to die together in war, we must learn to
live together in peace.

    With firm faith in our hearts, to sustain us along the hard
road to victory, we will find our way to a secure peace, for the
ultimate benefit of all humanity.

    We must build a new world - a far better world - one in which
the eternal dignity of man is respected. . . .

Differences soon surfaced between the Truman Administration and the Soviet Union centering on Soviet policy in Eastern Europe. Within the Administration, a debate ensued as to the appropriate strategy for dealing with the Soviets and, at the same time, ensuring the continuance of postwar U.S.-Soviet cooperation. Central to these deliberations was the role that the prospective development of the atomic bomb would have on U.S.-Soviet relations. Involved here were not only questions pertaining to whether the U.S. atomic monopoly could be used as a form of diplomatic leverage, but whether or not the United States should share the secret with the Soviet Union and attempt to work out some form of international control mechanism to resolve the problems posed by this potentially far-reaching development. Secretary of War Henry Stimson's July 19, 1945 memorandum aptly captures the ambivalence and cross-currents then shaping U.S. policy toward the Soviets, and particularly involving the role of the atomic bomb.

(75) <u>MEMO, SECRETARY OF WAR HENRY STIMSON TO PRESIDENT TRUMAN</u>, July 19, 1945 [Extract]

Source: *Foreign Relations of the United States: Conference of Berlin (Potsdam), 1945.* Washington: U.S. Government Printing Office, 1960, Vol. I, pp. 1155-1157.

1. With each International Conference that passes and, in fact, with each month that passes between conferences, it becomes clearer that the great basic problem of the future is the stability of the relations of the Western democracies with Russia.

2. With each such time that passes it also becomes clear that that problem arises out of the fundamental differences between a nation of free thought, free speech, free elections, in fact, a really free people with a nation which is not basically free but which is systematically controlled from above by Secret Police and in which free speech is not permitted.

3. It also becomes clear that no permanently safe international relations can be established between two such fundamentally different national systems. With the best efforts we cannot understand each other. Furthermore, in an autocratically controlled system, policy cannot be permanent. It is tied up with the life of one man. Even if a measure of mental accord is established with one head the resulting agreement is liable to be succeeded by an entirely different policy coming from a different successor.

4. Daily we find our best efforts for coordination and sympathetic understanding with Russia thwarted by the suspicion which basically and necessarily must exist in any controlled organization of men.

5. Thus every effort we make at permanent organization of such a world composed of two such radically different systems is subject to frustration by misunderstandings arising out of mutual suspicion.

6. The great problem ahead is how to deal with this basic difference which exists as a flaw in our desired accord. I believe we must not accept the present situation as permanent for the result will then almost inevitably be a new war and the destruction of our civilization.

I believe we should direct our thoughts constantly to the time
and method of attacking the basic difficulty and the means we may
have in hand to produce results. That something can be accomplished is not an idle dream. Stalin has shown an indication of
his appreciation of our system of freedom by his proposal of a
free constitution to be established among the Soviets. To read
this Constitution would lead one to believe that Russia had in
mind the establishing of free speech, free assembly, free press
and the other essential elements of our Bill of Rights and would
not have forever resting upon every citizen the stifling hand of
autocracy. He has thus given us an opening. . . .

7. The foregoing has a vital bearing upon the control of the
vast and revolutionary discovery of . . . [atomic energy] which
is now confronting us. Upon the successful control of that energy
depends the future successful development or destruction of the
modern civilized world. The Committee appointed by the War Department which has been considering that control has pointed this
out in no uncertain terms and has called for an international
organization for that purpose. After careful reflection I am of
the belief that no world organization containing as one of its
dominant members a nation whose people are not possessed of free
speech but whose governmental action is controlled by the auto-
cratic machinery of a secret political police, cannot [can] give
effective control of this new agency with its devastating possibilities.

I therefore believe that before we share our new discovery
with Russia we should consider carefully whether we can do so
safely under any system of control until Russia puts into effective action the proposed constitution which I have mentioned. If
this is a necessary condition, we must go slowly in any disclosures or agreeing to any Russian participation whatsoever and
constantly explore the question how our head-start in . . . [atomic
energy] and the Russian desire to participate can be used to bring
us nearer to the removal of the basic difficulties which I have
emphasized.

(76) STATEMENT, JOINT DECLARATION OF ATOMIC ENERGY (UNITED STATES,
GREAT BRITAIN, CANADA), November 15, 1945 [Extract]

Source: *Public Papers of the Presidents: Harry S. Truman, 1945.*
Washington: U.S. Government Printing Office, 1961, pp. 472-475.

****

1. We recognize that the application of recent scientific
discoveries to the methods and practice of war has placed at the
disposal of mankind means of destruction hitherto unknown, against
which there can be no adequate military defense, and in the employment of which no single nation can in fact have a monopoly.

2. We desire to emphasize that the responsibility for devising means to ensure that the new discoveries shall be used for
the benefit of mankind, instead of as a means of destruction,
rests not on our nations alone, but upon the whole civilized
world. Nevertheless, the progress that we have made in the development and use of atomic energy demands that we take an initiative

in the matter, and we have accordingly met together to consider
the possibility of international action:

(a) To prevent the use of atomic energy for destructive purposes.

(b) To promote the use of recent and future advances in scientific knowledge, particularly in the utilization of atomic
energy, for peaceful and humanitarian ends.

3. We are aware that the only complete protection for the
civilized world from the destructive use of scientific knowledge
lies in the prevention of war. No system of safeguards that can
be devised will of itself provide an effective guarantee against
production of atomic weapons by a nation bent on aggression. Nor
can we ignore the possibility of the development of other weapons,
or of new methods of warfare, which may constitute as great a
threat to civilization as the military use of atomic energy.

4. Representing, as we do, the three countries which possess
the knowledge essential to the use of atomic energy, we declare
at the outset our willingness, as a first contribution, to proceed
with the exchange of fundamental scientific information and the
interchange of scientists and scientific literature for peaceful
ends with any nation that will fully reciprocate.

5. We believe that the fruits of scientific research should
be made available to all nations, and that freedom of investigation and free interchange of ideas are essential to the progress
of knowledge. In pursuance of this policy, the basic scientific
information essential to the development of atomic energy for
peaceful purposes has already been made available to the world.
It is our intention that all further information of this character
that may become available from time to time shall be similarly
treated. We trust that other nations will adopt the same policy,
thereby creating an atmosphere of reciprocal confidence in which
political agreement and cooperation will flourish.

6. We have considered the question of the disclosure of detailed information concerning the practical industrial application
of atomic energy. The military exploitation of atomic energy depends, in large part, upon the same methods and processes as would
be required for industrial uses.

We are not convinced that the spreading of the specialized
information regarding the practical application of atomic energy,
before it is possible to devise effective, reciprocal, and enforceable safeguards acceptable to all nations, would contribute
to a constructive solution of the problem of the atomic bomb. On
the contrary we think it might have the opposite effect. We are,
however, prepared to share, on a reciprocal basis with others of
the United Nations, detailed information concerning the practical
industrial application of atomic energy just as soon as effective
enforceable safeguards against its use for destructive purposes
can be devised.

7. In order to attain the most effective means of entirely
eliminating the use of atomic energy for destructive purposes and
promoting its widest use for industrial and humanitarian purposes,
we are of the opinion that at the earliest practicable date a
Commission should be set up under the United Nations Organization
to prepare recommendations for submission to the Organization.

The Commission should be instructed to proceed with the utmost dispatch and should be authorized to submit recommendations from time to time dealing with separate phases of its work. . . .

8. The work of the Commission should proceed by separate stages, the successful completion of each one of which will develop the necessary confidence of the world before the next stage is undertaken. Specifically, it is considered that the Commission might well devote its attention first to the wide exchange of scientists and scientific information, and as a second stage to the development of full knowledge concerning natural resources of raw materials.

9. Faced with the terrible realities of the application of science to destruction, every nation will realize more urgently than before the overwhelming need to maintain the rule of law among nations and to banish the scourge of war from the earth. This can only be brought about by giving wholehearted support to the United Nations Organization, and by consolidating and extending its authority, thus creating conditions of mutual trust in which all peoples will be free to devote themselves to the arts of peace. It is our firm resolve to work without reservation to achieve these ends. . . .

Recent historians have differed over whether, on assuming the Presidency, Harry Truman repudiated Franklin Roosevelt's conciliatory policy toward the Soviet Union thereby contributing significantly to the origins of the Cold War. Undeniably, under Truman a tactical shift occurred in the conduct of U.S. policy as his Administration adopted a more self-righteous and rigid bargaining stance. Nonetheless, in 1945 the Truman Administration remained committed to seeking to resolve U.S.-Soviet differences through negotiations and thereby to provide the basis for a lasting and just peace. In part because of this commitment and in part because of the belief that direct negotiations among the heads of state might contribute to a reduction in tensions and suspicions, Administration officials supported the convening of another summit conference among the Big Three (the U.S., the Soviet Union, and Great Britain) which was held in Potsdam, Germany (a suburb of Berlin) from July 16 through August 2, 1945. Interrupted by the British elections, Potsdam turned out to be the last summit conference of the World War II period; thereafter Big Three negotiations were conducted either on the ambassadorial level or, until 1947, through the Council of Foreign Ministers. The major decisions of the Potsdam Conference are highlighted in the following excerpts from the Protocol released on August 1, 1945. In its public statements, at least through 1946, moreover, the Truman Administration emphasized its commitment to internationalism and to furthering individual rights. Although reflecting a particular conception of internationalism and human rights, this public posture of 1945-1946 differed substantively from the Truman Administration's post 1947 position when international cooperation was no longer emphasized.

(77) PROTOCOL OF THE PROCEEDINGS OF THE BERLIN (OR POTSDAM) CONFERENCE, August 1, 1945 [Extract]

Source: *Foreign Relations of the United States: Conference of Berlin (Potsdam), 1945*. Washington: U.S. Government Printing Office, 1960, Vol. I, pp. 1478-1479, 1483-1485, 1490ff.

I. ESTABLISHMENT OF A COUNCIL OF FOREIGN MINISTERS

The Conference reached the following agreement for the establishment of a Council of Foreign Ministers to do the necessary preparatory work for the peace settlements:

(1) There shall be established a Council composed of the Foreign Ministers of the United Kingdom, the Union of Soviet Socialist Republics, China, France and the United States. . . .

(3) (i) As its immediate important task, the Council shall be authorized to draw up, with a view to their submission to the United Nations, treaties of peace with Italy, Roumania, Bulgaria, Hungary and Finland, and to propose settlements of territorial questions outstanding on the termination of the war in Europe. The Council shall be utilized for the preparation of a peace settlement for Germany to be accepted by the Government of Germany when a government adequate for the purpose is established. . . .

III. GERMAN REPARATION

1. Reparation claims of the U.S.S.R. shall be met by removals from the zone of Germany occupied by the U.S.S.R., and from appropriate German external assets.

2. The U.S.S.R. undertakes to settle the reparation claims of Poland from its own share of reparations.

3. The reparations claims of the United States, the United Kingdom and other countries entitled to reparations shall be met from the Western Zones and from appropriate German external assets.

4. In addition to the reparations to be taken by the U.S.S.R. from its own zone of occupation, the U.S.S.R. shall receive additionally from the Western Zones:

(a) 15 per cent of such usable and complete industrial equipment, in the first place from the metallurgical, chemical and machine manufacturing industries as is unnecessary for the German peace economy and should be removed from the Western Zones of Germany, in exchange for an equivalent value of food, coal, potash, zinc, timber, clay products, petroleum products, and such other commodities as may be agreed upon.

(b) 10 per cent of such industrial capital equipment as is unnecessary for the German peace economy and should be removed from the Western Zones, to be transferred to the Soviet Government on reparations account without payment or exchange of any kind in return. . . .

5. The amount of equipment to be removed from the Western Zones on account of reparations must be determined within six months from now at the latest.

6. Removals of industrial capital equipment shall begin as soon as possible and shall be completed within two years from the determination specified in paragraph 5. . . . The determination

of the amount and character of the industrial capital equipment
unnecessary for the German peace economy and therefore available
for reparation shall be made by the Control Council under policies
fixed by the Allied Commission on Reparations, with the participation of France, subject to the final approval of the Zone Commander in the Zone from which the equipment is to be removed. . . .

IX.   POLAND

A. Declaration

We have taken note with pleasure of the agreement reached
among representative Poles from Poland and abroad which has made
possible the formation, in accordance with the decisions reached
at the Crimea Conference, of a Polish Provisional Government of
National Unity recognised by the Three Powers. The establishment
by the British and United States Governments of diplomatic relations with the Polish Provisional Government has resulted in the
withdrawal of their recognition from the former Polish Government
in London, which no longer exists.

The Three Powers note that the Polish Provisional Government
in accordance with the decisions of the Crimea Conference has
agreed to the holding of free and unfettered elections as soon as
possible on the basis of universal suffrage and secret ballot in
which all democratic and anti-Nazi parties shall have the right
to take part and to put forward candidates; and that representatives of the Allied Press shall enjoy full freedom to report to
the world upon developments in Poland before and during the elections. . . .

X.   CONCLUSION OF PEACE TREATIES AND ADMISSION
TO THE UNITED NATIONS ORGANISATION

The Three Governments consider it desirable that the present
anomalous position of Italy, Bulgaria, Finland, Hungary and
Roumania should be terminated by the conclusion of Peace Treaties.
. . .

. . . The conclusion of Peace Treaties with recognised Governments in these States will also enable the Three Governments to
support applications from them for membership of the United Nations. The Three Governments agree to examine each separately
in the near future, in the light of the conditions then prevailing, the establishment of diplomatic relations with Finland
Roumania, Bulgaria, and Hungary to the extent possible prior to
the conclusion of peace treaties with those countries. . . .

(78) STATEMENT, PRESIDENT TRUMAN, December 15, 1945 [Extract]

Source: *Public Papers of the Presidents: Harry S. Truman, 1945.*
Washington: U.S. Government Printing Office, 1961, pp. 543-545.

The Government of the United States holds that peace and
prosperity of the world in this new and unexplored era ahead depend upon the ability of the sovereign nations to combine for
collective security in the United Nations organization.

. . . a strong, united and democratic China is of the utmost
importance to the success of this United Nations organization and
for world peace. A China disorganized and divided either by for-

eign aggression, such as that undertaken by the Japanese, or by violent internal strife, is an undermining influence to world stability and peace, now and in the future. The United States Government has long subscribed to the principle that the management of internal affairs is the responsibility of the peoples of the sovereign nations. Events of this century, however, would indicate that a breach of peace anywhere in the world threatens the peace of the entire world. It is thus in the most vital interest of the United States and all the United Nations that the People of China overlook no opportunity to adjust their internal differences promptly by methods of peaceful negotiation.

The Government of the United States believes it essential:

(1) That a cessation of hostilities be arranged between the armies of the National Government and the Chinese Communists and other dissident Chinese armed forces for the purpose of completing the return of all China to effective Chinese control, including the immediate evacuation of the Japanese forces.

(2) That a national conference of representatives of major political elements be arranged to develop an early solution to the present internal strife - a solution which will bring about the unification of China.

The United States and the other United Nations have recognized the present National Government of the Republic of China as the only legal government in China. It is the proper instrument to achieve the objective of a unified China. . . .

. . . the United States has been assisting and will continue to assist the National Government of the Republic of China in effecting the disarmament and evacuation of Japanese troops in the liberated areas. The United States Marines are in north China for that purpose.

The United States recognizes and will continue to recognize the National Government of China and cooperate with it in international affairs and specifically in eliminating Japanese influence from China. The United States is convinced that a prompt arrangement for a cessation of hostilities is essential to the effective achievement of this end. United States support will not extend to United States military intervention to influence the course of any Chinese internal strife. . . .

The United States is cognizant that the present National Government of China is a "one-party government" and believes that peace, unity and democratic reform in China will be furthered if the basis of this Government is broadened to include other political elements in the country. Hence, the United States strongly advocates that the national conference of representatives of major political elements in the country agree upon arrangements which would give those elements a fair and effective representation in the Chinese National Government. . . . this would require modification of the one-party "political tutelage" established as an interim arrangement in the progress of the nation toward democracy by the father of the Chinese Republic, Doctor Sun Yat-sen.

The existence of autonomous armies such as that of the Communist army is inconsistent with, and actually makes impossible, political unity in China. With the institution of a broadly representative government, autonomous armies should be eliminated as such and all armed forces in China integrated effectively into the Chinese National Army.

. . . the United States Government considers that the detailed steps necessary to the achievement of political unity in China must be worked out by the Chinese themselves and that intervention by any foreign government in these matters would be inappropriate. The United States Government feels, however, that China has a clear responsibility to the other United Nations to eliminate armed conflict within its territory as constituting a threat to world stability and peace - a responsibility which is shared by the National Government and all Chinese political and military groups.

As China moves toward peace and unity along the lines described above, the United States would be prepared to assist the National Government in every reasonable way to rehabilitate the country, improve the agrarian and industrial economy, and establish a military organization capable of discharging China's national and international responsibilities for the maintenance of peace and order. In furtherance of such assistance, it would be prepared to give favorable consideration to Chinese requests for credits and loans under reasonable conditions for projects which would contribute toward the development of a healthy economy throughout China and healthy trade relations between China and the United States.

(79) SPEECH, SECRETARY OF STATE JAMES BYRNES, February 28, 1946 [Extract]

Source: *Department of State Bulletin*, March 10, 1946, pp. 355-358.

I should be lacking in candor if I said to you that world conditions today are sound or reassuring. All around us there is suspicion and distrust, which in turn breeds suspicion and distrust.

Some suspicions are unfounded and unreasonable. Of some others that cannot be said. That requires frank discussion between great powers of the things that give rise to suspicion. At the Moscow conference [of foreign ministers of December 1945] there was such frank discussion. It was helpful. . . .

Unless the great powers are prepared to act in the defense of law, the United Nations cannot prevent war. We must make it clear in advance that we do intend to act to prevent aggression, making it clear at the same time . . . we will not use force for any other purpose. . . .

The present power relationships of the great states preclude the domination of the world by any one of them. Those power relationships cannot be substantially altered by the unilateral action of any one great state without profoundly disturbing the whole structure of the United Nations.

Therefore, if we are going to do our part to maintain peace in the world we must maintain our power to do so; and we must make it clear that we will stand united with other great states in defense of the Charter. . . .

Much as we desire general disarmament and much as we are prepared to participate in a general reduction of armaments, we cannot be faithful to our obligations to ourselves and to the world if we alone disarm.

. . . we must be able and ready to provide armed contingents that may be required on short notice. We must also have a trained citizenry able and ready to supplement those armed contingents without unnecessarily prolonged training.

I am convinced that there is no reason for war between any of the great powers. Their present power relationships and interests are such that none need or should feel insecure in relation to the others, as long as each faithfully observed the purposes and principles of the Charter. . . .

Our diplomacy must not be negative and inert. It must be capable of adjustment and development in response to constantly changing circumstances. . . .

Though the status quo is not sacred and unchangeable, we cannot overlook a unilateral gnawing away at the status quo. The Charter forbids aggression, and we cannot allow aggression to be accomplished by coercion or pressure or by subterfuges such as political infiltration. . . .

In our relations with the other great powers there are many problems which concern two or three of us much more than the others of us. I see no objection to conferences between the big three or the big four or the big five. . . .

But in such conferences, so far as the United States is concerned, we will gang up against no state. We will do nothing to break the world into exclusive blocs or spheres of influence. In this atomic age we will not seek to divide a world which is one and indivisible. . . .

We will not and we cannot stand aloof if force or the threat of force is used contrary to the purposes and principles of the Charter.

We have no right to hold our troops in the territories of other sovereign states without their approval and consent freely given.

We must not unduly prolong the making of peace and continue to impose our troops upon small and impoverished states.

No power has a right to help itself to alleged enemy properties in liberated or ex-satellite countries before a reparation settlement has been agreed upon by the Allies. We have not and will not agree to any one power deciding for itself what it will take from these countries.

We must not conduct a war of nerves to achieve strategic ends.

We do not want to stumble and stagger into situations where no power intends war but no power will be able to avert war.

We must not regard the drawing of attention to situations which might endanger the peace, as an affront to the nation or nations responsible for those situations. . . .

There are ideological differences in the world. . . . But in this world there is room for many people with varying views and

many governments with varying systems. None of us can foresee
the far-distant future and the ultimate shape of things to come.
But we are bound together as part of a common civilization. . . .

(80) STATEMENT, ACTING SECRETARY OF STATE DEAN ACHESON, October
11, 1946 [Extract]
Source: Philleo Nash Files, Harry S. Truman Library.

I have been asked if I would . . . make some comment or statement about the trial and conviction of [Yugoslav] Archbishop
Stepinac . . . What I should like to say is that we have for a
long time been concerned about civil liberties in Yugoslavia. . . .
at the time we recognized the Government of Yugoslavia, we drew
their attention to what we thought was the undesirable situation
in that field and reminded them of their undertakings under the
United Nations Charter in which all of these matters are specifically dealt with and urged that the matter be rectified as soon
as possible. We have since recognition unhappily had to take up
a very considerable number of cases with the Yugoslav Government
where we have felt that trials of our own citizens were unfairly
conducted. It is this aspect of the Archbishop's trial which
. . . now concerns us. We do not have, of course, a record of
the trial, nor have we had a specific report from our Embassy in
regard to it. Therefore, our information about it is . . . that
which has been conveyed through the press.

It is the civil liberties aspect of the thing which causes
us concern, aspects which raise questions as to whether the trial
has any implications looking toward the impairment of freedom of
religion and of worship. . . .

You will recall that under the Constitution and law of the
United States, fairness of trial is guaranteed under the 14th
Amendment and the Supreme Court of the United States has set aside
as not being legal procedure at all, trials in which the court
room has been dominated by feelings adverse to the defendant by
demonstrations of prejudice. That is deeply inherent in the
American system, that the very essence of due process of law is
that in trials we shall lean over backwards in being fair to the
defendant, in the atmosphere in the court room, in forbidding
demonstrations of spectators, in opportunity of facing and cross-
examining witnesses, - all these matters seem to us to be absolutely inherent in the matter of a fair trial. It is that aspect
of the thing on which one can have no final evidence until a record and detailed reports are available, which cause us concern
and deep worry.

****

*Although seeking to resolve U.S.-Soviet differences through
diplomacy in 1945-1946, the Truman negotiating position was based
on maintaining a position of superior military strength. Agreement could come and peace could be assured not because American
principles were morally right and politically sound (although
Truman believed that the American position was principled and
responsible) but because potential adversaries or aggressors must*

respect American power. Truman believed that in the past the U.S. failure to maintain a strong military had undermined U.S. influence. Accordingly, in 1945 he lobbied for congressional enactment of universal military training. In addition, the Administration sought to use "universal training" as a means of altering public opinion, undermining a still-powerful anti-military tradition. Unsuccessful in the immediate postwar years, Truman nonetheless continued to lobby until 1948 for the concept of universal military training and eventually obtained (in the midst of the Berlin crisis of June 1948) congressional approval of selective service. Until selective service came under attack in the 1970s in the wake of the controversy over the Viet-nam War, U.S. military planning was based on the existence of a conscript army. At the same time, the President sought to shape the public debate to ensure support for military aid to the Latin American states and for military research and development on the premise that such measures were essential to furthering the cause of peace.

(81) <u>ADDRESS TO CONGRESS, PRESIDENT TRUMAN</u>, October 23, 1945 [Extract]

Source: *Public Papers of the Presidents: Harry S. Truman, 1945.* Washington: U.S. Government Printing Office, 1961, pp. 404-413..

. . . I now present to the Congress my recommendations with respect to . . . universal training.

The United States now has a fighting strength greater than at any other time in our history. It is greater than that of any other nation in the world. . . .

With our strength comes grave responsibility. With it must also come a continuing sense of leadership in the world for justice and peace.

For years to come the success of our efforts for a just and lasting peace will depend upon the strength of those who are determined to maintain that peace. We intend to use all our moral influence and all our physical strength to work for that kind of peace. We can ensure such a peace only so long as we remain strong. We must face the fact that peace must be built upon power, as well as upon good will and good deeds.

Our determination to remain powerful denotes no lack of faith in the United Nations Organization. On the contrary, with all the might we have, we intend to back our obligations and commitments under the United Nations Charter. . . . It is only by strength that we can impress the fact upon possible future aggressors that we will tolerate no threat to peace or liberty.

To maintain that power we must act now. The latent strength of our untrained citizenry is no longer sufficient protection. If attack should come again, there would be no time under conditions of modern war to develop that latent strength into the necessary fighting force.

. . . Our geographical security is now gone - gone with the advent of the robot bomb, the rocket, aircraft carriers and modern airborne armies.

The surest guaranty that no nation will dare again to attack us is to remain strong in the only kind of strength an aggressor understands - military power.

To preserve the strength of our nation, . . . [we should] rely upon a comparatively small regular Army, Navy and Air Force, supported by well trained citizens, who in time of emergency could be quickly mobilized.

. . . The backbone of our military force should be the trained citizen who is first and foremost a civilian, and who becomes a soldier or a sailor only in time of danger - and only when Congress considers it necessary. . . .

In such a system, however, the citizen reserve must be a trained reserve. We can meet the need for a trained reserve in only one way - by universal training.

Modern war is fought by experts . . . Now it takes many months for men to become skilled in electronics, aeronautics, ballistics, meteorology, and all the other sciences of modern war. If another national emergency should come, there would be no time for this complicated training. . . .

The sooner we can bring the maximum number of trained men into service, the sooner will be the victory and the less tragic the cost. Universal training is the only means by which we can be prepared right at the start to throw our great energy and our tremendous force into the battle. . . .

I recommend that we create a postwar military organization which will contain the following basic elements:

First - A comparatively small regular Army, Navy, and Marine Corps;

Second - A greatly strengthened National Guard and Organized Reserve for the Army, Navy, and Marine Corps;

Third - A General Reserve composed of all the male citizens of the United States who have received training.

The General Reserve would be available for rapid mobilization in time of emergency, but it would have no obligation to serve, either in this country or abroad, unless and until called to the service by an Act of the Congress.

In order to provide this General Reserve, I recommend to the Congress the adoption of a plan for Universal Military Training. . . .

It has been suggested in some quarters that there should be no universal training until the shape of the peace is better known, and until the military needs of this country can be estimated and our commitments under the United Nations Organization can be determined. But it is impossible today to foresee the future. It is difficult at any time to know exactly what our responsibilities will require in the way of force. We do know that if we are to have available a force when needed, the time to begin is right now. . . .

The argument has been made that compulsory training violates traditional American concepts of liberty and democracy, and even that it would endanger our system of government by creating a

powerful military caste. The purpose of the program, however,
. . . is not to train professional soldiers. It is to train
citizens, so that if and when the Congress should declare it necessary for them to become soldiers, they could do so more quickly
and more efficiently. A large trained reserve of peace-loving
citizens would never go to war or encourage war, if it could be
avoided. . . .

There are some who urge that the development of rocket weapons
and atomic bombs and other new weapons indicates that scientific
research, rather than universal training, is the best way to safeguard our security. . . .

. . . there must be continuous exploration into new fields of
science in order to keep ahead in the discovery and manufacture
of new weapons. No matter what the cost, we cannot afford to fall
behind in any of the new techniques of war or in the development
of new weapons of destruction.

Until we are sure that our peace machinery is functioning
adequately, we must relentlessly preserve our superiority on land
and sea and in the air. Until that time, we must also make sure
that by planning - and by actual production - we have on hand at
all times sufficient weapons of the latest nature and design with
which to repel any sudden attack, and with which to launch an
effective counter-attack.

That _is_ the only way we can be sure - until we are sure that
there is another way.

But research, new materials, and new weapons will never, by
themselves, be sufficient to withstand a powerful enemy. We must
have men trained to use these weapons. As our armed forces become more and more mechanized, and as they use more and more complicated weapons, we must have an ever-increasing number of
trained men. Technological advances do not eliminate the need
for men. They increase that need. . . .

Any system which is intended to guarantee our national defense
will, of course, cause some inconvenience - and perhaps even some
hardship - to our people. But we must balance that against the
danger which we face unless we are realistic and hard-headed
enough to be prepared. Today universal training is the only adequate answer we have to our problem in this troubled world.

There will be better answers, we hope, in the days to come.
The United States will always strive for those better answers -
for the kind of tried and tested world cooperation which will make
for peace and harmony among all nations. It will continue to
strive to reach that period quickly. But that time has not yet
arrived. . . .

(82) <u>ADDRESS, PRESIDENT TRUMAN</u>, March 17, 1948 [Extract]

Source: *Public Papers of the Presidents: Harry S. Truman, 1948.*
Washington: U.S. Government Printing Office, 1964 pp. 185-186.

****

Until the free nations of Europe have regained their strength,
and so long as Communism threatens the very existence of democracy,

the United States must remain strong enough to support those countries of Europe which are threatened with Communist control and police-state rule.

I believe that we have learned the importance of maintaining military strength as a means of preventing war. We have found that a sound military system is necessary in time of peace if we are to remain at peace. Aggressors in the past, relying on our apparent lack of military force, have unwisely precipitated war. . . .

Universal training is the only feasible means by which the civilian components of our armed forces can be built up to the strength required if we are to be prepared for emergencies. Our ability to mobilize large numbers of trained men in time of emergency could forestall future conflict and, together with other measures of national policy, could restore stability to the world.

The adoption of universal training by the United States at this time would be unmistakable evidence to all the world of our determination to back the will to peace with the strength for peace. . . .

I also recommend the temporary reenactment of selective-service legislation in order to maintain our armed forces at their authorized strength. . . .

We cannot meet our international responsibilities unless we maintain our armed forces. It is of vital importance, for example, that we keep our occupation forces in Germany until the peace is secure in Europe. . . .

The recommendations I have made represent the most urgent steps toward securing the peace and preventing war.

We must be ready to take every wise and necessary step to carry out this great purpose. This will require assistance to other nations. It will require an adequate and balanced military strength. We must be prepared to pay the price of peace, or assuredly we shall pay the price of war.

We in the United States remain determined to seek, by every possible means, a just and honorable basis for the settlement of international issues. We shall continue to give our strong allegiance to the United Nations as the principal means for international security based on law, not on force. We shall remain ready and anxious to join with all nations - I repeat, with all nations - in every possible effort to reach international understanding and agreement.

The door has never been closed, nor will it ever be closed, to the Soviet Union or any other nation which will genuinely cooperate in preserving the peace.

At the same time, we must not be confused about the central issue which confronts the world today.

The time has come when the free men and women of the world must face the threat to their liberty squarely and courageously.

The United States has a tremendous responsibility to act according to the measure of our power for good in the world. We have learned that we must earn the peace we seek just as we earned victory in war, not by wishful thinking but by realistic effort.

At no time in our history has unity among our people been so vital as it is at the present time.

Unity of purpose, unity of effort, and unity of spirit are essential to accomplish the task before us.

. . . The world situation is too critical, and the responsibilities of this country are too vast, to permit party struggles to weaken our influence for maintaining peace.

The American people have the right to assume that political considerations will not affect our working together. They have the right to assume that we will join hands, whole-heartedly and without reservation, in our efforts to preserve peace in the world. . . .

(83) SPECIFIC MESSAGE TO CONGRESS, PRESIDENT TRUMAN, May 6, 1946 [Extract]

Source: *Public Papers of the Presidents: Harry S. Truman, 1946.* Washington: U.S. Government Printing Office, 1962, pp. 233-235.

I submit herewith for the consideration of the Congress a bill to be entitled "The Intra-American Military Cooperation Act" authorizing a program of military collaboration with other American States including the training, organization, and equipment of the armed forces of those countries. . . .

Under the bill transmitted herewith, the Army and Navy, acting in conjunction with the Department of State, would be permitted to continue in the future a general program of collaboration with the armed forces of our sister republics with a view to facilitating the adoption of similar technical standards. Certain additional training activities, not covered by existing legislation, would be permitted. The President would also be authorized to transfer military and naval equipment to the Governments of other American States by sale or other method. . . .

A special responsibility for leadership rests upon the United States in this matter because of the preponderant technical, economic and military resources of this country. There is a reasonable and limited purpose for which arms and military equipment can rightfully be made available to the other American States. This Government will not, I am sure, in any way approve of, nor will it participate in, the indiscriminate or unrestricted distribution of armaments, which would only contribute to a useless and burdensome armaments race. It does not desire that operations under this bill shall raise unnecessarily the quantitative level of armament in the American republics. . . .

. . . any operations under this bill, which the Congress may authorize, shall be in every way consistent with the wording and spirit of the United Nations Charter. The bill has been drawn up primarily to enable the American nations to carry out their obligations to cooperate in the maintenance of inter-American peace and security under the Charter and the Act of Chapultepec . . .

It is incumbent upon this Government to see that military developments in which we have a part are guided towards the maintenance of peace and security and that military and naval establishments are not encouraged beyond what security considerations require. In this connection the bill provides that operations thereunder are subject to any international agreement for the regulation of armaments to which the United States may become a party. . . .

In executing this program it will be borne in mind, moreover, that it is the policy of this Government to encourage the establishment of sound economic conditions in the other American republics which will contribute to the improvement of living standards and the advancement of social and cultural welfare. Such conditions are a prerequisite to international peace and security. Operations under the proposed legislation will be conducted with full and constant awareness that no encouragement should be given to the imposition upon other people of any useless burden of armaments which would handicap the economic improvement which all countries so strongly desire. The execution of the program authorized by the bill will also be guided by a determination to guard against placing weapons of war in the hands of any groups who may use them to oppose the peaceful and democratic principles to which the United States and other American nations have so often subscribed. . . .

(84) STATEMENT, PRESIDENT TRUMAN, October 17, 1946 [Extract]

Source: *Public Papers of the Presidents: Harry S. Truman, 1946.* Washington: U.S. Government Printing Office, 1962, p. 456.

I have [today] signed Executive Order 9791 . . . [establishing] a Presidential Research Board . . .

The order directs the Reconversion Director to prepare a report of (1) his findings with respect to the Federal research program and his recommendations for providing coordination and improved efficiency therein; and, (2) his findings with respect to non-Federal research, development and training activities, a statement of the interrelationship of Federal and non-Federal research and development, and his recommendations for planning, administering and staffing Federal research programs to insure that the scientific personnel, training and research facilities of the Nation are used most effectively in the national interest.

National security and the development of the domestic economy depend upon the extension of fundamental scientific knowledge and the application of basic principles to the development of new techniques and processes. The Nation has a vast reservoir of war-accelerated technological development which must be applied speedily and effectively to the problems of peace - stepping up productivity in both industry and agriculture, creation of new farm and factory products and advancement of medical science. . . .

The Federal Government has played and will play an important role in all areas of research, but the share of our national income which can be devoted to research has definite limits. The order lays the groundwork for a general plan designed to insure that Federal scientific research will promote the most effective allocation of research resources between the universities, the research foundations, industry and the Federal Government. . . .

In contrast to its public posture of 1945-1946 that a negoti-
ated agreement with the Soviet Union was possible, by early 1946
the Administration had opted for what came to be described as the
containment policy. This conception of Soviet expansionism and
untrustworthiness and accordingly of the proper U.S. role was most
sharply articulated by George Kennan, chargé d'affaires *in Moscow*
and soon called to Washington to head the State Department's
Policy Planning Staff, in the reprinted February 1946 cablegram.
The premises of the Kennan cable were formally adopted with the
enunciation of the so-called Truman Doctrine (approved by Congress
on May 22, 1947), both during the intra-Administration delibera-
tions leading to the formulation of this important policy and in
President Truman's dramatic address to a joint session of Congress
on March 12, 1947 calling for congressional approval of economic
and technical aid to the Greek and Turkish governments. If the
Truman Doctrine's emphasis was anti-Communist, and thus anti-
Soviet, nonetheless the rationale originally offered in 1947 was
that economic assistance could successfully curb Communist expan-
sion. By February 1948, however, the Administration's emphasis
shifted from the need to promote "economic recovery" to the need
to establish "internal security." The underlying premise, the
so-called domino theory, continued to determine U.S. foreign pol-
icy until the 1970s.

(85) CABLE, GEORGE KENNAN, February 22, 1946 [Extract]

Source: *Foreign Relations of the United States: 1946, Vol. VI*
Eastern Europe; the Soviet Union. Washington: U.S. Government
Printing Office, 1969, pp. 696-709.

. . . BASIC FEATURES OF POST-WAR SOVIET OUTLOOK, AS PUT FOR-
WARD BY OFFICIAL PROPAGANDA MACHINE . . . :

(A) USSR still lives in antagonistic "capitalist encirclement"
with which in the long run there can be no permanent peaceful coexistence. . . .

(B) Capitalist world is beset with internal conflicts, inherent in nature of capitalist society. These conflicts are insoluble by means of peaceful compromise. Greatest of them is that
between England and US.

(C) Internal conflicts of capitalism inevitably generate wars.
Wars thus generated may be of two kinds: intra-capitalist wars
between two capitalist states, and wars of intervention against
socialist world. Smart capitalists, vainly seeking escape from
inner conflicts of capitalism, incline toward latter.

(D) Intervention against USSR, while it would be disastrous
to those who undertook it, would cause renewed delay in progress
of Soviet socialism and must therefore be forestalled at all
costs.

(E) Conflicts between capitalist states, though likewise
fraught with danger for USSR, nevertheless hold out great possibilities for advancement of socialist cause, particularly if USSR
remains militarily powerful, ideologically monolithic and faithful
to its present brilliant leadership.

(F) It must be borne in mind that capitalist world is not all bad. In addition to hopelessly reactionary and bourgeois elements, it includes (one) certain wholly enlightened and positive elements united in acceptable communistic parties and (two) certain other elements (now described for tactical reasons as progressive or democratic) whose reactions, aspirations and activities happen to be "objectively" favorable to interests of USSR. These last must be encouraged and utilized for Soviet purposes.

(G) Among negative elements of bourgeois-capitalist society, most dangerous of all are those whom Lenin called false friends of the people, namely moderate-socialist or social-democratic leaders (in other words, non-communist left-wing). These are more dangerous than out-and-out reactionaries, for latter at least march under their true colors, whereas moderate left-wing leaders confuse people by employing devices of socialism to serve interests of reactionary capital.

So much for premises. To what deductions do they lead from standpoint of Soviet policy? . . . :

(A) Everything must be done to advance relative strength of USSR as factor in international society. Conversely, no opportunity must be missed to reduce strength and influence, collectively as well as individually, of capitalist powers.

(B) Soviet efforts, and those of Russia's friends abroad, must be directed toward deepening and exploiting of differences and conflicts between capitalist powers. If these eventually deepen into an "imperialist" war, this war must be turned into revolutionary upheavals within the various capitalist countries.

(C) "Democratic-progressive" elements abroad are to be utilized to maximum to bring pressure to bear on capitalist governments along lines agreeable to Soviet interests.

(D) Relentless battle must be waged against socialist and social-democratic leaders abroad.

PART TWO: BACKGROUND OF OUTLOOK

****

First, [Communist party line] does not represent natural outlook of Russian people. Latter are, by and large, friendly to outside world, eager for experience of it, eager to measure against it talents they are conscious of possessing, eager above all to live in peace and enjoy fruits of their own labor. Party line only represents thesis which official propaganda machine puts forward with great skill and persistence to a public often remarkably resistant in the stronghold of its innermost thoughts. But party line is binding for outlook and conduct of people who make up apparatus of power - party, secret police and government - and it is exclusively with these that we have to deal.

Second, . . . Experience has shown that peaceful and mutually profitable coexistence of capitalist and socialist states is entirely possible. Basic internal conflicts in advanced countries are no longer primarily those arising out of capitalist ownership of means of production, but are ones arising from advanced urbanism and industrialism as such, which Russia has thus far been spared not by socialism but only by her own backwardness. Internal rivalries of capitalism do not always generate wars, and not all wars are attributable to this cause. To speak of possibility of intervention against USSR today . . . is sheerest nonsense. If not provoked by forces of intolerance and subversion "capitalist" world of today is quite capable of living at peace with itself and Russia. Finally, no sane person has reason to doubt sincerity of moderate socialist leaders in western countries. Nor is it fair to deny success of their efforts to improve conditions for working population whenever, as in Scandinavia, they have been given chance to show what they could do. . . .

Nevertheless, all these theses, however baseless and disproven, are being boldly put forward again today. What does this indicate? It indicates that Soviet party line is not based on any objective analysis of situation beyond Russia's borders; . . . that it arises mainly from basic inner-Russian necessities which existed before recent war and exist today.

At bottom of Kremlin's neurotic view of world affairs is traditional and instinctive Russian sense of insecurity. . . . Russian rulers have invariably sensed that their rule was relatively archaic in form, fragile and artificial in its psychological foundation, unable to stand comparison or contact with political systems of western countries. For this reason they have always feared foreign penetration, feared direct contact between western world and their own, feared what would happen if Russians learned truth about world without or if foreigners learned truth about world within. And they have learned to seek security only in patient but deadly struggle for total destruction of rival power, never in compacts and compromises with it.

It was no coincidence that Marxism, which had smouldered ineffectively for half a century in Western Europe, caught hold and blazed for first time in Russia. Only in this land which had never known a friendly neighbor or indeed any tolerant equilibrium of separate powers, either internal or international, could a doctrine thrive which viewed economic conflicts of society as insoluble by peaceful means. After establishment of Bolshevist regime, Marxist dogma, rendered even more truculent and intolerant by Lenin's interpretation, became a perfect vehicle for sense of insecurity with which Bolsheviks, even more than previous Russian rulers, were afflicted. In this dogma, with its basic altruism of purpose, they found justification for their instinctive fear of outside world, for the dictatorship without which they did not know how to rule, for cruelties they did not dare not to inflict, for sacrifices they felt bound to demand. In the name of Marxism they sacrificed every single ethical value in their methods and tactics. . . . Without it they would stand before history, at best, as only the last of that long succession of cruel and wasteful Russian rulers who have relentlessly forced country on to ever new heights of military power in order to guarantee external security of their internally weak regimes. This is why Soviet purposes must always be solemnly clothed in trappings of Marxism, and why no one should underrate importance of dogma in Soviet affairs. Thus Soviet leaders are driven necessities of their own past and present position to put forward a dogma which [views] outside world as evil, hostile and menacing; but as bearing within itself germs of creeping disease and destined to be wracked with growing internal convulsions until it is given final coup de

grace by rising power of socialism and yields to new and better
world. This thesis provides justification for that increase of
military and police power of Russian state, for that isolation of
Russian population from outside world, and for that fluid and constant pressure to extend limits of Russian police power which are
together the natural and instinctive urges of Russian rulers.
Basically this is only the steady advance of uneasy Russian nationalism, a centuries old movement in which conceptions of offense
and defense are inextricably confused. But in new guise of international Marxism, with its honeyed promises to a desperate and war
torn outside world, it is more dangerous and insidious than ever
before.

It should not be thought from above that Soviet party line is
necessarily disingenuous and insincere on part of all those who
put it forward. Many of them are too ignorant of outside world
and mentally too dependent to question . . . self-hypnotism, and
who have no difficulty making themselves believe what they find
it comforting and convenient to believe. Finally we have the un-
solved mystery as to who, if anyone, in this great land actually
receives accurate and unbiased information about outside world.
In atmosphere of oriental secretiveness and conspiracy which per-
vades this government, possibilities for distorting or poisoning
sources and currents of information are infinite. The very dis-
respect of Russians for objective truth - indeed, their disbelief
in its existence - leads them to view all stated facts as instruments for furtherance of one ulterior purpose or another. There
is good reason to suspect that this government is actually a conspiracy within a conspiracy; and I for one am reluctant to believe
that Stalin himself receives anything like an objective picture
of outside world. . . . Inability of foreign governments to place
their case squarely before Russian policy makers - extent to
which they are delivered up in their relations with Russia to good
graces of obscure and unknown advisers whom they never see and
cannot influence - this to my mind is most disquieting feature of
diplomacy in Moscow, . . .

PART THREE: PROJECTION OF SOVIET OUTLOOK IN
PRACTICAL POLICY ON OFFICIAL LEVEL

. . . Soviet policy, . . . is conducted on two planes: (one)
official plane represented by actions undertaken officially in
name of Soviet Government; and (two) subterranean plane of actions
undertaken by agencies for which Soviet Government does not admit
responsibility. . . .

On official plane we must look for following:

(A) Internal policy devoted to increasing in every way
strength and prestige of Soviet state's intensive military-
industrialization; maximum development of armed forces; great dis-
plays to impress outsiders; continued secretiveness about internal
matters, designed to conceal weaknesses and to keep opponents in
dark.

(B) Whereever it is considered timely and promising, efforts
will be made to advance official limits of Soviet power. For the
moment, these efforts are restricted to certain neighboring points
conceived of here as being of immediate strategic necessity, such
as Northern Iran, Turkey, possibly Bornholm. However, other
points may at any time come into question, if and as concealed

Soviet political power is extended to new areas. Thus a "friend-ly" Persian Government might be asked to grant Russia a port on Persian Gulf. Should Spain fall under communist control, question of Soviet base at Gibraltar Strait might be activated. But such claims will appear on official level only when unofficial prepara-tion is complete.

(C) Russians will participate officially in international or-ganizations where they see opportunity of extending Soviet power or of inhibiting or diluting power of others. . . . Thus Soviet attitude toward UNO [United Nations] will depend largely on loyal-ty of other nations to it, and on degree of vigor, decisiveness and cohesion with which these nations defend in UNO the peaceful and hopeful concept of international life, which that organization represents to our way of thinking. . . .

(D) Toward colonial areas and backward or dependent peoples, Soviet policy, even on official plane, will be directed toward weakening of power and influence and contacts of advanced western nations, on theory that in so far as this policy is successful, there will be created a vacuum which will favor communist-Soviet penetration. . . .

(E) Russians will strive energetically to develop Soviet rep-resentation in, and official ties with, countries in which they sense strong possibilities of opposition to western centers of power. This applies to such widely separated points as Germany, Argentina, Middle Eastern countries, etc.

(F) In international economic matters, Soviet policy will really be dominated by pursuit of autarchy for Soviet Union and Soviet-dominated adjacent areas taken together. . . . As far as official line is concerned, position is not yet clear. Soviet Government has shown strange reticence since termination hostil-ities on subject foreign trade. If large scale long term credits should be forthcoming, I believe Soviet Government may eventually again do lip service, as it did in nineteen-thirties to desirabil-ity of building up international economic exchange in general. Otherwise I think it possible Soviet foreign trade may be re-stricted largely to Soviet's own security sphere, including oc-cupied areas in Germany, and that a cold official shoulder may be turned to principle of general economic collaboration among nations. . . .

PART FOUR: . . . IMPLEMENTATION OF BASIC SOVIET
POLICIES ON UNOFFICIAL, OR SUBTERRANEAN
PLANE, . . .

One. Inner central core of communist parties in other coun-tries. . . . many of persons who compose this category . . . are in reality working closely together as an underground operating directorate of world communism, a concealed Comintern tightly co-ordinated and directed by Moscow. . . .

Two. Rank and file of communist parties. . . . Whereas form-erly foreign communist parties represented a curious (and from Moscow's standpoint often inconvenient) mixture of conspiracy and legitimate activity, now the conspiratorial element has been neatly concentrated in inner circle and ordered underground, while rank and file - no longer even taken into confidence about realities of movement - are thrust forward as bona fide internal partisans of certain political tendencies within their respective countries, genuinely innocent of conspiratorial connection with foreign states. Only in certain countries where communists are numerically strong do they now regularly appear and act as a body. As a rule they are used to penetrate . . . other organizations less likely to be suspected of being tools of Soviet Government, with a view to accomplishing their purposes through these organizations, rather than by direct action as a separate political party.

Three. A wide variety of national associations or bodies which can be dominated or influenced by such penetration. These include: labor unions, youth leagues, womens organizations, racial societies, religious societies, social organizations, cultural groups, liberal magazines, publishing houses, etc.

Four. International organizations which can be similarly penetrated through influence over various national components. Labor, youth and womens organizations are prominent among them. . . . In this, Moscow sees possibility of side-tracking western governments in world affairs and building up international lobby capable of compelling governments to take actions favorable to Soviet interests in various countries and of paralyzing actions disagreeable to USSR. . . .

Seven. Governments or governing groups willing to lend themselves to Soviet purposes in one degree or another, such as present Bulgarian and Yugoslav governments, North Persian regime, Chinese Communists, etc. Not only propaganda machines but actual policies of these regimes can be placed extensively at disposal of USSR.

It may be expected that component parts of this far-flung apparatus will be utilized.

(A) To undermine general political and strategic potential of major western powers. Efforts will be made in such countries to disrupt national self-confidence, to hamstring measures of national defense, to increase social and industrial unrest, to stimulate all forms of disunity. All persons with grievances, whether economic or racial, will be urged to seek redress not in mediation and compromise, but in defiant violent struggle for destruction of other elements of society. . . .

(B) On unofficial plane particularly violent efforts will be made to weaken power and influence of western powers of colonial, backward, or dependent peoples. On this level, no holds will be barred. Mistakes and weaknesses of western colonial administration will be mercilessly exposed and exploited. Liberal opinion in western countries will be mobilized to weaken colonial policies. Resentment among dependent peoples will be stimulated. And while latter are being encouraged to seek independence of western powers, Soviet dominated puppet political machines will be undergoing preparation to take over domestic power in respective colonial areas when independence is achieved.

(C) Where individual governments stand in path of Soviet purposes pressures will be brought for their removal from office. This can happen where governments directly oppose Soviet foreign policy aims (Turkey, Iran), where they seal their territories off against Communist penetration (Switzerland, Portugal), or where they compete too strongly, like Labor Government in England, for moral domination among elements which it is important for Communists to dominate. . . .

(D) In foreign countries Communists will, as a rule, work toward destruction of all forms of personal independence, economic, political or moral. Their system can handle only individuals who have been brought into complete dependence on higher power. . . .

(E) Everything possible will be done to set major western powers against each other. . . . Where suspicions exist, they will be fanned; where not, ignited. No effort will be spared to discredit and combat all efforts which threaten to lead to any sort of unity or cohesion among other [nations] from which Russia might be excluded. Thus, all forms of international organization not amenable to communist penetration and control, whether it be the Catholic [Church's] international economic concerns, or the international fraternity of royalty and aristocracy, must expect to find themselves under fire. . . .

(F) In general, all Soviet efforts on unofficial international plane will be negative and destructive in character, designed to tear down sources of strength beyond reach of Soviet control. . . . behind all this will be applied insistent, unceasing pressure for penetration and command of key positions in administration and especially in police apparatus of foreign countries. The Soviet regime is a police regime par excellence, reared in the dim half world of Tsarist police intrigue, accustomed to think primarily in terms of police power. This should never be lost sight of in gauging Soviet moves.

PART FIVE

In summary, we have here a political force committed fanatically to the belief that with US there can be no permanent modus vivendi, that it is desirable and necessary that the internal harmony of our society be disrupted, our traditional way of life be destroyed, the international authority of our state be broken, if Soviet power is to be secure. This political force has complete power of disposition over energies of one of world's greatest peoples and resources of world's richest national territory, and is borne along by deep and powerful currents of Russian nationalism. In addition, it has an elaborate and far flung apparatus for exertion of its influence in other countries, an apparatus of amazing flexibility and versatility, managed by people whose experience and skill in underground methods are presumably without parallel in history. Finally, it is seemingly inaccessible to considerations of reality in its basic reactions. For it, the vast fund of objective fact about human society is not, as with us, the measure against which outlook is constantly being tested and re-formed, but a grab bag from which individual items are selected arbitrarily and tendenciously to bolster an outlook already preconceived. . . . Problem of how to cope with this force is undoubtedly greatest task our diplomacy has ever faced and probably greatest it will ever have to face. . . . It should be approached with same thoroughness and care as solution of major strategic problem in war, and if necessary, with no smaller outlay in planning effort. . . . I would like to record my conviction that problem is within our power to solve – and that without recourse to any general military conflict. . . .

(One) Soviet power, unlike that of Hitlerite Germany, is neither schematic nor adventuristic. It does not work by fixed plans. It does not take unnecessary risks. Impervious to logic of reason, and it is highly sensitive to logic of force. For this reason it can easily withdraw - and usually does - when strong resistance is encountered at any point. Thus, if the adversary has sufficient force and makes clear his readiness to use it, he rarely has to do so. If situations are properly handled there need be no prestige engaging showdowns.

(Two) Gauged against western world as a whole, Soviets are still by far the weaker force. Thus, their success will really depend on degree of cohesion, firmness and vigor which western world can muster. And this is factor which it is within our power to influence.

(Three) Success of Soviet system, as form of internal power, is not yet finally proven. It has yet to be demonstrated that it can survive supreme test of successive transfer of power from one individual or group to another. Lenin's death was first such transfer, and its effects wracked Soviet state for 15 years after. Stalin's death or retirement will be second. But even this will not be final test. Soviet internal system will now be subjected, by virtue of recent territorial expansions, to series of additional strains which once proved severe tax on Tsardom. We here are convinced that never since termination of civil war have mass of Russian people been emotionally farther removed from doctrines of communist party than they are today. In Russia, party has now become a great and - for the moment - highly successful apparatus of dictatorial administration, but it has ceased to be a source of emotional inspiration. Thus, internal soundness and permanence of movement need not yet be regarded as assured.

(Four) All Soviet propaganda beyond Soviet security sphere is basically negative and destructive. It should therefore be relatively easy to combat it by any intelligent and really constructive program. . . .

(One) Our first step must be to apprehend, and recognize for what it is, the nature of the movement with which we are dealing. . . .

(Two) We must see that our public is educated to realities of Russian situation. . . . It must be done mainly by government, which is necessarily more experienced and better informed on practical problems involved. . . . I am convinced that there would be far less hysterical anti-Sovietism in our country today if realities of this situation were better understood by our people. . . . if there is any real risk here involved, it is one which we should have courage to face, and sooner the better. But I cannot see what we would be risking. . . . We have here no investments to guard, no actual trade to lose, virtually no citizens to protect, few cultural contacts to preserve. Our only stake lies in what we hope rather than what we have; and I am convinced we have better chance of realizing those hopes if our public is enlightened and if our dealings with Russians are placed entirely on realistic and matter of fact basis.

(Three) Much depends on health and vigor of our own society. . . . Every courageous and incisive measure to solve internal problems of our own society, to improve self-confidence, discipline, morale and community spirit of our own people, is a diplomatic victory over Moscow worth a thousand diplomatic notes and joint communiques. If we cannot abandon fatalism and indifference in face of deficiencies of our own society, Moscow will profit - Moscow cannot help profiting by them in its foreign policies.

(Four) We must formulate and put forward for other nations a much more positive and constructive picture of sort of world we would like to see than we have put forward in past. It is not enough to urge people to develop political processes similar to our own. Many foreign peoples, in Europe at least, are tired and frightened by experiences of past, and are less interested in abstract freedom than in security. They are seeking guidance rather than responsibilities. We should be better able than Russians to give them this. And unless we do, Russians certainly will.

(Five) Finally we must have courage and self-confidence to cling to our own methods and conceptions of human society. After all, the greatest danger that can befall us in coping with this problem of Soviet Communism, is that we shall allow ourselves to become like those with whom we are coping.

(86) MEMO, JOSEPH JONES (STATE DEPARTMENT OFFICIAL) TO ASSISTANT SECRETARY OF STATE WILLIAM BENTON, February 26, 1947

Source: Joseph Jones Papers, Truman Doctrine, Harry S. Truman Library.

There are many signs that the world is approaching this year
. . .

. . . primarily an economic crisis centered in Britain and Empire, France, Greece, and China. But this economic crisis will have the most profound political repercussions imaginable. For the crisis spots are precisely the areas from which the United States has in the past received its greatest protection and from which United States foreign policy now draws its greatest strength. The chief areas involved are those where there exists, or we hope will exist, friendly and democratic bases for United States foreign policy.

If these areas are allowed to spiral downwards into economic anarchy, then at best they will drop out of the U.S. orbit and try an independent nationalistic policy; at worst they will swing into the Russian orbit.

We will then face the world alone. What will then be the cost, in dollars and cents, of our armaments and of our economic isolation? I do not see how we could possibly avoid a depression far greater than that of 1929-1932 and crushing taxes to pay for the direct commitments we would be forced to make around the world.

While we progress rapidly towards this crisis, the front pages of today's papers are filled with accounts of the compromises which the President and [Under Secretary of State William] Clayton and [William McChesney] Martin [Chairman] of the Export-Import Bank are obliged to make with Congress on trade pacts, foreign relief, and foreign loans. These compromises will partially sterilize even existing authority in meeting this year's economic crisis, and the full existing authority is pathetically inadequate.

I think we must admit the conclusion that Congress and the people of this country are not sufficiently aware of the character and dimensions of the crisis that impends, and of the measures that must be taken in terms of relief, loans, gifts, constructive development programs and liberal trade policies - all these on a scale hitherto unimagined - if disaster is to be avoided. The people and Congress do not know the imcomparably greater cost to them if the chief supporters of our trade and political policies around the world are forced to abandon us, if the United States should be obliged to shoulder directly responsibilities that are now only contingent, for peace and security in all areas of the world.

The State Department knows. Congress and the people do not know.

We thus face a situation similar to that prevailing prior to Pearl Harbor: a powerlessness on the part of the Government to act because of Congressional or public unawareness of the danger or cost of inaction.

I wish to raise the question of whether we have learned the lessons of past disasters sufficiently to undertake the kind of information program necessary to inform the people and convince Congress adequately with respect to today's crisis.

Such a program will require first bold action at the top. It will require a grave, frank statesmanlike appeal to the people by Secretary [of State George] Marshall, who is the only one in the Government with the prestige to make a deep impression. In this appeal the danger should be described fully and the cost of both action and inaction estimated. . . .

With such a lead our information service could then get under-way and keep the ball rolling. But I am afraid the most we can do without top leadership will be scarcely noticeable.

(87) <u>SPEECH TO JOINT SESSION OF CONGRESS, PRESIDENT TRUMAN,</u> March 12, 1947 [Extract]

Source: U.S. Congress, *Congressional Record*, 80th Congress, 1st Session, pp. 1980-1981.

. . . The United States has received from the Greek Government an urgent appeal for financial and economic assistance. Preliminary reports from the American economic mission now in Greece and reports from the American Ambassador in Greece corrob-orate the statement of the Greek Government that assistance is imperative if Greece is to survive as a free nation.

I do not believe that the American people and the Congress wish to turn a deaf ear to the appeal of the Greek Government.

Greece is not a rich country. Lack of sufficient natural resources has always forced the Greek people to work hard to make both ends meet. Since 1940, this industrious and peace-loving country has suffered invasion, 4 years of cruel enemy occupation, and bitter internal strife. . . .

As a result of these tragic conditions, a militant minority, exploiting human want and misery, was able to create political chaos which, until now, has made economic recovery impossible. . . .

The very existence of the Greek state is today threatened by the terrorist activities of several thousand armed men, led by Communists, who defy the Government's authority at a number of points, particularly along the northern boundaries. . . .

. . . the Greek Government is unable to cope with the situation. The Greek Army is small and poorly equipped. It needs supplies and equipment if it is to restore the authority of the Government throughout Greek territory.

Greece must have assistance if it is to become a self-supporting and self-respecting democracy.

The United States must supply this assistance. We have already extended to Greece certain types of relief and economic aid but these are inadequate.

There is no other country to which democratic Greece can turn.

No other nation is willing and able to provide the necessary support for a democratic Greek Government. . . .

We have considered how the United Nations might assist in this crisis. But the situation is an urgent one requiring immediate action, and the United Nations and its related organizations are not in a position to extend help of the kind that is required. . . .

No government is perfect. One of the chief virtues of a democracy, however, is that its defects are always visible and under democratic processes can be pointed out and corrected. The Government of Greece is not perfect. Nevertheless it represents 85 percent of the members of the Greek Parliament who were chosen in an election last year. . . .

The Greek Government has been operating in an atmosphere of chaos and extremism. It has made mistakes. The extension of aid by this country does not mean that the United States condones everything that the Greek Government has done or will do. We have condemned in the past, and we condemn now, extremist measures of the right or the left. We have in the past advised tolerance, and we advise tolerance now.

Greece's neighbor, Turkey, also deserves our attention.

The future of Turkey as an independent and economically sound state is clearly no less important to the freedom-loving peoples of the world than the future of Greece. The circumstances in which Turkey finds itself today are considerably different from those of Greece. Turkey has been spared the disasters that have beset Greece. And during the war, the United States and Great Britain furnished Turkey with material aid.

Nevertheless, Turkey now needs our support.

Since the war, Turkey has sought financial assistance from Great Britain and the United States for the purpose of effecting that modernization necessary for the maintenance of its national integrity.

That integrity is essential to the preservation of order in the Middle East. . . .

As in the case of Greece, if Turkey is to have the assistance it needs, the United States must supply it. We are the only country able to provide that help.

I am fully aware of the broad implications involved if the United States extends assistance to Greece and Turkey, . . .

One of the primary objectives of the foreign policy of the United States is the creation of conditions in which we and other nations will be able to work out a way of life free from coercion. . . .

To insure the peaceful development of nations, free from coercion, the United States has taken a leading part in establishing the United Nations. The United Nations is designed to make possible lasting freedom and independence for all its members. We shall not realize our objectives, however, unless we are willing to help free peoples to maintain their free institutions and their national integrity against aggressive movements that seek to impose upon them totalitarian regimes. This is no more than a frank recognition that totalitarian regimes imposed on free peoples, by direct and indirect aggression, undermine the foundations of international peace and hence the security of the United States.

The peoples of a number of countries of the world have recently had totalitarian regimes forced upon them against their will. The Government of the United States has made frequent protests against coercion and intimidation, in violation of the Yalta agreement, in Poland, Rumania, and Bulgaria. I must also state that in a number of other countries there have been similar developments.

At the present moment in world history nearly every nation must choose between alternative ways of life. The choice is too often not a free one.

One way of life is based upon the will of the majority, and is distinguished by free institutions, representative government, free elections, guarantees of individual liberty, freedom of speech and religion, and freedom from political oppression.

The second way of life is based upon the will of a minority forcibly imposed upon the majority. It relies upon terror and oppression, a controlled press and radio, fixed elections, and the suppression of personal freedoms.

I believe that it must be the policy of the United States to support free peoples who are resisting attempted subjugation by armed minorities or by outside pressures.

I believe that we must assist free people to work out their own destinies in their own way.

I believe that our help should be primarily through economic and financial aid, which is essential to economic stability and orderly political processes.

The world is not static and the status quo is not sacred. But we cannot allow changes in the status quo in violation of the Charter of the United Nations by such methods as coercion, or by such subterfuges as political infiltration. In helping free and independent nations to maintain their freedom, the United States will be giving effect to the principles of the Charter of the United Nations.

It is necessary only to glance at a map to realize that the survival and integrity of the Greek nation are of grave importance in a much wider situation. If Greece should fall under the control of an armed minority, the effect upon its neighbor, Turkey, would be immediate and serious. Confusion and disorder might well spread throughout the entire Middle East.

Moreover, the disappearance of Greece as an independent state would have a profound effect upon those countries in Europe whose peoples are struggling against great difficulties to maintain their freedoms and their independence while they repaired the damages of war. . . .

Should we fail to aid Greece and Turkey in this fateful hour, the effect will be far reaching to the West as well as to the East.

We must take immediate and resolute action. . . .

In addition to [the requested $400 million in] funds, I ask the Congress to authorize the detail of American civilian and military personnel to Greece and Turkey, at the request of those countries, to assist in the tasks of reconstruction, and for the purpose of supervising the use of such financial and material assistance as may be furnished. I recommend that authority also be provided for the instruction and training of selected Greek and Turkish personnel. . . .

The seeds of totalitarian regimes are nurtured by misery and want. They spread and grow in the evil soil of poverty and strife. They reach their full growth when the hope of a people for a better life has died.

We must keep that hope alive.

The free peoples of the world look to us for support in maintaining their freedoms.

If we falter in our leadership, we may endanger the peace of the world - and we shall surely endanger the welfare of our own Nation. . . .

(88) SPECIAL MESSAGE TO CONGRESS, PRESIDENT TRUMAN, February 16, 1948 [Extract]

Source: *Public Papers of the Presidents: Harry S. Truman, 1948.* Washington: U.S. Government Printing Office, 1964, pp. 140-141.

Pursuant to the provisions of [the Truman Doctrine] . . . , I submit herewith the second quarterly report on aid to Greece and Turkey, covering the period from the inception of the program to December 31, 1947.

Since the [November 7, 1947] report . . . Greece has been subjected to ever-increasing pressure by the Communist minority, which, subservient to the foreign influences from which it draws support, would impose its will on the Greek people by force of arms. . . .

These bands which traffic in human misery and chaos are small, too small to claim any truly representative character. They total about 20,000, of which a large proportion are known to have been unwillingly impressed into the guerrilla ranks under threat of death to themselves and their families. . . .

This policy is sapping the economic strength of Greece at the same time that the American Mission for Aid to Greece is seeking to build it up through reconstruction and economic assistance. This is, of course, the intent of the guerrillas, for a healthy Greece on the road to economic recovery would not be receptive to Communist ideology. . . .

The American Mission is doing all in its power to assist, and its accomplishments have been considerable. Owing to the Communist obstruction it is increasingly clear, however, that economic recovery in Greece must await the establishment of internal security. Although economic programs most effective under the circumstances will continue to be actively prosecuted, the benefits from them can be fully realized only when the warfare against the guerrillas has been successfully concluded.

To aid the Greek Government in the prosecution of the warfare against the guerrillas, the American Mission at the close of the year transferred . . . funds from the economic to the military program, . . . These additional funds will be used to support the formation of an additional 58 National Defense Corps battalions, . . . these battalions will take over the task of protecting the villages of the provinces from which they are recruited, thereby freeing the Greek National Army to conduct a more offensive warfare. If the guerrilla menace should increase as a result of greater outside assistance, a new situation would be created which would have to be dealt with in the light of circumstances prevailing at that time.

While recent developments are adverse, in that they have lengthened the time necessary for Greece's ultimate recovery, . . . Greece is still a free country. The recent announcement of a "government" by the Communist guerrillas, who do not effectively control territory in which to exercise any of the functions of government, appears to have been an act of desperation and not of strength. The transparent device of declaring the "free government" has not materially changed the existing situation, except to reveal more clearly to the Greeks and to the world the true character of Greece's enemy. The United States Government has already made known its view that recognition of this group by other governments would have serious implications and would be clearly contrary to the principles of the United Nations Charter. . . .

I am pleased to be able to report that the Turkish aid program is proceeding in an orderly manner. Careful planning and procurement are now resulting in deliveries which can be expected to flow at a fairly uniform rate.

Continued economic assistance to Greece will be provided under the European Recovery Program [the Marshall Plan], if that program is authorized by the Congress. The European Recovery Program will not provide, however, for any additional military assistance required for Greece and Turkey, which will, at the appropriate time, be sought from the Congress . . .

Concurrent with the formulation of the Truman Doctrine the Truman Administration undertook an even more important policy, first the formulation and then the selling of the Marshall Plan. Also based on the objective of containing Soviet influence the Marshall Plan differed from the Truman Doctrine in terms of its political problems. First, the costs, and potentially inflationary impact, of this program must be sold to a fiscally conservative Congress in the immediate aftermath of a debate wherein conservative congressmen had raised questions about the globalist character and inflationary impact of the Truman Doctrine. Second, and no less important, the support of Western European leaders and general public must be assured. The anti-Communist, domino theory emphasis which had proved successful for selling the Truman Doctrine at home could undermine support abroad for an economic recovery program, even though U.S. economic assistance could benefit Western Europe. The Administration's public and private assessment of the need for the Marshall Plan and the strategy needed to ensure public and congressional support thereby was based on these complex and contradictory political considerations.

(89) MEMO, JOSEPH JONES (STATE DEPARTMENT AIDE) TO MSSRS. HARLIK, CLEVELAND, STOKES, STINEBOWER, NESS, AND RUSSELL (STATE DEPARTMENT OFFICIALS), May 20, 1947

Source: Joseph Jones Papers, Marshall Plan Speech, Harry S. Truman Library.

The attached draft speech was begun at the direction of the Secretary [of State George Marshall] at the time he thought he might go out to Wisconsin to accept a degree. The Secretary felt at that time that he would like to "develop further" the line taken by [Under Secretary of State Dean] Acheson in his Mississippi speech on May 8.

Although the Secretary abandoned the Wisconsin trip, I have completed the speech. It is my understanding that the Secretary will give several addresses during June, of which one may be on this subject.

I would therefore appreciate it if you would consider this draft carefully and let me have your criticism and suggestions at the earliest moment.

Except for the first four pages, which sound warnings similar to those of Mr. Acheson in Mississippi, this speech is written primarily with a view to its effect abroad. The indications of suspicion and skepticism with which foreign peoples are beginning to view American aid are alarming and it would seem to be of first importance to spell out our design for reconstruction and to give a positive concept about which peoples of Europe especially can rally and upon which they can pin their hopes. The political and economic policy of the Department has led up to an expression of this sort and now seems the psychological time to launch it. We have a great deal to gain by convincing the world that we have something positive and attractive to offer, and not just anti-Communism.

(90) COMMENCEMENT ADDRESS, HARVARD UNIVERSITY, SECRETARY OF STATE GEORGE MARSHALL, June 5, 1947 [Extract]

Source: U.S. Congress, *Congressional Record*, 80th Congress, 1st session, p. A3248.

I need not tell you gentlemen that the world situation is very serious. . . . the problem is one of such enormous complexity that the very mass of facts presented to the public by press and radio make it exceedingly difficult for the man in the street to reach a clear appraisal of the situation. Furthermore, the people of this country are distant from the troubled areas of the earth and it is hard for them to comprehend the plight and consequent reactions of the long-suffering peoples, and the effect of those reactions on their governments in connection with our ef forts to promote peace in the world.

In considering the requirements for the rehabilitation of Europe, the physical loss of life, the visible destruction of cities, factories, mines, and railroads was correctly estimated, but . . . this visible destruction was probably less serious than the dislocation of the entire fabric of European economy. For the past 10 years conditions have been highly abnormal. The feverish preparation for war and the more feverish maintenance of the war effort engulfed all aspects of national economies. Machinery has fallen into disrepair or is entirely obsolete. Under the arbitrary and destructive Nazi rule, virtually every possible enterprise was geared into the German war machine. Long-standing commercial ties, private institutions, banks, insurance companies and shipping companies disappeared through loss of capital, absorption through nationalization or by simple destruction. In many countries, confidence in the local currency has been severely shaken. The breakdown of the business structure of Europe during the war was complete. Recovery has been seriously retarded by the fact that 2 years after the close of hostilities a peace settlement with Germany and Austria has not been agreed upon. But even given a more prompt solution of these difficult problems, the rehabilitation of the economic structure of Europe quite evidently will require a much longer time and greater ef-fort than had been foreseen. . . .

The truth of the matter is that Europe's requirements for the next 3 or 4 years of foreign food and other essential products – principally from America – are so much greater than her present ability to pay that she must have substantial additional help, or face economic, social, and political deterioration of a very grave character.

The remedy lies in breaking the vicious circle and restoring the confidence of the European people in the economic future of their own countries and of Europe as a whole. . . .

Aside from the demoralizing effect on the world at large and the possibilities of disturbances arising as a result of the desperation of the people concerned, the consequences to the economy of the United States should be apparent to all. It is logical that the United States should do whatever it is able to do to assist in the return of normal economic health in the world, without which there can be no political stability and no assured peace. Our policy is directed not against any country or doctrine but against hunger, poverty, desperation, and chaos. Its purpose should be the revival of a working economy in the world so as to permit the emergence of political and social conditions in which free institutions can exist. Such assistance . . . must not be on a piecemeal basis as various crises develop. Any assistance that this Government may render in the future should provide a cure rather than a mere palliative. Any government that is willing to assist in the task of recovery will find full cooperation, I am sure, on the part of the United States Government. Any government which maneuvers to block the recovery of other countries cannot expect help from us. Furthermore, governments, political parties, or groups which seek to perpetuate human misery in order to profit therefrom politically or otherwise will encounter the opposition of the United States.

. . . before the United States Government can proceed much further in its efforts to alleviate the situation and help start the European world on its way to recovery, there must be some agreement among the countries of Europe as to the requirements of the situation and the part those countries themselves will take in order to give proper effect to whatever action might be undertaken by this Government. It would be neither fitting nor efficacious for this Government to undertake to draw up unilaterally a program designed to place Europe on its feet economically. . . . The initiative, I think, must come from Europe. The role of this country should consist of friendly aid in the drafting of a European program and of later support of such a program so far as it may be practical for us to do so. The program should be a joint one, agreed to by a number, if not all European nations.

An essential part of any successful action on the part of the United States is an understanding on the part of the people of America of the character of the problem and the remedies to be applied. . . . With foresight, and a willingness on the part of our people to face up to the vast responsiblity which history has clearly placed upon our country, the difficulties I have outlined can and will be overcome.

(91) LETTER, PRESIDENT TRUMAN TO CHAIRMEN OF CONGRESSIONAL COM-MITTEES, October 1, 1947 [Extract]

Source: *Public Papers of the Presidents: Harry S. Truman, 1947.* Washington: U.S. Government Printing Office, 1963, p. 451.

The situation in western Europe has, in the last few months, become critical. This is especially true in the cases of France and Italy, where slow recovery of productivity, particularly of goods for export, combined with the increasing drain on their dollar resources, has produced acute distress.

The unusually bad harvests in western Europe, together with rising costs of imports, the unfortunate results of the temporary cessation of sterling convertibility and the near exhaustion of gold and dollar reserves, have placed these two countries in a position where they are without adequate food and fuel supplies for the fall and winter, and without sufficient dollars with which to purchase these essentials. They cannot, by their own efforts, meet this major crisis which is already upon them.

Political groups that hope to profit by unrest and distress are now attempting to capitalize on the grave fears of the French and Italian people that they will not have enough food and fuel to survive the coming winter.

The prospect of a successful general economic recovery program for Europe is one of the major hopes for peace and economic security in the world. The Congress will soon be called upon to consider the part which the United States should play in aiding this program. But the program will have no chance of success if economic collapse occurs in Europe before the program can be put into operation. Prompt and effective aid to meet the urgent needs of the present is essential, lest the strains become too great and result in an expanding economic depression which would engulf western Europe and, eventually, spread over much of the rest of the world.

I have examined with great care the means now available to the executive branch of the Government to provide the necessary assistance. They may meet the urgent needs of the next few weeks, but it is clear that they cannot provide the necessary assistance beyond December, if as long as that. Requirements beyond that time can be met only if further authority is granted by the Congress.

The problems arising out of these circumstances are of such importance that they should be considered by the Congress at the earliest practicable time. The early convening of your committee, together with other appropriate Congressional committees, is a necessary first step in this consideration.

. . . Time is of critical importance in this matter, however, and I earnestly hope that arrangements can be made for convening your committee at an early date. . . .

(92) THE MARSHALL PLAN, April 2, 1948 [Extract]

Source: 62 Stat. 137 (1948).

Sec. 102. (a) Recognizing the intimate economic and other relationships between the United States and the nations of Europe, and recognizing that disruption following in the wake of war is not contained by national frontiers, the Congress finds that the existing situation in Europe endangers the establishment of a lasting peace, the general welfare and national interest of the United States, and the attainment of the objectives of the United Nations. The restoration or maintenance in European countries of principles of individual liberty, free institutions, and genuine independence rests largely upon the establishment of sound economic conditions, stable international economic relationships, and the achievement by the countries of Europe of a healthy economy independent of extraordinary outside assistance. The accomplishment of these objectives calls for a plan of European recovery open to all such nations which cooperate in such plan, based upon a strong production effort, the expansion of foreign trade, the creation and maintenance of internal financial stability and the development of economic cooperation, including all possible steps to establish and maintain equitable rates of exchange, and to bring about the progressive elimination of trade barriers. Mindful of the advantages which the United States has enjoyed through the existence of a large domestic market with no internal trade barriers, and believing that similar advantages can accrue to the countries of Europe, it is declared to be the policy of the people of the United States to encourage these countries through a joint organization to exert sustained common efforts as set forth in the report of the Committee of European Economic Cooperation signed at Paris in September 22, 1947, which will speedily achieve that economic cooperation in Europe which is essential for lasting peace and prosperity. It is further declared to be the policy of the people of the United States to sustain and strengthen principles of individual liberty, free institutions, and genuine independence in Europe through assistance to those countries of Europe which participate in a joint recovery program based upon self-help and mutual cooperation: <u>Provided</u>, That no assistance to the participating countries herein contemplated shall seriously impair the economic stability of the United States. It is further declared to be the policy of the United States that continuity of assistance provided by the United States should, at all times, be dependent upon continuity of cooperation among countries participating in the program. . . .

It is the purpose of this title to effectuate the policy . . . by furnishing material and financial assistance to the participating countries in such a manner as to aid them, through their own individual and concerted efforts, to become independent of extraordinary outside economic assistance within the period of operations under this title, by –

      (1) promoting industrial and agricultural production in the participating countries;

      (2) furthering the restoration or maintenance of the soundness of European currencies, budgets, and finances; and

      (3) facilitating and stimulating the growth of international trade of participating countries with one another and with other countries by appropriate measures including reduction of barriers which may hamper such trade. . . .

Sec. 115. (a) The Secretary of State, after consultation with the Administrator [for Economic Cooperation, created to administer the program], is authorized to conclude, with individual participating countries or any number of such countries or with an organization representing any such countries, agreements in furtherance of the purposes of this title. . . . In addition to continued mutual cooperation of participating countries in such a program, each such country shall conclude an agreement with the United

States in order for such country to be eligible to receive assistance under this title. . . .

Despite its public emphasis in 1948-1949 on the importance of international cooperation and thus the United Nations and on the need to promote European economic recovery to ensure peace, in private the Truman Administration based its diplomacy on the attainment of superior military strength. A radical shift had occurred in Administration policy by 1949 outlined first privately in policy planning papers of early 1949 stressing the importance of military aid to Western Europe and culminating in the drafting of the North Atlantic Treaty Organization (NATO). These considerations influenced the Administration's response to the successful explosion of a Soviet atomic bomb in September 1949 and the resultant decision to accept the risk of a nuclear arms race by proceeding with the development of thermonuclear weapons (the so-called H-bomb).

(93) FACC D-3, POLICY PAPER APPROVED BY THE FOREIGN ASSISTANCE CORRELATION COMMITTEE (COMPOSED OF REPRESENTATIVES FROM DEPARTMENT OF STATE, THE DEPARTMENT OF DEFENSE, AND THE ECONOMIC COOPERATION ADMINISTRATION), February 7, 1949 [Extract]

Source: *Foreign Relations of the United States: 1949 Vol. I National Security Affairs, Foreign Economic Policy.* Washington: U.S. Government Printing Office, 1976, pp. 250-257.

It is the policy of this Government to provide military and other assistance to free nations, whose security is of critical importance to the United States, which require strengthened military capabilities, and which make determined efforts to resist communist expansion.

In light of present circumstances the military assistance program . . . may, in general, include:

(1) Finished armaments, munitions and implements of war, . . .

(3) Raw materials, machinery and other items required for the production in recipient countries, . . .

(4) Technical assistance and information to, and training of, armed forces;

(5) Reimbursement for costs arising out of diversion of resources, including manpower, required to implement approved military programs; . . .

The policy stated above and those underlying it are an essential and integral part of our basic foreign policies which derive from (1) our fundamental national ideals and interests; (2) our recognized position as the leading Power of the free world; and (3) the policies and programs of Soviet Russia and international communism. The foreign policies of this country, however, deal with a constantly changing world environment and require constant review. . . .

It is also a basic policy of this country to so act that the Soviet Government will recognize the practical undesirability of acting on the basis of its present concepts and the necessity of complying with the precepts of international conduct as set forth in the purposes and principles of the UN Charter.

As a part of this policy it is our purpose to help to strengthen the free nations of the non-Soviet world in their effort to resist Soviet Communist aggression, external and internal, and to help increase the economic and political stability and the military capability of such of those nations as are willing to make an important contribution to US security. In so strengthening these nations it is our purpose not only to reduce the likelihood of further Soviet-Communist aggression and to improve the ability of those nations to resist if attacked, but also to create an atmosphere of confidence and security within which the chances for success of economic recovery programs may be enhanced and a more favorable atmosphere for the accomplishment of the principles and purposes of the UN established.

Basic military security policies with respect to military assistance are to:

1. strengthen the security of the US and its probable allies,

2. Strengthen the morale and material resistance of the free nations,

3. support their political and military orientation toward the U.S.,

4. augment US military potential by improvement of our armament industries, . . .

Under existing policies the following considerations must govern the determination of priorities:

(1) The strategic relationship of the area or country to the United States, which includes:

a. The Political Factor. The political factor includes consideration of: the relative importance to the US of keeping any given country free from Soviet communist domination; each country's inherent internal political stability; the strengthening of anti-communistic activity within each country; the strengthening of internal political conditions through improvement of the economic stability therein; and the degree of orientation of each country toward the United States in its own political philosophy.

b. The Military Factor. The principal elements of the military factor comprise the location and terrain of each country or group of countries and its importance to US strategic plans; the economic ability of each country or group of countries to support a military program; and the military capability of each country or group of countries to utilize military assistance.

(2) Since events have indicated that political or indirect aggression is most likely to succeed in the proximity of the Soviet army, general precedence in assistance should be given to those countries on the periphery of the Soviet world, subject to modifications required by obvious politico-strategic considerations, such as keeping open lines of communication through the

Mediterranean and preserving the United Kingdom for use as a source of production and as an advanced base.

(3) It is the present policy of the United States that . . . first priority should be given to Western Europe. Negotiations are currently in progress looking toward a collective defense arrangement for the North Atlantic area in which the United States and certain other countries would be full participants. . . .

(4) There are current military understandings with Brazil, Canada, and Mexico which affect defense coordination with the United States.

(5) The United States is committed to providing military assistance to certain specified areas and countries, notably Greece, Turkey, Iran and Korea.

(6) The United States is committed by its ratification of the Rio de Janeiro treaty to the general principles accepted by the signatory nations of common defense against aggression. . . .

It is the policy of this government, with respect to the relationship between military and economic recovery programs, that a program of mutual aid and self help supplemented by military assistance from the US must be so designed as to enable the recipients to stand on their own feet, economically, politically, and, so far as practicable, militarily. In this connection, economic recovery is basic and military assistance must facilitate recovery through the increased confidence attendant upon attaining increased security. It is our policy that economic recovery must not be sacrificed to rearmament and must continue to be given a clear priority. . . . Of basic importance is recognition of the limits of US financial and economic aid available. A balance must be struck between the needs of our domestic economy, our own armament requirements, our contribution to the recovery of recipient states and our contribution to their rearmament. . . .

The program is designed to strengthen international security which is a major objective of the United Nations Charter. Under existing conditions the purposes and principles of the Charter will be advanced by arrangements for collective self-defense and mutual assistance designed to enable free nations which are acting in support of such purposes and principles to preserve their independence and freedom, to promote respect for human rights, and to fulfill effectively their obligations under the Charter. . . .

Under this program it is not contemplated that direct military assistance will be granted the UN as an organization. . . .

Effective implementation of a policy of strengthening the military capabilities of free nations would be facilitated by the early enactment of legislation broadening the authority of the President to provide, suspend or withdraw military assistance in the interest of the national security and the political interests of the United States.

It is not possible to predict with any degree of exactness the period of time for which military assistance will be required nor as to the overall amounts that will be needed. The US does not have control over the concepts and policies of the Soviet Union which have made the military assistance program necessary and may continue to do so for an indefinite period. . . .

The Congress must be advised that military assistance to foreign nations will undoubtedly be required over a period of years, but that it is not now possible to determine in what total volume or for how long a period, and accordingly, legislative authorization should be sought for an indefinite period, . . .

The primary return sought by the United States is the preservation of the security of the United States and its probable allies.

(1) North Atlantic Pact Countries. Assuming the consummation of a North Atlantic Pact, a principal benefit in the way of reciprocal assistance from members thereof is the participation of those countries in a coordinated defense program under which each country will contribute, commensurate with its resources, economic condition, and geographic location what it most effectively can in facilities, manpower, resources, production capacity or raw or finished materials.

In the case of those countries, the United States should require as a matter of principle, that reciprocal assistance, such as base rights, materials, labor, services or other forms, be granted, where necessary, to the United States and its allies. Should individual members prove uncooperative with respect to such reciprocal assistance this would be a highly important factor to be taken into account in the determination of military aid programs; and if the lack of cooperation was serious, this would mean no military aid at all. . . .

(2) Other Countries. The amount of reciprocal assistance to be obtained from countries which do not participate in such a coordinated defense program but to whom it is determined that military assistance should be provided is not anticipated as likely to balance intangible material values the amounts we may give them. Nevertheless, it is the policy of the United States in each such case to determine what reciprocal assistance in the way of material benefits such as base rights, materials, labor, services or other forms, is vital to the security of the United States and in so far as practicable in the light of political and strategic considerations, to require the recipients to grant such benefits as a condition of our assistance.

(3) Among the principal benefits in all cases as a result of military assistance are an increase in the determination of these countries to withstand communist pressures, an increase in their confidence that they can successfully do so, and a decrease in the tendency to temporize with communism, or to withhold support from efforts at resistance to communism, out of fear that communist pressures may prove irresistible. . . .

****

(94) PPS/50, REPORT BY THE POLICY PLANNING STAFF, DEPARTMENT OF STATE, March 22, 1949 [Extract]

Source: *Foreign Relations of the United States: 1949. Vol. I National Security Affairs, Foreign Economic Policy.* Washington: U.S. Government Printing Office, 1976, p. 270.

1. U.S. security and welfare are closely bound up with the peace and security of the world community. Aggression, anywhere, may jeopardize the security of the US. Such aggression may be direct, i.e. through armed force, or indirect, i.e. through measures short of armed force by one nation to deprive another of its independence.

2. Another world war would probably be a crippling blow to civilization.

3. Even with sincere and determined efforts to settle international differences by peaceful means, aggression, direct or indirect, may occur which would present such a critical threat to the security of the United States as to require the use of armed force.

CONCLUSIONS

4. The policies of the United States should be directed to the promotion of conditions of peace, the prevention of armed aggression, and the countering of indirect aggression.

5. The United States should seek security not only through its own national strength but also through the United Nations and collective and other arrangements consistent with the Charter.

6. Collective arrangements should ensure immediate and effective counter measures against those who violate the peace by armed attack.

7. It should be borne constantly in mind that, as a result of acts of indirect aggression, the U.S. may be presented with a critical threat to its security, or to the integrity of nations whose security is vital to our own. In such event the US should consult with other countries whose security is similarly menaced with a view to taking appropriate action.

****

(95) DRAFT REPORT, NATIONAL SECURITY COUNCIL STAFF, March 30, 1949 [Extract]

Source: *Foreign Relations of the United States: 1949 Vol. I National Security Affirs, Foreign Economic Policy.* Washington: U.S. Government Printing Office, 1976, pp. 271-277.

1. Introduction. To counter the threats to our national security and well being posed by the USSR and to achieve our general objectives with respect to Russia, the following measures are deemed essential. In implementing these measures, care must be taken to avoid unduly impairing our economy and the fundamental values and institutions inherent in our way of life. . . .

2. Military readiness. The United States should develop a level of military readiness adequate as a basis for immediate

military commitments and for rapid mobilization should war prove unavoidable. This level should be such that it can be maintained as long as it is necessary for United States forces to act as a deterrent to Soviet aggression. . . .

To this end the National Military Establishment should, to the extent permitted by budget limitations, provide for . . .

a. Forces in being or capable of prompt activation . . .

(1) To insure the integrity of the Western Hemisphere and to promote and develop its war-making capacity.

(2) In conjunction with our allies to secure such base areas as are essential for the projection of offensive operations.

(3) To secure, maintain, and defend in conjunction with our allies such bases, land and sea areas, and lines of communication as are required for the prosecution of the war.

(4) To conduct, at the earliest practicable date, a strategic air offensive against the vital elements of the Soviet war-making capacity, and other air offensive operations as are required for the prosecution of the war.

(5) To initiate development of the offensive power of the armed forces for such later operations as may be necessary for achievement of the national war objectives.

(6) To support the war efforts of our allies by the provision of all feasible military assistance.

(7) To exploit at the earliest practicable date the psychological warfare plans developed under the provisions of the NSC 10 series, and to conduct other special operations.

(8) To fulfill our occupational functions and other international commitments.

b. Improvement of our strategic potential to the extent practicable under existing or future agreements by arranging for the coordination of military effort between the United States and nations likely to be associated with us, and through appropriate reciprocal assistance.

c. Improvement and exploitation of our technical potential through development of new improved material and methods.

3. Economic potential and mobilization. The United States should develop and maintain a constant state of peacetime economic preparedness, a prerequisite for which is the continuous balancing of military, war-supporting industrial, and civilian requirements against the resources to be available for meeting them. Policies should be shaped toward the following essentials.

a. Economic stabilization measures designed to strengthen the U.S. peacetime economy plus readiness measures which can be quickly invoked in the event of emergency.

b. Industrial facilities and essential utilities sufficient to meet immediate requirements in the event of war, plus plans for additional capacity to meet peak war requirements and to offset estimated losses caused by sabotage or direct enemy action.

c. Strengthening of the US industrial potential thru encouragement of scientific research and technological improvements.

d. Development of transportation and communication facilities adequate to serve current needs, plus planned reserves for estimated war requirements. . . .

e. Dispersion of industries, services, governmental and military activities now dangerously vulnerable, without undue detriment to essential operations.

f. Development of dependable sources of critical and strategic materials.

g. Stockpiling in appropriate areas of essential quantities of critical and strategic materials. . . .

l. A program for economic warfare and related wartime economic activities.

m. Organization of the Executive Branch of the Government to provide for efficient transition from peace to war and war to peace.

n. Standby emergency powers legislation and executive orders required in the event of war.

4. _Intelligence_. The United States should increase and improve US intelligence and counter-intelligence activity, and in particular assure that activities both at home and abroad are closely coordinated.

5. _Internal security_. In accordance with the provisions of the NSC 17 series, the United States should establish and maintain the highest practicable state of domestic security preparedness, recognizing that further measures will be required in the event of war. The essential minimum requirements include:

a. Establishing and maintaining more effective controls to prevent the penetration of the United States by potentially or actually dangerous persons through legal or illegal entry.

b. Providing closer controls of imports and exports as well as of incoming and outgoing travellers for the purpose of:

(1) Preventing the introduction into the United States of sabotage and espionage devices.

(2) Preventing the removal from the United States of information, materials and equipment which if in the possession of potentially hostile powers would adversely affect the national security.

c. Scrutinizing, curtailing, and counteracting, to the maximum extent possible the open and clandestine activities of communists and other subversive groups, whether party members or not.

d. Safeguarding critical governmental, industrial and other installations and utilities, affording priority to those considered absolutely essential.

e. Ready for application in the event of war, civil defense machinery to aid existing agencies in the protection of the nation's population and resources.

f.   Insuring that the various statutes in the United States Code pertaining to internal security, particularly the Espionage Act of 1917, provide an adequate legal basis for the internal security of the United States in the light of present and probably future conditions.

g.   Readying a program for controlling the activities, in the event of a war-related emergency, of US citizens and aliens who constitute threats to the nation's internal security, by apprehension and detention or by other appropriate measures, this program to provide the greatest practicable procedural safeguards to the individual.

h.   Preparation of a censorship program to be invoked in the event of war or at such time as the Congress may authorize.

6.   Collective strength of non-Soviet nations.   The United States should take the lead in increasing the collective strength of non-Soviet nations by:

a.   Effectively implementing the provisions of the North Atlantic Pact.

b.   Seeking . . . to facilitate economic recovery and promote multi-lateral commercial and financial relations among all parts of the non-Soviet world, to the end that their economic strength shall be mutually increased and self-sustained.

c.   Developing a balanced and coordinated program of economic and military assistance to selected nations of the non-Soviet world able and willing to make important contributions to our security.   Such a program should include:

(1) Continuing the Economic Cooperation program so long as US security is thereby enhanced, to the extent that recipient nations demonstrate their ability and willingness by self-help and mutual cooperation to utilize US assistance in establishing political and economic stability and thereby increasing the over-all potential of the non-Soviet world.

(2) Providing a flexible and comprehensive program of military assistance in the form of supplies, equipment and technical advice in accordance with the approved conclusion of the NSC 14 series.

(3) Coordinating the economic and military assistance programs and establishing flexibility of transfer between them, with a view to furnishing each recipient over-all assistance balanced to conform to changing circumstances and the requirements of US security.

d.   Engaging in economic mobilization planning with selected nations when appropriate.

e.   To the extent that it increases world stability and US security:

(1) Strengthening world organization by encouraging development of the United Nations and other international organizations, both regional and functional.

(2) Wherever practicable, utilizing international organizations for the handling of international problems and disputes.

f.   Securing, as soon as politically feasible, timely access to and use of those areas throughout the world considered strategically essential to US security.

7.   Political and economic activities.   The United States should by all available means . . .

a.   Encourage in all appropriate ways the political and economic unification of Europe.

b.   Seek to make the Kremlin fear that it is ideologically dangerous to keep an army abroad.

c.   Develop internal dissension within the USSR and disagreements among the USSR and Soviet orbit nations.

d.   Encourage, develop and support anti-Soviet activist organizations within the Soviet orbit.

e.   Defeat communist activities in countries outside the Soviet orbit where such activities constitute a serious threat to US security.

f.   Minimize the export of strategic materials and equipment from the United States and other non-Soviet nations to areas within the Soviet sphere, and conversely, increase the flow of strategic materials now needed for US production and stockpiling purposes.

g.   Prevent the USSR from achieving a dominant economic or political position in countries in which trade with the United States is essential to our national security.

8.   Foreign information program.   The United States should strengthen, maintain and intensify for as long as necessary, a vigorous coordinated foreign information program directed primarily toward the USSR and its armies, Soviet satellites, countries where there is a serious communist threat, and countries not sufficiently aware of real Soviet objectives.   This program should:

a.   Stress the fact that the Western way of life increasingly offers greatest and most enduring benefits to the individual, and is therefore destined to prevail over the communist ideology with its inevitable police state methods.

b.   Strive to eradicate the myth by which people remote from direct Soviet influence are held in a position of subservience to Moscow, and to cause the world at large to see and understand the true nature of the USSR and the world communist party, and to adopt a logical and realistic attitude toward them.

c.   Endeavor to strain the relationships between Moscow and satellite governments by encouraging the latter to take independent action within the United Nations and elsewhere.

d.   Encourage the revival of the national life of major national groups within the USSR without committing us to irrevocable or premature decisions respecting independence for national minorities.

e.   Discreetly convey to the Russian and Satellite peoples and soldiers the feeling that Americans are friendly to them, though not to their governments.

9. <u>Psychological warfare</u>. In accordance with the provisions of the NSC 43 series, the United States should plan and make preparations for the conduct of foreign information programs and overt psychological operations abroad, in the event of war or threat of war as determined by the President. . . .

10. <u>Domestic information</u>. The United States should establish programs to:

a. Keep the United States public fully informed of Soviet aims and tactics and the threats to our national security arising therefrom, so that the public will be prepared to support measures which we must accordingly adopt.

b. Explain and support the need of:

(1) U.S. world leadership and US willingness to assume the responsibilities arising therefrom.

(2) Non-partisan support of our foreign policy.

c. Keep the US public informed of the specific nature and types of domestic security threats existing, and of the measures which should be adopted to counteract them.

d. Provide for a wartime domestic information service in accordance with the provisions of the NSC 43 series.

11. <u>Economic soundness</u>. In carrying out the above measures, the greatest possible attention must be paid to evaluating essential military, foreign aid, and other national security requirements in the light of the ability of the United States to support such requirements, with the realization that military preparedness and foreign aid on a scale larger than we have been accustomed to may have to be continued indefinitely. The relative share of government in the total national product and the direction of investment at home and abroad must be carefully scrutinized. The size, timing, and distribution of drafts on materials, facilities, and manpower must be articulated with the operating needs and practices of industry, commerce, and finance so as not to fan inflation, demoralize markets, or weaken incentives to production, any one of which would eventually impair our military capability.

The United States should endeavor to restrict national security programs from going beyond the level at which fiscal and monetary measures, selective voluntary allocation and standby mandatory allocations meet the needs. If it should be decided to raise expenditures beyond this sensitive zone, this should be done with the full awareness that more comprehensive controls, including price and wage controls may be required, which if long continued might develop resistance to decontrol. . . .

(96) <u>STATEMENT, SECRETARY OF STATE DEAN ACHESON</u>, March 18, 1949 [Extract]

Source: *Department of State Bulletin*, March 27, 1949, pp. 384-388.

The very basis of western civilization . . . is the ingrained spirit of restraint and tolerance. This is the opposite of the Communist belief that coercion by force is a proper method of hastening the inevitable. Western civilization has lived by mutual restraint and tolerance. This civilization permits and stimulates free inquiry and bold experimentation. It creates the environment of freedom, from which flows the greatest amount of ingenuity, enterprise, and accomplishment.

These principles of democracy, individual liberty, and the rule of law have flourished in [the North] Atlantic community. They have universal validity. They are shared by other free nations and find expression on a universal basis in the Charter of the United Nations; they are the standards by which its members have solemnly agreed to be judged. They are the elements out of which are forged the peace and welfare of mankind. . . .

It is clear that the North Atlantic pact is not an improvisation. It is the statement of the facts and lessons of history. We have learned our history lesson from two world wars in less than half a century. That experience has taught us that the control of Europe by a single aggressive, unfriendly power would constitute an intolerable threat to the national security of the United States. We participated in those two great wars to preserve the integrity and independence of the European half of the Atlantic community in order to preserve the the integrity and independence of the American half. It is a simple fact, proved by experience, that an outside attack on one member of this community is an attack upon all members. . . .

Successful resistance to aggression in the modern world requires modern arms and trained military forces. As a result of the recent war, the European countries joining in the pact are generally deficient in both requirements. The treaty does not bind the United States to any arms program. But we all know that the United States is now the only democratic nation with the resources and the productive capacity to help the free nations of Europe to recover their military strength.

Therefore, we expect to ask the Congress to supply our European partners some of the weapons and equipment they need to be able to resist aggression. We also expect to recommend military supplies for other free nations which will cooperate with us in safeguarding peace and security.

In the compact world of today, the security of the United States cannot be defined in terms of boundaries and frontiers. A serious threat to international peace and security anywhere in the world is of direct concern to this country. Therefore it is our policy to help free peoples to maintain their integrity and independence, not only in Western Europe or in the America, but wherever the aid we are able to provide can be effective. . . .

In providing military assistance to other countries, both inside and outside the North Atlantic pact, we will give clear priority to the requirements for economic recovery. We will carefully balance the military assistance program with the capacity and requirements of the total economy, both at home and abroad.

. . . article 5 [of the NATO treaty] deals with the possibility . . . that the nations joining together in the pact may have to face the eventuality of an armed attack. In this article, they agree that an armed attack on any of them, in Europe or North America, will be considered an attack on all of them. In the event of such an attack, each of them will take, individually and in concert with the other parties, whatever action it deems necessary to restore and maintain the security of the North Atlantic area, including the use of armed force.

This does not mean that the United States would be automatically at war if one of the nations covered by the pact is subjected to armed attack. Under our Constitution, the Congress alone has the power to declare war. We would be bound to take promptly the action which we deemed necessary to restore and maintain the security of the North Atlantic area. That decision would be taken in accordance with our constitutional procedures. . . . If we should be confronted again with a calculated armed attack such as we have twice seen in the twentieth century, I should not suppose that we would decide any action other than the use of armed force effective either as an exercise of the right of collective self-defense or as necessary to restore the peace and security of the North Atlantic area. That decision will rest where the Constitution has placed it.

This is not a legalistic question. It is a question we have frequently faced, the question of faith and principle in carrying out treaties. Those who decide it will have the responsibility for taking all appropriate action under the treaty. Such a responsibility requires the exercise of will - a will disciplined by the undertaking solemnly contracted to do what they decide is necessary to restore and maintain the peace and security of the North Atlantic area. That is our obligation under this article 5. It is equally our duty and obligation to the security of our own country. . . .

. . . we are determined, on the one hand, to make it unmistakably clear that immediate and effective counter measures will be taken against those who violate the peace and, on the other, to wage peace vigorously and relentlessly.

Too often peace has been thought of as a negative condition - the mere absence of war. . . . Peace is positive, and it has to be waged with all our thought, energy and courage, and with the conviction that war is not inevitable. . . .

The United States is waging peace by throwing its full strength and energy into the struggle, and we shall continue to do so.

We sincerely hope we can avoid strife, but we cannot avoid striving for what is right. We devoutly hope we can have genuine peace, but we cannot be complacent about the present uneasy and troubled peace.

A secure and stable peace is not a goal we can reach all at once and for all time. It is a dynamic state, produced by effort and faith, with justice and courage. The struggle is continuous and hard. The prize is never irrevocably ours. . . .

(97) NORTH ATLANTIC TREATY (NATO), April 4, 1949 [Extract]
Source: 63 Stat. 2242 (1949).

The Parties to this Treaty reaffirm their faith in the purposes and principles of the Charter of the United Nations and their desire to live in peace with all peoples and all governments.

They are determined to safeguard the freedom, common heritage and civilization of their peoples, founded on the principles of democracy, individual liberty and the rule of law.

They seek to promote stability and well-being in the North Atlantic area.

They are resolved to unite their efforts to collective defense and for the preservation of peace and security.

They therefore agree to this North Atlantic Treaty:

Article 1. The Parties undertake . . . to settle any international disputes in which they may be involved by peaceful means in such a manner that international peace and security, and justice, are not endangered, and to refrain in their international relations from the threat or use of force in any manner inconsistent with the purposes of the United Nations.

Article 2. The Parties will contribute toward the further development of peaceful and friendly international relations by strengthening their free institutions, by bringing about a better understanding of the principles upon which these institutions are founded, and by promoting conditions of stability and well-being. They will seek to eliminate conflict in their international economic policies and will encourage economic collaboration between any or all of them.

Article 3. In order more effectively to achieve the objectives of this Treaty, the Parties, separately and jointly, by means of continuous and effective self-help and mutual aid, will maintain and develop their individual and collective capacity to resist armed attack.

Article 4. The Parties will consult together whenever, in the opinion of any of them, the territorial integrity, political independence or security of any of the Parties is threatened.

Article 5. The Parties agree that an armed attack against one or more of them in Europe or North America shall be considered an attack against them all; and consequently they agree that, if such an armed attack occurs, each of them in exercise of the right of individual or collective self-defense recognized by Article 51 of the Charter of the United Nations, will assist the Party or Parties so attacked by taking forthwith, individually and in concert with the other Parties, such action as it deems necessary, including the use of armed force, to restore and maintain the security of the North Atlantic area.

Any such armed attack and all measures taken as a result thereof shall immediately be reported to the Security Council. Such measures shall be terminated when the Security Council has taken the measures necessary to restore and maintain international peace and security.

Article 6. For the purpose of Article 5 an armed attack on one
or more of the Parties is deemed to include an armed attack on
the territory of any of the Parties in Europe or North America,
on the Algerian departments of France, on the occupation forces
of any Party in Europe, on the islands under the jurisdiction of
any Party in the North Atlantic area north of the Tropic of Cancer
or on the vessels or aircraft in this area of any of the Parties.
. . .

Article 9. The Parties hereby establish a council, on which each
of them shall be represented, to consider matters concerning the
implementation of this Treaty. The council shall be so organized
as to be able to meet promptly at any time. . . .

Article 10. The Parties may, by unanimous agreement, invite any
other European state in a position to further the principles of
this Treaty and to contribute to the security of the North
Atlantic area to accede to this Treaty. Any state so invited may
become a party to the Treaty by depositing its instrument of
accession with the Government of the United States of America.
. . .

(98) SPECIAL MESSAGE TO SENATE, PRESIDENT TRUMAN, April 12, 1949
[Extract]

Source: *Public Papers of the Presidents: Harry S. Truman, 1949.*
Washington: U.S. Government Printing Office, 1964, pp. 206 207.

I transmit herewith for the consideration of the Senate a copy
of the North Atlantic Treaty signed at Washington on April 4,
1949, together with a report of the Secretary of State.

This Treaty is an expression of the desire of the people of
the United States for peace and security, for the continuing opportunity to live and work in freedom.

Events of this century have taught us that we cannot achieve
peace independently. The world has grown too small. The oceans
to our east and west no longer protect us from the reach of
brutality and aggression.

We have also learned - learned in blood and conflict - that
if we are to achieve peace we must work for peace.

This knowledge has made us determined to do everything we can
to insure that peace is maintained. . . . we cannot escape the
great responsibility that goes with our great stature in the
world. . . .

The twelve nations which have signed this Treaty undertake to
exercise their right of collective or individual self-defense
against armed attack, in accordance with Article 51 of the United
Nations Charter, and subject to such measures as the Security
Council may take to maintain and restore international peace and
security. The Treaty makes clear the determination of the people
of the United States and of our neighbors in the North Atlantic
community to do their utmost to maintain peace with justice and
to take such action as they may deem necessary if the peace is
broken.

The people of the North Atlantic community have seen solemn agreements, designed to assure peace and the rights of small nations, broken one by one and the people of those nations deprived of freedom by terror and oppression. They are resolved that their nations shall not, one by one, suffer the same fate. . . .

The security and welfare of each member of this community depend upon the security and welfare of all. None of us alone can achieve economic prosperity or military security. None of us alone can assure the continuance of freedom.

Together, our joint strength is of tremendous significance to the future of free men in every part of the world. For this Treaty is clear evidence that differences in language and in economic and political systems are no real bar to the effective association of nations devoted to the great principles of human freedom and justice.

This Treaty is only one step - although a long one - on the road to peace. No single action, no matter how significant, will achieve peace. We must continue to work patiently and carefully, advancing with practical, realistic steps in the light of circumstances and events as they occur, building the structure of peace soundly and solidly. . . .

(99) SANACC 360/11, REPORT BY STATE-NAVY-AIR FORCE COORDINATING COMMITTEE, August 18, 1948 [Extract]

Source: *Foreign Relations of the United States: 1949 Vol. I National Security Affairs; Foreign Economic Policy*. Washington: U.S. Government Printing Office, 1976. p. 265.

****

5. The United States is now engaged in the political phase of a conflict with the Soviet-dominated world. Under these conditions, the security interests of the United States, insofar as action by other countries is involved, may be advanced most effectively by preventing Soviet Communist expansion, which may take place either by political means or by direct military action. The purpose, then, of military aid is to prevent indirect and to deter direct Soviet-inspired aggression. Politically, United States military aid will strengthen the determination of recipient countries to resist aggression. By strenthening internal security forces, such aid will act as a preventive of Communist political expansion. Further, United States military aid will enhance the capabilities of the recipient countries to resist armed aggression. Events have indicated that political or indirect aggression is most likely to succeed in the proximity of the Soviet Army. These concepts suggest a broad approach to the problem by giving general precedence in assistance to those countries on the periphery of the Soviet world, subject to modifications required by obvious strategic considerations, such as keeping open lines of communications through the Mediterranean and preserving the United Kingdom for use as a source of production and as an advanced base. . . .

(100) REPORT TO PRESIDENT, SPECIAL COMMITTEE OF THE NATIONAL SECURITY COUNCIL, March 2, 1949 [Extract]

Source: *Foreign Relations of the United States: 1949 Vol. I National Security Affairs; Foreign Economic Policy*. Washington: U.S. Government Printing Office, 1976, p. 449.

****

1. The Nature of the Weapon.

The atomic bomb should neither be considered an absolute weapon which can win wars by itself nor "just another weapon" which should be treated as all others. The importance of the atomic bomb can best be evaluated in the light of the predominant position it has been given in the strategic war plans of this Government and the United Kingdom Government as well. The common war plans are built around the concept that atomic bombs will form the central core of our offensive capabilities in the case of the outbreak of war. It is considered that the bomb will provide immediate means of counter attack and retaliation; it will provide our only offensive in the early months of conflict; and it will accomplish in a short space of time what conventional weapons could accomplish only over a much longer period. Moreover, the initial paralyzing impact of atomic bombs will, at minimum, furnish the time required to mount an offensive combined with more conventional means of warfare. It is in this sense that the atomic bomb, while neither absolute nor ordinary, must be considered a unique weapon. This evaluation of the nature of the bomb is reinforced by the fact that as of the present the United States alone possesses them. Once the Soviet Union has atomic bombs a critical reexamination of our war plans will probably be required.
. . .

(101) MINUTES, POLICY PLANNING STAFF, DEPARTMENT OF STATE, October 12, 1949

Source: *Foreign Relations of the United States: 1949 Vol. I National Security Affairs; Foreign Economic Policy*. Washington: U.S. Government Printing Office, 1976, pp. 191-192.

Mr. Kennan explained that at the request of the Secretary we were undertaking to reassess the U.S. position on international control of atomic energy. In this connection we would of course examine the military implications of the [recent, September 1949] atomic explosion in Russia.

Colonel [Don] Zimmerman [Plans and Operations, Department of the Army] explained that he and his associates did not speak for the JCS [Joint Chiefs of Staff] or the NME [National Military Establishment]. He also explained that he and his associates had always considered the problem of atomic warfare on the assumption that the U.S. and its antagonist would each have a stockpile of bombs.

Col Zimmerman and Col. [George] Beller [Plans and Operations, Department of the Army] . . . [then stated]:

1. If the USSR should occupy Western Europe, the United States would not be able to develop the superiority necessary to

retake the continent, in view of the advantages which would be with the defensive in such an operation, given the use of ABC [atomic bomb armaments]. The US would then be faced with a military stalemate during which it could not be assumed that time would be running in our favor. To win a war against the USSR, therefore, it would be essential for the U.S. to hold Western Europe. The United States could not hold Western Europe by means of conventional armaments. With ABC built into balanced military forces we could defend it, assuming we had air superiority.

2. The knowledge of the existence in the US of ABC potential with balanced military forces would be the best deterrent to war.

3. The U.K. would probably not "cave in" as a result of atomic attack or threat of attack.

4. Russia would use the atomic bomb in war if she found that it would be desirable and effective; the threat of retaliation would not deter Russia from using it.

5. Although no explicit decision has been made as to whether the U.S. would use the bomb in war, the fact that our military establishment is being built around it makes the nature of the decision almost a foregone conclusion.

6. The subject of general disarmament has never been properly approached and it may be possible to devise a plan which would be both workable and acceptable to the U.S.S.R.

7. This is the worst possible time for us to have the majority UN plan accepted as we now have such a tremendous superiority in our stockpile of atomic weapons.

8. It seems likely that the Russians from now on will develop atomic weapons rapidly and make more efficient use of raw materials than we have up to this point.

9. In summary, the U.S. should continue the development of a balanced military force and ABC, including the modernizing of our atomic production facilities; we should immediately go in for a program for civilian defense; we should plan for the defense of Western Europe; and simultaneously we should work up a program for general disarmament.

(102) PRESS CONFERENCE, PRESIDENT TRUMAN, October 19, 1949 [Extract]

Source: *Public Papers of the Presidents: Harry S. Truman, 1949.* Washington: U.S. Government Printing Office, 1964, p. 519.

Question: Mr. President, there's a lot of interest in the United Nations on the atomic question, as a result of your announcement about the Russians. I was wondering if you could give us any idea as to the way your thinking is going? There seem to be two ways of going at it in the General Assembly. One might be that the United States would agree not to use the bomb except on authorization of the Security Council, without the veto, and of course that will be on the . . .

THE PRESIDENT: Don't you think it probable Russia would veto that?

Question: It wouldn't be subject to the veto.

THE PRESIDENT: The Russians would veto it before we had a chance to use it. They would bring one over here, and use it. What are you going to do about that?

Question: No - but a vote would be taken. Another was the possible change in our proposals for international control.

THE PRESIDENT: How would we change that?

Question: Well, I am asking you, sir?

THE PRESIDENT: How would you change that? We made the best proposition that has ever been made in the history of the world. No nation in the history of the world has ever done what we did in the proposition.

Question: You don't feel that cooperation . . .

THE PRESIDENT: We have given them everything we have got, but we want something in return. We want assurance that we will get the same treatment that we have given. That's all we are asking.

Someone was in to see me just recently, and he asked why we didn't go ahead and make peace. "Why don't you get to the Russians and fix this thing up?" he said. I said, "All right, we will give them Berlin, we will give them Germany, we will give them Korea, we will give them Japan, we will give them East Asia. Then they will settle. Is that what you want?" "Oh no, that isn't what we want at all, " he said. That's what they want.

(103) <u>MEMORANDUM, CARLTON SAVAGE (POLICY PLANNING STAFF, DEPT. OF STATE) AND ROBERT HOOKER (ASSOCIATE CHIEF, DIVISION OF EASTERN EUROPEAN AFFAIRS, DEPT. OF STATE) TO GEORGE KENNAN (DIRECTOR OF POLICY PLANNING STAFF)</u>, November 14, 1949 [Extract]

Source: *Foreign Relations of the United States: 1949 Vol. I National Security Affairs; Foreign Economic Policy*. Washington: U.S. Government Printing Office, 1976, p. 221.

****

<u>National Commission</u>. We <u>do not</u> favor the appointment of a National Commission to reassess the U.S. position on international control. We <u>do</u> favor continuing the investigation of the subject in the Executive Branch of the Government under the leadership of the State Department, but with the counsel of authorities outside the Government. This should produce the same results as a National commission without the dangers inherent in the naming of a public body. . . .

(104) MEMORANDUM, OMAR BRADLEY (CHAIRMAN, JOINT CHIEFS OF STAFF) TO SECRETARY OF DEFENSE LOUIS JOHNSON, November 23, 1949

Source: *Foreign Relations of the United States: 1949 Vol. I National Security Affairs; Foreign Economic Policy.* Washington: U.S. Government Printing Office, 1976, pp. 595-596.

The Joint Chiefs of Staff have studied the subject matter of this memorandum and have reached the following conclusions:

That the United States military position with respect to the development of the thermonuclear weapon should be:

a. Possession of a thermonuclear weapon by the USSR without such possession by the United States would be intolerable.

b. There is an imperative necessity of determining the feasibility of a thermonuclear explosion and its characteristics. Such determination is essential for US defense planning, preparations for retaliation, and direction of research. It will have a profound effect on policy in the field of international affairs.

c. If a thermonuclear weapon is determined to be feasible, the following additional considerations pertaining to military requirements are currently evident:

(1) Possession of such weapons by the United States may act as a possible deterrent to war.

(2) Possession of such weapons by the United States will provide an offensive weapon of the greatest known power possibilities thereby adding flexibility to our planning and to our operations in the event of hostilities.

d. The cost in money, materials, and industrial effort of developing a thermonuclear weapon appears to be within the capabilities of the United States. Available information indicates that such a weapon may likewise be within the capability of the USSR.

e. It is reasonable to anticipate, and in some cases it is known, that a number of thermonuclear weapons can substitute for a greater number of fission bombs. Further, the thermonuclear weapon promises in the high ranges of energy release to be more efficient in utilization of available ore and production capacity per unit area of damage.

f. The foregoing considerations decisively outweigh the possible social, psychological and moral objections which may be considered to argue against research and development leading to a thermonuclear weapon by the United States.

g. Any decisions or actions pertaining to the United States' effort to develop a thermonuclear weapon or any determination of its feasibility constitute a military secret of the highest classification. It should be possible to maintain secrecy on a subject of such importance to the security of the United States.

h. A unilateral decision on the part of the United States not to develop a thermonuclear weapon will not prevent the development of such a weapon elsewhere.

(105) REPORT TO THE PRESIDENT, SPECIAL COMMITTEE OF THE NATIONAL SECURITY COUNCIL, January 31, 1950 [Extract]

Source: *Foreign Relations of the United States: 1950 Vol. I National Security Affairs; Foreign Economic Policy.* Washington: U.S. Government Printing Office, 1977, pp. 513-517.

1. By letter to Mr. [Sidney] Souers [Executive Secretary, NSC] dated November 19, 1949, the President designated the Secretary of State, the Secretary of Defense, and the Chairman of the Atomic Energy Commission as a special Committee of the National Security Council to make recommendations

a. "as to whether and in what manner the United States should undertake the development and possible production of 'super' atomic weapons," and

b. "as to whether and when any publicity should be given to this matter."

ANALYSIS

2. . . . The question presented is whether the United States should undertake at this time an accelerated program to determine the feasibility of a thermonuclear weapon, should continue its research at the present rate, or should place a moratorium on further work in this field.

3. An all-out effort leading to both a feasibility test and quantity production of "supers" would seriously impair the efficiency and output of the fission bomb program, . . . an accelerated research and development program to test the feasibility of such a weapon (as distinguished from a quantity production program) would require a minimum time of three years; that with such a target date other weapon developments now under way, principally lighter and smaller weapons aimed at improved deliverability . . . could probably still be carried out, but not with the care and refinement originally planned; that this probable decrease in refinement would not be sufficiently important to serve as a deterrent to an accelerated effort on thermonuclear research and development . . . the important consideration from a military point of view appears to be that the most advantageous rate and scale of effort would be such as to produce a weapon for testing as soon as possible without significant impairment to the quantity output of fission weapons as scheduled . . .

4. In the present state of knowledge, it appears that there is at least a 50-50 chance that a thermonuclear weapon will be feasible, but this cannot be determined except by actual test . . .

5. It is estimated on the basis of technical studies . . . that an accelerated program including ordnance and carrier development, is within the capabilities of the United States from the point of view of money, materials, and industrial effort.

6. Knowledge as to whether the thermonuclear bomb is or is not feasible and knowledge as to its potentialities and limitations, if feasible, are of importance to military planning and foreign policy planning . . .

7. It must be considered whether a decision to proceed with a program directed toward determining feasibility prejudices the more fundamental decisions (a) as to whether, in the event that a test of a thermonuclear weapon proves successful, such weapons should be stockpiled, or (b) if stockpiled, the conditions under which they might be used in war. If a test of a thermonuclear weapon proves successful, the pressures to produce and stockpile such weapons to be held for the same purposes for which fission bombs are then being held will be greatly increased. The question of use policy can be adequately assessed only as a part of a general reexamination of this country's strategic plans and its objectives in peace and war. Such reexamination would need to consider national policy not only with respect to possible thermonuclear weapons, but also with respect to fission weapons - viewed in the light of the probable fission bomb capability and the possible thermonuclear bomb capability of the Soviet Union. The moral, psychological, and political questions involved in this problem would need to be taken into account and be given due weight. The outcome of this reexamination would have a crucial bearing on the further question as to whether there should be a revision in the nature of the agreements, including the international control of atomic energy, which we have been seeking to reach with the U.S.S.R.

8. There is evidence which leads to the belief that the Soviet Union prefers to put its chief reliance on winning the cold war rather than precipitating a hot war. There is also ground for the belief that the Soviet Union would prefer not to use weapons of mass destruction except in the event of prior use by others. These assumptions might appear to argue for renunciation by the United States of work in the field of thermonuclear weapons. We cannot safely assume, however, that these hypotheses are correct. Even if they are correct, it cannot be assumed that the Soviet Union would forego development of the fission bomb. Sole possession by the Soviet Union of this weapon would cause severe damage not only to our military posture but to our foreign policy position.

9. There is also the question of possible effect on Soviet attitudes and actions of a decision to proceed with a program to test the feasibility of thermonuclear weapons.

a. Would a decision on the part of the United States to go ahead with an accelerated program cause the Soviet Union to press ahead in this field more vigorously? . . . The Soviet Union probably has felt it could not make any other assumption than that the United States is working on such a weapon, especially in view of the public discussion that has already taken place. It is difficult to escape the conclusion that the Soviet Union will make an intensive effort to produce thermonuclear weapons. A decision to accelerate our program may cause the Soviet Union to increase the priority of these efforts. Knowledge by the U.S.S.R. that we had successfully completed development of a thermonuclear weapon might have the effect of increasing the probability that the USSR would successfully develop a similar weapon. These are risks which are difficult to measure, but which we must frankly face up to if a decision is made to accelerate our development program.

b. It does not appear likely that the character of United States military developments will have a decisive effect on Soviet military developments or be the cause of an arms race. The Soviet decision to reequip its armies and devote major energies to developing war potential, after the end of the war and at a time when we were disbanding our armies, was based on considerations more profound than our possession of the atomic weapon.

10. a. The possibility of the Russians developing a thermonuclear weapons capability, added to their probably growing fission bomb capability, re-emphasizes the importance of effective international control of the entire field of atomic energy. Even if we can find a new approach to the control of atomic energy which would be acceptable to us and to our allies, and which offers greater prospect than the UN plan of being negotiable with Russia, the necessary negotiations probably could not be completed in less than a year and a half or two years. But to delay an accelerated program of development for such a period in the absence of adequate assurance that work in the Soviet Union had been similarly delayed, would measurably increase the prospect of prior Soviet possession of thermonuclear weapons.

b. It has been suggested that a decision should be deferred until an approach has been made to the Soviet Union proposing that both nations forego work in the field of thermonuclear weapons. If such a proposal were coupled with a plan for the necessary safeguards to insure that the renunciation was in fact being carried out – these safeguards necessarily involving an opening up of Soviet territory – it is the view of the Department of State that the proposition would be unacceptable to the Soviet Union to the same degree that the United Nations plan for the control of atomic energy is unacceptable. If not coupled with safeguards, it is not believed that sufficient assurance would be gained from such an agreement to make it worth while.

11. In the light of the foregoing considerations, the following recommendations are made:

a. That the President direct the Atomic Energy Commission to proceed to determine the technical feasibility of a thermonuclear weapon, the scale and rate of effort to be determined jointly by the Atomic Energy Commission and the Department of Defense; and that the necessary ordnance development and carrier program be undertaken concurrently;

b. That the President direct the Secretary of State and the Secretary of Defense to undertake a reexamination of our objectives in peace and war and of the effect of these objectives on our strategic plans, in the light of the probable fission bomb capability and possible thermonuclear bomb capability of the Soviet Union;

c. That the President indicate publicly the intention of this Government to continue work to determine the feasibility of a thermonuclear weapon, and that no further official information on it be made public without the approval of the President. . . .

(106) STATEMENT, PRESIDENT TRUMAN, January 31, 1950

Source: *Public Papers of the Presidents: Harry S. Truman, 1950.*
Washington: U.S. Government Printing Office, 1965, p. 138.

It is part of my responsibility as Commander in Chief of the
Armed Forces to see to it that our country is able to defend itself against any possible aggressor. Accordingly, I have directed
the Atomic Energy Commission to continue its work on all forms of
atomic weapons, including the so-called hydrogen or superbomb.
Like all other work in the field of atomic weapons, it is being
and will be carried forward on a basis consistent with the overall
objectives of our program for peace and security.

This we shall continue to do until a satisfactory plan for
international control of atomic energy is achieved. We shall also
continue to examine all those factors that affect our program for
peace and this country's security.

*The impact of the Soviet Union's development of an atomic
bomb on Administration officials was not confined to assessing
whether to proceed with thermonuclear weapons development. Already convinced that Soviet leaders were bent on world conquest
and interpreting radical or revolutionary developments as either
directed by the Soviet Union or benefitting Soviet interests,
Truman Administration officials began to assess the required measures to defeat this challenge. The economic and political costs
of their preferred policy - including whether the nation could or
should bear the costs - were outlined sharply in NSC #68. These
costs caused Administration officials to hesitate. Their hesita-
tion, however, was based principally on domestic political considerations: how best to sell this policy to a basically ignorant and short-sighted public. One result was to accentuate elitist tendencies within the Administration - after all the policy
was right but the Administration's opponents were irrational. A
second result was the decision to adopt an alarmist rhetoric to
"scare the hell" out of the public and the Congress as the most
effective means for securing the needed support for this costly
and risky policy. In the midst of this intra-Adminstration assessment came the Korean War. The political difficulties of conducting such a war - adopting an alarmist posture emphasizing the
costs of failure but seeking to limit the war militarily and avert
its escalation to a global conflict - bedevilled the Administration throughout its remaining years in power.*

(107) DRAFT MEMORANDUM, GEORGE KENNAN TO SECRETARY OF STATE
ACHESON, February 17, 1950 [Extract]

Source: *Foreign Relations of the United States: 1950 Vol. I
National Security Affairs; Foreign Economic Policy.* Washington:
U.S. Government Printing Office, 1977, pp. 166-167.

****

4. I think it quite essential that we find a new and much
more effective approach to the problem of making our policies
understood within this Government and among our own people. This

relates particularly to those interrelationships of policy which are of a relatively subtle nature and for the understanding of which some knowledge of the theory of foreign relations is essential. Up to this time, it seems to me, we have been quite unsuccessful in this. You still have the most distinguished and influential of our columnists and diplomatic observers making statements which reflect an almost incredible ignorance of basic elements of our foreign policy, to say nothing of the state of mind of Congressional circles.

The first prerequisite for people who are to concern themselves with explaining policy to others is that they themselves should understand it. It is not uncharitable to point out that this qualification is not generally obtained without considerable experience and intellectual discipline. We have gone thus far on the principle that the teachers themselves require no teaching; that they imbibe what they need to know by their mere presence and activity within the institution of the Department of State. This is our first mistake.

Our second is the belief that we can achieve our purposes in this field without real ideological discipline. I think that we must not fear the principle of indoctrination within the government service. The Secretary of State is charged personally by the President with the conduct of foreign affairs, and there is no reason why he should not insist that his views and interpretations be those of the entire official establishment. There is no reason why every responsible officer of the Department and Foreign Service should not be schooled and drilled in the handling of the sort of questions concerning our foreign policy which are raised morning after morning by Lippmann and Krock and others. What we need here is a section of the Department charged not only with the briefing, but with the training and drilling, of our official personnel on political matters. And this operation should extend beyond the walls of this Department and into other departments closely concerned with foreign policy, particularly the armed services and the Treasury.

The elaboration of a body of policy thought and rationale which can be taught in this manner will do more than anything I can think of not only to improve our general impact on press and Congress and public. Without this type of discipline and singleness of purpose, I do not think the problem can be mastered. And unless it is mastered, there seems to me to be serious and urgent danger that our present policy toward the Soviet Union will founder on the lack of popular support.

(108) <u>MEMORANDUM, ASSISTANT SECRETARY OF STATE EDWARD BARRETT TO SECRETARY OF STATE ACHESON</u>, April 6, 1950 [Extract]

Source: *Foreign Relations of the United States: 1950 Vol. I National Security Affairs; Foreign Economic Policy*. Washington: U.S. Government Printing Office, 1977, pp. 225-226.

****

My most important point: the whole paper seems to me to point to a gigantic armament race, a huge buildup of conventional arms that quickly become obsolescent, a greatly expanded military

establishment in being. I think that, however much we whip up
sentiment, we are going to run into vast opposition among informed
people to a huge arms race. We will be warned that we are heading
toward a "garrison state". Moreover, even if we should sell the
idea, I fear that the U.S. public would rapidly tire of such an
effort. In the absence of real and continuing crises, a dictatorship can unquestionably out last a democracy in a conventional
armament race.

On the other hand, I believe the American public can be sold
on programs to build up our strength in those fields in which we
have natural superiority. . . .

This whole plan underscores again the wisdom of the current
proposal for a cold war headquarters, probably attached directly
to the White House.

If and when this whole project is approved by the President,
the public education campaign must obviously receive the most
careful study. I will forward within the next few days some detailed recommendations for this campaign. In the meantime, I
would like to point out the following: The first step in the campaign is obviously building up a full public awareness of the
problem. This might take three months or it might require no more
than ten days. My hunch is that it will be nearer ten days. We
must be sure that the Government is in a position to come forward
with positive steps to be taken just as soon as the atmosphere is
right. It is imperative, for both domestic and overseas reasons,
that there should not be too much of a time lag between the creation of a public awareness of the problem and the setting forth of
a positive Government program to solve that problem.

In other words, we should have at least the broad proposals
for action well in hand before the psychological "scare campaign"
is started.

(109) NATICNAL SECURITY COUNCIL DIRECTIVE 68, NSC-68, April 7,
1950 [Extract]

Source: *Foreign Relations of the United States: 1950 Vol. I
National Security Affairs; Foreign Economic Policy*. Washington:
U.S. Government Printing Office, 1977, pp. 262-272, 282-288, 290-
292.

. . . the integrity and vitality of our system is in greater
jeopardy than ever before in our history. Even if there were no
Soviet Union we would face the great problem of the free society,
accentuated many fold in this industrial age, of reconciling
order, security, the need for participation, with the requirements
of freedom. We would face the fact that in a shrinking world the
absence of order among nations is becoming less and less tolerable. The Kremlin design seeks to impose order among nations
by means which would destroy our free and democratic system. The
Kremlin's possession of atomic weapons puts new power behind its
design, and increases the jeopardy to our system. It adds new
strains to the uneasy equilibrium-without-order which exists in
the world and raises new doubts in men's minds whether the world
will long tolerate this tension without moving toward some kind
of order, on somebody's terms.

The risks we face are of a new order of magnitude, commensurate with the total struggle in which we are engaged. . . . These risks crowd in on us, in a shrinking world of polarized power, so as to give us no choice, ultimately, between meeting them effectively or being overcome by them.

. . . the Kremlin seeks to bring the free world under its dominion by the methods of the cold war. The preferred technique is to subvert by infiltration and intimidation. Every institution of our society is an instrument which it is sought to stultify and turn against our purposes. Those that touch most closely our material and moral strength are obviously the prime targets, labor unions, civic enterprises, schools, churches, and all media for influencing opinion. The effort is not so much to make them serve obvious Soviet ends as to prevent them from serving our ends, and thus to make them sources of confusion in our economy, our culture and our body politic. The doubts and diversities that in terms of our values are part of the merit of a free system, the weaknesses and the problems that are peculiar to it, the rights and privileges that free men enjoy, and the disorganization and destruction left in the wake of the last attack on our freedoms, all are but opportunities for the Kremlin to do its evil work. Every advantage is taken of the fact that our means of prevention and retaliation are limited by those principles and scruples which are precisely the ones that give our freedom and democracy its meaning for us. . . .

At the same time the Soviet Union is seeking to create overwhelming military force, in order to back up infiltration with intimidation. . . . it is seeking to demonstrate to the free world that force and the will to use it are on the side of the Kremlin, that those who lack it are decadent and doomed. In local incidents it threatens and encroaches both for the sake of local gains and to increase anxiety and defeatism in all the free world.

The possession of atomic weapons at each of the opposite poles of power, and the inability (for different reasons) of either side to place any trust in the other, puts a premium on a surprise attack against us. It equally puts a premium on a more violent and ruthless prosecution of its design by cold war, especially if the Kremlin is sufficiently objective to realize the improbability of our prosecuting a preventive war. It also puts a premium on piecemeal aggression against others, counting on our unwillingness to engage in atomic war unless we are directly attacked. . . .

The risk that we may thereby be prevented or too long delayed in taking all needful measures to maintain the integrity and vitality of our system is great. The risk that in this manner a descending spiral of too little and too late, of doubt and recrimination, may present us with ever narrower and more desperate alternatives, is the greatest risk of all. . . .

The risk of having no better choice than to capitulate or precipitate a global war at any of a number of pressure points is bad enough in itself, but it is multiplied by the weakness it imparts to our position in the cold war. Instead of appearing strong and resolute we are continually at the verge of appearing and being alternately irresolute and desperate; yet it is the cold war which we must win, because both the Kremlin design, and our fundamental purpose give it the first priority. . . .

But there are risks in making ourselves strong. A large measure of sacrifice and discipline will be demanded of the American people. They will be asked to give up some of the benefits which they have come to associate with their freedoms. Nothing could be more important than that they fully understand the reasons for this. The risks of a superficial understanding or of an inadequate appreciation of the issues are obvious and might lead to the adoption of measures which in themselves would jeopardize the integrity of our system. . . . Our fundamental purpose is more likely to be defeated from lack of the will to maintain it, than from any mistakes we may make or assault we may undergo because of asserting that will. No people in history have preserved their freedom who thought that by not being strong enough to protect themselves they might prove inoffensive to their enemies.

. . . The United States now has an atomic capability . . . to deliver a serious blow against the war-making capacity of the U.S.S.R. It is doubted whether such a blow, even if it resulted in the complete destruction of the contemplated target systems, would cause the U.S.S.R. to sue for terms or prevent Soviet forces from occupying Western Europe against such ground resistance as could presently be mobilized. A very serious initial blow could, however, so reduce the capabilities of the U.S.S.R. to supply and equip its military organization and its civilian population as to give the United States the prospect of developing a general military superiority in a war of long duration.

2. As the atomic capability of the U.S.S.R. increases, it will have an increased ability to hit at our atomic bases and installations and thus seriously hamper the ability of the United States to carry out an attack such as that outlined above. It is quite possible that in the near future the U.S.S.R. will have a sufficient number of atomic bombs and a sufficient deliverability to raise a question whether Britain with its present inadequate air defense could be relied upon as an advance base from which a major portion of the U.S. attack could be launched.

It is estimated that, within the next four years, the U.S.S.R. will attain the capability of seriously damaging vital centers of the United States, provided it strikes a surprise blow and provided further that the blow is opposed by no more effective opposition than we now have programmed. Such a blow could so seriously damage the United States as to greatly reduce its superiority in economic potential. . . .

3. In the initial phases of an atomic war, the advantages of initiative and surprise would be very great. A police state living behind an iron curtain has an enormous advantage in maintaining the necessary security and centralization of decision required to capitalize on this advantage.

4. For the moment our atomic retaliatory capability is probably adequate to deter the Kremlin from a deliberate direct military attack against ourselves or other free peoples. However, when it calculates that it has a sufficient atomic capability to make a surprise attack on us, nullifying our atomic superiority and creating a military situation decisively in its favor, the Kremlin might be tempted to strike swiftly and with stealth. . . .

5. A further increase in the number and power of our atomic weapons is necessary in order to assure the effectiveness of any

U.S. retaliatory blow, . . . Greatly increased general air, ground and sea strength, and increased air defense programs would also be necessary to provide reasonable assurance that the free world could survive an initial surprise atomic attack of the weight which it is estimated the U.S.S.R. will be capable of delivering by 1954 and still permit the free world to go on to the eventual attainment of its objectives. Furthermore, such a build-up of strength could safeguard and increase our retaliatory power, and thus might put off for some time the date when the Soviet Union could calculate that a surprise blow would be advantageous. This would provide additional time for the effects of our policies to produce a modification of the Soviet system.

6. If the U.S.S.R. develops a thermonuclear weapon ahead of the U.S., the risks of greatly increased Soviet pressure against all the free world, or an attack against the U.S., will be greatly increased.

7. If the U.S. develops a thermonuclear weapon ahead of the U.S.S.R., the U.S. should for the time being be able to bring increased pressure on the U.S.S.R. . . .

In the event of a general war with the U.S.S.R., it must be anticipated that atomic weapons will be used by each side in the manner it deems best suited to accomplish its objectives. In view of our vulnerability to Soviet atomic attack, it has been argued that we might wish to hold our atomic weapons only for retaliation against prior use by the U.S.S.R. To be able to do so and still have hope of achieving our objectives, the non-atomic military capabilities of ourselves and our allies would have to be fully developed and the political weaknesses of the Soviet Union fully exploited. In the event of war, however, we could not be sure that we could move toward the attainment of these objectives without the U.S.S.R.'s resorting sooner or later to the use of its atomic weapons. Only if we had overwhelming atomic superiority and obtained command of the air might the U.S.S.R. be deterred from employing its atomic weapons as we progressed toward the attainment of our objectives.

In the event the U.S.S.R. develops by 1954 the atomic capability which we now anticipate, it is hardly conceivable that, if war comes, the Soviet leaders would refrain from the use of atomic weapons unless they felt fully confident of attaining their objectives by other means.

In the event we use atomic weapons either in retaliation for their prior use by the U.S.S.R. or because there is no alternative method by which we can attain our objectives, it is imperative that the strategic and tactical targets against which they are used be appropriate and the manner in which they are used be consistent with those objectives.

. . . we should produce and stockpile thermonuclear weapons in the event they prove feasible and would add significantly to our net capability. Not enough is yet known of their potentialities to warrant a judgment at this time regarding their use in war to attain our objectives.

. . . In our present situation of relative unpreparedness in conventional weapons, . . . a declaration [not to use atomic weapons except in retaliation against prior use] would be interpreted

by the U.S.S.R. as an admission of great weakness and by our
allies as a clear indication that we intended to abandon them.
Furthermore, it is doubtful whether such a declaration would be
taken sufficiently seriously by the Kremlin to constitute an important factor in determining whether or not to attack the United
States. . . .

Unless we are prepared to abandon our objectives, we cannot
make such a declaration in good faith until we are confident that
we will be in a position to attain our objectives without war, or,
in the event of war, without recourse to the use of atomic weapons
for strategic or tactical purposes. . . .

No system of international control could prevent the production and use of atomic weapons in the event of a prolonged war.
Even the most effective system of international control could, of
itself, only provide (a) assurance that atomic weapons had been
eliminated from national peacetime armaments and (b) immediate
notice of a violation. In essence, an effective international
control system would be expected to assure a certain amount of
time after notice of violation before atomic weapons could be used
in war. . . .

The most substantial contribution to security of an effective
international control system would, of course, be the opening up
of the Soviet Union, . . . Such opening up is not, however, compatible with the maintenance of the Soviet system in its present
rigor. . . .

The studies which began with the Acheson-Lilienthal committee
[of 1945] and culminated in the present U.S. plan [introduced in
1946] made it clear that inspection of atomic facilities would not
alone give the assurance of control; but that ownership and operation by an international authority of the world's atomic energy
activities from the mine to the last use of fissionable materials
was also essential. The delegation of sovereignty which this
implies is necessary for effective control and, therefore, is as
necessary for the United States and the rest of the free world as
it is presently unacceptable to the Soviet Union.

It is also clear that a control authority not susceptible directly or indirectly to Soviet domination is equally essential.
As the Soviet Union would regard any country not under its domination as under the potential if not the actual domination of the
United States, it is clear that what the United States and the
non-Soviet world must insist on, the Soviet Union must at present
reject.

The principal immediate benefit of international control would
be to make a surprise atomic attack impossible, assuming the elimination of large reactors and the effective disposal of stockpiles
of fissionable materials. But it is almost certain that the
Soviet Union would not agree to the elimination of large reactors,
unless the impracticability of producing atomic power for peaceful purposes had been demonstrated beyond a doubt. By the same
token, it would not now agree to elimination of its stockpile of
fissionable materials.

Finally, the absence of good faith on the part of the U.S.S.R.
must be assumed until there is concrete evidence that there has
been a decisive change in Soviet policies. It is to be doubted

whether such a change can take place without a change in the nature of the Soviet system itself.

The above considerations make it clear that at least a major change in the relative power positions of the United States and the Soviet Union would have to take place before an effective system of international control could be negotiated. The Soviet Union would have had to have moved a substantial distance down the path of accommodation and compromise before such an arrangement would be conceivable. . . .

In short, it is impossible to hope that an effective plan for international control can be negotiated unless and until the Kremlin design has been frustrated to a point at which a genuine and drastic change in Soviet policies has taken place. . . .

[There are] four possible courses of action by the United States . . . :

a. Continuation of current policies, with current and currently projected programs for carrying out these policies;

b. Isolation;

c. War; and

d. A more rapid building up of the political, economic, and military strength of the free world than provided under a, with the purpose of reaching, if possible, a tolerable state of order among nations without war and of preparing to defend ourselves in the event that the free world is attacked. . . .

****

A more rapid build-up of political, economic, and military strength and thereby of confidence in the free world than is now contemplated is the only course which is consistent with progress toward achieving our fundamental purpose. The frustration of the Kremlin design requires the free world to develop a successfully functioning political and economic system and a vigorous political offensive against the Soviet Union. These, in turn, require an adequate military shield under which they can develop. It is necessary to have the military power to deter, if possible, Soviet expansion, and to defeat, if necessary, aggressive Soviet or Soviet-directed actions of a limited or total character. . . .

. . . U.S. military capabilities are strategically more defensive in nature than offensive and are more potential than actual. . . . there is now and will be in the future no absolute defense. The history of war also indicates that a favorable decision can only be achieved through offensive action. Even a defensive strategy, if it is to be successful, calls not only for defensive forces to hold vital positions while mobilizing and preparing for the offensive, but also for offensive forces to attack the enemy and keep him off balance. . . .

. . . a build-up of military strength by the United States and its allies [is required] to a point at which the combined strength will be superior . . . , both initially and throughout a war, to the forces that can be brought to bear by the Soviet Union and its satellites. . . . it is not essential to match item for item with the Soviet Union, but to provide an adequate defense

against air attack on the United States and Canada and an adequate
defense against air and surface attack on the United Kingdom and
Western Europe, Alaska, the Western Pacific, Africa, and the Near
and Middle East, and on the long lines of communication to these
areas. . . . in building up our strength, we [must] enlarge upon
our technical superiority by an accelerated exploitation of the
scientific potential of the United States and our allies.

Forces of this size and character are necessary not only for
protection against disaster but also to support our foreign policy. . . . larger forces in being and readily available are [more]
necessary to inhibit a would-be aggressor than to provide the
nucleus of strength and the mobilization base on which the tremendous forces required for victory can be built. . . . it is clear
that a substantial and rapid building up of strength in the free
world is necessary to support a firm policy intended to check and
to roll back the Kremlin's drive for world domination.

Moreover, the United States and the other free countries do
not now have the forces in being and readily available to defeat
local Soviet moves with local action, but must accept reverses or
make these local moves the occasion for war - for which we are not
prepared. This situation makes for great uneasiness among our
allies, particularly in Western Europe, for whom total war means,
initially, Soviet occupation. Thus, unless our combined strength
is rapidly increased, our allies will tend to become increasingly
reluctant to support a firm foreign policy on our part and increasingly anxious to seek other solutions, even though they are
aware that appeasement means defeat. An important advantage in
adopting the fourth course of action lies in its psychological
impact - the revival of confidence and hope in the future. . . .
any announcement of the recommended course of action could be
exploited by the Soviet Union in its peace campaign and would have
adverse psychological effects in certain parts of the free world
until the necessary increase in strength had been achieved.
Therefore, in any announcement of policy and in the character of
the measures adopted, emphasis should be given to the essentially
defensive character and care should be taken to minimize, so far
as possible, unfavorable domestic and foreign reactions.

. . . The immediate objectives - to the achievement of which
such a build-up of strength is a necessary though not a sufficient condition - are a renewed initiative in the cold war and a
situation to which the Kremlin would find it expedient to accom-
modate itself, first by relaxing tensions and pressures and then
by gradual withdrawal. The United States cannot alone provide the
resources required for such a build-up of strength. The other
free countries must carry their part of the burden, but their
ability and determination to do it will depend on the action the
United States takes to develop its own strength and on the adequacy of its foreign political and economic policies. . . .

At the same time, we should take dynamic steps to reduce the
power and influence of the Kremlin inside the Soviet Union and
other areas under its control. The objective would be the establishment of friendly regimes not under Kremlin domination. Such
action is essential to engage the Kremlin's attention, keep it
off balance and force an increased expenditure of Soviet resources
in counteraction. . . .

A program for rapidly building up strength and improving political and economic conditions will place heavy demands on our courage and intelligence; it will be costly; it will be dangerous. . . . Budgetary considerations will need to be subordinated to the stark fact that our very independence as a nation may be at stake.

A comprehensive and decisive program to win the peace and frustrate the Kremlin design should be so designed that it can be sustained for as long as necessary to achieve our national objectives. It would probably involve:

(1) The development of an adequate political and economic framework for the achievement of our long-range objectives.

(2) A substantial increase in expenditures for military purposes . . .

(3) A substantial increase in military assistance programs, designed to foster cooperative efforts, which will adequately and efficiently meet the requirements of our allies . . .

(4) Some increase in economic assistance programs and recognition of the need to continue these programs until their purposes have been accomplished. . . .

(6) Development of programs designed to build and maintain confidence among other peoples in our strength and resolution, and to wage overt psychological warfare calculated to encourage mass defections from Soviet allegiance and to frustrate the Kremlin design in other ways.

(7) Intensification of affirmative and timely measures and operations by covert means in the fields of economic warfare and political and psychological warfare with a view to fomenting and supporting unrest and revolt in selected strategic satellite countries.

(8) Development of internal security and civilian defense program.

(9) Improvement and intensification of intelligence activities.

(10) Reduction of Federal expenditures for purposes other than defense and foreign assistance, if necessary by the deferment of certain desirable programs.

(11) Increased taxes.

Essential as prerequisites to the success of this program would be (a) consultations with Congressional leaders designed to make the program the object of non-partisan legislative support, and (b) a presentation to the public of a full explanation of the facts and implications of present international trends.

The program will be costly, but it is relevant to recall the disproportion between the potential capabilities of the Soviet and non-Soviet worlds . . . The Soviet Union is currently devoting about 40 percent of available resources . . . to military expenditures (14 percent) and to investment (26 percent), much of which is in war-supporting industries. . . .

The United States is currently devoting about 22 percent of its gross national product . . . to military expenditures (6 percent), foreign assistance (2 percent), and investment (14 percent), little of which is in war-supporting industries. . . .

From the point of view of the economy as a whole, the program might not result in a real decrease in the standard of living, for the economic effects of the program might be to increase the gross national product by more than the amount being absorbed for additional military and foreign assistance purposes. . . .

The comparison gives renewed emphasis to the fact that the problems faced by the free countries in their efforts to build a successfully functioning system lie not so much in the field of economics as in the field of politics. The building of such a system may require more rapid progress toward the closer association of the free countries in harmony with the concept of the United Nations. It is clear that our long-range objectives require a strengthened United Nations, or a successor organization, to which the world can look for the maintenance of peace and order in a system based on freedom and justice. It also seems clear that a unifying ideal of this kind might awaken and arouse the latent spiritual energies of free men everywhere and obtain their enthusiastic support for a positive program for peace going far beyond the frustration of the Kremlin design and opening vistas to the future that would outweigh short-run sacrifices.

The threat to the free world involved in the development of the Soviet Union's atomic and other capabilities will rise steadily and rather rapidly. For the time being, the United States possesses a marked atomic superiority over the Soviet Union which, together with the potential capabilities of the United States and other free countries in other forces and weapons, inhibits aggressive Soviet action. This provides an opportunity for the United States, in cooperation with other free countries, to launch a build-up of strength which will support a firm policy directed to the frustration of the Kremlin design. . . . By acting promptly and vigorously . . . we would permit time for the process of accommodation, withdrawal and frustration to produce the necessary changes in the Soviet system. Time is short, however, and the risks of war attendant upon a decision to build up strength will steadily increase the longer we defer it.

CONCLUSIONS AND RECOMMENDATIONS

CONCLUSIONS

The foregoing analysis indicates that the probable fission bomb capability and possible thermonuclear bomb capability of the Soviet Union have greatly intensified the Soviet threat to the security of the United States. . . . In particular, the United States now faces the contingency that within the next four or five years the Soviet Union will possess the military capability of delivering a surprise atomic attack of such weight that the United States must have substantially increased general air, ground, and sea strength, atomic capabilities, and air and civilian defenses to deter war and to provide reasonable assurance, in the event of war, that it could survive the initial blow and go on to the eventual attainment of its objectives. In turn, this contingency requires the intensification of our efforts in the fields of intelligence and research and development. . . .

In the light of present and prospective Soviet atomic capabilities, the action which can be taken under present programs and plans, however, becomes dangerously inadequate, in both timing and scope, to accomplish the rapid progress toward the attainment of the United States political, economic, and military objectives which is now imperative.

A continuation of present trends would result in a serious decline in the strength of the free world relative to the Soviet Union and its satellites. This unfavorable trend arises from the inadequacy of current programs and plans rather than from any error in our objectives and aims. These trends lead in the direction of isolation, not by deliberate decision but by lack of the necessary basis for a vigorous initiative in the conflict with the Soviet Union.

Our position as the center of power in the free world places a heavy responsibility upon the United States for leadership. We must organize and enlist the energies and resources of the free world domination by creating a situation in the free world to which the Kremlin will be compelled to adjust. Without such a cooperative effort, led by the United States, we will have to make gradual withdrawals under pressure until we discover one day that we have sacrificed positions of vital interest.

It is imperative that this trend be reversed by a much more rapid and concerted build-up of the actual strength of both the United States and the other nations of the free world. The analysis shows that this will be costly and will involve significant domestic financial and economic adjustments.

The execution of such a build-up, however, requires that the United States have an affirmative program beyond the solely defensive one of countering the threat posed by the Soviet Union. This program . . . must envisage the political and economic measures with which and the military shield behind which the free world can work to frustrate the Kremlin design by the strategy of the cold war; for every consideration of devotion to our fundamental values and to our national security demands that we achieve our objectives by the strategy of the cold war, building up our military strength in order that it may not have to be used. The only sure victory lies in the frustration of the Kremlin design by the steady development of the moral and material strength of the free world and its projection into the Soviet world in such a way as to bring about an internal change in the Soviet system. Such a positive program - harmonious with our fundamental national purpose and our objectives - is necessary if we are to regain and retain the initiative and to win and hold the necessary popular support and cooperation in the United States and the rest of the free world.

This program should include a plan for negotiation with the Soviet Union, developed and agreed with our allies and which is consonant with our objectives. . . . The present world situation, however, is one which militates against successful negotiations with the Kremlin - for the terms of agreements on important pending issues would reflect present realities and would therefore be unacceptable, if not disastrous, to the United States and the rest of the free world. After a decision and a start on building up the strength of the free world has been made, it might then be desirable for the United States to take an initiative in seeking negotiations in the hope that it might facilitate the process of accommodation by the Kremlin to the new situation. Failing that, the unwillingness of the Kremlin to accept equitable terms of its bad faith in observing them would assist in consolidating popular opinion in the free world in support of the measures necessary to sustain the build-up.

In summary, we must, by means of a rapid and sustained build-up of the political, economic, and military strength of the free world, and by means of an affirmative program intended to wrest the initiative from the Soviet Union, confront it with convincing evidence of the determination and ability of the free world to frustrate the Kremlin design of a world dominated by its will. Such evidence is the only means short of war which eventually may force the Kremlin to abandon its present course of action and to negotiate acceptable agreements on issues of major importance.

The whole success of the proposed program hangs ultimately on recognition by this Government, the American people, and all free peoples, that the cold war is in fact a real war in which the survival of the free world is at stake. Essential prerequisites to success are consultations with Congressional leaders designed to make the program the object of non-partisan legislative support, and a presentation to the public of a full explanation of the facts and implications of the present international situation. The prosecution of the program will require of us all the ingenuity, sacrifice, and unity demanded by the vital importance of the issue and the tenacity to persevere until our national objectives have been attained.

RECOMMENDATIONS

That the President:

a. Approve the foregoing Conclusions.

b. Direct the National Security Council . . . to coordinate and insure the implementation of the Conclusions herein on an urgent and continuing basis for as long as necessary to achieve our objectives. . . .

(110) NSC 68/2, REPORT TO NATIONAL SECURITY COUNCIL BY NSC EXECU-TIVE SECRETARY JAMES LAY, September 3, 1950 [Extract]

Source: *Foreign Relations of the United States: 1950 Vol. I National Security Affairs; Foreign Economic Policy.* Washington: U.S. Government Printing Office, 1977, p. 400.

At the 68th [National Security] Council meeting, with the President presiding . . . draft reports on "United States Objectives and Programs for National Security" (NSC 68 and NSC68/1), [were considered], and:

a. Adopted the Conclusions of NSC 68 as a statement of policy to be followed over the next four or five years, and agreed that the implementing programs will be put into effect as rapidly as feasible, with the understanding that the specific nature and estimated costs of these programs will be decided as they are more firmly developed.

b. Deferred acton on NSC 68/1 pending a revision of that report to be prepared by the NSC Staff for Council consideration not later than November 15, 1950.

c. Noted the President's instructions that there should be no public discussion of this program, and specifically no public quotation of figures, until the appropriate time as determined by the President.

d. The President has this date approved the Conclusions of NSC 68 as a statement of policy to be followed over the next four or five years, and directed their implementation by all appropriate executive departments and agencies of the U.S. Government. . . .

(111) LETTER, SECRETARY OF STATE ACHESON TO PRESIDENT TRUMAN, January 20, 1950 [Extract]

Source: *Public Papers of the Presidents: Harry S. Truman, 1950.* Washington: U.S. Government Printing Office, 1965, p. 120.

The Department of State received with concern and dismay the report that the House of Representatives had rejected the Korean Aid Bill of 1949 by a vote of 193 to 191. This action, if not quickly repaired, will have the most far-reaching adverse effects upon our foreign policy, not only in Korea but in many other areas of the world. It has been fundamental to our policy that in those areas where a reasonable amount of American aid can make the difference between the maintenance of national independence and its collapse under totalitarian pressure, we should extend such aid within a prudent assessment of our capabilities. . . .

The Republic of Korea [South Korea] owes its existence in large measure to the United States, which freed the country from Japanese control. The peoples of the Republic of Korea, the other peoples of Asia, and the members of the United Nations under whose observation a government of the Republic was freely elected, alike look to our conduct in Korea as a measure of the seriousness of our concern with the freedom and welfare of peoples maintaining their independence in the face of great obstacles. We have not only given the Republic of Korea independence; since then we have provided the economic, military, technical, and other assistance necessary to its continued existence. . . . It is our considered judgment that if our limited assistance is continued the Republic will have a good chance of survival as a free nation. Should such further aid be denied, that chance may well be lost and all our previous efforts perhaps prove to have been in vain.

We are concerned not only about the consequences of this abrupt about-face in Korea, . . . but we are also deeply concerned by the effect which would be created in other parts of the world where our encouragement is a major element in the struggle for freedom. . . .

In our judgment it would be disastrous for the foreign policy of the United States for us to consider this action by the House of Representatives as its last word on the matter.

(112) NSC 56/2, REPORT BY THE NATIONAL SECURITY COUNCIL TO THE PRESIDENT, May 18, 1950 [Extract]

Source: *Foreign Relations of the United States: 1950 Vol. I National Security Affairs; Foreign Economic Policy*. Washington: U.S. Government Printing Office, 1977, pp. 628-629, 633.

1. To determine the policies of the United Staes with respect to military collaboration among the American states. . . .

3. In July 1945, the President approved a statement . . . that the United States insofar as possible should:

a. Establish U.S. military training missions in the other American republics.

b. Provide training in the United States for Latin American military personnel.

c. Participate in the making of combined joint plans for hemisphere defense.

d. Provide military equipment to the other American republics. . . .

13. The principal strategic military objectives of the United States in Latin America are:

a. The continued and increasing production and delivery of essential strategic materials.

b. While allowing scope for normal political change, the maintenance within each nation of political stability and of internal security to insure protection of the installations upon which the productions and delivery of strategic materials depend.

c. The mutual cooperation of all of the Latin American nations in support of the United States.

d. The protection of vital lines of communication.

e. The provision, development, operation and protection of those bases that may be required for the use of the United States and for the protection of lines of communication.

f. The coordinated protection of Latin America from invasion and from raids.

g. The provision of those Latin American armed forces necessary for the accomplishment of the foregoing.

h. The provision by Latin American nations, for the support of collective action in other theaters, of those forces beyond their requirements for the accomplishment of the foregoing. . . .

****

(113) LETTER, PRESIDENT TRUMAN TO SPEAKER OF THE HOUSE SAM RAYBURN, July 13, 1950 [Extract]

Source: *Public Papers of the Presidents: Harry S. Truman, 1950*. Washington: U.S. Government Printing Office, 1965, p. 521.

I have the honor to transmit herewith . . . supplemental estimates of appropriation for the fiscal year 1951 in the amount of $89,000,000 for the Department of State and the General Services Administration.

On several recent occasions I have directed the attention of the Congress and the Nation to the growing abuse and vilification of communist propaganda. Unsuccessful in its attempts to win Western Europe through ideological appeals, communism is seeking to discredit the United States and its actions throughout the world. If it succeeds in this effort to create distrust and hatred of our Government and its motives, the gains we have recently made in Western Europe may be substantially nullified. Our material assistance, to be fully effective, must be complemented by a full-scale effort in the field of ideas.

The free nations of the world have a great advantage in that truth is on their side. Communist leaders have repeatedly demonstrated that they fear the truth more than any weapon at our command. We must now throw additional resources into a campaign of truth which will match in vigor and determination the measures we have adopted in meeting postwar economic and military problems. . . .

This expanded program . . . does not propose a general worldwide expansion of our information and educational exchange efforts. Instead it is concentrated on the most critical areas in the world today. Each of these critical areas has been studied with great care; our objectives for each area have been defined. . . .

I regard such an expanded campaign of truth as vital to our National Security. We will never attain real security until people everywhere recognize that the free nations of the world are the true seekers of permanent peace. . . .

(114) MEMORANDUM, SECRETARY OF STATE DEAN ACHESON, July 14, 1950 [Extract]

Source: *Foreign Relations of the United States: 1950 Vol. I National Security Affairs; Foreign Economic Policy*. Washington: U.S. Government Printing Office, 1977, pp. 344-346.

At the Cabinet meeting this morning the Secretary [of State] made the following statement on the Korean crisis and related possible developments:

. . . [queried about] probable danger spots . . . with reference to possible further communist or Soviet moves [the Secretary of State] said that he did not think that it was profitable for him to go over specific spots again, since General Bradley had reviewed these military danger spots, and the next crisis might arise at any one of a dozen places. . . . the State Department and the Pentagon were agreed on the following general points:

1.   The Soviet Union has the military capability at the present time of taking, or inspiring through satellites, military action ranging from local aggression on one or more points along the periphery of the Soviet world to all-out general war.

2.   While estimates of probabilities of Soviet action vary it is completely agreed that there is not sufficient evidence to justify a firm opinion that the Soviet Union will not take any one or all of the actions which lie within its military capabilities.

3.   There is unanimous agreement, therefore, that the present world situation is one of extreme danger and tension which, either by Soviet desire or by the momentum of events arising from the Korean situation in which actual warfare is in progress, could present the United States with new outbreaks of aggression possibly up to and including general hostilities.

That is the situation we face, and it is one of gravest danger. It is becoming apparent to the world that we do not have the capabilities to face the threat, and the feeling in Europe is changing from one of elation that the United States has come into the Korean crisis to petrified fright.   People are questioning whether NATO [North Atlantic Treaty Organization] really means anything, since it means only what we are able to do.   Our intentions are not doubted, but are [our] capabilities are doubted.

In Asia the fear is manifested in two places - Japan and India.   In Japan the Socialist Party has adopted officially the principle that there must be a treaty with the Soviet Union as well as with the other belligerents; that Japan should be neutralized and that American troops should be withdrawn.   This is evidence that they believe association with the U.S. is dangerous to them.

In this situation the question is what the United States can do to affect these trends.   Obviously it must do all possible to deal with Korean situation and other present dangers, but it must do more now. . . . In the very early days of next week some action must be announced.   Whether that action is the best possible action is less important than that some effective action be taken and announced.

The Secretary listed the actions and announcements which must be made: The President's action regarding increased forces must be announced.   He must ask for money, and if it is a question of asking for too little or too much, he should ask for too much. He should stress production and ask for powers of allocation and limitation. . . . what we announce as to military steps will be of some reassurance to our friends, but will not deter our enemies; whereas what we do in the line of stepping up production will strike fear into our enemies, since it is in this field that our great capabilities and effectiveness lie.   Finally, the President should state that what we are doing in production - one of the great reasons for increased production - is to help our allies speed up their own capabilities, so that the free world can deal with obvious dangers.

The President said he agreed.

Defense and State are agreed on these recommendations, which had been made by State, and action will be taken on Tuesday.

(115) DRAFT PAPER, JOHN DREIER (DIRECTOR, OFFICE OF REGIONAL AMERICAN AFFAIRS, DEPARTMENT OF STATE) TO NATIONAL SECURITY COUNCIL, August 3, 1950

Source: *Foreign Relations of the United States: 1950 Vol. I National Security Affairs; Foreign Economic Policy.* Washington: U.S. Government Printing Office, 1977, pp. 642-644.

To determine the policy of the United States Government with respect to the extension by the Latin American countries of military assistance to the UN forces in Korea. . . .

Consideration of whether this Government should . . . encourage Latin American military assistance to Korea involves an analysis of the benefits which the participation of Latin American countries in the Korean conflict might bring to the United States. . . .

1. From the viewpoint of manpower alone, it would appear desirable to tap the resources of Latin America at this stage of world conflict with Soviet Communism in order to avoid too great a commitment of United States manpower. There exists in Latin America a relatively large potential fighting force and a considerable disposition to participate in the UN effort to restore peace and security. . . .

2. The political advantage of active participation by Latin American forces in the UN action in Korea (or in any other similar situation) would be enormous. The Latin American peoples as a whole are relatively remote from the Asian scene and they are tempted by the thought, which is encouraged by Communist propaganda, that the present crisis is merely a struggle for power between the USA and USSR. If, however, Latin American troops participate with the UN forces, the nationalism and patriotism of the Latin American people will be aroused in support of the entire UN action against Communist aggression. The Latin American countries will be accordingly more closely than ever lined with the position of the United States in the world at large, and more directly committed to the UN.

3. A further political advantage from the active participation of Latin Americans in the UN action in Korea concerns the attitude of the Latin American countries towards Communism at home. The commitment of Latin American manpower against aggressive Communism in Korea will also arouse public opinion in Latin America more firmly than ever against Communist programs and activities within their own countries. Since a major concern of the United States with respect to Latin America under wartime conditions is the possibility of sabotage of the production and transportation of strategic materials, a strong public support of the UN position against Communist aggression should have far-reaching consequences favorable to our interests in Latin America. . . .

(116) NATImplNAL SECURITY COUNCIL REPORT, NSC 73/4, August 25, 1950
[Extract]

Source: *Foreign Relations of the United States: 1950 Vol. I
National Security Affairs; Foreign Economic Policy.* Washington:
U.S. Government Printing Office, 1977, pp. 385-389.

****

31. The Korean war is only an additional and more acute mani-
festation of the chronic world situation resulting from the
Kremlin design for world domination through the international communist conspiracy. This situation requires many measures designed
to enable the free world to regain the initiative, to deter further aggression, and to increase ability to defeat aggression if
it occurs. . . . These measures should be taken regardless of
future Soviet action so long as the USSR retains its present capabilities and intention to threaten the security of the United
States.

32. The United States should as rapidly as possible increase
the build-up of its military and supporting strength in order to
reach at the earliest possible time and maintain for as long as
necessary a level of constant military readiness adequate to support U.S. foreign policy, to deter Soviet aggression, and to form
the basis for fighting a global war should war prove unavoidable.
The program for the increased military stature and preparedness
of the U.S. should proceed without regard to possible temporary
relaxation of international tension and without regard to isolated
instances of aggression unless the latter provide evidence of the
imminence of war, which would call for full preparation at full
speed.

33. The United States should urgently press forward to obtain,
through appropriate channels, knowledge or understanding as to
the willingness of United Nations members to hold Russia responsible at a proper time within the structure of the United Nations,
for satellite aggression. . . .

35. In the event of an overt attack by organized USSR military
forces against the territory or armed forces of the United States,
the immediate action of the United States should be to react to
the attack in accordance with existing directives, and to proceed
with full preparation at full speed to meet the situation created.
In the event of any attack covered by the terms of the North
Atlantic Treaty, which includes attack on Germany and Austria,
the United States would respond in accordance with its obligations
under that Treaty.

36. In case of other overt aggression by organized USSR military forces, or in case of further Soviet-inspired aggression in
Europe, and depending upon the nature of the aggression and the
country attacked, the United States in common prudence would
have to proceed on the assumption that global war is probably
imminent. Accordingly, . . . the United States immediately:

a. Make every effort in the light of the circumstances to
localize the action, to stop the aggression by political measures
and to ensure the unity of the free world if war nevertheless
follows. These measures should include direct diplomatic action
and resort to the United Nations with the objectives of:

(1) In the case of Soviet-inspired overt aggressions, accelerating measures to identify the true source of the aggression in order that at a time most advantageous to the United States, the Soviet Union itself could be exposed as the aggressor.

(2) Making clear to the world United States preference for a peaceful settlement and the conditions upon which the United States would, in concert with other members of the United Nations, accept such a settlement.

(3) Consulting with members of the United Nations regarding their willingness to join with the United States in military opposition, if necessary, to the aggression.

In addition, the United States should give consideration to the possibility of a direct approach to the highest Soviet leaders. . . .

c. Place itself in the best possible position to meet the eventuality of global war, and therefore prepare to execute emergency war plans; but should, in so far as it has any choice, enter into full-scale hositilities only at the moment and in the manner most favorable to it in the light of the situation then existing.

d. While minimizing United States military commitments in areas of little strategic significance, take action with reference to the aggression to the extent and in the manner best contributing to the implementation of United States national war plans.

37. Specific immediate actions to be taken . . .

a. In the event of overt attack by organized USSR military forces against:

(1) <u>Finland or Afghanistan</u>: The United States should itself take no military action in these countries to oppose the aggression. The emphasis of the action taken would be placed upon political and psychological measures, . . .

(2) <u>Yugoslavia</u>: The United States should implement existing policy (NSC 18/4) pending a review of that policy, with the purpose of denying to the USSR effective control of this country.

(3) <u>Greece or Turkey</u>: The United States should provide accelerated military assistance to Greece or Turkey and deploy such United States forces to the support of those countries as can be made available without jeopardizing United States national security. . . .

(4) <u>Iran</u>: The United States should initially rely on the United Kingdom for principal responsibility to assist Iran in meeting the aggression, should endeavor to induce Pakistan and India to take a leading role, and should deploy such forces to the Near and Middle East and the Persian Gulf areas as can be made available without jeopardizing United States security or its ability to implement emergency war plans.

b. In the event of Soviet-inspired satellite aggression against <u>Yugoslavia</u> or <u>Greece</u>, the United States should take the same action as if the attack were directly by Soviet forces, . . .

c. <u>Germany</u>. In the event of a major attack by East German para-military forces on Berlin or on West Germany, such attack should be resisted by Allied occupation forces.

38. In the event of any new single overt act of aggression by Soviet satellite armed forces in the Far East, the United States . . . should:

a. Attempt to localize the conflict.

b. Take all possible counter-measures short of seriously impairing the ability to execute emergency war plans.

c. Seek the support of its allies and take appropriate steps in the UN.

d. Concurrently recognize the increased strain on the fabric of world peace arising from a further act of aggression following on the Korean episode.

39. <u>Formosa</u>. . . . In the event of a Chinese Communist attack on Formosa or the Pescadores, the United States should repel the assault in accordance with existing directives but should not permit itself to become engaged in a general war with Communist China. In any event, US ground forces should not be committed on Formosa. In the event the Chinese Communists succeed in defeating the Chinese Nationalist forces, the United States, bearing in mind its desire to avoid general war with Communist China, should review the situation to determine its further action and to decide whether to cease all military operations against the Chinese Communists.

40. <u>Korea</u>. . . .

a. In the event that North Korean forces, alone or plus such reinforcements as may covertly be brought into action, are powerful enough to compel the withdrawal of UN forces in Korea, the South Korean Government should be evacuated from the Korean mainland and established at an appropriate place in the area, if practicable.

b. In the event of the overt use of Organized Chinese Communist forces in Korea:

"(1) The United States should not permit itself to become engaged in a general war with Communist China.

(2) As long as action by UN military forces now committed or planned for commitment in Korea offers a reasonable chance of successful resistance, such action should be continued and extended to include authority to take appropriate air and naval action outside Korea against Communist China. The latter action should be continued pending a review of US military commitments in the light of conditions then existing to determine further US courses of action."

41. <u>Other Far Eastern Areas</u>. . . .

a. In the event of Chinese Communist aggression against Chinese inshore islands, Tibet, or Macao, the United States should take political action but would not expect to take military action.

b. If such aggression were directed against Burma, the United States acting through the British, should accelerate its assistance to that government and endeavor to induce states in the neighborhood of Burma to commit ground forces to resist the aggression.

c. If such aggression were directed against Hong Kong the United States should consider furnishing relief assistance to the British and such military assistance as may be appropriate in the light of our own military commitments and capabilities at that time.

d. In the event of overt attack by organized Chinese communist forces against Indochina, the United States should not permit itself to become engaged in a general war with Communist China but should, in concert with the UK, support France and the associated states, and accelerate and expand the present miliary assistance program. . . .

44. Iran. In the event of internal subversion leading toward the establishment of a communist-dominated government in Iran, the United States should:

a. Accelerate its assistance to the legitimate Iranian Government.

b. Consider seeking an agreement in the UN in charging the USSR with direct responsibility for conditions in Iran.

45. While recognizing the importance of United States assistance and support of the United Nations, and while wholly supporting its aims and objectives, the United States cannot yet rely on the United Nations as the sole instrumentality for safeguarding essential United States security interests. . . .

(117) RADIO AND TELEVISION ADDRESS, PRESIDENT TRUMAN, September 1, 1950 [Extract]

Source: *Public Papers of the Presidents: Harry S. Truman, 1950.* Washington: U.S. Government Printing Office, 1965, pp. 609-610, 611-613.

. . . Two months ago Communist imperialism turned from the familiar tactics of infiltration and subversion to a brutal attack on the small Republic of Korea. When that happened, the free and peace-loving nations of the world faced two possible courses.

One course would have been to limit our action to diplomatic protests, while the Communist aggressors went ahead and swallowed up their victim. That would have been the course of appeasement. . . . If aggression were allowed to succeed in Korea, it would be an open invitation to new acts of aggression elsewhere.

The other course is the one which the free world chose. The United Nations made its historic decision to meet military aggression with armed force. The effects of that decision will be felt far beyond Korea. The firm action taken by the United Nations is our best hope of achieving world peace.

It is your liberty and mine which is involved. What is at stake is the free way of life - the right to worship as we please, the right to express our opinions, the right to raise our children in our own way, the right to choose our jobs, the right to plan our future and to live without fear. . . .

We cannot hope to maintain our own freedom if freedom elsewhere is wiped out. . . .

The Soviet Union has repeatedly violated its pledges of international cooperation. It has destroyed the independence of its neighbors. It has sought to disrupt those countries it could not dominate. It has built up tremendous armed forces far beyond the needs of its own defense. . . .

In these circumstances, the free nations have been compelled to take measures to protect themselves against the aggressive designs of the Communists. . . .

Right now the battle in Korea is the front-line in the struggle to build a world in which a just and lasting peace can be maintained.

That is why we in the United States must increase our own defensive strength over and above the forces we need in Korea. That is why we must continue to work with the other free nations to increase our combined strength. . . .

The Armed Forces of the United States are a key element in the strength of the free world. In view of the threats of aggression which now face us, we shall have to increase these forces and we shall have to maintain larger forces for a long time to come. . . .

In addition to increasing the size of our Armed Forces, we must step up sharply the production of guns, tanks, planes, and other military equipment. We shall also have to increase our stockpile of essential materials, and to expand our industrial capacity to produce military supplies. . . .

In order to increase our defense effort, rapidly enough to meet the danger that we face, we shall have to make many changes in our way of living and working here at home. We shall have to give up many things we enjoy. We shall have to work harder and longer. To prevent runaway inflation and runaway prices, we shall have to impose certain restrictions upon ourselves. . . .

As we now move forward to arm ourselves more quickly in the days ahead, and as we strive with the United Nations for victory in Korea, we must keep clearly in mind what we believe in and what we are trying to do. . . .

First: We believe in the United Nations. When we ratified its charter, we pledged ourselves to seek peace and security through this world organization. We kept our word when we went to the support of the United Nations in Korea 2 months ago. . . .

Second: We believe the Koreans have a right to be free, independent, and united - as they want to be. Under the direction and guidance of the United Nations, we, with others, will do our part to help them enjoy that right. . . .

Third: We do not want the fighting in Korea to expand into a general war. It will not spread unless Communist imperialism draws other armies and governments into the fight of the aggressors against the United Nations.

Fourth: We hope in particular that the people of China will not be misled or forced into fighting against the United Nations and against the American people, who have always been and still are their friends. Only the Communist imperialism, which has already started to dismember China, could gain from China's involvement in the war. . . .

Fifth: We do not want Formosa or any part of Asia for ourselves. We believe that the future of Formosa . . . should be settled [peacefully] by international action, and not by the decision of the United States or any other state alone. The mission of the 7th Fleet is to keep Formosa out of the conflict. . . .

Sixth: We believe in freedom for all the nations of the Far East. That is one of the reasons why we are fighting under the United Nations for the freedom of Korea. We helped the Philippines become independent and we have supported the national aspirations to independence of other Asian countries. Russia has never voluntarily given up any territory it has acquired in the Far East; it has never given independence to any people who have fallen under its control. . . .

Seventh: We do not believe in aggressive or preventive war. Such war is the weapon of dictators, not of free democratic countries like the United States. We are arming only for the defense against aggression. Even though Communist imperialism does not believe in peace, it can be discouraged from new aggression if we and other free peoples are strong, determined, and united.

Eighth: We want peace and we shall achieve it. Our men are fighting for peace today in Korea. We are working for peace constantly in the United Nations and in all the capitals of the world. Our workers, our farmers, our businessmen, all our vast resources, are helping now to create the strength which will make peace secure. . . .

(118) <u>STATEMENT, PRESIDENT TRUMAN</u>, November 30, 1950 [Extract]

Source: *Public Papers of the Presidents: Harry S. Truman, 1950.* Washington: U.S. Government Printing Office, 1965, pp. 724-725.

Recent developments in Korea confront the world with a serious crisis. The Chinese Communist leaders have sent their troops from Manchuria to launch a strong and well-organized attack against the United Nations forces in North Korea. This has been done despite prolonged and earnest efforts to bring home to the Communist leaders of China the plain fact that neither the United Nations nor the United States has any aggressive intentions toward China. Because of the historic friendship between the people of the United States and China, it is particularly shocking to us to think that Chinese are being forced into battle against our troops in the United Nations command.

The Chinese attack was made in great force, and it still continues. It has resulted in the forced withdrawal of large parts of the United Nations command. . . . But the forces of the United Nations have no intention of abandoning their mission in Korea.

The forces of the United Nations are in Korea to put down an aggression that threatens not only the whole fabric of the United Nations, but all human hopes of peace and justice.

If the United Nations yields to the forces of aggression, no nation will be safe or secure. If aggression is successful in Korea, we can expect it to spread throughout Asia and Europe to this hemisphere. We are fighting in Korea for our own national security and survival. . . .

We shall continue to work in the United Nations for concerted action to halt this aggression in Korea.

We shall intensify our efforts to help other free nations strengthen their defenses in order to meet the threat of aggression elsewhere.

We shall rapidly increase our own military strength. . . .

Some had hoped that the normal peaceful process of discussion and negotiation . . . could be successfully entered into with the present Chinese Communist delegation [to the UN] at Lake Success. There is, however, no indication that the representatives of Communist China are willing to engage in this process. Instead of discussing the real issues, they have been making violent and wholly false statements of the type which have often been used by the Soviet representatives in an effort to prevent the Security Council from acting.

We hope that the Chinese people will not continue to be forced or deceived into serving the ends of Russian colonial policy in Asia.

I am certain that, if the Chinese people now under the control of the Communists were free to speak for themselves, they would denounce this aggression against the United Nations.

Because this new act of aggression in Korea is only a part of a worldwide pattern of danger to all the free nations of the world, it is more necessary than ever before for us to increase at a very rapid rate the combined military strength of the free nations. It is more necessary than ever that integrated forces in Europe under a supreme command be established at once.

With respect to our own defense, I shall submit a supplemental request for appropriations needed immediately to increase the size and effectiveness of our Armed Forces. The request will include a substantial amount for the Atomic Energy Commission in addition to large amounts for the Army, the Navy, and the Air Force. . . .

(119) ADDRESS, PRESIDENT TRUMAN, December 5, 1950 [Extract]

Source: *Public Papers of the Presidents: Harry S. Truman, 1950.* Washington: U.S. Government Printing Office, 1965, pp. 733-735.

As we meet here today, the serious crisis in world affairs overshadows all that we do. This country of ours, together with the other members of the United Nations, is engaged in a critical struggle to uphold the values of peace and justice and freedom.

We are struggling to preserve our own liberty as a nation. More than that, we are striving to cooperate with other free nations to uphold the basic values of freedom - of peace based on justice - which are essential for the progress of mankind. . . .

All of us are aware of the grave risk of general conflict which has been deliberately caused by the Chinese Communist leaders. Their action greatly changes the immediate situation with which we are confronted. It does not change our fundamental purpose to work for the cause of a just and peaceful world.

No matter how the immediate situation may develop, we must remember that the fighting in Korea is but one part of the tremendous struggle of our time - the struggle between freedom and Communist slavery. This struggle engages all our national life, all our institutions, and all our resources. For the effort of the evil forces of communism to reach out and dominate the world confronts our Nation and our civilization with the greatest challenge in our history.

I believe the single most important thing our young people will need to meet this critical challenge in the years ahead is moral strength - and strength of character. . . .

If we are to give our children the training that will enable them to hold fast to the right course in these dangerous times, we must clearly understand the nature of the crisis. We must understand the nature of the threat created by international communism.

In the first place, it is obviously a military threat. The Communist dominated countries are maintaining large military forces - far larger than they could possibly need for peaceful purposes. And they have shown by their actions in Korea that they will not hesitate to use these forces in armed aggression whenever it suits their evil purposes.

Because of this military threat, we must strengthen our military defenses. . . . In no other way can we insure our survival as a nation.

. . . Our objective [also] is to help build up the collective strength of the free nations - the nations which share the ideals and aspirations of free men everywhere.

As a matter of defense, we need the combined resources and the common determination of the free world to meet the military threat of communism.

But our problem . . . and our objective is to build a world order based on freedom and justice. We have worked with the free nations to lay the foundations of such a world order in the United Nations. . . . That is the only way out of an endless circle of force and retaliation, violence and war - which will carry the human race back to the Dark Ages if it is not stopped now. . . .

The threat of communism has other aspects than the military aspect. In some ways the moral and spiritual dangers that flow from communism are a much more serious threat to freedom than is its military power.

The ideology of communism is a challenge to all the values of our society and of our way of life. . . .

Communism attacks our main basic values, our belief in God, our belief in the dignity of man and the value of human life, our belief in justice and freedom. It attacks the institutions that are based on these values. It attacks our churches, our guarantees of civil liberty, our courts, our democratic form of government. . . .

We must fight against the moral cynicism - the materialistic view of life - on which communism feeds. We must teach the objectives that lie behind our institutions, and the duty of all our citizens to make those institutions work more perfectly. Nothing is more important than this. . . .

(120) RADIO AND TV ADDRESS, PRESIDENT TRUMAN, December 15, 1950 [Extract]

Source: *Public Papers of the Presidents: Harry S. Truman, 1950.* Washington: U.S. Government Printing Office, 1965, pp. 741-746.

. . . Our homes, our Nation, all the things we believe in, are in great danger. This danger has been created by the rulers of the Soviet Union.

For 5 years we have been working for peace and justice among nations. We have helped to bring the free nations of the world together in a great movement to establish a lasting peace. Against this movement for peace, the rulers of the Soviet Union have been waging a relentless attack. They have tried to undermine or overwhelm the free nations one by one. They have used threats and treachery and violence. . . .

That is why we are in such grave danger.

The future of civilization depends on what we do - on what we do now, and in the months ahead.

We have the strength and we have the courage to overcome the danger that threatens our country. We must act calmly and wisely and resolutely. . . .

Though the present situation is highly dangerous, we do not believe that war is inevitable. There is no conflict between the legitimate interests of the free world and those of the Soviet Union that cannot be settled by peaceful means. We will continue to take every honorable step we can to avoid general war.

But we will not engage in appeasement. . . .

The danger we face exists not only in Korea. Therefore, the second thing we are going to do is to increase our efforts, with other free nations, to build up defenses against aggression in other parts of the world. In dealing with the Korean crisis, we are not going to ignore the danger of aggression elsewhere.

There is actual warfare in the Far East, but Europe and the rest of the world are also in very great danger. The same menace - the menace of Communist aggression - threatens Europe as well as Asia.

To combat this menace, other free nations need our help, and we need theirs. We must work with a sense of real partnership and common purpose with these nations. . . .

Working together, the free nations can present the common
front, backed by strength, which is necessary if we are to be in
a position to negotiate successfully with the Kremlin for peaceful settlements.

Working together, we hope we can prevent another world war.
. . .

. . . to meet the present danger [we must also] step up our
defense program.

We are expanding our Armed Forces very rapidly.

We are speeding up the production of military equipment for
our Armed Forces and for our allies. . . .

. . . measured against the danger that confronts us, our
forces are not adequate.

On June 25, when the Communists invaded the Republic of Korea,
we had less than 1½ million men and women in our Army, Navy, and
Air Force. Today, the military strength has reached about 2½ million. Our next step is to increase the number of men and women
on active duty to nearly 3½ million. . . .

At the same time we will have a very rapid speedup in the
production of military equipment. Within 1 year we will be turning out planes at five times the present rate of production.
Within 1 year combat vehicles will be coming off the production
line at four times today's rate. Within 1 year the rate of production of electronics equipment for defense will have multiplied
4½ times.

. . . [The weapons] will constitute an arsenal for the defense
of freedom. Out of this arsenal we will be able to send weapons
to other free nations, to add to what they can produce for their
own defenses. And in this same arsenal we will provide a large
reserve of weapons to equip additional units in our Armed Forces
whenever that may be necessary.

Furthermore, . . . we will also expand our training and production facilities so as to make possible a very rapid expansion
to full mobilization if that becomes necessary. . . .

If we are to make the weapons we need soon enough, we shall
have to cut back on many lines of civilian production. . . . We
must [also] produce more - more steel, more copper, more aluminum,
more electric power, more food, more cotton, more of many other
things.

A defense effort of the size we must now undertake will inevitably push up prices, unless we take positive action to hold
them down.

We have already taken a number of steps in that direction.
We have put restrictions on credit buying. We have increased
taxes. And I hope that the Congress will enact an excess profits
tax at this session. Still further taxes will be needed. We
cannot escape paying the cost of our military program. The more
we pay by taxes now, the better we can hold prices down. . . .

I have also instructed the Director of the [Bureau of the
Budget] to reduce the nonmilitary expenditures in the new Federal

budget to the minimum required to give effective support to the defense effort. . . .

As we move ahead with this mobilization effort, there will be increased need for central control over the many Government activities in this field. Accordingly, I am establishing an Office of Defense Mobilization . . . [to direct] all mobilization activities of the Government, including production, procurement, manpower, transportation, and economic stabilization.

The Government is also moving forward with preparations for civil defense. . . .

In addition, I have recommended legislation to the Congress which will authorize the Federal Government to help the States and cities in their civil defense preparations. . . .

Our freedom is in danger.

Sometimes we may forget just what freedom means to us. It is as close to us, as important to us, as the air we breathe. Freedom is in our homes, in our schools, in our churches. It is in our work and our Government and the right to vote as we please. Those are the things that would be taken from us if communism should win. . . .

Because of all these things . . . I will issue a proclamation tomorrow morning declaring that a national emergency exists. This will call upon every citizen to put aside his personal interests for the good of the country. All our energies must be devoted to the tasks ahead of us.

No nation has ever had a greater responsibility than ours has at this moment. We must remember that we are the leaders of the free world. We must understand that we cannot achieve peace by ourselves, but only by cooperating with other free nations and with the men and women who love freedom everywhere. . . .

****

President Truman's decision to dismiss General Douglas MacArthur as UN Commander in the Far East sharply highlighted the Administration's political dilemma, dramatized by this contradictory posture of emphasizing the threat which a Communist victory in Korea posed to U.S. security interests while at the same time pursuing a military strategy intended to limit the Korean conflict. The vain and ambitious General had since 1945 barely tolerated policy direction from the White House, and, since September 1950, had used his reputation and the Conservative Republican Congressional leadership's policy difference with the Truman Administration to seek to effect what he believed to be a successful military strategy. MacArthur's insubordination, and indirect challenge to civilian supremacy over the military, left the President with but one option. By dismissing the popular General, who appealed to the then-popular conviction that victory over the Soviet Union (the Anti-Christ) required full utilization of the nation's military resources, Truman had created a real political crisis. MacArthur returned to the United States a war hero; his prescriptions for "victory" commanding the adulation of the American public. Concurrently, many in the Congress and in the press called for Truman's impeachment and the purging of the pusillanimous and treasonous State Department bureaucracy. As such, the Truman Administration's limited war strategy for waging the Korean War enhanced the appeal of a McCarthyite politics.

(121) <u>RADIO ADDRESS, PRESIDENT TRUMAN</u>, April 11, 1951 [Extract]

Source: *Public Papers of the Presidents: Harry S. Truman, 1951.* Washington: U.S. Government Printing Office, 1965, pp. 223-227.

I want to talk . . . about what we are doing in Korea and about our policy in the Far East.

In the simplest terms, what we are doing in Korea is this: We are trying to prevent a third world war. . . .

It is right for us to be in Korea . . .

I want to remind you why this is true.

The Communists in the Kremlin are engaged in a monstrous conspiracy to stamp out freedom all over the world. If they were to succeed, the United States would be numbered among their principal victims. It must be clear to everyone that the United States cannot - and will not - sit idly by and await foreign conquest. The only question is: What is the best time to meet the threat and how is the best way to meet it?

The best time to meet the threat is in the beginning. . . . And the best way to meet the threat of aggression is for the peace-loving nations to act together. . . .

If history has taught us anything, it is that aggression anywhere in the world is a threat to the peace everywhere in the world. When the aggression is supported by the cruel and selfish rulers of a powerful nation who are bent on conquest, it becomes a clear and present danger to the security and independence of every free nation.

This is a lesson that most people in this country have learned thoroughly. . . . And, since the end of World War II, we have been putting that lesson into practice - we have been working with other free nations to check the aggressive designs of the Soviet Union before they can result in a third world war.

That is what we did in Greece, when that nation was threatened by the aggression of international communism. . . .

The aggression against Korea is the boldest and most dangerous move the Communists have yet made.

The attack on Korea was part of a greater plan for conquering all of Asia. . . .

The question we have had to face is whether the Communist plan of conquest can be stopped without a general war. Our Government and other countries associated with us in the United Nations believe that the best chance of stopping it without a general war is to meet the attack in Korea and defeat it there. . . .

So far, by fighting a limited war in Korea, we have prevented aggression from succeeding, and bringing on a general war. And the ability of the whole free world to resist Communist aggression has been greatly improved.

We have taught the enemy a lesson. He has found that aggression is not cheap or easy. Moreover, men all over the world who want to remain free have been given new courage and new hope. They know now that the champions of freedom can stand up and fight, and that they will stand up and fight.

Our resolute stand in Korea is helping the forces of freedom now fighting in Indochina and other countries in that part of the world. It has already slowed down the timetable of conquest.

In Korea itself there are signs that the enemy is building up his ground [and air] forces for a new mass offensive. . . .

If a new attack comes, I feel confident it will be turned back. The United Nations fighting forces . . . are fighting for a just cause. They are proving to all the world that the principle of collective security will work. . . .

The Communist side must now choose its course of action. The Communist rulers may press the attack against us. They may take further action which will spread the conflict. . . . The Communists also have the choice of a peaceful settlement which could lead to a general relaxation of the tensions in the Far East. The decision is theirs, because the forces of the United Nations will strive to limit the conflict if possible.

We do not want to see the conflict in Korea extended. We are trying to prevent a world war - not to start one. And the best way to do that is to make it plain that we and the other free countries will continue to resist the attack.

But . . . why can't we take other steps to punish the aggressor. Why don't we bomb Manchuria and China itself? Why don't we assist the Chinese Nationalist troops to land on the mainland of China?

If we were to do these things we would be running a very grave risk of starting a general war. If that were to happen, we would have brought about the exact situation we are trying to prevent.

If we are to do these things, we would become entangled in a vast conflict on the continent of Asia and our task would become immeasurably more difficult all over the world.

What would suit the ambitions of the Kremlin better than for our military forces to be committed to a full-scale war with Red China?

It may well be that . . . the Communists may spread the war. But it would be wrong - tragically wrong - for us to take the initative in extending the war.

The dangers are great. . . . Behind the North Koreans and Chinese Communists in the front lines stand additional millions of Chinese soldiers. And behind the Chinese stand the tanks, the planes, the submarines, the soldiers, and the scheming rulers of the Soviet Union. . . .

The course we have been following is the one best calculated to avoid an all-out war. It is the course consistent with our obligation to do all we can to maintain international peace and security. . . .

First of all- it is clear that our efforts in Korea can blunt the will of the Chinese Communists to continue the struggle. The United Nations forces . . . have inflicted very heavy casualities on the enemy. Our forces are stronger now than they have been before. . . .

Second, the free world as a whole is growing in military strength every day. In the United States, in Western Europe, and throughout the world, free men are alert to the Soviet threat and are building their defenses. . . .

If the Communist authorities realize that they cannot defeat us in Korea, if they realize it would be foolhardy to widen the hostilities beyond Korea, then they may recognize the folly of continuing their aggression. . . .

Then we may achieve a settlement in Korea which will not compromise the principles and purposes of the United Nations.

I have thought long and hard about this question of extending the war in Asia. I have discussed it many times with the ablest military advisers in the country. I believe with all my heart that the course we are following is the best course.

I believe that we must try to limit the war to Korea . . . to make sure that the precious lives of our fighting men are not wasted; to see that the security of our country and the free world is not needlessly jeopardized; and to prevent a third world war.

A number of events have made it evident that General [Douglas] MacArthur did not agree with that policy. I have therefore considered it essential to relieve General MacArthur [as UN Commander in Korea] so that there would be no doubt or confusion as to the real purposes and aim of our policy. . . .

The change in commands in the Far East means no change whatever in the policy of the United States. We will carry on the fight in Korea with vigor and determination in an effort to bring the war to a speedy and successful conclusion. . . .

. . . I want to be clear about our military objective. We are fighting to resist an outrageous aggression in Korea. We are trying to keep the Korean conflict from spreading to other areas. But at the same time we must conduct our military activities so as to insure the security of our forces. This is essential if they are to continue the fight until the enemy abandons its ruthless attempt to destroy the Republic of Korea.

That is our military objective - to repel attack and to restore peace.

In the hard fighting in Korea, we are proving that collective action among nations is not only a high principle but a workable means of resisting aggression. Defeat of aggression in Korea may be the turning point in the world's search for a practical way of achieving peace and security. . . .

We do not want to widen the conflict. We will use every effort to prevent that disaster. And in so doing, we know that we are following the great principles of peace, freedom, and justice.

To Administration officials, the MacArthur imbroglio confirmed the wisdom of a policy based upon an elitist disdain for public and congressional participation in policy making. Unwilling to reassess the wisdom or costs of current policy, these officials viewed the resultant McCarthyite upsurge as simply requiring better public relations. The result was an even more simplistic and alarmist public position, with Administration officials self-righteously extolling the magnitude and pervasiveness of the Soviet threat.

(122) MEMO, PRESIDENTIAL PRESS SECRETARY JOSEPH SHORT TO PRESI-
DENT TRUMAN, April 20, 1951 [Extract]

Source: Harry S. Truman Papers, Official Files 386, Harry S. Truman Library.

In view of developments of the last ten days, it seems more important than ever that administration spokesmen hammer away with explanations of our Asian policy and its relation to our global policy, with particular emphasis on the theme that the President's recent actions have one primary objective: Prevention of the extension of the fighting in Korea into a full-scale World War.

I therefore suggest that you urge Department heads making speeches within the next two weeks to give special attention to this subject. It would not be necessary for them to base their speeches on foreign policy. In fact, I think it would be desirable if the speeches were on other subjects but included a reference of several paragraphs to this burning issue of the day.

Another thought that I would like to see repeated all across the land is that the President's action in relieving General MacArthur from command followed a unanimous recommendation for the General's relief from the top Presidential civilian and military advisers, including the Joint Chiefs of Staff. This might not be appropriate speech material but the travelling Cabinet and sub-Cabinet officers might make a point of telling as many people as possible that this were true. . . .

A number of speeches are scheduled by Cabinet and sub-Cabinet officers during the next two weeks. The schedules have been furnished me by members of my working group. With your permission, I will ask the working group member from each Department to furnish each of the speakers with material along the lines indicated.

You also might wish to take up the subject at your Cabinet meeting this morning.

(123) LETTER, PRESIDENT TRUMAN TO SPEAKER OF THE HOUSE SAM
RAYBURN, April 30, 1951 [Extract]

Source: *Public Papers of the Presidents: Harry S. Truman, 1951.* Washington: U.S. Government Printing Office, 1965, pp. 254-256.

I transmit herewith . . . my budget recommendations for the military functions of the Department of defense for the fiscal year ending June 30, 1952.

My recommendations for appropriations amount to
$57,604,254,390, . . . In addition, I am submitting an estimate
of $4,500,000,000, which represents the funds needed in 1952 for
a large military public works program . . . This makes a total of
$60,679.414,690, . . .

The major expansion in our defense expenditures is one part
of our total program . . . to save the world from another and
more frightful global war. It is also a program to enable us, if
general war should be thrust upon us, to halt the enemy's forces
and strike back decisively at the center of the enemy's power.

The aggression in Korea is only part of the Kremlin strategy
to achieve world domination. The Soviet Union is prepared to use
armed force elsewhere in the world, and is using many other methods than military force to gain its ends.

The struggle which the Kremlin has initiated is global in
scope, and involves almost every aspect of human endeavor. All
the free nations . . . are affected by the aggressive designs
of the despots in the Kremlin. . . . not only by the military
power these men control, but also by their attacks upon the economic, social and moral life of free men.

To meet this threat the free world must strengthen its military defenses and its economic and social foundations. The free
nations must carry the attack to the enemy in the realm of the
minds and convictions of men.

This budget estimate represents, therefore, but one of the
parts of our national security program. Other parts [include]
. . . proposals for needed legislation to enable our economy to
carry out our defense production plans. . . . recommendations for
the expansion of our campaign of truth. . . . [and] an integrated
program to help other free nations build up their military and
economic strength, in combination with ours. . . .

In money terms, by far the largest part of this total security
program is the cost of building up our own military strength.
The funds I am today recommending will carry forward the rapid
build-up in military strength upon which our Nation embarked,
when the aggression in Korea showed that the Soviet rulers were
willing to push the world to the brink of a general war to get
what they want. . . .

The major element in this threat is the military strength and
military production of the Soviet Union. The armed forces of the
Soviet Union today far exceed any reasonable defense requirements.
Its economy is harnessed to war production.

If the Soviet Union chooses to unleash a general war, the
free world must be in a position to stop the attack and strike
back decisively and at once at the seats of Soviet power. We believe that the best path to peace is through building combined
defenses for the free world sufficiently powerful to insure disaster for the aggressors if they launch a new world war. . . .

The major emphasis of this budget estimate is upon building up our Armed Forces and our productive capacity toward the level of preparedness necessary in the event of all-out war. In addition to maintaining our forces on active duty, funds are provided for a war reserve of supplies and equipment and for the creation of a mobilization base . . . to enable us to mobilize quickly, if necessary, for an all-out war effort. At the same time, the level of preparedness which this budget is designed to create is one which is well within our ability to maintain for many years, if necessary.

This budget is based on our estimate at this time of the military build-up required to meet our security objectives. . . . In the event of a change in the international situation, [however] the present program may have to be substantially modified.

Most of the funds in this military budget will be spent for military equipment and supplies, and for constructing bases, camps, and other facilities. Of the total of 60.7 billion dollars of the new obligational authority, about 43 billion dollars is for procurement and construction. About 34.7 billion dollars will be used to purchase heavy equipment such as ships, planes, tanks, artillery, trucks, ammunition, guided missiles, and electronics. . . .

We shall, at the same time, continue to step up the research and development program. The funds in this budget will support a program about 20 percent larger than in the current fiscal year and about two-and-one-half times as large as in fiscal year 1950.

This military program will have an increasing impact on our economy, especially as equipment orders are translated into actual production.

The present plans for our military and other security programs . . . are estimated to require about 20 percent of the total national output by the end of fiscal year 1952. . . . and will involve a rapid and substantial shift of resources. It will give us serious production problems and will require forceful action against inflation.

In my message of April 26 . . . I urged renewal of the authority under which we are now regulating the flow of scarce materials, so as to assure the performance of defense contracts. I also outlined the tax increases and other measures which must be taken in order to offset these inflationary pressures. . . . The national defense will be seriously hampered if [these recommendations] are not enacted.

The necessity which is now thrust upon the Government to draw heavily upon manpower, materials, and industrial facilities, for national defense, requires efficient scheduling of procurement, production, and facilities expansion. Both the civilian and military agencies of Government are concerned with these matters, and both are moving to improve their effectiveness as the defense program grows.

This military budget is essential to our national security. The outbreak of aggression, the threat of general war that overhangs the world, make it imperative to increase our defenses rapidly and efficiently. . . .

(124) <u>ADDRESS, PRESIDENT TRUMAN</u>, May 7, 1951 [Extract]

Source: *Public Papers of the Presidents: Harry S. Truman, 1951.*
Washington: U.S. Government Printing Office, 1965, pp. 265-269.

. . . The lives of many millions of our fellow citizens may depend on the development of a strong civil defense.

The threat of atomic warfare is one which we must face, . . . We can never afford to forget that the terrible destruction of cities, and the civilization as we know it, is a real possibility.

There are two things our country must do to face this awesome and terrible possibility.

One of them is to look to our civil defense [on June 21, 1951, Truman requested a $535 million appropriation for civil defense]. So long as there is any chance at all that the atomic bombs may fall on our cities, we cannot gamble on being caught unprepared. . . .

The other thing we must do is to try to prevent atomic war from coming. . . . That is what our foreign policy is all about.

The foreign policy of the United States is based on an effort to attain world peace. Every action we have taken has had this aim in view.

These two things - civil defense and foreign policy - . . . are closely tied together. And they are both concerned with a form of warfare which is more destructive than anything the world has ever known before in its history.

Our civil defense problem starts with a few basic facts.

Because there was an atomic explosion in the Soviet Union in 1949, we must act on the assumption that they do have atomic bombs.

They have planes that could drop atomic bombs upon our cities.

No matter how good our air defense may be, or how big an air force we build, a determined air attack by the Soviet Union could drop bombs upon this country. . . .

The purpose of atomic attacks would be to strike a death blow at our cities, to burn out our centers of production, and to create panic among our people.

There is no complete protection against an atomic bomb attack. But there is a lot we can do to reduce the number of deaths and injuries and to check panic.

We must organize ourselves - in every city, factory, office, and home. Civil defense is a responsibility which begins with the individual. . . . It is shared with the city, the State, and the Nation.

We have two immediate jobs. One is to teach all our people how to protect themselves in the event of an enemy attack. The other is to organize and train millions of volunteers as active members of the United States Civil Defense Corps. . . .

But even with such an organization, our losses in an atomic war . . . would be terrible. Whole cities . . . might be destroyed. And they could be destroyed.

Even with such losses, frightful as they would be, I think this country would survive and would win an atomic war. But even if we win, an atomic war would be a disaster.

The best defense against the atomic bomb is to prevent the outbreak of another world war and to achieve a real peace. We must bend all our energy to the job of keeping our free way of life, and to keep it without another war. . . .

Our best chance to keep the peace and to stay free is for nations that believe in freedom to stick together and to build their strength together. . . .

We have been trying . . . to build a system of collective security among those countries who really believe in the principles of the United Nations.

I think we have made a lot of progress. . . .

There are cynics who scorn the United Nations, who are indifferent to the need for cooperation among the free peoples. They do not understand that our best hope for peace is to bind together the nations that are striving for peace and to increase their strength to stop aggression.

The United Nations is being severely tested today because of the Korean conflict. The fighting there is requiring great sacrifices. In a time of crisis there is a tendency to look for some easy way out regardless of the consequences. But we must not be misled. We must not lose sight of the world picture and the critical importance of the United Nations if we are to reach a permanent solution.

Communist aggression in Korea is a part of the worldwide strategy of the Kremlin to destroy freedom. It has shown men all over the world that Communist imperialism may strike anywhere, anytime.

The defense of Korea is part of the worldwide effort of all the free nations to maintain freedom. It has shown free men that if they stand together, and pool their strength, Communist aggression cannot succeed. . . .

We have been urged to take measures which would spread the fighting in the Far East. We have been told that this would bring the Korean conflict to a speedy conclusion; that it would save the lives of our troops. . . . I believe we have a better chance of stopping aggression in Korea, at a smaller cost in the lives of our troops and those of our allies, by following our present course. . . .

. . . the question of limited war or all-out war cannot be decided in the light of Korea alone. It is not a local question. It affects Korea and Japan, and the security of our troops in those places. But it also reaches Europe, and the future of the North Atlantic Treaty, and the security of free people there everywhere else in the world. It is a decision that affects the future of the United Nations and the future of the world.

I have refused to extend the area of the conflict in the Far East, under the circumstances which now prevail, . . .

. . . first on military grounds. The best military advice I have been able to obtain - the best collective military advice in this country - is that this course of action would not lead to a quick and easy solution of the Korean conflict.

On the contrary, it could very well lead to a much bigger and much longer war. . . .

Furthermore, a deep involvement on our part in a war in China, whatever the outcome there, would have critical military consequences in Europe. There is nothing that would give the Kremlin greater satisfaction than to see our resources committed to an all-out struggle in Asia, leaving Europe exposed to the Soviet armies. . . .

Our allies agree with us in the course we are following. They do not believe that we should take the initiative to widen the conflict in the Far East. If the United States were to widen the conflict, we might well have to go it alone.

If we go it alone in Asia, we may destroy the unity of the free nations against aggression. Our European allies are nearer to Russia than we are. They are in far greater danger. If we act without regard to the danger that faces them, they may act without regard to the dangers that we face. Going it alone brought the world to the disaster of World War II. We cannot go it alone in Asia and go it in company in Europe. . . . Going it alone in Asia might wreck the United Nations, the North Atlantic Treaty, and the whole system of collective security we are helping to set up.

That would be a tremendous victory for the Soviet Union.

The path of collective security is our only sure defense against the dangers that threaten us. It is the path to peace in Korea; it is the path to peace in the world.

We are determined to do our utmost to limit the war in Korea. We will not take any action which might place upon us the responsibility of initiating a general war - a third world war. But if the aggressor takes further action which threatens the security of the United Nations forces in Korea, we will meet and counter that action. . . .

Remember this, if we do have another world war, it will be an atomic war. We could expect many atomic bombs to be dropped on American cities, and a single one of them could cause many more times the casualties than we have suffered in all the fighting in Korea. . . .

Some people do not understand how the free world can ever win this long struggle without fighting a third world war. These people overlook the inner weaknesses of the Soviet dictatorship. They forget that the free world is stronger - stronger in its determination, stronger in its staying power, stronger in its human resources - than any system of slavery under a totalitarian dictatorship.

The Kremlin's system of terror, which appears to be its main strength, is one of its greatest weaknesses. Dictatorships are based on fear. They cannot give their people happiness and peace. They have nothing to offer except aggression and slavery.

As the aggressive tactics of the Kremlin are checked by the collective defenses of a free world, the futility of the whole Communist program is becoming more and more apparent to the people under Soviet control. . . .

We must remember that the peoples under the Soviet rule of terror are not only our friends but our allies. They are victims of a terrible tyranny. We do not hate them. We have had friendly relations with them in the past, and we can have such friendship again.

As the free nations build their strength and unity, this fact will compel a change in the Soviet drive for power and conquest. The Soviet rulers are faced with the growing strength of the free world, the increasing cost of aggression, and the increasing difficulty of driving their people to greater and greater hardships. They will be forced by these pressures from within and without to give up aggression. . . .

(125) <u>PRESS CONFERENCE, PRESIDENT TRUMAN</u>, September 20, 1951 [Extract]

Source: *Public Papers of the Presidents: Harry S. Truman, 1951.* Washington: U.S. Government Printing Office, 1965, pp. 527, 528.

Question: Mr. President, on Monday, at the Library of Congress, you said that a Russian agreement wasn't worth the paper it was written on. If that is the case, will this country continue to seek agreements with Russia?

THE PRESIDENT: Yes. When you are in the position to enforce those agreements, they will be kept. That is the reason for the defense program. . . .

Question: Mr. President, would it be correct to infer from what you have just said about Russia, that in the future we will place our reliance on force rather than diplomacy in dealing with Russia?

THE PRESIDENT: Under the circumstances it is necessary. And I dislike it very much. That is what we organized the United Nations for - was to argue these things out without the use of force - but it has become impossible. Korea is the example. . . . I can name you several [other] examples . . . : Greece, Turkey, Korea, and Berlin. Trieste in the beginning.

Question: Mr. President, when you speak of the use of force, you are referring in a general way to all the areas of disagreement?

THE PRESIDENT: To our ability to meet force with force. That is all we are aiming at. We don't want to misuse that force. Our idea is a free and happy world. That is what we are going to continue to fight for.

Question: The other fellow has to use the force first.

THE PRESIDENT: I didn't say that. That is what brought on the Korean thing.

2. Expansion of the Power of the Intelligence Agencies

The National Security Act of 1947 might have delimited the CIA's authority to gathering and disseminating
intelligence information. Nonetheless, the Agency's
role expanded radically almost immediately. Administration officials' perceptions of the subversive and worldwide character of the Soviet threat and elitist disdain
for public opinion and the Congress encouraged them to
rely increasingly on the CIA for the conduct and execution of certain policy objectives. In contrast to the
State Department, the CIA both provided an instrumentality for the secretive conduct of potentially controversial policy and possessed the personnel willing to consider operations which more legalistic officials in the
Foreign Service and State Department might not have
countenanced. The initial expansion of the CIA's role
was confined to psychological warfare. In time, CIA
officials either were directed or independently devised
other more extensive functions. These included subsidizing pro-Western political parties and universities,
devising covert operation capabilities (i.e., planning
and or subsidizing coups), and at least considering
assassinating unfriendly foreign leaders. CIA officials'
mentality of all-out-war with the Soviets, and alarmist
conceptions of Soviet subversive influence, not unnatur-
ally made them responsive to measures, such as the initiation in 1952 of an illegal mail cover operation in
New York City, which directly violated the 1947 Act's
prohibition against any internal security role. By
1953, then, the CIA was no longer the institution
specifically authorized by the 1947 Act and the institutional framework for the far-reaching abuses of power,
publicized only in the 1970s, had been forged.

This development was not, however, the inevitable
byproduct of the Cold War. Rather it derived from the
prevailing political philosophy of those holding high-
level positions in the Administration and the intelligence community. A September 1954 report of a special
committee, the Doolittle Committee, appointed by President Eisenhower to evaluate and recommend changes in the
operation of the CIA starkly captures this philosophy:

> As long as it remains national policy, another
> important requirement is an aggressive covert
> psychological, political and paramilitary organ-
> ization more effective, more unique, and if nec-
> essary, more ruthless than that employed by the
> enemy. No one should be permitted to stand in
> the way of the prompt, efficient, and secure
> accomplishment of this mission.

> It is now clear that we are facing an impla-
> cable enemy whose avowed objective is world
> domination by whatever means and at whatever

cost. There are no rules in such a game.
Hitherto acceptable norms of human conduct do
not apply. If the United States is to survive,
long-standing American concepts of "fair play"
must be reconsidered. We must develop effective espionage and counter-espionage services.
We must learn to subvert, sabotage and destroy
our enemies by more clever, more sophisticated,
and more effective methods than those used
against us. It may become necessary that the
American people be made acquainted with, understand and support this fundamentally repugnant
philosophy.

(126) STAFF REPORT, SENATE SELECT COMMITTEE ON INTELLIGENCE
ACTIVITIES, CIA COVERT ACTION AUTHORITY, 1976 [Extract]

Source: U.S. Senate, Select Committee to Study Governmental
Operations with respect to Intelligence Activities, *Final Report,
Foreign and Military Intelligence*, Book I, 94th Congress 2d ses-
sion, pp. 476-480, 483-496.

Although it has been cited as authority for the CIA to engage
in covert action, the National Security Act of 1947 does not
specifically mention covert action. A review of the hearings,
committee reports and floor debates on the Act reveals no substantial evidence that Congress intended by passage of the Act to
authorize covert action by the CIA. . . .

Congress did intend to provide the newly created CIA with sufficient flexibility so that it would be able to respond to changing circumstances. There is no evidence, however, that the flexibility was intended to allow the creation of a peacetime agency
engaged in activities such as paramilitary action or attempted
assassination.

Although the evidence strongly suggests that the executive
branch did not intend through the language of the National Security Act to obtain authorization from Congress for the conduct of
covert action, the record is not absolutely clear. Whether it did
or did not so intend, the executive branch soon seized upon the
broad language of the National Security Act. Facing what was perceived as an extraordinary threat from the Soviet Union and her
allies, coming to believe that the only possible course of action
for the United States was to respond to covert action with covert
action, the NSC authorized the CIA to conduct covert action. . . .

Nowhere in the National Security Act is covert action specifically authorized. Section 102(d)(5) of the Act, however, . . .
authorizes the CIA to "perform such other functions and duties
related to intelligence affecting the national security as the
National Security Council may from time to time direct." . . .

On its face, the clause might be taken to authorize an enormous range of activities not otherwise specified in the National
Security Act. An important limitation on the authorization, however, is that the activities must be "related to intelligence
affecting the national security." . . . Some covert actions are at

least arguably "related to intelligence affecting the national
security." . . .

. . . Many covert operations, such as the invasion of the Bay
of Pigs, have, at best, only the most limited relationship to
intelligence affecting the national security. As the General
Counsel of the CIA wrote in [September 25,] 1947:

> Taken out of context and without knowledge of its
> history, these Sections [102(d) (4) and (5)] could bear
> almost unlimited interpretation, provided that the ser-
> vices performed could be shown to be of benefit to an
> intelligence agency or related to national intelligence.

> Thus black propaganda, primarily designed for sub-
> version, confusion, and political effect, can be shown
> incidentally to benefit positive intelligence as a
> means of checking reliability of informants, effective-
> ness or penetration, and so forth. Even certain forms
> of S.O. [special operations] work could be held to bene-
> fit intelligence by establishment of W/T [wireless tele-
> graph] teams in accessible areas, and by opening pene-
> tration points in confusion following sabotage or riot.
> In our opinion, however, either activity would be an
> unwarranted extension of the functions authorized in
> Sections 102(d) (4) and (5). This is based on our under-
> standing of the intent of Congress at the time these
> provisions were enacted. . . .

. . . Only the most strained interpretation of "intelligence
affecting the national security" would allow certain covert actions by the CIA such as paramilitary activities or the attempted
assassination of foreign leaders to come under Section 102(d) (5).
As some covert actions are more directly "related to intelligence
affecting the national security," however, it is important to
examine the legislative history of the National Security Act to
determine if these forms of covert action were within the range of
activities which Congress intended to authorize or whether they
represent what the CIA's former General Counsel called "an unwarranted extension of the functions authorized in Sections 102(d)
(4) and (5)." Congressional intent is particularly important in
this instance as Congress required the language of Section 102 to
be written into law rather than incorporating an earlier Presidential Directive by reference. This was done because several
Members of Congress believed that if the CIA's missions were not
set out in the statute, the President could change them at any
time simply by amending the Directive.

. . . it is [also] important to note that Section 102(d) (5)
sets out a second condition - the CIA must be directed by the NSC
to perform the "other functions and duties." . . . General
Vandenberg, who headed the Central Intelligence Group, the CIA's
predecessor body, expressed to the drafters of the National Security Act his belief that the CIA should not have to come continually to the NSC for approval for action. . . . Vandenberg was
told that the CIA would need to come to the NSC only on such
specific matters as the NSC required. . . .

. . . On January 22, 1946, President Truman issued a Presidential Directive which established the National Intelligence

Authority under the direction of the Director of Central Intelligence. . . . Under the Directive, the NIA was to be "assisted by" the Central Intelligence Group, a coordinating body which drew funds and personnel from other agencies of the executive. The CIG was to collect, evaluate, and disseminate intelligence relating to the national security, plan for the coordination of intelligence agencies, and perform "such services of common concern" as the National Intelligence Authority determines can be more efficiently accomplished centrally. The CIG was also to perform "such other functions and duties related to intelligence affecting the national security as the President and the National Intelligence Authority may from time to time direct."

Although the . . . CIG was [purportedly] assigned the "function of conducting covert action" the former General Counsel of the CIA noted that at the time of the CIG draft directive "there was really . . . no contemplation whatsoever of a program of what might be called covert action." In fact, the CIG does not appear to have been engaged in any covert action abroad. The covert action capability of the government which had been lodged in OSS [Office of Strategic Services] and then transferred to SSU [Strategic Services Unit] in the War Department had been, in early 1946, almost totally liquidated. The absence of a covert action program and the decline of the capability suggests that a covert action mission for the CIA was not clearly anticipated by either the executive or the Congress. . . .

In January 1947, . . . Clark Clifford, Charles Murphy, Vice Admiral Forest Sherman, and Major General Lauris Norstad, began to consider proposals for an agency to supercede the CIG, this time in the context of a proposal which would unify the Armed Services. On February 26, 1947, President Truman submitted to the Congress a draft entitled, "The National Security Act of 1947." Title 2 of Section 202 provided for a Central Intelligence Agency (CIA), which would report to a National Security Council (NSC). The NSC was to take over the duties of the NIA while the CIA was to have the functions, personnel, property, and records of the CIG.

The section in the draft legislation dealing with the CIA did not spell out, in any detail, its relationship to the rest of the executive branch or its functional responsibilities. As the framers were primarily concerned with the unification of the armed services, the draft legislation . . . eliminated "any and all controversial material insofar as it referred to central intelligence which might in any way hamper the successful passage of the Act." The legislation incorporated by reference the functions of the CIG as set out in the Presidential Directive of January 22, 1946. . . .

There is little in the public record of this process to indicate congressional intent with respect to the CIA's authority to engage in covert action. The records of public hearings and floor debates on the National Security Act, as well as the proceedings of a committee meeting in executive session, support the view that Congress as a whole did not anticipate that the CIA would engage in such activities.

The record is ambiguous, however, in part because the legislators and witnesses were concerned that United States security might be compromised by too full and frank a discussion of American intelligence needs on the floor of Congress. . . . Related to this point is the possibility that ambiguous language was expressly chosen in order not to offend world opinion. The former General Counsel of the CIA recalled that some Members of Congress sought to put in the statutory language the authorization to conduct espionage and counterespionage. But this was deleted, in "light of the argument that they didn't want it advertised that this country was going to engage in such activities."

An additional problem in interpreting the available evidence is that in 1947 no term was clearly understood to mean covert action as the term is used [in the 1970s]. Members of Congress and witnesses used terms such as "operational activities," "special operations," [or/and] "direct activities," but these remarks were as likely to have meant clandestine collection of Intelligence as covert action. The following exchange between Representative [Fred] Busbey and Secretary [of the Navy James] Forrestal in public hearings before the House Committee on Expenditures in the Executive Departments illustrates this problem:

> Mr. Busbey. Mr. Secretary, this Central Intelligence Group, as I understand it under the bill, is merely for the purpose of gathering, disseminating, and evaluating information to the National Security Council, is that correct?
>
> Secretary Forrestal. That is a general statement of their activity.
>
> Mr. Busbey. I wonder if there is any foundation in the rumors that have come to me to the effect that through the Central Intelligence Agency, they are contemplating *operational activities*?
>
> Secretary Forrestal. I would not be able to go into the details of their operations, Mr. Busbey. The major part of what they do, their major function, as you say, is the collection and collation and evaluation of information from Army Intelligence, Navy Intelligence, the Treasury, Department of Commerce, and most other intelligence, really. Most intelligence work is not of a mystical or mysterious character; it is simply the intelligence gathering of available data throughout this Government. . . . As to the nature and extent of any *direct operational activities*, I think I should rather have General Vandenberg respond to that question. [Emphasis added.]

Another example is contained in a letter . . . from Allen Dulles, then a private citizen but later Director of Central Intelligence, to the Senate Armed Services Committee. Dulles recommended that the CIA have its own appropriations, but be able to supplement these with funds from other agencies, "in order to carry on special operations which may, from time to time, be deemed necessary by the President, the Secretary of State, and the Secretary of National Defense."

Finally, Representative [James] Patterson stated during the floor debates that while he clearly wanted "an independent intelligence agency working without direction by our armed services, with full authority in operation procedures," he knew that it was "impossible to incorporate such broad authority in the bill now before us. . . . "

These exhaust the statements in open session - in hearings or on the floor - which arguably deal with covert action - although . . . they may also be read to refer to clandestine intelligence gathering. There is no clear explanation of or proposal for covert action. No justification for covert action was presented by the Executive. . . .

The legislating committees met extensively in executive session to consider the bill and to discuss the Central Intelligence Agency portions of it. . . . At [a June 27, 1947] meeting the wisdom of centralizing the clandestine intelligence collection function in the CIA was discussed in some detail. Although the Members and witnesses could put aside the security constraints which might have inhibited them in open session, this record too is ambiguous. . . .

The CIA has cited two exchanges at this executive session for the proposition that the House Committee on Expenditures "had full knowledge of the broad implications" of the Presidential Directive and understood it to authorize the CIG to engage in covert action. . . .

The first exchange quoted was between Representative Clarence Brown and General Hoyt S. Vandenberg, Director of Central Intelligence. The full context of the remarks which the Agency quoted, however, clearly indicates that the broad language of the 1946 Directive had been read to authorize clandestine collection of intelligence.

The CIA also cited the executive session testimony of Peter Vischer, who opposed the "other functions and duties" clause. . . . calling it a loophole "because it enabled the President to direct the CIG to perform almost any operations." The CIA notes this opposition, implies that Vischer opposed the clause as it authorized covert action, and claims congressional authorization for covert action because the clause was included in the National Security Act. The full record shows, however, that Vischer spoke specifically in opposition to centralizing clandestine collection in the CIA. He objected to the "other functions and duties" language as it would authorize such collection. . . .

The only clear reference to the activities which are now referred to as covert action took place in the executive session during an exchange between Representative [Robert] Rich and [CIG executive secretary] General [Hoyt] Vandenberg. Representative Rich asked, "Is this agency [the CIG] used in anyway as a propaganda agency?" General Vandenberg responded, "No, sir." . . .

. . . [the inability] to locate transcripts of the other executive sessions [makes] it impossible to state conclusively that covert action was not explicitly mentioned during these meetings. However, none of the participants queried [by the Senate Select Committee on Intelligence Activities] recalled any such discussions and none of the committee reports contain any references to covert action.

A memorandum by the CIA's General Counsel . . . noted that "We do not believe that there was any thought in the minds of Congress that the Central Intelligence Agency, under this authority, would take positive action for subversion and sabotage." In that September 25, 1947 memorandum to the Director, the General Counsel wrote:

A review of debates indicates that Congress was primarily interested in an agency for coordinating intelligence and orginally did not propose any overseas collection activities for CIA. The strong move to provide specifically for such collection overseas was defeated, and, as a compromise, Sections 102(d) (4) and (5) were enacted, which permitted the National Security Council to determine the extent of the collection work to be performed by CIA. We do not believe that there was any thought in the minds of Congress that the Central Intelligence Agency under this authority would take positive action for subversion and sabotage. A bitter debate at about the same time on the State Department's foreign broadcast service tends to confirm our opinion. Further confirmation is found in the brief and off-the-record hearings on appropriations for CIA. . . . It is our conclusion, therefore, that neither M.O. [morale operations] nor S.O. [special operations] should be undertaken by CIA without previously informing Congress and obtaining its approval of the functions and the expenditure of funds for those purposes.

. . . The issue of covert action simply was not raised in the course of the legislation's enactment. . . . Rather than authorizing covert action, the broad language of 102(d) (5) appears to have been intended to authorize clandestine collection of intelligence and to provide the CIA with the "maximum flexibility" necessary to deal with problems which, due to America's inexperience with a peacetime intelligence agency, might not be foreseen.

. . . the executive branch presented no justification to the Congress for the conduct of covert action by the CIA. Yet even while the National Security Act of 1947 was being drafted, introduced, debated, and passed the Coordinating Committee of the Departments of State, War, and the Navy (SWNCC) prepared a paper establishing procedures for psychological warfare during peacetime as well as wartime. On April 30, 1947, SWNCC established a Subcommittee on Psychological Warfare to plan and execute psychological war.

These plans took on new importance as the United States became concerned over the course of events in Western Europe and the Near East. Tension soon became so high that in December of 1947, the Department of State advised the NSC that covert operations mounted by the Soviet Union and her allies threatened the defeat of American foreign policy objectives. The Department recommended that the U.S. supplement its own foreign policy activity with covert action.

At its first meeting in December, 1947, the National Security Council approved NSC-4, which empowered the Secretary of State to coordinate information activities designed to counter communism. A top secret annex took cognizance of the "vicious psychological efforts of the USSR, its satellite countries, and Communist groups to discredit and defeat the activities of the U.S. and other Western powers." The NSC determined that "in the interests of world peace and U.S. national security the foreign information activities of the U.S. government must be supplemented by covert psychological operations."

The CIA was already engaged in clandestine collection of intelligence and, as the NSC put it, "The similarity of operational methods involved in covert psychological and intelligence activities and the need to ensure their secrecy and obviate costly duplication renders the CIA the logical agency to conduct such operations." Therefore, acting under the authority of section 102(d)(5) of the National Security Act of 1947, the NSC instructed the Director of Central Intelligence to initiate and conduct psychological operations that would counteract Soviet and Soviet-inspired covert actions and which would be consistent with U.S. foreign policy and overt foreign information activities.

In the following months the CIA was involved in a number of covert actions. As the Soviet threat loomed larger and larger, the need for covert action, beyond psychological operations, seemed more pressing. On June 18, 1948, the NSC issued NSC-10/2 which superseded NSC-4-A, and vastly expanded the range of covert activities. The CIA was authorized to undertake economic warfare, sabotage, subversion against hostile states (including assistance to guerrilla and refugee liberation groups), and support of indigenous anti-communist elements in threatened countries.

The NSC noted that CIA was already charged with espionage and counterespionage abroad. Because of this, . . . it was "desirable" for "operational reasons" to assign covert action authority to the CIA rather than to create a new unit. Therefore, . . . the NSC ordered the establishment in CIA of the Office of Special Projects (OSP), to conduct covert action. The Chief of OSP was to receive policy guidance from the Secretary of State and the Secretary of Defense. OSP . . . was to operate independently of all components of the CIA to the maximum degree consistent with efficiency.

. . . Language [in the National Security Act] intended to authorize clandestine intelligence gathering and to provide flexibility for unforeseen circumstances was broadened by the executive to cover sabotage, subversion and paramilitary activities. The executive branch did not heed the advice offered by the CIA's General Counsel in 1947 that congressional authorization was still necessary.

Two years after the enactment of the National Security Act and after the NSC had directed the CIA to engage in various covert activities, Congress passed the Central Intelligence Agency Act of 1949. The 1949 legislation was an enabling act containing administrative provisions necessary for the conduct of the Agency's mission. As such, it did not add to the missions of the Agency. . . .

The Act included a number of administrative provisions which clearly were designed to assure the security of some sort of clandestine activity by the CIA. These included the waiver of normal restrictions placed on governmental acquisition of matériel, hiring, and perhaps more important, accounting for funds expended. . . .

The Central Intelligence Agency has argued that passage of the Central Intelligence Agency Act of 1949 "clearly reflects Congress' determination that the Agency be able to conduct activities such as covert action, similar to those conducted by the OSS." Although members of the House Armed Services Committee were aware that the Central Intelligence Agency was conducting covert operations and that the administrative provisions would be "essential to the flexibility and security" of these operations, there is no evidence that Congress as a whole knew the range of clandestine activities, including covert action, which was being undertaken by the CIA. The committee reports on the Central Intelligence Agency Act include no reference to covert action. The floor debates contain only one reference to covert action, and strongly suggest that the Congress knew only that clandestine intelligence gathering was going on.

In addition, the provisions of the 1949 Act are not uniquely designed to facilitate covert action. They would serve the needs of an organization performing espionage equally well; Members of Congress, in fact, described the Act as an "espionage bill." Thus even a careful reader of the Act would not infer from its provisions that the Agency was conducting covert action. . . .

The bill which was to become the Central Intelligence Agency Act of 1949 was first introduced in Congress in 1948. The Director of Central Intelligence appeared before the House Armed Services Committee on April 8, 1948, to discuss the bill. The Director noted:

> It was thought when we started back in 1946, that at least we would have time to develop this mature service over a period of years . . . Unfortunately, the international situation has not allowed us the breathing space we might have liked, and so as we present this bill, we find ourselves in operations up to our necks, and we need the authorities contained herein as a matter of urgency.

It is clear that the operations that the Director referred to were understood by the executive branch to include covert action. In describing the provision of the bill which would eliminate the normal government advertising requirements, the Director stated that there were urgent requests from overseas which required immediate operational response. As an example, he provided: "Any possible action in connection with the Italian election." In later remarks on the same section, the Director cited the need to avoid advertising for contracts for the production of certain materiél, listing among his examples explosives and silencers. Such materiél was clearly not for the purposes of clandestine intelligence gathering reporting.

In his 100-page statement, the Director also explained the provision for unvouchered funds . . . .:

> In view of the nature of the work which must be conducted by the CIA under the National Security Act and applicable directives of the National Security Council, it is necessary to use funds for various covert or semi-covert operations and other purposes where it is either impossible to conform with existing government procedures and regulations or conformance therewith would materially

injure the national security. It is not practicable, and in some cases impossible, from either a record or security viewpoint to maintain the information and data which would be required under usual government procedures and regulations. In many instances, it is necessary to make specific payments or reimbursements on a project basis where the background information is of such a sen sitive nature from a security viewpoint that only a gen eral certificate, signed by the Director of CIA, should be processed through even restricted channels. To do otherwise would obviously increase the possiblities of penetration with respect to any specific activity or general project. The nature of the activities of CIA are such that items of this nature are recurring and, while in some instances the confidential or secret aspects as such may not be of primary importance, the extraordinary situations or the exigencies of the particular transac tion involved warrant the avoidance of all normal chan nels and procedures.

On the basis of this presentation, it can be concluded that at least the House Armed Services Committee, one of the committees which had jurisdiction over the CIA, knew that the CIA was con ducting or would in the future conduct covert action. The Commit tee also knew that the administrative provisions would enhance the Agency's covert action capability.

The evidence, however, is not entirely clear. While the present day reader may interpret "covert or semicovert operations" to mean covert action, the Members had had little exposure to these terms. Covert or semicovert operations could easily have been interpreted to mean clandestine intelligence gathering oper ations; the CIA's role in clandestine intelligence gathering had been discussed in a hearing before the same committee, as well as in the press.

Even if it were assumed, moreover, that the House and Senate Armed Services Committees fully understood that the CIA was en gaging in covert action, there is no evidence that the Congress as a whole knew that the CIA was engaged in covert action or that the administrative provisions were intended to facilitate it. The hearings on the CIA Act of 1949 were held almost entirely in executive session. The committee reports on the Act did not men tion covert action at all. They were bland and uninformative - the provision to provide the secret funding of the CIA through transfers from appropriations to other government agencies was described as providing "for the annual financing of Agency opera tions without impairing security." They were strikingly incom plete. As the House Armed Services Committee report itself noted, the report:

> does not contain a full and detailed explanation of all
> the provisions of the proposed legislation in view of
> the fact that much of such information is of a highly
> confidential nature.

The floor debates contain only one indication that covert action, as opposed to clandestine intelligence gathering, was being, or would be undertaken by the CIA. The debates strongly suggest that rather than approving covert action by the CIA,

Congress was attempting to facilitate clandestine intelligence gathering by the Agency.

Prior to the passage of the Act there had been discussion in the press of CIA involvement in clandestine intelligence gathering. Clandestine intelligence gathering was mentioned on the floor; . . . . Members referred to the CIA Act of 1949 as an "espionage bill." Senator Tydings, the Chairman of the Senate Armed Services Committee, stated, "The bill does not provide for new activity, but what it does particularly is to seek to safeguard information procured by agents of the government so that it will not fall into the hands of enemy countries or potential enemy countries who would use the information to discover who the agents were and kill them." . . .

(127) NSC ACTIONS 7-12, November 14, 1947 [Extract]

Source: National Security Council Files, National Archives.

****

9. POSITION OF THE US WITH RESPECT TO ITALY
    (NSC 1)

>   a. Adopted NSC 1 subject to the following amendments:
>
>   (1) Revise Paragraph 8-a-(3) to read: "Further assistance to the Italian armed forces in the form of technical advice to increase their capacity to deal with threats to Italian internal security and territorial integrity."
>
>   (2) On page 6, first line, substitute "at an appropriate time" for "now".
>
>   (3) Revise paragraph 12-e to read: "If the Communists seize control of all or part of Italy prior to December 15, 1947, the US should suspend withdrawal of its troops from Italy pending a consideration of the status of the Peace Treaty and of the US military situation at that time."

****

(NOTE: NSC 1/1, which includes the above amendments, was transmitted on November 14, 1947 to the Secretary of State for submission to the President. Comments of the Joint Chiefs of Staff were transmitted to the President with the minutes of the meeting.)

(128) NOTE, NSC EXECUTIVE SECRETARY SIDNEY SOUERS TO NATIONAL SECURITY COUNCIL, November 14, 1947 [Extract]

Source: National Security Council Files, National Archives.

The enclosed Report is a revision of NSC 1 in the form accepted by the National Security Council at its second meeting.

The enclosed Report will be submitted to the President by the Secretary of State, with a notation that the section entitled

"Conclusions" constitutes an expression of the Council's advice to the President.

NSC 1/1, REPORT BY THE NATIONAL SECURITY COUNCIL

on

THE POSITION OF THE UNITED STATES WITH RESPECT TO ITALY

****

3. The basic objective of the United States in Italy is to establish and maintain in that key country conditions favorable to our national security. Current US policies toward Italy include measures intended to preserve Italy as an independent, democratic state, friendly to the United States, and capable of effective participation in the resistance to Communist expansion.

4. The Italian Government, ideologically inclined toward western democracy, is weak and is being subjected to continuous attack by a strong Communist Party. The Communists were excluded from the Italian Government in June 1947. They resent this exclusion and are exerting increasing pressure to regain lost ground. The ultimate goal of the Italian Communist Party is its complete control of Italy and Italy's alignment with the USSR. The Italian Government is in urgent need of political support, dollar credits favorable material allocations, and military assistance in the form of equipment and technical advice.

5. The Italian Peace Treaty came into effect on September 15, 1947, and under its terms the small US and UN forces in Italy must be withdrawn by December 15, 1947. Under Annex VII of the Italian Treaty, 5000 US, 5400 British, and 5000 Yugoslav troops are to remain in the Free Territory of Trieste until such time as the Governor of the Free Territory shall declare to the Security Council of the UN that their services are no longer required. Although it is estimated that the Government forces are strong enough to cope with a general Communist armed uprising, it is nevertheless possible that the Communists may gain, and hold for the time being, control of northern Italy. It is probable that the Italian Communist Party will not attempt to seize control of Italy until US and British troops have been withdrawn at the end of the ninety-day period. The rise of Communism to power in Italy would seriously menace US security interests. . . .

7. The United States has security interests of primary importance in Italy and the measures to implement our current policies to safeguard those interests should be strengthened without delay.

8. The United States should:

a. Give full support to the present Italian Government to equally satisfactory successive governments by means of measures such as the following:

****

(3) Further assistance to the Italian armed forces in the form of technical advice to increase their capacity to deal with threats to Italian internal security and territorial integrity. . . .

(5) Directive to Foreign Liquidation Commission to transfer, "in the national interest", to the Italian

armed forces . . . certain non-combat equipment essential to the proper function of the armed forces. . . .

e. Actively combat Communist propaganda in Italy by an effective US information program and by all other practicable means, including the use of unvouchered funds. . . .

10. In the event that the situation in Italy develops in such a way that it becomes impossible for the Italian Government to carry out terms of the Italian Peace Treaty, the United States should take the position that a treaty is a contract binding upon all parties thereto, and that unless all parties are in a position to carry out the contract the treaty ceases to be binding upon any of the signatories. The United States then should announce that it must reconsider its position with respect to the terms of the Italian Peace Treaty in the light of the new situation.

11. The United States should not use US armed force in a civil conflict of an internal nature in Italy.

12. In the event that a Communist-dominated Government is set up in all or part of Italy by civil war or illegal means, the United States should continue to recognize the legal government and actively assist it. Such Communist aggression in Italy should immediately be countered by steps to extend the strategic disposition of United States armed forces in Italy and other parts of the Mediterranean area. A specific plan should include the following measures:

a. The Italian Government should inform the Ambassadors of the US, UK, France, and the USSR in Rome (with the request that they notify the other signatories of the Italian Peace Treaty) that it is no longer able to maintain effective authority throughout Italy and that it consequently cannot accept responsibility for the executive of the terms of the Peace Treaty.

b. The United States should immediately and publicly express concern over the fact that disorder has broken out in Italy so soon after the entry into effect of the Peace Treaty and should notify the Italian Government and the UN that, in the light of the new situation, the United States must reconsider its position with respect to the terms of the Treaty.

c. The Italian Government should inform the US Government that in view of its inability to carry out the terms of the Peace Treaty it will take all action within the limits of its ability to cooperate with the US under the changed situation. The US should then inform the Italian Government that it will require additional military facilities for the time being. Upon agreement with the Italian Government, the US should utilize selected naval and air bases in Italy. In order to accomplish preparations for such use of Italian air bases, steps should be taken at an appropriate time to have the Italian Government make available such facilities to the US for training flights of US air units.

d. The United States should announce the suspension of aid to Communist-dominated areas of Italy under the UN relief program, at the same time making it clear that this aid will be continued for areas under the jurisdiction of the Italian Government.

e. If Communists seize control of all or part of Italy prior to December 15, 1947, the US should suspend withdrawal of its troops from Italy pending a consideration of the status of the Peace Treaty and of the US military situation at that time.

13. In the event that the elections in March 1948 should result in the establishment of a Communist Government in Italy, reconsideration of US policy with respect to Italy would be necessary. With that end in view, the present report should be revised not less than 45 days before the elections in the light of the political situation existing at that time.

(129) MEMORANDUM, SECRETARY OF STATE DEAN ACHESON TO JAMES LAY (EXECUTIVE SECRETARY, NSC), October 26, 1950

Source: *Foreign Relations of the United States: 1950 Vol. I National Security Affairs; Foreign Economic Policy.* Washington: U.S. Government Printing Office, 1977, pp. 402-403.

During the last few years there have been a number of instances in which communist skill in utilizing guerrilla forces and tactics has been apparent. This was true in Greece and is at present notably the case in Indochina, in Malaya, and in the Philippines. Examples in Korea, and elsewhere could also be cited. While there has been a certain amount of exchanges of views between military representatives, as in the case of the British and French in Southeast Asia, it does not appear that an organized effort has been made to pool information, skills and techniques among the friendly nations who have a common interest in defeating this kind of activity. It is to be anticipated that the international communist movement will continue to utilize similar tactics in the future. We have recognized the need for a cooperative defense on formal military lines in the North Atlantic Treaty area. We have also begun coordination of information and propaganda activities particularly with the British and French both in Europe and in Asia. It would seem appropriate and important to extend the scope of such guerrilla warfare, mobilizing the experience gained in jungle fighting during the war, in operations in Greece, in Korea, Malaya and elsewhere, as well as taking into account the successes and failures of both political and military action, or inaction in the field of anti-guerrilla activity.

Accordingly, I recommend that the NSC Senior Staff arrange for a study of this matter, and submit a report on it for the consideration of the Council. The report might include a brief statement of the problem from the military point of view as well as indicating the most desirable and effective means for bringing about the desired collaboration. In this connection, attention would need to be paid to possible political sensibilities of the governments whose collaboration is sought. It would be desirable also to indicate how many governments should be approached, for example, whether Burma and Indonesia should be included.

It should be noted that no part of the foregoing recommendation is concerned with the field of special political operations, which presumably could provide useful assistance and support in the areas concerned, inasmuch as it is understood that adequate means already exist for the exchange of information in that field.

(130) ANNEXES TO NSC 68/3, REPORT TO THE NATIONAL SECURITY COUN-
CIL BY NSC EXECUTIVE SECRETARY JAMES LAY, December 8, 1950
[Extract]

Source: *Foreign Relations of the United States: 1950, Vol. I
National Security Affairs; Foreign Economic Policy.* Washington:
U.S. Government Printing Office, 1977, pp. 448-450, 452, 453, 461.

****

The Economic Cooperation Administration is . . . charged with a direct responsibility for conducting a foreign information program with regard to one specific aspect of the foreign policy of the United States. The great majority of its information work consists of thoroughly informing the people of the Marshall Plan countries of the achievements and objectives of the Plan.

While conducting this information program, the Economic Cooperation Administration, in order to promote the success of the Marshall Plan, is involved in many aspects of the international information program carried on by the Department of State. . . .

The foreign information program of the Economic Cooperation Administration has been, and still is most vigorously conducted in the sixteen countries of western Europe which are recipients of Economic Cooperation Adminstration assistance. Foreign information services are being developed in the countries of Southeast Asia where the Economic Cooperation Administration is administering programs.

From the beginning the Economic Cooperation Administration has decentralized the operations of its foreign information program. The largest information operation is in the Office of the ECA Special Representative in Paris. That office assists the Mission Information officers . . . [and] also functions on a Western Europe-wide basis to produce, in various media, materials showing the overall achievements and objectives of the Marshall Plan in all the Western European members. . . .

The ECA has also operated on the principle of vigorous participation by indigenous governments and peoples. It has paid close attention to organized labor in Europe, especially in countries like France and Italy where the Communists still control the largest labor confederations. It has labor information officers in the majority of the Missions. . . .

In conformity with NSC 59/1, the ECA foreign information program is coordinated with other foreign information activities of the United States Government in support of national objectives. Policy coordination is assured through the participation of the representative of the ECA on the Interdepartmental Foreign Information Organization. It is further assured by the activities of committees set up in the capital of each nation in which the ECA is functioning. These committees consist of the Public Affairs Officer, the ECA Information Officer, the ECA Labor Information Officer, an administrative officer of the ECA Mission and an administrative officer of the Embassy. Their task is to discuss the information activities of USIS and ECA in that country and to work out joint projects where possible. Such joint projects are financed with ECA counterpart funds. . . .

1. <u>The Task of Information and Educational Exchange</u>. The frustration of the design of the Kremlin will result primarily from concrete decisions taken and vigorous measures executed in the political, military and economic fields by the people and the governments of the free world under the leadership of the United States. The task of the United States foreign information and educational exchange programs is to assure that the psychological implications of these actions are, first, fully developed and second, effectively conveyed to the minds and the emotions of groups and individuals who may importantly influence governmental action and popular attitudes in other nations and among other peoples. . . .

3. <u>The Development of Psychological Resistance</u>. The development and maintenance of psychological resistance to the design of the Kremlin calls for continuous and highly detailed exposure of the ways in which Soviet Communism threatens the interest shared by other peoples and nations. These may be revealed in the contradiction between the deeds and the words of the Kremlin, between the ideals proclaimed abroad and the conditions of poverty, oppression and terror prevailing within the Soviet Union and its satellites and between the professions of peace and the facts of massive armed force and of imperial aggression. By concrete example of what Soviet Communism has done within its orbit and intends to do wherever its agents seize authority, the myth can be destroyed that it stands for national freedom, international peace, social progress, economic development and human betterment.

Exposure of the nature, the intentions and the capabilities of the Soviet Union is part of a program to induce peoples and nations outside its sphere:

a. To face up to the fact that Soviet Communism is the implacable enemy of all free nations and peoples and of their common aspiration.

b. To participate in effective actions to deter or, if necessary to repel direct, or indirect aggression by the Soviet Union and its satellites.

c. To sacrifice leisure and comforts in order to resist Soviet Communism.

d. To maintain efficient governments, stable economies and the discipline required to support resistance to Soviet Communism.

e. To prevent the infiltration of agents of Soviet Communism into the armed forces, the government, labor unions, educational institutions, press and radio and other key organizations and to bring about the elimination of those already in such positions.

f. To cooperate with other nations and peoples in a spirit of accommodation for mutually desired ends.

g. To carry on these actions for as long as necessary to frustrate the design of the Kremlin. . . .

1. It is axiomatic that the situation appreciated in NSC 68 and the policy proposed to meet it require the improvement and

intensification of U.S. foreign intelligence and related activities, as a safeguard against political or military surprise, and
as essential to the conduct of the affirmative program envisaged.

2.   The Director of Central Intelligence and Intelligence
Advisory Committee have taken and are taking action directed toward the improvement and intensification of foreign intelligence
and related activities.   For reasons of security, the specific
programs undertaken and contemplated, and their budgetary requirements, are not set forth here.   It has been determined, however,
that even the substantially increased budgets now projected would
be inconsiderable in relation to the grand total of the other
programs projected in this report. . . .

(131)   FINAL REPORT, SENATE SELECT COMMITTEE ON INTELLIGENCE
ACTIVITIES, PROGRAM BRANCH 7, 1976 [Extract]

Source: U.S. Senate: Select Committee to Study Governmental
Operations with respect to Intelligence Activities, *Final Report,
Supplementary Detailed Staff Reports on Foreign and Military
Intelligence*, Book IV, 94th Congress, 2d session, pp. 128-133.

Boris T. Pash, an Army colonel specializing in intelligence
and counterintelligence, was assigned to the CIA from March 3,
1949, to January 3, 1952, . . . In the formative years of the CIA,
Pash served as Chief of Program Branch 7 (PB/7), a "special operations" unit within the Office of Policy Coordination [OPC] the
original clandestine services organization . . . The responsibility for standard forms of covert action was assigned to the six
other program branches within OPC's Staff 3:   political warfare,
psychological warfare, economic warfare, escape and evasion,
sabotage, and countersabotage.   According to Colonel Pash, PB/7
was responsible for "such activities which the other six branches
didn't specifically have."   Pash testified that PB/7 was "not
operations," but rather involved in the planning of "special operations" such as promoting defections from Communist countries,
facilitating the escape of prominent political refugees, disseminating anti-Communist propaganda behind the Iron Curtain, and contingency planning for the death of foreign leaders, such as
Stalin.

. . . [However, former CIA official Howard] Hunt stated that,
based on "hearsay" from his superiors in the CIA's Southeast
Europe division in the early 1950s, he had the "distinct impression" that Colonel Boris Pash had run a unit which would arrange
an assassination mission if it were required.

The Director of Operations Planning for OPC, who supervised
program branches, confirmed the fact that Colonel Pash's Program,
7 unit was responsible for assassinations and kidnapping as well
as other "special operations."   The supervisor testified that he
consulted with Frank Wisner, the Director of OPC, who agreed that
Pash should have jurisdiction over assassinations.   Kidnapping
was also part of PB/7's "catch-all function," according to the
supervisor - "kidnapping of personages behind the Iron Curtain
. . . if they were not in sympathy with the regime, and could
be spirited out of the country by our people for their own safety;
or kidnapping of people whose interests were inimical to ours."

Boris Pash testified [before the Senate Select Committee on Intelligence Activities] . . . .

It is conceivable to me that, if someone in OPC had thought that an assassination program and policy should be developed, the requirement might have been levied on PB/7 because of the "catch-all" nature of its responsibility . . . I was never asked to undertake such planning. It was not my impression that such planning was my responsibility. However, because of the "catch-all" nature of my unit, it is understandable to me that others on the PP [Political and Psychological Warfare] Staff could have had the impression that my unit would undertake such planning.

The Deputy Chief of PB/7, who served under Pash, testified, however, that he had a clear recollection that the written charter of the "special operations" unit included the following language:

PB/7 will be responsible for assassination, kidnapping and such other functions as from time to time may be given it . . . by higher authority.

He said that the charter also assigned to PB/7 responsibility for any functions not specifically assigned to the other program branches. The Deputy Chief did not recall any discussion at the CIA of the assassination of kidnapping aspects of this charter because, compared to the charters of the other program branches, he believed that PB/7's charter was "more secret than any of the others." He construed the charter's reference to "higher authority" to include "State Department, Defense Department, National Security Council, the President of the United States."

Boris Pash did not recall "particular wording" in a charter that included a reference to assassinations, but he did not dispute the accuracy of the Deputy Chief's testimony: "It could have been there without my recalling it, but I didn't give it any serious consideration because I knew that . . . it would be beyond us."

The Director of Operations Planning did not recall the charter of PB/7, but he testified that whether or not there was a written directive "it was clear" to everyone in OPC that assassination and kidnapping "was within the purview" of Pash's responsibilities. The Director testified that "the heads of the program branch" were all involved in general discussions of assassination as a tactic, although the subject did not have a high priority. . . .

None of the witnesses testified that any actual assassination operation or planning was ever undertaken by PB/7, which was disbanded along with the other program branches when the DDP [Directorate for Plans] was formed in late 1952. Pash testified that he was "never in charge of or involved in any assassination planning, nor ever requested to do so." Pash's Deputy said that no action or planning was ever undertaken pursuant to that portion of the PB/7 charter which assigned responsibility for assassination and kidnapping. The Director of Operations Planning testified that he knew of no assassination mission or planning, including contingency planning, by Pash or anyone in OPC. The only consideration of assassinations that the Director was aware of was the general discussion among Pash and other program branch chiefs in the process of establishing OPC. . . .

Howard Hunt testified that he once met with Boris Pash and his Deputy to discuss "on hypothetical basis" a method of dealing with a situation in which the CIA suspected that a double-agent was undermining the Agency's liaison with a group in West Germany. . . . Hunt described his inquiry to Pash as "a search mission to determine the alleged capability of Colonel Pash in 'wet affairs' . . . that is, liquidations, would have any relevance to our particular problem." Hunt said that Pash "seemed a little startled at the subject. He indicated that it was something that would have to be approved by higher authority and I withdrew and never approached Colonel Pash again." Nonetheless, it was Hunt's impression even after leaving the meeting with Pash that assassination was one function of Pash's unit.

Hunt testified: "I never asked [Pash] to plan an assassination mission, I simply asked if he had the capability." . . .

Colonel Pash testified . . . : "I deny that I have ever talked to [Hunt] about [assassination] and that he ever asked me about it." Pash did not recall "any discussion of any double-agent-type activity anyplace." The Deputy Chief of PB/7 also said that he knew "absolutely nothing" about the incident recounted by Hunt.

Pash [and the Deputy Chief] stated that PB/7 would not have dealt with double-agent problems because his unit was more oriented to planning rather than "operational" activity.

The Director of Operations Planning testified, however, that Pash's unit would have had responsibility for the planning aspects of dealing with a double-agent problem. But the Director was not aware of any specific instances in which the "Special Operations" unit had to handle a double-agent problem. The Director said that assassination or complete isolation was generally regarded as the means of dealing with a suspected double-agent. . . .

The Deputy Chief [of the "Special Operations" unit] testified that in the summer of 1949, while he was serving as Acting Chief of PB/7 because Boris Pash was out of the country, the Chief of the CIA's political warfare program branch approached him to request the assassination of an Asian leader. After attending a planning meeting at the State Department, the Chief of the political branch - who was the CIA's liaison with the State Department - told Pash's deputy that the Asian leader "must be sent to meet his ancestors." The Deputy Chief of PB/7 testified that the political branch chief assured him that there was "higher authority" for this request.

The Deputy Chief referred the request to OPC Director Frank Wisner's assistant. Soon thereafter Wisner's assistant told the Deputy Chief: "It has gone right to the top, and the answer is no . . . we don't engage in such activities." He instructed the Deputy Chief to inform anyone involved of this position and to destroy any document related to the incident. The Deputy Chief followed these instructions. . . .

(132) <u>PRESS CONFERENCE, PRESIDENT TRUMAN</u>, July 26, 1951 [Extract]

Source: *Public Papers of the Presidents: Harry S. Truman, 1951.*
Washington: U.S. Government Printing Office, 1965, p. 427.

Question: Mr. President, would you care to clarify the functions of the newly formed Gordon Gray board? There seems to be
a great deal of misunderstanding as to it.

THE PRESIDENT: The Psychological Warfare Board is just what
it says. That board is for the purpose of coordinating things
that will psychologically help win the peace. I think Gordon Gray
can give you a detailed statement on the subject that will cover
every phase of it. I would have to talk all afternoon to do that.

Question: May I ask one more question, sir?

THE PRESIDENT: Go ahead.

Question: Do you intend for it to be a permanent board?

THE PRESIDENT: Yes, it is a part of the Central Intelligence
Agency.

(133) <u>MEMO, CIA DIRECTOR WALTER B. SMITH TO THE PRESIDENT</u>, March
21, 1952 [Extract]

Source: Charles Murphy Files, Harry S. Truman Library.

****

The proposals in the [President's] message [on special immigration programs to aid refugees from communism] respecting the
reception, care, and movement of escapees from the Soviet orbit
seem entirely satisfactory. In its revised form there is no objection, as far as this agency is concerned, to the general language with regard to possible education and training in Europe.
However, such education and training, if carried out in Europe
through European institutions, should not become, <u>overtly</u>, an
American governmental enterprise. As you know, this agency has been
<u>covertly</u> aiding a significant educational project for iron curtain
escapees at the University of Strasbourg. Our connection with
this project has not been disclosed and should not be.

(134) <u>CIA INSPECTOR GENERAL'S SURVEY OF THE OFFICE OF SECURITY,
CIA, ANNEX II</u>, undated but written during the early 1960s [Extract]

Source: U.S. Senate, Select Committee to Study Governmental Operations with respect to Intelligence Activities, *Hearings on Intelligence Activities*, Vol. 4 Mail Opening, 94th Congress, 1st session, pp. 175-180, 182-186.

PROJECT SCPOINTER/HGLINGUAL

1. This project is a sensitive mail intercept program started by the Office of Security in 1952 in response to a request from
the SR [Soviet] Division. Under the original project, named
SCPOINTER, representatives of the Office of Security obtained access to mail to and from the USSR and copied the names of the
addressees and addressors. In 1955 the DD/P [Deputy Director of

Plans] transferred the responsibilities in his area for this program from SR Division to the CI [Counterintelligence] Staff, the
program was gradually expanded, and its name was changed to
HGLINGUAL. Since then the program has included not only copying
information from the exteriors of envelopes, but also opening and
copying selected items.

2. The activity cannot be called a "project" in the usual
sense, because it was never processed through the approval system
and has no separate funds. The various components involved have
been carrying out their responsibilities as a part of their normal staff functions. Specific DD/P approval was obtained for certain budgetary practices in 1956 and for the establishment of a
TSD [Technical Services Division] lab in 1960, but the normal pro-
gramming procedures have not been followed for the project as a
whole. However, the DCI [CIA Director], the DD/P, and the DD/S
[Deputy Director of Security] have been aware of the project since
its inception and their approval may thus be inferred.

3. The mechanics of the project can be summarized as follows.
Mail to and from the USSR and other countries is processed through
the branch post office at LaGuardia Airport in New York City.
The postal authorities agreed ⌊in 1952⌋ to a screening of mail by
Agency representatives at this central point, and office space
has been established there for three Agency officers and one representative of the postal service. As mail is received it is
screened by the Agency team and the exteriors of the envelopes
are photographed on the site. . . . the Agency team selects approximately 60 items a day which are set aside and covertly removed from the post office at the end of the day. These are carried to the Manhattan Field Office (MFO) and during the evening
they are steamed open, reproduced and then resealed. The letters
are replaced in the mails the following morning. The films are
forwarded to the Office of Security at [CIA] headquarters and
thence to the CI Staff, where dissemination is controlled.

4. The total flow of mail through the LaGuardia post office
is not screened. The intercept team can work there only when the
postal representative is on duty which is usually the normal five-
day, 40-hour week. Mail, of course, is received and processed at
the post office 24 hours a day, seven days a week. Thus much of
the overseas mail simply is not available for screening. Regis-
tered mail also is not screened because it is numbered and carefully controlled; however, on occasion, it has been possible to
remove and process individual items on a priority basis. . . .

5. Three Security officers at the MFO work fulltime on the
project, and one clerical employee helps. Most of the officers'
time is spent at the LaGuardia post office screening and photo-
graphing the exteriors of envelopes and supervising the actual
openings during the evening. . . .

6. The principal guidance furnished to the interception team
is the "watch list" of names compiled by the CI Staff. Names may
be submitted by the SR Division, the FBI, the CI Staff, or the
Office of Security. . . . The list itself is not taken to the
LaGuardia post office, and the three team members have to memor-
ize it. Headquarters has compared the actual watch list intercepts with the photographs of all exteriors, and there has not
yet been a case of a watch list item having been missed by inter-

ceptors. Of the total items opened, about one-third are on the
watch list and the others are selected at random. Over the years,
however, the interceptors have developed a sixth sense or intui-
tion, and many of the names on the watch list were placed there as
a result of interest created by the random openings. . . .

7. One of the uncertainties of the project is lack of specific knowledge concerning early agreements with postal authorities
and any commitments which the Agency may have made. Senior postal authorities in Washington approved the earlier phases of the
activity. There are no documents to support this, however. After
the initial acceptance of the project by postal authorities, liaison responsibilities were transferred to the Office of Security
and have since been handled by the chief of MFO. The designated
liaison officer for the postal service is the head of its Inspection Service in New York. The Agency has been fortunate in that
the same persons have been associated with the project since its
inception. Details of agreements and conversations have not been
reduced to writing, however, and there is now some uncertainty as
to what the postal authorities may have been told or what they
might reasonably be expected to have surmised. This is important
because the New York facility is being expanded in the expectation
that we will continue to have access to the mail. The very nature
of the activity, however, makes it impossible at this point to
try and have a firm understanding with postal authorities. There
thus seems to be no alternative except to continue relying on the
discretion and judgment of the persons involved.

8. The postal representative designated to work with the inter-
ceptor team at LaGuardia is a relatively junior but highly intelligent mail clerk. He probably suspects but has not been informed
that the Agency is sponsoring the program. He is not a member of
the postal Inspection Service, but reports to it on matters concerned with the project. . . . Because of the mail clerk's long
association with the activity it should be assumed that he knows
our basic objectives. On the other hand, there is no evidence
that he has ever communicated this knowledge to his New York superiors. It is possible, of course, that key postal officials both
in New York and Washington suspect the true nature of the activity
and have decided not to make an issue of it so long as they are
not required officially to sanction it. In any event, the success
of the project depends upon the cooperation of the mail clerk because mail cannot be removed without his knowledge. If he should
be replaced it would probably be necessary to withdraw from the
operation until his successor could be evaluated. . . .

12. Disseminations to the FBI [which began in 1958] are approximately equal to those made to SR Division. Since the information is largely domestic CI/CE [Counterintelligence/Counterespi-
onage], it is not difficult to conclude that the FBI is receiving
the major benefit from this project.

13. The annual cost of this activity cannot be estimated accurately because both administration and operations have always
been decentralized. The costs are budgeted by the contributing
components as a part of their regular operating programs. . . .
This dispersal of costs throughout the budgets of other components
is an effective security device and should be continued but we
believe that it is nevertheless necessary that exact cost figures
be developed to permit Agency management to evaluate the activity.

14. There is no coordinated procedure for processing information received through the program; each component has its own system. . . .

15. The general security of the project has always been maintained at a very high level. When intelligence information is disseminated the source is concealed and no action can be taken until a collateral source is found. [*Officially deleted.*] The Office of Security has not obtained full clearances on post office personnel with whom it is dealing. This should be done in the case of the mail clerk who can be presumed to know much of what is going on. Another oversight is the absence of any emergency plan for use if the project should be exposed and time prevented consultation with headquarters. On the whole, security has been exceptionally good.

16. Probably the most obvious characteristic of the project is the diffusion of authority. Each unit is responsible for its own interests and in some areas there is little coordination. . . . There is no single point in the Agency to which one might look for policy and operational guidance on the project as a whole. . . . The greatest disadvantages of this diffusion of authority are (a) there can be no effective evaluation of the project if no officer is concerned with all its aspects, and (b) there is no central source of policy guidance in a potentially embarrassing situation.

17. We do not advocate a change in the methods of operation, nor do we believe that the responsibilities of the participating components should be diluted, but we feel that the activity has now developed to the point that clear command and administrative channels for the over-all project are essential. We also believe that a formal evaluation of the project is required.

18. Operational evaluation should include an assessment of overall potential. It is improbable that anyone inside Russia would wittingly send or receive mail containing anything of obvious intelligence or political significance. It should also be assumed that Russian tradecraft is as good as our own and that Russian agents communicating with their headquarters would have more secure channels than the open mails. On the other hand, many seemingly innocent statements can have intelligence significance. . . . No intercept program can cover the entire flow of mail, and the best that can be done is to develop techniques which will provide a highly selective examination of a small portion. With the limitations imposed by budgetary and personnel ceilings, as well as by policy considerations, it must be recognized that the full potential of this project is not likely to be developed. However, it does provide a basic apparatus which could be expanded if the need arose.

Recommendation No. 41:

a. The DD/P and the DD/S direct a coordinated evaluation of this project, with particular emphasis on costs, potential and substantive contribution to the Agency's mission.

b. An emergency plan and cover story be prepared for the possibility that the operation might be blown.

Through a covert relationship with the three international telegraph companies headquartered in the United States during World War II, the Army had acquired access to the telegraphic messages of adversary powers transmitted through these companies' facilities. With the end of the war, military officials sought to continue this potentially beneficial relationship, directed now at the Soviet Union. Yet, company officials hesitated to continue to provide this service as they were concerned about their companies' vulnerability given the illegality of this operation (violating the ban against the interception and divulgence of wire and radio messages of Section 605 of the Federal Communications Act of 1934). The military, however, soon encountered in the Truman Administration a more than willing participant in the effort to undercut these officials' hesitancy. Both Secretary of Defense Forrestal and Attorney General Tom Clark encouraged these company officials in their continued violation of the law. Moreover, the Administration drafted and, unsuccessfully as it turned out, sought to secure congressional passage of legislation to legalize this operation. When legislative action proved impossible, the Administration proceeded as if such action were not needed. This program, Operation SHAMROCK, continued until publicly exposed in 1975. After its establishment by a secret executive order of President Truman in 1952, the National Security Agency assumed responsibility for this program. (See also Official Secrets Section, pp. 370-373.)

(135) STATEMENT AND REPORT, SENATOR FRANK CHURCH, CHAIRMAN SENATE SELECT COMMITTEE ON INTELLIGENCE ACTIVITIES, November 6, 1975 [Extract]

Source: U.S. Senate, Select Committee to Study Governmental Operations with respect to Intelligence Activities, *Hearings on Intelligence Activities*, Vol. 5 The National Security Agency and Fourth Amendment Rights, 94th Congress, 1st session, pp. 57-60.

SHAMROCK was the cover name given to a message-collection program [conducted by the National Security Agency, NSA] in which the Government persuaded three international telegraph companies, RCA Global, ITT World Communications, and Western Union International, to make available in various ways certain of their international telegraph traffic to the U.S. Government. For almost 30 years [beginning in 1945], copies of most international telegrams originating in or forwarded through the United States were turned over to the National Security Agency and its predecessor agencies.

. . . in the midst of the program, the Government's use of the material turned over by the companies changed. At the outset, the purpose apparently was only to extract international telegrams relating to certain foreign targets. Later, the Government began [at least in 1967 and until 1975] to extract the telegrams of certain U.S. citizens. . . . the Government did not tell [these three companies] that it was selecting out and analyzing the messages of certain U.S. citizens. On the other hand the companies knew they were turning over to the Government most international telegrams, including those of U.S. citizens and organizations. There is no evidence . . . that they ever asked what the Government was doing with that material or took steps to make sure the Government did not read the private communications of Americans.

The Senate [select committee] on intelligence activities made its first inquiries into this operation last May. It was not until early September, however, that the select committee . . . obtained preliminary briefings from NSA operational personnel. Subsequently, we examined three NSA officials, including former Deputy Director Louis Tordella. These persons were the only ones at NSA with substantial knowledge of the SHAMROCK operation. The committee also reviewed all existing documentation relating to the operation. . . . Sworn testimony was taken from officials in each company [of the three], and company counsel have worked with the committee to reconstruct, as nearly as possible, what has taken place over the last 30 years.

During World War II, all international telegraph traffic was screened by military censors, located at the companies, as part of the wartime censorship program. During this period, messages of foreign intelligence targets were turned over to military intelligence.

. . . the Department [of Defense] sought in 1947 [sic, 1945] to renew the part of this arrangement whereby the telegraph traffic of foreign intelligence targets had been turned over to it. At that time, most of these foreign targets did use the paid message facilities of the international carriers . . .

At meetings with Secretary of Defense James Forrestal in 1947, representatives of the three companies were assured that if they co-operated with the Government in this program they would suffer no criminal liability and no public exposure, at least as long as the current administration was in office. They were told that such participation was in the highest interests of national security.

Secretary Forrestal also explained that the arrangements had the approval of President Truman and his Attorney General, Tom C. Clark. Forrestal explained to the companies, however, that he could not bind his successors by these assurances. He told the companies, moreover, that Congress would consider legislation in its forthcoming session which would make clear that such activity was permissible. . . .

In 1949, the companies sought renewed assurances from Forrestal's successor, Louis D. Johnson, and were told again that President Truman and Attorney General Clark had been consulted and had given their approval of these arrangements. . . . neither the Department of Defense nor any of the participating private companies has any evidence that such assurances were ever sought again.

The Army Security Agency (ASA) was the first Government agency which had operational responsibility for SHAMROCK. When the Armed Forces Security Agency was created in 1949, however, it inherited the program; and, similarly, when NSA was created in 1952, it assumed operational control.

There are no documents at NSA or the Department of Defense which reflect the operational arrangements between the Government and the telegraph companies. The companies decided at the outset that they did not want to keep any documents, and the Government has none today other than those relating to the 1947 and 1949 discussions . . . [additional documents were provided by NSA officials in March 1976, allegedly only then discovered].

. . . it appears, however, that the companies were given to understand at the outset that only traffic of foreign intelligence targets would be gleaned by NSA. . . .

In the early 1960's, there was a change in technology which had a significant impact upon the way in which SHAMROCK was run. RCA Global and ITT World Communications began to store their international paid message traffic on magnetic tapes, and these were turned over to NSA. Thereafter, . . . telegrams to or from, or even mentioning, U.S. citizens whose names appeared on the watch list in the late sixties and early seventies, would have been sent to NSA analysts, and many would subsequently be disseminated to other agencies.

The NSA officials examined by us had no recollection of NSA's ever informing the companies how NSA was handling the information they were providing. They furthermore had no recollection of any of the companies making such an inquiry, even after NSA began receiving magnetic tapes from two of the companies. Several company officials corroborated this testimony, . . .

No one examined from NSA or the companies knew of any effort by the companies since 1949 to seek renewed assurances from the Government for their continued participation in SHAMROCK. Indeed, each of the companies has given sworn statements to the committee that they did not think the arrangements with NSA were ever considered by the executive levels of their respective companies. Moreover, Dr. Tordella, the former Deputy Director, told us that he would have known if additional assurances had ever been sought and testified that to his knowledge they were not. . . .

NSA never received any domestic telegrams from these companies. Indeed, none of these companies, at least since 1963, has had domestic operations. . . .

Of all the messages made available to NSA each year, it is estimated that NSA in recent years selected about 150,000 messages a month for NSA analysts to review. Thousands of these messages in one form or another were distributed to other agencies in response to "foreign intelligence requirements."

Until current controversy arose, only a handful of officials in the executive branch over the last 30 years were apparently aware of the SHAMROCK operation. Dr. Tordella testified that to the best of his knowledge no President since Truman had been informed of it.

SHAMROCK terminated by order of the Secretary of Defense on May 15, 1975.

(136) FINAL REPORT, SENATE SELECT COMMITTEE ON INTELLIGENCE
ACTIVITIES. OPERATION SHAMROCK, 1976 [Extract]

Source: U.S. Senate, Select Committee to Study Governmental
Operations with respect to Intelligence Activities, *Final Report,*
Supplementary Detailed Staff Reports on Intelligence Activities
and the Rights of Americans, Book III, 94th Congress, 2d session,
pp. 767-771.

During World War II, under the wartime censorship laws, all
international message traffic was made available to military censors. Copies of pertinent foreign traffic were turned over to
military intelligence. With the cessation of the War in 1945,
this practice was to end.

In August 1945, the Army sought to continue that part of the
wartime arrangement which had allowed military intelligence access to certain foreign traffic. At that time, most of this traffic was still conveyed via the facilities of three carriers.

On August 18, 1945, two representatives of the Army Signal
Security Agency were sent to New York

> to make the necessary contacts with the heads of the
> Commercial Communications Companies in New York, secure
> their approval of the interception of all Governmental
> traffic entering the United States, leaving the United
> States, or transiting the United States, and make the
> necessary arrangements for this photographic intercept
> work.

They first approached an official at ITT, who "very definitely
and finally refused" to agree to any of the Army proposals. The
Army representatives then approached a vice president of Western
Union Telegraph Company, who agreed to cooperate unless the Attorney General of the United States ruled that such intercepts were
illegal.

Having succeeded with Western Union, the Army representatives
returned to ITT on August 21, 1945, and suggested to an ITT vice
president that "his company would not desire to be the only non-
cooperative company on this project." The vice president decided
to reconsider and broached the matter the same day with the president of the company. The ITT president agreed to cooperate with
the Army, provided that the Attorney General decided that the
program was not illegal.

These Army representatives also met with the president of RCA
on August 21, 1945. The RCA president indicated his willingness
to cooperate, but withheld final approval until he, too, had
heard from the Attorney General.

After their trip, the Army representatives reported to their
superiors that . . .

> Two very evident fears existed in the minds of the heads
> of each of these communications companies. One was the
> fear of the illegality of the procedure according to
> present FCC regulations. In spite of the fact that favor-
> able opinions have been received from the Judge Advocate
> General of the Navy and the Judge Advocate General of
> the Army, it was feared that these opinions would not

hold in civil court and, as a consequence, the companies
would not be protected. If a favorable opinion is handed
down by the Attorney General, this fear will be completely allayed, and cooperation may be expected for the
complete intercept coverage of this material. The second
fear uppermost in the minds of these executives is the
fear of . . . the communications union. This union has
reported on many occasions minor infractions of FCC regulations and it is feared that a major infraction, such
as the proposed intercept coverage, if disclosed by the
Union, might cause severe repercussions.

. . . the companies had consulted their corporate attorneys
during these three days of discussions, and that their attorneys
uniformly advised against participation in the proposed intercept
program. The company executives were apparently willing to ignore
this advice if they received assurances from the Attorney General
that he would protect them from any consequences.

The new documentary evidence made available [in March 1976]
to the [Senate Select] Committee [on Intelligence Activities] did
not reveal that the Attorney General at that time, Tom C. Clark,
actually made the assurances that the companies desired. It is
clear, however, that the program began shortly after the August
meetings: ITT and Western Union began their participation by
September 1, and RCA by October 9, 1945.

. . . a letter from the Army Signal Security Agency to the
Army Chief of Staff on March 19, 1946, . . . indicates that
SHAMROCK was well underway, but that concerns about its legality
had not vanished:

It can be stated that both [Western Union and RCA] have
placed themselves in precarious positions since the legality of such operations has not been established and has
necessitated the utmost secrecy on their part in making
these arrangements. Through their efforts, only two or
three individuals in the respective companies are aware
of the operation.

. . . the Office of Secretary of Defense James Forrestal attempted unsuccessfully in June 1948 to have Congress pass an
amendment to relax the disclosure restrictions of Section 605 of
the Federal Communications Act of 1934. Agencies designated by
the President would have been allowed to obtain the radio and
wire communications of foreign governments. If the amendment had
passed, the SHAMROCK program, as it was originally conceived,
would have been authorized by law.

The proposed amendment sought to allay concerns of the companies on the legality of their participation in SHAMROCK. The
companies were demanding assurances in 1947 not only from the
Secretary of Defense and the Attorney General, but also from the
President that their participation was essential to the national
interest and that they would not be subject to prosecution in the
Federal Courts. Secretary Forrestal, who stated he was speaking
for the President, gave ITT and RCA representatives these assurances at a December 16, 1947, meeting in Washington, D.C.
Forrestal warned, however, that the assurances he was making could
not bind his successors in office.

Representatives of Western Union were not present at this meeting. [Other] documents . . . indicate that the President and Operating Vice President of Western Union were briefed in January 1948 on the earlier meeting with RCA and ITT.

In early June 1948, the Chairmen of the Senate and House Judiciary Committees were informed of the Government's need for a relaxation of Section 605 and of its position with the telegraph companies. The delicacy of the problem and the top secret nature of the information were made clear to these two Chairmen. The amendment was considered in an executive session of the Senate Judiciary Committee on June 16, 1948, and approved. Since support for the bill was not unanimous, however, the Committee voted to leave it to the Chairman's discretion whether or not to release the bill to the Senate floor. The representative of the Secretary of Defense then told the Senate Judiciary Chairman that "we did not desire an airing of the whole matter on the Floor of the Senate at this late date in the session." The bill apparently was not reported out.

A Defense Department official expressed the view that they thought a great deal had already been accomplished and that the administration had sufficient ammunition to be able to effect a continuation of the present practices with the companies. Apparently no other statutory attempts were made to authorize the companies' participation in SHAMROCK. . . .

None of the telegraph companies could find any record of an agreement with NSA or its predecessors wherein the companies would provide copies of telegrams to the Government, or which reflected anything about arrangements with NSA. No one interviewed by the Committee had any recollection or knowledge that the Government had given the companies specific assurances to ensure their co operation in 1945, 1947, 1949, or at any time thereafter.

Apparently only a few people in each company - apart from those who physically turned over the materials - had any knowledge of the NSA arrangement. These were primarily mid-level executives charged with the operational aspects of the companies' business. All assumed that the arrangement was valid when it was made and thus continued it. No witness from the telegraph companies recalled that there had ever been a review of the arrangements at the executive levels of their respective companies. . . .

Under procedures refined during the early years of Truman's presidency, legislative recommendations of federal agencies and departments had to be submitted for clearance to the Bureau of the Budget. These legislative recommendations were reviewed by the staff of the Budget Bureau to ascertain their consistency with the President's legislative priorities as outlined in his State of the Union address. Concurrently, Budget Bureau officials would refer the proposed legislation to other interested departments or agencies for their assessment and input. Because the Department of the Treasury had objected to another internal security bill submitted by the Department of Justice for Budget clearance in February 1948 (and particularly to the provision of that proposed bill concerning wiretapping), its views on the proposed legislation to legalize Operation SHAMROCK were sought.

Indirectly, then, this legislative review confirms that at least in 1948 President Truman had been apprised of this ongoing program and the attendant legal problem.

(137) LETTER, SECRETARY OF THE TREASURY JOHN SNYDER TO BUREAU OF BUDGET DIRECTOR, June 8, 1948 [Extract]

Source: John Snyder Papers, Bureau of Budget Files, Harry S. Truman Library.

Reference is made to Assistant [Bureau of the Budget] Director [Elmer] Staats' letter of June 3, 1948, requesting an expression of Treasury's views with respect to a draft of a bill "To amend section 605 of the Communications Act of 1934 in order to increase the security of the United States, and for other purposes", submitted by the Secretary of Defense [James Forrestal]; and to a letter of June 4, 1948, from Mr. Staats stating that your office has been informally advised that the Office of the Secretary of Defense would have no objection to the addition of the following sentence at the end of the draft bill submitted with the June 3 letter:

"Provided that nothing herein shall authorize the interception of interstate or local telephonic communications."

As modified by this additional sentence, it is our understanding that the draft bill is intended to permit the interception, receipt, or utilization, in the interests of national security, of the contents of any communication within the scope of the Communications Act of 1934 by telegraph, cable, radio, or otherwise (but not interstate and local telephone) of any foreign government, as broadly defined in the draft bill. Such action could be taken, under the terms of the draft bill, by any Federal agency designated by the President for this purpose under rules and regulations approved by him.

If our understanding (as set out above) of the purpose of the draft bill as modified is correct, the Treasury would have no objection to this proposed legislation, . . .

This Department heartily approves fixing the power in the President to designate the agencies which may exercise this authority under regulations to be prescribed by him, rather than specifically naming the agencies in the bill. . . .

B. *Internal Security*

1. *The Federal Employee Loyalty/Security Program*

Since the inception of the Roosevelt New Deal, congressional conservatives had sought to raise public doubts about the loyalty of federal employees and therefore in 1938 had supported the creation of the Special House Committee on Un-American Activities (HUAC's authority was renewed annually until it was made a permanent committee in 1945). Nonetheless, until the Cold War years, this particular conservative political effort had limited impact. To the extent that such charges could be portrayed as partisan in nature - i.e., anti-New Deal - they could be undercut. Only with the development of an obsession over Soviet subversion would such charges command widespread support. At the same time, conservative politicians refined these charges and advanced the thesis that liberal or radical federal employees had acted to further not domestic reform but the interests of a foreign power, the Soviet Union. The foremost practitioner of this altered conservative strategy was Wisconsin Republican Senator Joseph McCarthy. In February, 1950 and thereafter, McCarthy charged that the presence of "Communists in the State Department" had resulted in the communization of Eastern Europe and China and the general crisis of the Cold War. McCarthy, however, had not originated this tactic; indeed, he capitalized on a climate and institutional changes which dated from mid-1946. In that year, responding to recent disclosures publicized with the arrest and indictment of individuals associated with a radical journal of Far Eastern affairs, **Amerasia**, and the release of a Canadian Royal Commission report claiming that Communist or pro-Communist Canadian officials had leaked state secrets to the Soviet Union, in July 1946 a House Subcommittee initiated hearings into federal employee loyalty procedures. In response to the impact of its report of that month, and then to the Republicans' decisive victory in November, 1946 congressional elections (winning control of Congress for the first time since 1930), President Truman established by executive order on November 25, 1946 a Temporary Commission on Employee Loyalty, and then on March 21, 1947 issued another executive order instituting a permanent federal employee loyalty program.

(138) <u>MEMO, FBI DIRECTOR J. EDGAR HOOVER TO ATTORNEY GENERAL TOM
CLARK</u>, July 25, 1946

Source: A Devitt Vanech Papers, ADV Loyalty Commission, Harry S.
Truman Library.

You will recall that a Subcommittee of the Civil Service
Committee of the House of Representatives submitted to Congress on
Saturday, July 20th, a report upon the Subcommittee's study concerning employee loyalty and employment policies and practices
of the various agencies of the Government.

The majority of the Committee recommended that a commission
be established to be composed of officials of the Departments of
Justice, War, Navy, State and Treasury, and the Civil Service
Commission, this Commission to make a thorough study of existing
laws and the adequacy of existing legislation, to study the problems raised by the Subcommittee's report concerning the standards,
procedures, techniques, needed funds and personnel necessary to
protect the Government from disloyal employees, and to present to
Congress at the earliest practicable time a complete and unified
program to correct the problems enumerated.

I think it would be well for the Department to be represented
on this Commission, if it is set up, by a representative who has
a broad, overall picture of the problems and policies of the various units of the Department of Justice, and accordingly I suggest
that if you are approached to designate a representative to represent you on this Commission, you give favorable consideration
to Mr. A. Devitt Vanech as your representative.

(139) <u>MEMO, ATTORNEY GENERAL TO FBI DIRECTOR,</u> July 31, 1946

Source: A. Devitt Vanech Papers, ADV Loyalty Commission, Harry
S. Truman Library.

In accordance with the suggestion contained in your memorandum
of July 25, I concur in your suggestion of Mr. A. Devitt Vanech
to serve as my representative on the inter-departmental commission
proposed by the Subcommittee of the Civil Service Committee . . .

(140) LETTER, THOMAS INGLIS (OFFICE OF NAVAL INTELLIGENCE) TO A.
DEVITT VANECH (CHAIRMAN, THE PRESIDENT'S TEMPORARY COMMISSION ON
EMPLOYEE LOYALTY), January 8, 1947
Source: Harry S. Truman Papers, Official Files 252-I, Harry S.
Truman Library.

****

There are no statistics which are available to me which would
indicate the total number of subversive cases handled by Naval
Intelligence. As you know, Naval Intelligence functions as a
service rather than an action agency in that all such data obtained by it are referred to the appropriate naval authority for
administrative decision. There have been a large number of such
cases in the past and they continue to be received at present.
Unfortunately, I cannot see that these cases will decrease materially in number in the future. . . .

I trust that the information forwarded herewith will be of
value to your committee. It is my personal opinion that the problem of employee loyalty as regards the Federal Service is one the
importance of which cannot be stressed too much.

Extent to which the subversive or disloyal person constitutes a
problem in or threat to Federal service.

As the Federal Service becomes increasingly important in
terms of the political, economic and social structure of the
United States, it becomes a higher priority target for subversive elements. During the past fourteen years, the executive
functions of the Federal Service have been expanded rapidly
in order to discharge responsibilities formerly carried out
by state and local authorities. This centralization of planning and administration invested our central government with
tremendous powers over local institutions for the first time
in the history of the Federal system. This control was expanded further during World War II on a scale unprecedented
in any democratic country, covering all phases of American
ingenuity, industry, resources, and development. Since these
sources of power are regarded with envy by other nations, it
is logical to assume that there is a constant threat to them
by other powers.

Techniques by which subversive or disloyal persons operate:

a. Infiltration.

From the point of view of a power seeking information, infiltration is a highly successful approach. From the point
of view of the protecting country, it is one of the most difficult to detect. The action of a seeking power cannot be
determined easily if agents of that power conduct themselves
discreetly and slowly encroach upon the knowledge available
to them during the course of their employment. . . . strenu-
ous efforts have been made and will continue to be made to
penetrate the governmental service, not only overtly to obtain
information, but to foment distrust of American practices,
ridicule American standards and breed discontent, dissatis-
faction and disaffection. Infiltration is attack at the roots
of American government and sows the seeds of unrest which

could ultimately lead to revolution. It is a practice which must be guarded against constantly, and all cases where there is any doubt as to an employee's wholehearted loyalty to the United States Democratic principles should be resolved to the benefit of the government. . . . Individuals in governmental service in any capacity, high or low, are public servants within the strictest meaning of that expression, and as such owe the highest degree of loyalty to this country.

b. Direct action.

Subversion, unlike revolution or mutiny, is difficult not only to observe but also to measure. Broadly speaking, it is any activity carried on by any person or group which is directed toward the overthrow wholly or in part of duly constituted authority. It may range from actual physical sabotage to the destruction by psychological methods of a program, activity or institution. It may be carried out directly and openly or covertly and by indirection. Subversive activities were observed during World War II not only in whispering campaigns launched against military leaders whose objectives were to undermine confidence in their abilities to plan and wage war but also in direct frontal attacks made on American institutions. Direct action may be timed to coincide with infiltration techniques to achieve a desired end.

c. "Front" organizations.

Because it has its roots in humanitarian principles, based on the "Rights of the Man," our Democracy is particularly susceptible to subversive attack. For that reason, it is a relatively simple matter for subversive individuals or organizations to accomplish their objective while masquerading as protectors of civil liberties or the promoters of the interests of individuals whose level of economy is declared to be sub-standard. Making an emotional appeal for the "down-trodden," such groups loudly demand "rights" for particular groups, but usually fail to point out the corresponding "duty" which logically arises from any Social Contract.

"Front" organizations, too numerous to name, are ideal for subversive use. In the first place, they will frequently associate with the enterprise, individuals well known to the public whose names are used as a "drawing power" to induce greater membership. In not a few cases, public or important persons have had their names used without their consent or knowledge. Also, the aims of these organizations are couched in lofty terms which belie the actual purpose to which the organization will be put and to throw off guard the unwary or unsuspecting person. Once he has joined such a group, efforts are made to persuade him to think along the lines desired by those controlling the group.

d. Propaganda.

Propaganda is always a potential and prolific source of trouble. It is usually of a subtle nature and, therefore, less susceptible to detection and proof, unless the circumstances require a more direct form of action. An illustration of the possible degree of danger manifest in propaganda efforts was reported in the Sunday press of 5 January 1947 in

connection with an attack by the President of the Federation
of Citizens Associations in the District of Columbia against a
report on racial conditions in Washington by the Council of
Social Agencies. If, as alleged in this attack, propaganda is
worth enough effort to concentrate on these matters, it is
being carried into more important fields of endeavor as well,
especially against the Federal service which must stand as a
bulwark against this and other insidious practices.

e. Other techniques.

    . . . enemies of Democracy will utilize any method avail-
able to accomplish their aims, whether it is by direct action,
indirect techniques, creation of distrust, or propaganda. All
are inter-related and cannot be isolated. All are apparent
and not mythical.

Difficulty of proof of subversive or disloyal connections and
activity:

a. Secrecy of membership.

    It is a well-established fact that an agent of a foreign
principal can achieve his best results if his true identity
remains unknown to the protecting power. Ostensibly, the
Comintern is dissolved; actually, the Communists seek more information now than ever before. Their trusted members are
instructed to show no affiliation with known Communists and
to adopt attitudes critical of Communists to gain access to
information. Secrecy of membership, therefore, is often difficult of tangible proof and serves to make more difficult
the task of dealing administratively with such cases. . . .

    The Office of Naval Intelligence is vitally interested in the
subject of National Security and favors legislation which will
add to the internal security of the United States. Any study
directed toward determining an improvement in the handling of
cases involving the loyalty of Federal employees must necessarily
concern itself with whether the statutes are adequate and whether
the Federal Government is amply protected by law from any efforts
at subversion of its functions.

(141) MINUTES, TEMPORARY COMMISSION, January 17, 1947 [Extract]

Source: Stephen Spingarn Papers, President's Temporary Commission, Harry S. Truman Library.

    The meeting was brought to order by the Chairman [A. Devitt
Vanech] who stated [FBI Assistant Director D. Milton] Ladd was
again before the Commission to furnish information to the Commission and Subcommittee members.

    In answer to the question as to whether the problem is acute,
Mr. Ladd stated that . . . it is a very serious problem . . . He
then stated that the Communists had established a separate group
for infiltration of the government, a group called the "government group". The members of this group are instructed to carry
no membership cards, attend no meetings of the organization and
to give no other indication that they are still active in the
organization. These instructions were issued by organization in

the latter part of November 1946. Answering the question as to
whether the problem was more serious than before the war, Mr. Ladd
stated there had been a decrease in the Communist vote; that the
Communist ticket and ballot was appearing in less of the States.
The question was then asked as to whether the claim that they were
instrumental in the defeat of certain Congressmen in the last
election. Mr. Ladd stated they were active in opposing those who
they felt would not be satisfactory from their standpoint. . . .
Mr. Ladd then called the Commission's attention to a publication
of the U.S. Chamber of Commerce dealing with Communist infiltration
of the United States, published in November 1946, in which the
opinion is expressed that Communists in the government have
reached a serious stage. Mr. Ladd then gave the Commission information relative to the Jaffe case involving six persons, three of
them government employees, who had been taking government documents, restricted, secret, etc., and turning them over to the
editor of Amerasia.

At this point General [Kenneth] Royall [of the War Department]
stated he felt the Commission should have something more than reports from the Chamber of Commerce, FBI, and Congress, to determine the size of the problem. He indicated the Commission had
insufficient data on which to evaluate, that he was interested in
figures and concrete facts. How many suspected of subversive
activities in the various departments? How many found to be subversive? How many found not to be subversive? How many has FBI
discovered throughout the Government? Some information as to the
type of activity they have engaged in. The type of evidence that
has led to a conclusion of innocence or guilt. Mr. [L. V.] Meloy
[of Civil Service Commission] then stated that over the five year
period beginning in 1940 there had been 1200 dismissals of persons found to be disloyal, and that of that number 547 were Communists. . . . In answer to questions he stated that they would have
been discharged regardless of the War; that the type of evidence
was party membership, attending meetings; following the party
line and disseminating Communist literature. . . . The next questions were: Where was the peak? Is it on the upgrade? Mr. Meloy
stated this would be difficult of determination. At this point
Mr. Ladd stated he had furnished figures relative to Hatch Act
cases at his previous appearance - that 101 had been dismissed.
In answer to the above questions it was stated that the first
year was the highest but that over the five year period it was on
the upgrade in new cases . . . Mr. Meloy then pointed out that the
difficulty with the Hatch Act and riders to the appropriation
acts was that the rule set up was too tough as you had to establish membership in secret organizations having secret names. The
question was asked as to the general type of the 101 cases. Mr.
Ladd stated it was principally membership and attending meetings.
. . .

Mr. [Stanley] Goodrich [of State Department] inquired concerning the difficulty of furnishing information to the various agencies. Mr. Ladd stated that the information was sent to the employing agency in all cases and that there was no difficulty if the
matter is handled through proper channels. Mr. Ladd was then
asked the approximate number of names in subversive files and Mr.
[John] Sullivan [of Navy Department] asked whether the Bureau had
a file of names of persons who could be picked up in the event of

a war with Russia. Mr. Ladd declined to answer because this matter was not within the scope of the Commission. The Chairman
suggested that the question involved a matter of policy and that
he would attempt to furnish Mr. Sullivan with the information
later. The request was also made that information be obtained
as to the size of the subversive file and how many of that number
were actually in the government today. Mr. [Edward] Foley [of
Treasury Department] suggested that information also be obtained
as to how many in each department and what constitutes sufficient
demonstration of a person's loyalty to get him on the list. . . .

Mr. Foley suggested that the Subcommittee meet this afternoon
to draft list of questions for consideration of the Commission.
The Commission was in general agreement that [FBI Director J.
Edgar] Hoover should be asked to appear and the Chairman was asked
to make the necessary arrangements for sometime early in the week.
No date was specified, the thought being that the Commission would
furnish Mr. Hoover with a list of questions they desired answers
on prior to his appearance.

(142) <u>MEMO, ATTORNEY GENERAL CLARK TO VANECH</u>, February 14, 1947

Source: Harry S. Truman Papers, Official Files 252-I, Harry S.
Truman Library.

On January 23, 1947, I appeared before your Commission in connection with the various aspects of the problem of employee loyalty. At that time I expressed my opinion regarding the seriousness
of the problem of subversive or disloyal persons in the Government.

My appearance was very informal and for that reason I think
it best to supplement it by this memorandum. The problem of subversive or disloyal persons in the Government is a most serious
one. While the number of such persons has not as yet reached
serious proportions, there is no doubt that the presence of any
in the government service or the possibility of their entering
Government service are serious matters, and should cause the
gravest concern to those charged with the responsibility of solv-
ing the problem. I do not believe that the gravity of the problem
should be weighed in the light of numbers, but rather from the
viewpoint of the serious threat which even one disloyal person
constitutes to the security of the Government of the United
States.

For this and other reasons, I do deem the problem to be very
grave. Hence, the existence and scope of the problem are indeed
very serious matters in terms of both the actual and potential
threats to the Government.

While on this subject and as an indication to the Commission
of my views, I also wish to state that I am convinced that a
Loyalty Review Board should be established by executive order and
this Board should be required to give its full time to the review
of all cases involving subversive or disloyal persons in the Government. It is also my conviction that such a Board should have
the authority to approve or overrule any action taken by the heads
of the various Government departments and agencies in loyalty
cases.

It is also my view that at the request of the head of any department or agency, the Federal Bureau of Investigation, where security considerations permit, should make available to such head, personally, or to any officer or officers designated by such head and approved by the Federal Bureau of Investigation, investigative material and information collected by it on any employee or prospective employee of the requesting department or agency. It is my further view that the Federal Bureau of Investigation within its sole discretion may refuse to disclose the names of confidential informants. However, where security considerations permit, the Federal Bureau of Investigation should furnish sufficient information about such informants on the basis of which the requesting department or agency can make an adequate evaluation of the information furnished by the Federal Bureau of Investigation.

In the light of past experience I am of the opinion that the Federal Bureau of Investigation should have the continuing responsibility to inquire into cases involving alleged subversive activities on the part of incumbent Federal employees.

(143) MEMO FOR THE FILES, STEPHEN SPINGARN (TREASURY DEPARTMENT REPRESENTATIVE ON TEMPORARY LOYALTY COMMISSION), February 20, 1947 [Extract]

Source: Stephen Spingarn Papers, President's Temporary Commission, Harry S. Truman Library.

The Commission and the Subcommittee met this afternoon at 3 o'clock to go over last moment changes and to sign the report.
. . .

. . . Mr. Vanech said that the word "alone" was being deleted from the last paragraph of the Attorney General's memorandum of February 14 to the Commission which prior to the deletion read as follows: "In the light of past experience I am of the opinion that the Federal Bureau of Investigation alone should have the continuing responsibility to inquire into cases involving alleged subversive activities on the part of incumbent Federal employees". The deletion of the word "alone" is an important and significant improvement which we very much desired, since the language previously indicated that the Attorney General thought that an agency should not investigate the loyalty of its own employees but would have to depend entirely on the FBI.

John Sullivan called the Commission's attention to page 1 of the Office of Naval Intelligence memorandum attached to Admiral Inglis' letter of January 8, 1947, to the Commission. Sullivan requested the elimination of the first two paragraphs under paragraph 2a of the ONI memorandum, dealing with the infiltration techniques by which subversive or disloyal persons operate. Sullivan wanted these two paragraphs eliminated and said he would substitute a corrected page as quickly as possible. The deletion was agreed to. The deleted paragraph reads as follows:

"As early as 1933, the 'progressive swing to liberalism' which characterized the 'socialized planning' of the next decade in American History, resulted in the introduction into the Federal system of large numbers of individuals whose concepts of democratic institutions had been developed abroad. At the same time, foreign-born 'special consultants' were brought into the Federal Service in order to advise not only on problems of relief and rehabilitation but also on related topics such as money and banking, labor and race relations, and government control of the instruments of production.

"Our liberal hiring policy as well as the absence of state-controlled dossiers on candidates for official positions, together with the traditional American practice of accepting individuals on their face value, offer ideal opportunities for subversion."

****

(144) EXECUTIVE ORDER 9835, March 21, 1947 [Extract]

Source: Charles Murphy Files, Harry S. Truman Library.

WHEREAS each employee of the Government of the United States is endowed with a measure of trusteeship over the democratic processes which are the heart and sinew of the United States; and

WHEREAS it is of vital importance that persons employed in the Federal service be of complete and unswerving loyalty to the United States; and

WHEREAS, although the loyalty of by far the overwhelming majority of all Government employees is beyond question, the presence within the Government service of any disloyal or subversive person constitutes a threat to our democratic processes; and

WHEREAS maximum protection must be afforded the United States against infiltration of disloyal persons into the ranks of its employees, and equal protection from unfounded accusations of disloyalty must be afforded the loyal employees of the Government:

NOW, THEREFORE, by virtue of the authority vested in me by the Constitution and statutes of the United States, . . . and as President and Chief Executive of the United States, it is hereby, in the interest of the internal management of the Government, ordered as follows:

PART I

INVESTIGATION OF APPLICANTS

1. There shall be a loyalty investigation of every person entering the civilian employment of any department or agency of the executive branch of the Federal Government.

a. Investigations of persons entering the competitive service shall be conducted by the Civil Service Commission, except in such cases as are covered by a special agreement between the Commission and any given department or agency.

b. Investigations of persons other than those entering the competitive service shall be conducted by the employing department or agency. Departments and agencies without investigative organizations shall utilize the investigative facilities of the Civil Service Commission.

****

4. Whenever derogatory information with respect to loyalty of an applicant is revealed a full field investigation shall be conducted. A full field investigation shall also be conducted of those applicants, or of applicants for particular positions, as may be designated by the head of the employing department or agency, such designations to be based on the determination by any such head in the best interests of national security.

PART II

INVESTIGATION OF EMPLOYEES

1. The head of each department and agency in the executive branch of the Government shall be personally responsible for an effective program to assure that disloyal civilian officers or employees are not retained in employment in his department or agency.

    a. He shall be responsible for prescribing and supervising the loyalty determination procedures of his department or agency, in accordance with the provisions of this order, which shall be considered as providing minimum requirements.

    b. The head of a department or agency which does not have an investigative organization shall utilize the investigative facilities of the Civil Service Commission.

2. The head of each department and agency shall appoint one or more loyalty boards . . . for the purpose of hearing loyalty cases arising within such department or agency and making recommendations with respect to the removal of any officer or employee of such department or agency on grounds relating to loyalty, and he shall prescribe regulations for the conduct of the proceedings before such boards.

    a. An officer or employee who is charged with being disloyal shall have a right to an administrative hearing before a loyalty board in the employing department or agency. He may appear before such board personally, accompanied by counsel or representative of his own choosing, and present evidence on his own behalf, through witnesses or by affidavit.

    b. The officer or employee shall be served with a written notice of such hearing in sufficient time, and shall be informed therein of the nature of the charges against him in sufficient detail, so that he will be enabled to prepare his defense. The charges shall be stated as specifically and completely as, in the discretion of the employing department or agency, security considerations permit, and the officer or employee shall be informed in the notice (1) of his right to reply to such charges in writing within a specified reasonable time, (2) of his right to an administrative hearing on such charges before a loyalty board, and (3) of his right to appear before such board personally, to be accompanied by counsel or representative of his own choosing, and to present evidence on his behalf, through witness or by affidavit.

3. A recommendation of removal by a loyalty board shall be subject to appeal by the officer or employee affected, prior to his removal, to the head of the employing department or agency or

to such person or persons as may be designated by such head, under such regulations as may be prescribed by him, and the decision of the department or agency concerned shall be subject to appeal to the Civil Service Commission's Loyalty Review Board, hereinafter provided for, for an advisory recommendation. . . .

PART III

RESPONSIBILITIES OF
CIVIL SERVICE COMMISSION

1. There shall be established in the Civil Service Commission a Loyalty Review Board of not less than three impartial persons, the members of which shall be officers or employees of the Commission.

    a. The Board shall have authority to review cases involving persons recommended for dismissal on grounds relating to loyalty by the loyalty board of any department or agency and to make advisory recommendations thereon to the head of the employing department or agency. . . .

3. The Loyalty Review Board shall currently be furnished by the Department of Justice the name of each foreign or domestic organization, association, movement, group or combination of persons which the Attorney General, after appropriate investigation and determination, designates as totalitarian, fascist, communist or subversive, or as having adopted a policy of advocating or approving the commission of acts of force or violence to deny others their rights under the Constitution of the United States, or as seeking to alter the form of government of the United States by unconstitutional means.

    a. The Loyalty Review Board shall disseminate such information to all departments and agencies.

PART IV

SECURITY MEASURES IN INVESTIGATIONS

1. At the request of the head of any department or agency of the executive branch an investigative agency shall make available to such head, personally, all investigative material and information collected by the investigative agency concerning any employee or prospective employee of the requesting department or agency, or shall make such material and information available to any officer or officers designated by such head and approved by the investigative agency.

2. Notwithstanding the foregoing requirement, however, the investigative agency may refuse to disclose the names of confidential informants, provided it furnishes sufficient information about such informants on the basis of which the requesting department or agency can make an adequate evaluation of the information furnished by them, and provided it advises the requesting department or agency in writing that it is essential to the protection of the informants or to the investigation of other cases that the identity of the informants not be revealed. Investigative agencies shall not use this discretion to decline to reveal sources of information where such action is not essential. . . .

PART V

STANDARDS

1. The standard for the refusal of employment or the removal from employment in an executive department or agency on grounds relating to loyalty shall be that, on all the evidence, reasonable grounds exist for belief that the person involved is disloyal to the Government of the United States.

2. Activities and associations of an applicant or employee which may be considered in connection with the determination of disloyalty may include one or more of the following:

a. Sabotage, espionage, or attempts or preparations therefor, or knowingly associating with spies or saboteurs;

b. Treason or sedition or advocacy thereof;

c. Advocacy of revolution or force or violence to alter the constitutional form of government of the United States;

d. Intentional, unauthorized disclosure to any person, under circumstances which may indicate disloyalty to the United States, of documents or information of a confidential or non-public character obtained by the person making the disclosure as a result of his employment by the Government of the United States;

e. Performing or attempting to perform his duties, or otherwise acting, so as to serve the interests of another government in preference to the interests of the United States.

f. Membership in, affiliation with or sympathetic association with any foreign or domestic organization, association, movement, group or combination of persons, designated by the Attorney General as totalitarian, fascist, communist, or subversive, or as having adopted a policy of advocating or approving the commission of acts of force or violence to deny other persons their rights under the Constitution of the United States, or as seeking to alter the form of government of the United States by unconstitutional means.

PART VI

MISCELLANEOUS

1. Each department and agency of the executive branch, to the extent that it has not already done so, shall submit, to the Federal Bureau of Investigation of the Department of Justice, either directly or through the Civil Service Commission, the names (and such other necessary identifying material as the Federal Bureau of Investigation may require) of all of its incumbent employees.

a. The Federal Bureau of Investigation shall check such names against its records of persons concerning whom there is substantial evidence of being within the purview of paragraph 2 of Part V hereof, and shall notify each department and agency of such information.

b. Upon receipt of the above-mentioned information from the Federal Bureau of Investigation, each department and

agency shall make, or cause to be made by the Civil Service
Commission, such investigation of those employees as the head
of the department or agency shall deem advisable.

2. The Security Advisory Board of the State-War-Navy Coordinating Committee shall draft rules applicable to the handling and
transmission of confidential documents and other documents and
information which should not be publicly disclosed, and upon approval by the President such rules shall constitute the minimum
standards for the handling and transmission of such documents and
information, and shall be applicable to all departments and agencies of the executive branch. . . .

*President Truman might have acceded unknowingly to FBI Direc-
tor Hoover's preference that A. Devitt Vanech be appointed as the
Justice Department representative on the Temporary Commission
(and the Chairman of the Commission). Truman, nonetheless, preferred a commission which would recommend a permanent loyalty
program. This preference is reflected in his appointment of the
other members of the Temporary Commission - all of whom had an
investigative background and were inclined to favor security considerations over civil liberties. These members included John
Peurifoy (State), Edward Foley (Treasury), Kenneth Royall (War),
John Sullivan (Navy), and Harry Mitchell (Civil Service). Subcommittee members included L. V. Meloy (Civil Service), Stanley
Goodrich (State), Stephen Spingarn (Treasury), Marvin Ottilie
(Navy), Kenneth Johnson (War), and Harold Baynton (Justice). In
addition, Innes Randolph (War) served as military advisor and
P. B. Nibecker (Navy) served as naval advisor. Despite its
security-oriented composition, however, when assessing the procedures of the to-be-established loyalty program, the commission
recommended vesting investigative control in the Civil Service
Commission and not the FBI. This recommendation derived from
the members' concern, that having loyalty decisions determined by
the FBI might precipitate an adverse reaction - commission member
Stephen Spingarn later contended that the commission had feared
that FBI investigations would be politically biased. Yet, despite
this provision of the recommended and established loyalty program,
the FBI immediately assumed investigative control. Not surprisingly, this decision precipitated a protest first from the Civil
Service Commission and then from other federal agencies, notably
the Treasury Department. In the final analysis, however, the FBI
prevailed.*

(145) LETTER, HARRY MITCHELL (PRESIDENT, U.S. CIVIL SERVICE COM-
MISSION) AND FRANCES PERKINS (COMMISSIONER) TO PRESIDENT TRUMAN,
April 25, 1947

Source: Harry S. Truman Papers, Official Files 252-K, Harry S.
Truman Library.

The Bureau of the Budget is now considering, for the approval
of the President, the appropriation to be made for the loyalty
investigations made necessary by Executive Order 9835.

To the undersigned it appears that the Budget's method of es-
timating the workload and consequent appropriation is entirely

contrary to the spirit of the President's Temporary Commission on Employee Loyalty and to the letter of the Executive order. Under the workload division proposed by the Budget, practically all loyalty investigations provided for by the order are to be made by the Federal Bureau of Investigation.

The members of the Loyalty Commission were strongly opposed to investigations by the FBI on the basis that whatever unfavorable reaction there was against the Executive order would be much stronger if the FBI made these investigations, than if the Civil Service Commission made them. If we understood you correctly in our conference with you, that also was your opinion.

After the issuance of your Executive order the FBI took the position that it was its duty, on the basis of the Hatch Act [of 1939] and an unpublished directive from the Attorney General, to investigate all persons already in the government service. You decided that such a plan might be beneficial as the FBI had already made investigations of many of these; and it was so agreed.

Now the FBI insists that it is its duty to also investigate probational employees named to positions subject to investigation by the Commission, and the Budget approves. That would mean a considerable majority of such appointees as it is very necessary for the Civil Service Commission in numerous cases to certify eligibles before it will be possible to complete an investigation. It is estimated by the Commission's Loyalty Board that about 70 per cent of the cases it has passed on have concerned persons who were appointed subject to investigation. Therefore, under the procedure which the Budget approves the Civil Service Commission would be investigating a proportionately smaller number of cases than it has in the past.

Other members of the Loyalty Commission have expressed themselves to the same effect as we are now doing, and express regret.

If you desire we would be glad to talk with you further before there is approval of the proposal by the Budget.

(146) MEMO, CLARK CLIFFORD (SPECIAL COUNSEL TO THE PRESIDENT) TO THE PRESIDENT, May 7, 1947 [Extract]

Source: George Elsey Papers, Internal Security, Harry S. Truman Library.

1. The Bureau of the Budget has submitted estimates of funds required by the Civil Service Commission and the F.B.I., from the present until June 30, 1948, to carry out the investigations on employee loyalty required by Executive Order 9835. The estimates are attached for your signature and transmittal to the Congress. . . .

3. On April 25, 1947, in a letter addressed to you, Mr. Mitchell and Miss Perkins of the Civil Service Commission expressed their concern over Budget's allocation of funds and the plan of investigations outlined above. They have no objection to the F.B.I.'s making investigations into the loyalty of persons now on the Federal payroll, but they do object to the F.B.I.'s making investigations into the loyalty of persons hereafter coming on the roll. . . .

4. Mr. Mitchell and Miss Perkins contend that . . . the Commission should complete whatever investigations, loyalty or other, become necessary, and that the Commission should not be obliged to call on F.B.I. to conduct the loyalty aspects of a new employee's investigation in those cases where a loyalty investigation appears necessary.

5. I cannot concur with Mr. Mitchell and Miss Perkins . . . I believe that the F.B.I. should [conduct loyalty investigations of new federal employees], and that the appropriation estimates prepared by Budget to this end should be approved.

6. Allowing Civil Service to make [such] loyalty investigations . . . would mean that both Civil Service and the F.B.I. would be making the same type of investigation because, of course, the F.B.I., under the authority of the Hatch Act, will continue its work on loyalty cases. Parallel and duplicating investigative organizations would be developed. Inasmuch as "undercover" and "infiltration" tactics may become necessary, duplication will be costly and would jeopardize the success of the efforts of both F.B.I. and Civil Service.

7. I believe that the F.B.I. is better qualified to conduct loyalty investigations than Civil Service. It has a highly trained, efficiently organized corps of investigators. . . .

8. Civil Service, on the other hand, has fewer than 100 investigators, none of whom is especially trained in the techniques required in loyalty investigation. It must recruit 600 more agents to make the general investigations for suitability, and if it were to conduct loyalty investigations for new Federal employees as well, Civil Service would need an additional 250 agents. . . .

9. Assigning loyalty investigations of new employees to the F.B.I., on the other hand, will require no increase in the number of F.B.I. agents. It would only slow up - slightly - the rate of decrease in the size of the F.B.I., inasmuch as the F.B.I. would retain about 250 of the 1,600 investigators now working on Atomic Energy employees instead of releasing them with the others when the Atomic investigations are concluded in another year.

10. I am fully cognizant of the dangers to our Civil Rights which we face in the matter of loyalty investigations, and I share your feelings of concern. It is precisely because of the dangers involved that I believe that the F.B.I. is a better agency than Civil Service to conduct loyalty investigations for new employees; the more highly trained, organized and administered an agency is, the higher should be its standards. The principal source of danger to our Civil Rights lies, not in the investigations, but what is done with the results of the investigations. That is a matter entirely divorced from the investigative activities of either F.B.I. or Civil Service and will require our continued careful supervision.

11. The only justification for the program of employee investigations is the discovery and dismissal of disloyal elements within the government. I believe that the F.B.I. is better qualified to ferret out such persons than is the as yet non-existent group of Civil Service investigators.

12. I therefore recommend the approval of the Budget's proposed estimates, and that you sign the attached letter to the
Speaker of the House. . . .

(147) MEMO, CLARK CLIFFORD TO PRESIDENT TRUMAN, May 9, 1947
[Extract]

Source: George Elsey Papers, Internal Security, Harry S. Truman
Library.

1. Following our discussion on May 7 on this subject, I requested Budget to continue its efforts to reach a settlement of
the differences of opinion between Civil Service and the F.B.I.
over loyalty investigations. Budget has now submitted a revised
estimate which should, I believe, be considerably more satisfactory to the Civil Service Commission than the previous estimate.

2. The revised estimate states:

"Whenever these checks bring to light derogatory information relating to the loyalty of persons seeking employment
in the competitive service and who have been appointed subject
to investigation, it will be the responsibility of the Civil
Service Commission to determine their eligibility for continued employment in the service. In the discharge of this responsibility, the Civil Service Commission may call upon the
Federal Bureau of Investigation to provide it with all the
information which it has or can develop, as a result of appropriate investigations, bearing on the question of loyalty."

3. You will note that it is no longer mandatory for Civil
Service to turn over loyalty cases to the F.B.I. It is a matter
of discretion on the part of the Commission which may, if it
wishes, call on the F.B.I. . . .

*Under Truman's loyalty program membership in certain proscribed
organizations would be considered as one ground for the denial of
a loyalty clearance. Yet, Truman's executive order had not outlined the criteria leading to listing an organization as "fascist,
communist, or subversive" - that was left to the Attorney General.
These criteria, outlined in the July 24, 1947, memorandum of
Edelstein and Duggan, were not of importance only for the administration of the loyalty program. Publicly released in December
1947, the so-called Attorney Generals list was in turn employed
by public officials (state and local governments, school boards)
and private employers (as CBS)* as a litmus test for judging the
loyalty of their employees.*

**CBS reliance on the Attorney General's list is discussed in
David Caute's* The Great Fear: The Anti-Communist Purge Under
Truman and Eisenhower *(New York: Simon and Schuster, 1978), pp.
528-529. Caute recounts similar uses of the Attorney General's
list by other private employers and by local and state agencies.
[Editor]*

(148) MEMO, DAVID EDELSTEIN AND JOSEPH DUGGAN (SPECIAL ASSISTANTS TO THE ATTORNEY GENERAL) TO ASSISTANT TO THE ATTORNEY GENERAL DOUGLAS McGREGOR, July 24, 1947 [Extract]

Source: A. Devitt Vanech Papers, Loyalty Criteria, Harry S. Truman Library.

In accordance with your request there is submitted for your consideration a set of criteria which, in our opinion, may be utilized by the Attorney General in designating those organizations in which membership may be cause for refusal of or removal from Government employment.

. . . the proposed criteria are designed to be elastic and flexible.

The formulation of criteria to be utilized to determine and recognize the true nature of an organization is unfortunately limited in scope by human frailty. . . definitions are particularly imperfect when it is intended to have them embrace the vast area of political, economic and social action which too often reside in the operation of the mind and are thus safeguarded from the ready detection which is possible when specific deeds detrimental to the United States are committed.

Organizations hostile to the United States are not eager to give evidence of their perfidy. Accordingly, they assume the guise of innocence the better to practice their policy of deception and disloyalty to the United States.

Their practices of hypocrisy and dissimulation make detection exceedingly difficult. Nevertheless, the spotlight of sound criteria focused by just and competent application can serve to ferret out the offending organizations and at the same time afford protection to those organizations which are inoffensive. . . .

The broad general criteria to be considered in determining whether any foreign or domestic organization should be designated by the Attorney General as within the purview of the standard . . . of Executive Order No. 9835 are whether, upon all the available evidence and information:

(1) the actual principles of such organizations may be deemed to be hostile or inimical to the American form of government, orderly democratic processes, and the constitutional guarantees of individual liberty so as to lead a person of reasonable prudence and discretion to conclude that such principles are opposed to or in contravention of the principles of the Constitution or laws of the United States;

(2) the aims, purposes, policies and programs of such organization promote the ideals and serve the interests of any foreign government or of any foreign political party;

(3) such organization is more concerned with the success or failure of foreign political and economic experiments which would result in the destruction or abolition of the republican form of government guaranteed by the Constitution or laws of the United States;

(4) the actual principles, methods and mode of operation of such organization indicate lack of bona-fide allegiance to

the government of the United States or lack of attachment to the principles of the Constitution;

(5) such organization may be fairly deemed to advocate, as part of its purpose and policy, political or economic changes by radical or revolutionary methods rather than by orderly, democratic, and constitutional processes;

(6) such organization is committed to an actual policy and program which sanctions the use of the techniques of conspiracy, force, intimidation, confusion, deceit, suppression of minority opinion, false propaganda and other similar devices to undermine confidence in the government of the United States, or to pervert or corrupt the integrity of its operations, or to overthrow it, by force and violence if necessary;

(7) such organization is committed to an actual policy and program which sanctions the use of the techniques enumerated in (6) above to deprive any person of rights guaranteed by the Constitution, or to suppress civil liberties, or to prevent any person from exercising any right or privilege secured to him by the laws of the United States. . . .

The specific criteria to be considered in determining whether any foreign or domestic organization should be designated by the Attorney General as within the purview of the standard . . . of Executive Order No. 9835 are as follows:

(1) a "totalitarian" organization is one which subscribes to the principles of, advocates the policies of, or favors or advances the methods of the unitary state characterized by a highly centralized government under the control of a political caste which allows no recognition of or representation to opposition parties or minority groups. . . . for practical purposes, a "totalitarian organization" is one which advocates the replacement of the American democratic form of government by the creation, establishment and perpetuation of such a state in the United States;

(2) in form, the totalitarian political and economic state may be either Fascist or Communist. In both instances it is monolithic and makes no provision for representative government. Hence, any organization which actually advocates the political, economic or social philosophy of either form may be aptly designated as "totalitarian";

(3) a "fascist" organization is one which advocates the principles, policies or methods of Fascism or Nazism as expressed through a highly centralized state, totalitarian in form, authoritarian and absolute in substance, and which is the negation of representative, democratic government in that it brooks no opposition to the ruling party, suppresses minorities, denies civil rights, and makes of the citizen a creature and chattel of the state;

(4) a "communist" organization is one which advocates the principles, policies and methods of the Communist Party (based upon the political and economic theories of Karl Marx, Friedrich Engels and Nicolai Lenin) as expressed through a highly centralized state, totalitarian in form,

authoritarian and absolute in substance, and in which representative, democratic government is replaced by the form of political organization known as the "dictatorship of the proletariat".

(5) In addition to the Communist Party itself, other organizations may be properly designated "communist" if they

(a) consistently follow the "Communist Party line" through one or more changes particularly where such change is in accord with the governmental policy of Soviet Russia and opposed to that of the United States;

(b) advocate revolution or the use of force, if necessary, in order to bring about political or economic changes;

(c) advocate Communist Party policies and objectives while subscribing to democratic forms and principles and generally through utilization of deceptive "fronts";

(d) consistently adhere to, approve and advocate Communist Party "causes" and the political and economic policies and programs of the government of Soviet Russia and its satellite nations in opposition to those of the government of the United States.

****

(7) A "subversive" organization is one which seeks to undermine confidence in, pervert or corrupt the integrity of the operations of, overthrow, ruin, betray, cause the downfall of, change by revolution or force, or subordinate to a foreign power the government of the United States. Advocacy of any such purposes categorizes an organization as subversive regardless of the means or methods adopted to effectuate such purposes.

The foregoing criteria have been formulated on the assumption that their use will be restricted to the Attorney General or his subordinates and that they are not for publication.

Given these priorities, not surprisingly the Administration after 1948 did not seriously consider those suggestions advocated by civil libertarians to curb abuses, ensure fairer procedures, and eliminate politically-motivated evaluations of the employee's loyalty. The only measures which received serious consideration were those intended to make the program more stringent or to undercut McCarthyite charges that existing procedures were inadequate. Accordingly, responding to the demonstrated political impact of McCarthyite charges during the 1950 congressional elections, in January 1951 President Truman appointed a special presidential commission, the Commission on Internal Security and Individual Rights, to study the general loyalty question. The Commission never became operative and did not issue a formal report owing to the Congress' refusal to enact special legislation waiving conflict of interest provisions for those appointed as commission members or staff employees. Despite the "Individual

Rights" theme in its title and President Truman's emphasis on the need to balance internal security and individual rights consider- ations, the only question which the Commission seriously consid- ered during its limited tenure involved a proposal to tighten the loyalty program's dismissal standard. President Truman in time formally adopted this recommendation advocated by security- oriented personnel and championed by Attorney General McGrath as early as 1949. By executive order 10241 of April 28, 1951, Truman amended the loyalty program's original dismissal standard ("rea- sonable grounds exist for the belief that the person is disloyal to the Government") to stipulate "reasonable doubt as to the loyalty of the individual involved to the Government." Based on the premise that federal employment was a privilege and not a right, the revised standard resulted in the review of the cases of 565 individuals who had been cleared earlier under the "disloyal- ty" standard and, in effect, indirectly confirmed the McCarthyite contention that earlier procedures were lax and ineffective. Foreign Service officer John Carter Vincent's case was one of the more dramatic of those reviewed under this revised standard be- cause it highlighted the political criteria (as opposed to espi- onage) which governed the Truman loyalty program. Vincent had been a Foreign Service officer since 1924, and during the World War II years had served variously as Counselor to the U.S. Embassy at Chungking (China), Chief of the State Department's Division of Chinese Affairs, and then Director of the Department's Division of Far Eastern Affairs. Denounced by Senator McCarthy as a Commu- nist sympathizer, Vincent became the subject of an intensive loyalty investigation which focused on his reporting and then assessment of reports on conditions in China. Because the re- ports had emphasized the corruption and unpopularity of the Chiang Kai-shek government, Vincent's "incorrect" assessment led the Loyalty Review Board to conclude, by a 3-2 vote, that his "whole course of conduct in connection with Chinese affairs" raised a "reasonable doubt" as to his loyalty.

(149) LETTER, ATTORNEY GENERAL J. HOWARD McGRATH TO DONALD DAWSON (ADMINISTRATIVE ASSISTANT TO PRESIDENT TRUMAN), December 23, 1949 [Extract]

Source: Harry S. Truman Papers, Official File 252-K, Harry S. Truman Library.

****

It is my considered opinion that the basic Loyalty Program, which resulted from the [President's Temporary] Commission's study, is quite satisfactory and that there are no sound grounds for criticizing its findings. Therefore, I believe the question as to whether the basic program should be re-examined at this time should be answered in the negative. However, experience gained in operating the program through the past two and one-half years has demonstrated, in my opinion, the desirability of an administrative review of the organizational structure, which is charged with carrying through the program, as well as some of the regulations and procedures which have been adopted. I would, therefore, recommend that the organization structure and the regu- lations and procedures be reviewed at this time with a view to meeting specific problems which those who have been directly con-

nected with the operation of the program have encountered during
the past two and one-half years. . . .

. . . observations . . . have been made to the effect that the
program should be a "Security" rather than a "Loyalty" Program.
This suggestion results, in my opinion, from a lack of understanding of the problem which the program was designed to meet. . . .
the President's Temporary Commission [had been directed to] . . .
study of ways and means of eliminating disloyal and subversive
persons from the Government service. It is probably natural that
some would feel that this endeavor leads directly into the much
broader question of testing whether or not employees are safe
from a security standpoint. There are certain weaknesses of
character, which, if present in an individual employee, might
make such individual a doubtful security risk and unsuitable for
Government employment, particularly in sensitive agencies or sensitive positions. Such persons should not, however, be grouped
with and judged on the same basis as disloyal and subversive persons, as would be the case if the Loyalty Program were changed to
a Security Program. These cases should, in my opinion, be handled
under the regular Civil Service procedures governing removals
from the service. However, it might be advisable to have the
Civil Service Commission review and make certain of the adequacy
of its procedures in this connection.

(150) STATEMENT, PRESIDENT TRUMAN, January 23, 1951 [Extract]
Source: *Public Papers of the Presidents: Harry S. Truman, 1951.*
Washington: U.S. Government Printing Office, 1964, pp. 119-120.

I have today established a Commission on Internal Security
and Individual Rights. . . . [to] consider in all its aspects
the question of how this Nation can best deal with the problem of
protecting its internal security and at the same time maintaining
the freedoms of its citizens. . . .

The Commission will make a thorough examination of the laws,
practices, and procedures concerning the protection of our Nation
against treason, espionage, sabotage, and other subversive activities, and of the operation of and any need for changes in such
laws, practices, and procedures. The Commission will also consider the methods used by public or private groups for the purpose
of protecting us against such activities. It will consider these
matters from the standpoint of protecting both the internal security of our country and the rights of individuals, and will seek
the wisest balance that can be struck between security and freedom. The Commission will report its conclusions and recommendations for legislative, administrative, or other action it deems
appropriate. . . .

Today, we are particularly concerned by the threat to our
Government and our national life arising from the activities of
the forces of Communist imperialism. In addition to the vigorous
action we are taking abroad to meet this threat, we must be sure
that our laws and procedures at home are adequate to protect our
system of government against unconstitutional attacks and to preserve our national security against treason, espionage, sabotage,
and other subversive acts designed to weaken or overthrow our

Government. At the same time, we are concerned lest the measures taken to protect us from these dangers infringe the liberties guaranteed by our Constitution and stifle the atmosphere of freedom in which we have so long expressed our thoughts and carried on our daily affairs.

These are problems of momentous importance for our country and its future, and for the future of our leadership in the world. They should be approached in a serious and fairminded way by all our citizens. We must not let our differences about how to solve these problems degenerate into partisan controversies. We must continue to protect our security within the framework of our historic liberties, without thought of partisan advantage or political gain.

To keep these great problems from falling into the arena of partisanship, I am appointing this Commission of distinguished citizens on a nonpartisan bases. I believe the people of this country will receive from them an authoritative judgment on these problems, based on the facts and formulated in the national interest, with no question of political advantage.

The Commission will undoubtedly wish to focus its primary attention on Federal laws and procedures. . . . I hope it will [also] consider afresh, in all its present-day ramifications, the recurrent question of how a free people protect their society from subversive attack without at the same time destroying their own liberties. . . .

One of the important matters for the Commission to consider is the operation of the Government employee loyalty and security programs. . . . The Commission will be expected to report on the effectiveness and fairness of the Government's loyalty and security programs. In doing this, the Commission . . . will be authorized to [inspect individual case files] to whatever extent it may determine to be necessary.

In connection with loyalty and security procedures, and also in considering the operation of such statutes as the Internal Security Act of 1950, the Commission will necessarily be reviewing information of very high security classifications. I am directing the Commission therefore, to take appropriate measures to safeguard the security of any classified or confidential information it may wish to examine.

I intend to do everything I can to enable this Commission to make a thorough and careful study. . . .

(151) MEMORANDUM, PRESIDENT TRUMAN TO SECRETARY OF STATE DEAN ACHESON, January 3, 1953

Source: *Public Papers of the Presidents: Harry S. Truman, 1952-53.* Washington: U.S. Government Printing Office, 1966, p. 1110.

I have read your memorandum of today concerning the case of John Carter Vincent. I think the suggestions which you make are well taken and I authorize and direct you to proceed in the manner which you have outlined.

(152) <u>MEMORANDUM SECRETARY OF STATE ACHESON TO PRESIDENT TRUMAN</u>,
January 3, 1953 [Extract]

Source: *Public Papers of the Presidents: Harry S. Truman, 1952-53*.
Washington: U.S. Government Printing Office, 1966, pp. 1110-1111.

I have recently been advised by Chairman [Hiram] Bingham of the
Loyalty Review Board that a panel of the Loyalty Review Board has considered the case of [foreign service officer] John Carter Vincent,
. . . [and] that while the panel did not find Mr. Vincent guilty of
disloyalty, it has reluctantly concluded that there is reasonable
doubt as to his loyalty to the Government of the United States.
Chairman Bingham further advised me that it is therefore the recommendation of the Board that the services of Mr. Vincent be terminated.

Such a recommendation by so distinguished a Board is indeed
serious and impressive and must be given great weight. The final
responsibility, however, for making a decision as to whether Mr.
Vincent should be dismissed is that of the Secretary of State. . . .

A most important item on which I must rely in exercising this
responsibility is the communication from Chairman Bingham in which
he advised me of the conclusion by his panel. . . .

In the first place, I note a statement that the panel has not
accepted or rejected the testimony of Mr. [Louis] Budenz [an ex-
Communist who became almost a professional informer during the
early Cold War years] that he recalls being informed by others that
Mr. Vincent was a Communist and under Communist discipline. The
panel also states that it does not accept or reject the findings
of the Committee on the Judiciary of the Senate with respect to
Mr. Vincent and the Institute of Pacific Relations or the findings
of the Committe with respect to the participation of Mr. Vincent
in the development of United States policy toward China in 1945.
The panel, however, proceeds to state that, although it has not
accepted or rejected these factors, it has taken them into account.
I am unable to interpret what this means. If the panel did take
these factors into account, this means that it must have relied
upon them in making its final determination. Yet I am unable to
understand how these factors could have played a part in the final
determination of the panel if these factors were neither accepted
nor rejected by the Board. . . .

The communication from the panel raises another issue which
goes to the heart of operation of the Department of State and the
Foreign Service. It is the issue of accurate reporting. The communication contains the following statement:

"The panel notes Mr. Vincent's studied praise of Chinese Communists and equally studied criticism of the Chiang Kai-shek
Government throughout a period when it was the declared and established policy of the Government of the United States to support
Chiang Kai-shek's Government."

Mr. Vincent's duty was to report the facts as he saw them. He
was not merely to report successes of existing policy but also to report on the aspects in which it was failing and the reasons therefor.
If this involved reporting that situations existed in the administration of the Chinese Nationalists which had to be corrected if the
Nationalist Government was to survive, it was his duty to report
this. If this involved a warning not to underestimate the combat

potential of the Chinese Communists, or their contribution to the war against Japan it was his duty to report this. . . .

I do not exclude the possibility that in this or in any other case a board might find that the reports of an officer might or might not disclose a bias which might have a bearing on the issue of his loyalty. But in so delicate a matter, affecting so deeply the integrity of the Foreign Service, I should wish to be advised by persons thoroughly familiar with the problems and procedures of the Department of State and the Foreign Service. This involves an issue far greater in importance than the disposition of a loyalty case involving one man. Important as it is to do full justice to the individual concerned, it is essential that we should not by inadvertence take any step which might lower the high traditions of our own Foreign Service to the level established by governments which will permit their diplomats to report to them only what they want to hear.

The memorandum from Mr. Bingham indicates that the Board also took into account "Mr. Vincent's failure properly to discharge his repsonsibilities as Chairman of the Far Eastern Subcommittee of State, War and Navy to supervise the accuracy or security of State Department documents emanating from that Subcommittee." The statement which refers to the security of the files seems to me to be inadvertent. Presumably it is a reference to the fact that State Department documents were involved in the Amerasia case. However, in the many Congressional investigations which have followed that case it has not been suggested that Mr. Vincent had any responsibility for those documents. I have not discovered any such evidence in the file in this case. The reference to the accuracy of the State Department documents emanating from that Committee is obscure. In any case, while it might be relative to Mr. Vincent's competence in performing his duties, it does not seem to me to have any bearing on the question of loyalty.

The report finally refers to Mr. Vincent's association with numerous persons "who, he had reason to believe," were either Communists or Communist sympathizers. This is indeed a matter which, if unexplained, is of importance and clearly relevant. It involves inquiry as to whether this association arose in the performance of his duties or otherwise. It further involves an inquiry as to the pattern of Mr. Vincent's close personal friends and whether he knew or should have known that any of these might be Communists or Communist sympathizers.

All these matters raised in my mind the necessity for further inquiry. . . . I find upon examining the documents [in this proceeding] that the recommendation made by the panel of the Loyalty Review Board was made by a majority of one, two of the members believing that no evidence had been produced which led them to have a doubt as to Mr. Vincent's loyalty. In this situation, I believe that I cannot in good conscience and in the exercise of my own judgment, which is my duty under law, carry out this recommendation of the Board. . . .

I, therefore, ask your permission to seek the advice of some persons who will combine the highest judicial qualifications of weighing the evidence with the greatest possible familiarity of the words and standards of the Department of State and the Foreign Service, both in reporting from the field and making decisions in the Department. If you approve, I should propose to ask the following five persons to examine the record in this case and to advise me as to what disposition in their judgment should be made in this case: . . .

I should ask them to read the record in this case and at their earliest convenience inform the Secretary of State of their conclusions.

Absolute security had become the objective of federal loyalty policy during the Truman years. To ensure this result, the Congress in August 1950 enacted Public Law 733 authorizing department and agency heads to dismiss summarily those employees whose continued employment would be inconsistent with the "national security" (thereby waiving the 1912 Lloyd-Lafollette Act's requirement assuring the right of hearings and due process). These same considerations motivated President Truman in 1952 to authorize an NSC review of the existing loyalty program and to recommend the adoption of administratively more uniform, but also more repressive, procedures based on the nebulous criterion of "suitability." Over time, then, the Truman loyalty program had evolved in a repressive direction. The original dismissal standard, requiring proof of disloyalty, entailed the prospect that termination judgments would be based on political criteria; this result was virtually assured when the dismissal standard became either "doubts as to loyalty" or "suitability."

(153) LETTER, DONALD MacPHAIL (BUREAU OF THE BUDGET ASSISTANT DIRECTOR) TO WILLIAM HOPKINS (WHITE HOUSE AIDE), August 25, 1950 [Extract]

Source: Bureau of the Budget Bill File, Harry S. Truman Library.

The Congress has enacted H.R. 7439 "To protect the national security of the United States by permitting the summary suspension of employment of civilian officers and employees of various departments and agencies of the Government, and for other purposes."

The purpose . . . is to protect the national security by permitting, notwithstanding the provisions of any other law, the summary suspension of the employment of civilian officers and employees of the Departments of Commerce, Justice, Defense, Army, Navy, Air Force, and Coast Guard, Atomic Energy Commission, National Security Resources Board and the National Advisory Committee for Aeronautics. The enactment further provides for the termination of employment of suspended employees of these agencies if subsequent investigation develops facts which support the suspension. Other departments and agencies could be brought within the coverage of the bill whenever their inclusion was deemed necessary in the interest of national security by the President, who, upon taking such action, would report that fact to the committees on Armed Services of the Congress. . . .

The present measure would supplement, not supersede, the President's loyalty program despite the fact that the broad authority which it contains would appear to sanction the suspension and dismissal of an employee of one of the agencies concerned on the grounds of disloyalty. The understanding with which it was proposed by the Department of Defense, cleared by the Bureau of the Budget, and enacted by the Congress was that it would be used to terminate the employment in sensitive agencies of employees who, although not disloyal, may, because of their habits, associations, affiliations or indiscretions, constitute as serious a menace to national security as if they were of questionable loyalty. It will be necessary for the various agency heads concerned to keep this distinction between security and loyalty constantly in mind if the two processes are to operate successfully side by side.

The sweeping powers over many Federal employees which this bill would confer on various agency heads is not new. Temporary and appropriation-act authority presently cover the employees of a number of agencies named here. While it appears that such authority has been employed with restraint in the past, this fact does not lessen the need for constant vigilance to properly safeguard individual liberties in a manner which, at the same time, will be consistent with the national security. This is particularly true with regard to legislation of the present type, legislation which furnishes few, if any, objective standards by which to judge the actions of government officials. For example, using criteria referred to above, when do habits, associations, affiliations or indiscretions of an employee categorize him as a security risk? Or, when is a charge as specific "as security considerations permit"? The highly successful manner in which equally intangible yardsticks have been applied in the loyalty program would appear to indicate that enlightened implementation of the authority provided here is possible without the necessity for sacrificing either national or individual interests. . . .

(154) LETTER, PRESIDENT TRUMAN TO ROBERT RAMSPECK (CHAIRMAN, CIVIL SERVICE COMMISSION), August 8, 1952 [Extract]

Source: *Public Papers of the Presidents: Harry S. Truman, 1952-53.* Washington: U.S. Government Printing Office, 1966, pp. 513-514.

On July 14, 1951, I requested the National Security Council to make an investigation of the administration of Federal employee security programs relating to the denial of employment and the suspension and removal of employees in the interest of national security. Pursuant to that request, a study was made by the Interdepartmental Committee on Internal Security. Its report, prepared in collaboration with the staff of the Civil Service Commission, has been submitted to me by the National Security Council.

This report recommends that certain uniform standards and procedures be established to apply to all agencies where employee security programs are in effect. It also recommends that provision be made for Civil Service Commission review of agency decisions in security risk cases.

In addition, the Interdepartmental Committee on Internal Security . . . called attention to the confused situation which exists by reason of there being three general programs dealing with the denial of employment and the suspension and separation of Government employees. These general programs were described by the Committee as relating to loyalty, security, and suitability under civil service regulations, respectively, and the Committee pointed out that it is extremely difficult if not impossible to draw clear lines of demarcation among them. In order to eliminate this confusion, the Committee recommended that a study be made to effect a single general program covering eligibility for employment in the Federal service, whether on grounds of loyalty, security, or suitability. It is my understanding that the Civil Service Commission agrees with this proposal.

I have given considerable thought to the recommendations contained in this report. I have concluded that the most desirable action at this time would be to merge the loyalty, security, and suitability programs, thus eliminating the overlapping, duplication, and confusion which apparently now exist. It is my understanding that the status of the incumbent employees loyalty program is now so advanced that there would be little or no obstacle to accomplishing this from the standpoint of the future needs of that phase of the loyalty program. Accordingly, I should like for the Civil Service Commission to take the necessary steps to provide me with a plan for combining the three existing programs into one at the earliest practicable date. . . .

Pending action to merge the existing three programs, it does not seem advisable to issue an Executive Order establishing uniform standards and procedures comprising an over-all Government employee security program, with provision for Civil Service Commission review of agency decisions. Such an Executive order would presumably have only temporary effect, since it would be superseded shortly by the new program I am requesting the Commission to prepare. I believe we can utilize our efforts most effectively by going straight to what we regard as the best solution.

In the meantime, however, departments and agencies having employee security programs should reexamine their procedures in the light of the findings and recommendations of the Interdepartmental Committee. The Committee's report . . . should provide valuable guidance for those responsible for the formulation and administration of personnel security procedures, and which should assist them in assuring adequate procedural safeguards for the protection of all personnel who are subject to employee security programs. . . .

2. FBI Political Surveillance Authority

The FBI possessed the statutory authority to investigate only those activities in violation or wherein there was a "probable cause" violation of federal statutes. FBI officials (particularly FBI Director J. Edgar Hoover) chafed under these restrictions. For these conservative bureaucrats, the espionage and sabotage statutes did not provide sufficient authority to investigate those groups and individuals whom FBI officials believed potentially threatened the internal security. Conducting these investigations anyway, FBI officials (and particularly the astute "complete bureaucrat" Hoover) nonetheless sought alternative authorization - in the form of presidential directives. The formal establishment of Truman's loyalty program provided one basis for FBI investigations of dissident political activities. The Bureau's responsibility to investigate incumbent employees, and applicants for federal employment, seemingly required (1) ascertaining whether particular organizations met the standards for inclusion on the Attorney General's list and (2) compiling files on disloyal or "potentially disloyal" individuals who might not have been federal employees but might in the future seek federal employment.

Not merely a bureaucratic empire-builder, FBI Director Hoover was committed to purging the federal bureaucracy of any taint of radicalism and to extending FBI investigative authority to include dissident political activities. These considerations underlay Hoover's interest in ensuring total FBI control over the investigative phase of the loyalty program.

(155) <u>MEMO, FBI DIRECTOR TO ATTORNEY GENERAL CLARK</u>, May 21, 1947

Source: A. Devitt Vanech Papers, FBI Loyalty, Harry S. Truman Library.

I wish to advise that this Bureau has noted an increasing number of instances wherein formation in the possession of the various government agencies indicating a violation . . . of the Hatch Act is not brought to the attention of this Bureau. Furthermore, in view of Executive Order 9835 prescribing procedures for the administration of an employee's loyalty program in the Executive Branch of the Government and of the President's determination that this Bureau is responsible under the Order of conducting all investigations or charges of disloyalty against government employees, it appears necessary that at this time the attention of the various government agencies be directed to our investigative jurisdiction.

. . . some agencies may not be aware of our jurisdiction under the Hatch Act and also of our responsibilities under this Executive Order and I, therefore, strongly urge that you direct a letter to the various government agencies informing them of our jurisdiction and of the necessity of referring such matters immediately to this Bureau.

There is attached for your assistance in this regard a suggested text for such a letter to the various agencies.

[Note by Attorney General: I think we should get up a letter along this line.]

The loyalty program provided one basis for FBI investigations of dissident political activities. A far more important basis, and the authority cited by FBI officials as justification for these investigations during the 1960s and 1970s when these investigative activities were first publicly challenged, were certain presidential directives of 1939, 1943, 1950, and 1953. The most important of these, however, from the standpoint of providing such authorization, was Truman's directive of July 24, 1950.

Following the outbreak of World War II with the German invasion of Poland, FBI Director Hoover urged that President Roosevelt issue a directive ostensibly to preclude the recurrence of the

*vigilante-type activities of the World War I period. A modified
version of the directive recommended by Hoover was in fact issued
on September 6, 1939.*

(156) STATEMENT, PRESIDENT ROOSEVELT, September 6, 1939

Source: U.S. House, Committee on Internal Security, *Hearings on
Domestic Intelligence Operations for Internal Security Purposes*,
Part 1, 93rd Congress, 2d session, p. 3697.

The Attorney General has been requested by me to instruct the
Federal Bureau of Investigation of the Department of Justice to
take charge of investigative work in matters relating to espionage, sabotage, and violations of the neutrality regulations.

This task must be coordinated in a comprehensive and effective
manner on a national basis, and all information must be carefully
sifted out and correlated in order to avoid confusion and irres-
ponsibility.

To this end I request all police officers, sheriffs, and all
other law enforcement officers in the United States promptly to
turn over to the nearest representative of the Federal Bureau of
Investigation any information obtained by them relating to espionage, counterespionage, sabotage, subversive activities and violation of the neutrality laws.

*Concerned about vigilante-type activities, on January 8,
1943, President Roosevelt issued a modified version of his September 1939 directive. In effect, the President extended his 1939
appeal to law enforcement officers to "patriotic organizations
and individuals."*

(157) STATEMENT, PRESIDENT ROOSEVELT, January 8, 1943

Source: U.S. House, Committee on Internal Security, *Hearings on
Domestic Intelligence Operations for Internal Security Purposes*,
Part 1, 93rd Congress, 2d session, pp. 3697-3698.

On September 6, 1939, I issued a directive providing that the
Federal Bureau of Investigation of the Department of Justice
should take charge of investigative work in matters relating to
espionage, sabotage and violations of the neutrality regulations,
pointing out that the investigations must be conducted in a comprehensive manner, on a national basis and all information carefully
sifted out and correlated in order to avoid confusion and irres-
ponsibility. I then requested all police officers, sheriffs, and
other law enforcement officers in the United States, promptly to
turn over to the nearest representative of the Federal Bureau of
Investigation any such information.

I am again calling the attention of all enforcement officers
to the request that they report all such information promptly to
the nearest field representative of the Federal Bureau of Investigation, which is charged with the responsibility of correlating
this material and referring matters which are under the jurisdic-

tion of any other Federal Agency with responsibilities in this field to the appropriate agency.

I suggest that all patriotic organizations and individuals likewise report all such information relating to espionage and related matters to the Federal Bureau of Investigation in the same manner.

I am confident that all law enforcement officers, who are now rendering such invaluable assistance toward the success of the internal safety of our country will cooperate in this matter.

Neither of Roosevelt's directives (whether of 1939 or 1943) had authorized FBI investigations of "subversive activities." Accordingly, in August 1948, in the guise of a suggestion that these directives be reaffirmed, Attorney General Tom Clark urged President Truman to issue a "third" statement.

(158) <u>MEMO, ATTORNEY GENERAL CLARK TO THE PRESIDENT</u>, August 17, 1948

Source: Harry S. Truman Papers, Official File 10-B, Harry S. Truman Library.

There is attached for your consideration a draft of a statement concerning investigations in the internal security field. Copies of the first [September 6, 1939] and the second [January 8, 1943] directives by President Roosevelt are attached. This appears to be the appropriate time for a third.

(159) <u>CLARK'S PROPOSED STATEMENT (BY PRESIDENT TRUMAN)</u> [undated submitted with Clark memo, August 17, 1948, above]

Source: Harry S. Truman, Official File 10-B, Harry S. Truman Library.

On September 6, 1939, and again on January 8, 1943, a Presidential directive was issued providing that the Federal Bureau of Investigation should take charge of investigative work in matters relating to espionage, sabotage, subversive activities, and in similar matters. It was requested that all law enforcement officers in the United States, and all patriotic organizations and individuals, promptly turn over to the Federal Bureau of Investigation any information concerning these matters.

The Federal Bureau of Investigation has fully carried out its responsibilities with respect to the internal security of the United States, under these directives. The cooperation rendered to the Federal Bureau of Investigation in accordance with the directives has been of invaluable assistance to it.

I wish to emphasize at this time that these directives continue in full force and effect.

Investigations in matters relating to the internal security of the United States to be effective must be conducted in a comprehensive manner, on a national basis, and by a single central agency. The Federal Bureau of Investigation is the agency designated for this purpose. At this time again, I request that all information concerning any activities within the United States, its territories or possessions, believed to be of a subversive nature, be reported promptly to the nearest field representative of the Federal Bureau of Investigation.

We do not know whether the FBI actually drafted the statement recommended to the President by Attorney General Clark. FBI officials, in any event, actively lobbied the White House on its behalf - claiming an interest in curbing "vigilante activities."

(160) <u>MEMO, STEPHEN SPINGARN (WHITE HOUSE AIDE) TO CLARK CLIFFORD (SPECIAL COUNSEL TO THE PRESIDENT</u>), September 21, 1948 [Extract]

Source: Harry S. Truman Papers, Official File 10-B, Harry S. Truman Library.

A file on this matter was passed to me by [White House aide George] Elsey on September 8. I have discussed the matter with Mr. Elsey and Admiral [Sidney] Souers [Executive Secretary, NSC].

On September 20, Mr. Ladd, Assistant Director of FBI, called [White House aide Donald] Dawson to urge early issuance of the statement by the President. He was referred to me. Mr. Ladd indicated that the purpose of the statement was to spike vigilante activity in the internal security field by private organizations and persons, making it clear that the FBI is the proper agency to handle such matters and that any information obtained on the subject should be reported promptly to that organization.

The Justice version of the proposed Presidential statement appears to go further than the statements on this subject made by President Roosevelt in 1939 and 1943 and to cut across the jurisdiction of other Federal investigative agencies. Admiral Souers has had a redraft of the statement prepared, which restricts its scope to that of the previous statements on the subject by President Roosevelt. In my opinion, if any statement is issued on the subject it should be the version prepared by Admiral Souers.

However, the issuance of such a statement at this time by the President might give rise to the impression that he was making a rather transparent show of activity on this matter as a result of needling from Congressional quarters, but that he was after all only echoing a statement by his predecessor.

I do not object to the issuance of the statement in the revised form suggested by Admiral Souers, but I suggest that it be held up until November when its issuance could not be misunderstood. . . .

In point of fact, the proposed statement would have substantially increased FBI investigative authority: providing the first direct presidential authorization for FBI investigations of "subversive activities" and designating the FBI as the "single central agency" in matters relating to internal security. The press of the 1948 presidential campaign and the fact that the NSC was then considering how to delimit the authority of the various federal intelligence agencies combined to avert any presidential action on this proposal. Eventually such a delimitation agreement was

recommended to the President by the National Security Council,
and was approved by President Truman on March 22, 1949. In the
interim, however, FBI and military intelligence officials had
independently concluded a delimitation agreement.

(161) DELIMITATION AGREEMENT OF FBI, OFFICE OF NAVAL INTELLIGENCE,
INTELLIGENCE DIVISION OF THE ARMY, AND OFFICE OF SPECIAL INVESTI-
GATIONS AIR FORCE, February 23, 1949 [Extract]

Source: U.S. House, Committee on Internal Security, *Hearings on*
Domestic Intelligence Operations for Internal Security Purposes,
Part 1, 93rd Congress, 2d session, p. 3369.

I. The undersigned have reviewed the directive contained in the
President's Memorandum of June 26, 1939, as augmented by his
Directive of September 6, 1939, the Delimitations Agreement of
February 9, 1942, and the Presidential Directive of October 30,
1947. In addition, cognizance has been taken of the provisions
of the Atomic Energy Act of 1946, . . . it is now agreed that responsibility for the investigation of all activities coming under
the categories of espionage, counterespionage, subversion and
sabotage (hereinafter referred to as "these categories") will be
delimited as indicated hereinafter. The responsibility assumed
by one organization in a given field carries with it the obligation to exchange freely and directly with the other subscribing
organizations all information of mutual interest. When the organization with primary operating responsibility is unable for any
reason to produce material in that field desired by the subscribing agencies, such special arrangements as may be legal or desirable will be worked out through negotiation at the national level
prior to activity by one agency in another agency's field. It is
recognized by the subscribers hereto that the Headquarters Department of the Army has decentralized such functions to its major
subordinate commanders. When the major subordinate commanders of
the Department of the Army cannot effect satisfactory special arrangements, the matter will be referred to the Director of Intelligence of the Army for further negotiations at the national
level. Close cooperation and coordination between the four subscribing organizations is a mutually recognized necessity. . . .

Neither the delimitation agreement approved by President
Truman on March 22, 1949 nor the agreement concluded between FBI
and military agency officials on February 23, 1949 (which merely
recognized but could not authorize FBI investigations of "sub-
versive activities") directly authorized FBI political investiga-
tions. Accordingly, in his capacity as head of the Interdepart-
mental Intelligence Conference, on July 5, 1950, FBI Director
Hoover recommended the issuance of another presidential directive.
Hoover's recommendation was vigorously supported by Attorney Gen-
eral J. Howard McGrath. On July 24, 1950, President Truman issued
a modified form of Hoover's proposal. At this time, and unknow-
ingly, President Truman apparently assumed that he was merely re-
affirming what President Roosevelt had authorized in 1939 and
1943 - that the FBI "take charge of investigative work in matters
relating to . . . subversive activities."

(162) <u>LETTER, ATTORNEY GENERAL McGRATH TO CHARLES MURPHY (SPECIAL COUNSEL TO THE PRESIDENT</u>), July 11, 1950

Source: Charles Murphy Files, National Security Council, Harry S. Truman Library.

The Interdepartmental Intelligence Conference on July 5, 1950, recommended to the National Security Council that a Presidential statement be issued to bring up to date and clarify prior Presidential Directives which were issued September 6, 1939, and January 8, 1943, outlining the responsibilities of the Federal Bureau of Investigation in connection with espionage, sabotage, subversive activities and related matters.

I am enclosing a proposed statement which I recommend for the President's signature. The effect of issuing this statement now will be to remind all agencies, patriotic organizations and individual citizens that the Federal Bureau of Investigation is charged with responsibility for investigating all matters pertaining to espionage, sabotage, subversive activities and related matters, and that it is also the agency charged with the responsibilty of being the central coordinating agency for all information relating to the same matters. For these reasons, the issuance of the statement at this time would be most helpful.

(163) <u>MEMO (WHITE HOUSE AIDE) GEORGE ELSEY TO (SPECIAL COUNSEL TO THE PRESIDENT) CHARLES MURPHY</u>, July 12, 1950

Source: Charles Murphy Files, National Security Council, Harry S. Truman Library.

The attached letter dated July 11 to you from the Attorney General, recommending that the President issue a statement outlining the responsibilities of the Federal Bureau of Investigation in connection with espionage and related matters, is distinctly out of bounds and an improper one for the Attorney General to have written at this time.

As McGrath admits in the opening sentence, this matter is now pending before the National Security Council. The Department of Justice should not have attempted an end run to the White House at a time when their proposal is in the NSC.

Before this letter arrived from your office, Jimmy Lay [NSC Executive Secretary] had told me about the recommendation and said that he would bring it to your attention as soon as all members of the National Security Council had responded to his request for their views on this matter.

Since there is no great rush, and since Lay will have the views of the various departments within the next two or three days, I recommend that you forward the McGrath letter to Lay. A memorandum for your signature is attached. [Murphy sent the memo on July 13, 1950.]

P.S. - I have talked with Steve Spingarn about this and he concurs in the above.

(164) <u>STATEMENT, PRESIDENT TRUMAN</u>, July 24, 1950

Source: George Elsey Papers, Central Intelligence, Harry S. Truman Library.

On September 6, 1939, and January 8, 1943, a Presidential directive was issued providing that the Federal Bureau of Investigation of the Department of Justice should take charge of investigative work in matters relating to espionage, sabotage, subversive activities and related matters. It was pointed out that the investigations must be conducted in a comprehensive manner on a national basis and all information carefully sifted out and correlated in order to avoid confusion. I should like to again call the attention of all enforcement officers, both Federal and State, to the request that they report all information in the above enumerated fields promptly to the nearest field representative of the Federal Bureau of Investigation, which is charged with the responsibility of correlating this material and referring matters which are under the jurisdiction of any other Federal Agency with responsibilities in this field to the appropriate agency.

I suggest that all patriotic organizations and individuals likewise report all such information relating to espionage, sabotage and subversive activities to the Federal Bureau of Investigation in this same manner.

Having thereby obtained formal presidential direction to investigate "subversive activities," FBI Director Hoover immediately exploited the Truman directive in a bold effort to influence public opinion.

(165) <u>STATEMENT, FBI DIRECTOR HOOVER</u>, July 26, 1950 [Extract]

Source: Eleanor Bontecou Papers, Internal Security File FBI, Harry S. Truman Library.

The internal security of the United States can be assured with the cooperation, aid and assistance of every law-abiding person in our Nation. The President of the United States in restating the responsibilities of the Federal Bureau of Investigation has called upon all law enforcement officers, patriotic organizations and individuals to report information pertaining to espionage, sabotage and subversive activities to the FBI. Plans have been made and are in operation whereby the law enforcement agencies of the Nation are working in close cooperation with the FBI.

The following suggestions are being made to assist patriotic organizations and individuals in complying with the President's request: . . .

  5. Once you have reported your information to the FBI do not endeavor to make private investigations. This can best be done by trained investigators who have access to data acquired over the years on individuals engaged in subversive activities. Hysteria, witch-hunts and vigilantes weaken internal security. Investigations involving internal security require care and painstaking effort. We all can contribute to our internal security by protecting the

innocent as well as by identifying the enemies within our midst. In cases involving espionage it is more important to identify spies, their contacts, sources of information, and methods of communications than to make immediate arrests.

6. Be alert. The greatest defenders against sabotage are the loyal American workmen who are producing the materials and weapons for our defense. They can be the "watch dogs" of defense in every walk of life.

7. The forces which are most anxious to weaken our internal security are not always easy to identify. Communists have been trained in deceit and secretly work toward the day when they hope to replace our American way of life with a Communist dictatorship. They utilize cleverly camouflaged movements, such as some peace groups and civil rights organizations, to achieve their sinister purposes. While they as individuals are difficult to identify, the Communist Party line is clear. Its first concern is the advancement of Soviet Russia and the godless Communist cause. It is important to learn to know the enemies of the American way of life.

3. FBI Electronic Surveillance Authority

When enacting Section 605 of the Federal Communications Act of 1934, Congress specifically forbad the "interception and divulgence" of any wire and radio communication. In rulings of 1937 and 1939 (Nardone v. U.S.), the U.S. Supreme Court held that this ban against wiretapping applied to federal agencies and further stipulated that such illegally obtained information could not be used to indict or convict any individual. Despite this ban, President Roosevelt decided to authorize the controlled use of wiretapping during "national defense" investigations.

(166) <u>MEMO, PRESIDENT ROOSEVELT TO ATTORNEY GENERAL ROBERT
JACKSON</u>, May 21, 1940

Source: Stephen Spingarn Papers, National Defense – Internal
Security, Harry S. Truman Library.

I have agreed with the broad purpose of the Supreme Court
decision [*Nardone v. U.S.*] relating to wire-tapping in investigations. The Court is undoubtedly sound both in regard to the use
of evidence secured over tapped wires in the prosecution of citizens in criminal cases; and is also right in its opinion that
under ordinary and normal circumstances wire-tapping by Government
agents should not be carried on for the excellent reason that it
is almost bound to lead to abuse of civil rights.

However, I am convinced that the Supreme Court never intended
any dictum in the particular case which it decided to apply to
grave matters involving the defense of the nation.

It is, of course, well known that certain other nations have
been engaged in the organization of propaganda of so-called "fifth
columns" in other countries and in preparation for sabotage, as
well as in actual sabotage.

It is too late to do anything about it after sabotage, assassinations and "fifth column" activities are completed.

You are, therefore, authorized and directed in such cases as
you may approve, after investigation of the need in each case, to
authorize the necessary investigating agents that they are at
liberty to secure information by listening devices direct to the
conversation or other communications of persons suspected of subversive activities against the Government of the United States,
including suspected spies. You are requested furthermore to limit
these investigations so conducted to a minimum and to limit them
insofar as possible to aliens.

*Roosevelt's 1940 wiretapping directive limited the uses of
wiretaps to aliens and to "national defense" investigations, and
thus did not meet the more expansive objectives of internal security bureaucrats. Accordingly, by misrepresenting Roosevelt's
directive (this time by deleting the authorization paragraph's
final sentence and not citing the qualifying language of the preceding paragraphs), Attorney General Tom Clark secured President*

Truman's approval for a radical expansion of FBI wiretapping authority to include such uses during investigations of "subversive activities." In point of fact, Clark had not drafted this letter. FBI Director Hoover actually wrote the letter and recommended to Clark that it be sent to the President. We do not know, however, whether Clark had reviewed Roosevelt's 1940 directive and thus understood the subterfuge basic to this effort to secure Truman's unknowing authorization for an extension of FBI electronic surveillance authority. In an interview with Ovid Demaris in the 1970s, Clark simply admitted: "When I came in [as Attorney General] Mr. Hoover asked me to write a letter which he had drafted to the White House to continue this arrangement [Roosevelt's wiretapping directive] which I did." (See, Ovid Demaris, The Director: An Oral Biography of J. Edgar Hoover. *New York: Harper's Magazine, 1975, p. 123.)*

(167) <u>LETTER, ATTORNEY GENERAL CLARK TO PRESIDENT TRUMAN</u>, July 17, 1946

Source: Stephen Spingarn Papers, National Defense - Internal Security, Harry S. Truman Library.

Under date of May 21, 1940, President Franklin D. Roosevelt, in a memorandum addressed to Attorney General Jackson, stated:

> "You are therefore authorized and directed in such cases as you may approve, after investigation of the need in each case, to authorize the necessary investigating agents that they are at liberty to secure information by listening devices directed to the conversation or other communications of persons suspected of subversive activities against the Government of the United States, including suspected spies."

This directive was followed by Attorneys General Jackson and Biddle, and is being followed currently in this Department. I consider it appropriate, however, to bring the subject to your attention at this time.

It seems to me that in the present troubled period in international affairs, accompanied as it is by an increase in subversive activity here at home, it is as necessary as it was in 1940 to take the investigative measures referred to in President Roosevelt's memorandum. At the same time, the country is threatened by a very substantial increase in crime. While I am reluctant to suggest any use whatever of these special investigative measures in domestic cases, it seems to me imperative to use them in cases vitally affecting the domestic security, or where human life is in jeopardy.

As so modified, I believe the outstanding directive should be continued in force. If you concur in this policy, I should appreciate it if you would so indicate at the foot of this letter.

In my opinion, the measures proposed are within the authority of law, and I have in the files of the Department materials indicating to me that my two most recent predecessors as Attorney General would concur in this view.

Despite the Roosevelt and Truman directives, FBI wiretapping remained illegal. The FBI's extensive reliance on wiretapping, accordingly, posed political problems when this practice became publicly known in 1949 during the Judith Coplon trial. An employee of the Department of Justice's alien registration section, Ms. Coplon was arrested on March 4, 1949, as she, allegedly, was about to deliver twenty-eight FBI documents to Valentin Gubitchev, a member of the Soviet Union's United Nations staff. During the resulting trial, Ms. Coplon's attorneys demanded that these twenty-eight documents be produced as evidence (a motion which the FBI and the Justice Department opposed on "national security" grounds). Ruling that the government could not try Ms. Coplon on "national security" grounds and then refuse to submit for defense examination the evidence supporting this claim, federal judge Albert Reeves ordered the production of the twenty-eight documents. Their release did not adversely affect the national security but did prove highly embarrassing to the FBI. One, the released documents confirmed the highly political nature of FBI investigations; two, the documents highlighted the Bureau's extensive use of wiretaps (since fifteen of the twenty-eight documents were based on wiretaps). To preclude the recurrence of this political problem, on July 8, 1949, FBI Director J. Edgar Hoover issued Bureau Bulletin No. 34. To date, we cannot ascertain how extensively this separate filing practice had been utilized in the effort to preclude the discovery of FBI wiretapping and other potentially embarrassing practices.

(168) MEMO, FBI DIRECTOR TO SAC (SPECIAL AGENT IN CHARGE) BOSTON, October 13, 1949

Source: FBI Files, Alger Hiss, Harvard University Library.

Reference is made to the report of Special Agent Francis D. O'Brien dated August 24, 1949, at Boston, Massachusetts, in the above-captioned case. [Alger Hiss]

Your attention is directed to the following sentence which appears in paragraph two on page four: "It is to be noted that [*name deleted*] is known to the Bureau, inasmuch as he is the subject of Bureau [*deleted but wiretap*]." Your attention is further directed to page five of Bureau Bulletin No. 34 dated July 8, 1949, where it is stated that "facts and information which are considered of a nature not expedient to disseminate or would cause embarrassment to the Bureau, if distributed," should be included in the administrative page of the report. [Handwritten notation "are these ever disclosed."]

In view of the above, page four of the aforementioned report has been rewritten and copies thereof are being furnished to the offices receiving this letter. In addition, the objectionable sentence aforementioned has been placed on page 10A which is also being enclosed herewith.

The New York Office should insert [this rewritten] page four in the copies of the report to be furnished Special Assistant to the Attorney General T. J. Donegan, and the United States Attorney for the Southern District of New York.

The Judith Coplon trial not only revealed that the FBI had wiretapped extensively and had kept dissident Americans under close surveillance, but also raised serious questions about the FBI's compliance with the law. Exploiting these revelations, the National Lawyers Guild, for one, attempted to convince President Truman to establish a special commission to investigate the FBI. Concerned that the President might decide upon this tactic, FBI Director Hoover forwarded derogatory reports about the Guild (compiled from FBI files) to the White House through Attorney General Clark. Hoover's objective, of convincing Truman not to honor this recommendation, succeeded. Another reason for its success (outlined in the concluding section on FBI political activities), was FBI officials' effective use of their contacts with conservative newspaper reporters, notably UPI Washington Bureau chief Lyle Wilson.

(169) LETTER, CLIFFORD DURR (PRESIDENT, NATIONAL LAWYERS GUILD) TO PRESIDENT TRUMAN, January 19, 1950

Source: Harry S. Truman Papers, Official File 10-B, Harry S. Truman Library.

On June 20, 1949 when the shocking disclosures of FBI practices emanating from the first [Judith] Coplon trial were fresh in our minds, we urged you "to appoint a Committee of outstanding citizens, including representatives of the national bar associations and civil liberties organizations, to undertake a comprehensive investigation into the operations and methods of the Federal Bureau of Investigation." We then expressed the view, which we still hold, that "The American people are entitled to full information on the extent to which the FBI has developed into a dangerous political secret police."

At that time we had available to us only the newspaper accounts of the FBI reports introduced in evidence. Since then we have carefully examined all of the trial record embodying the FBI reports. Two copies of our analysis of this FBI material, made available for public inspection for the first time through the trial, is enclosed. Affixed to our analysis, as appendices, is the full text of one of the reports and summaries of all of the others.

We believe that the Coplon reports demonstrate beyond any reasonable doubt extensive illegal practices by the FBI, and not only in wiretapping; that wiretapping has by no means been limited to the publicly admitted classes of cases; that the FBI has long been conducting a vast "loyalty" program of compiling "dossiers" or making investigations of private persons who are not government employees or applicants for government employment; that with few exceptions, the investigations described in the Coplon reports were attempts to determine not what crimes the subject had committed, but rather his social, economic and political views, his personal associations and organizational affiliations.

The disclosures issuing from the second Coplon trial strengthen our conviction that the liberties of the American people not safe so long as the FBI continues on its present path. The shocking and unprecedented violation of the confidential nature of communications between attorney and client which was there disclosed has no doubt come to your attention. We firmly believe that when this relationship is thus invaded by agencies of the government in clear violation of law, the foundations of justice are inevitably undermined.

We believe that there is already sufficient evidence to show that the Federal Bureau of Investigation is failing in its proper function; that it is bringing the administration of justice into disrepute, and that it's dossiers and investigations of the social, economic and political views and associations of private citizens strike at the very roots of our civil liberties. Who can say that men are free when their private communications, relations and ideas may be spied upon at any time, though they violate no law?

But it is only through a thorough and impartial investigation of the policies and practices of the FBI that there can be known the full steps that must be taken to correct all improper activities, including any not yet revealed.

It is our hope that on the basis of the enclosed report, and the further disclosures at the second Coplon trial, you will now conclude that the public interest requires such an investigation as we have here urged.

(170) <u>LETTER, ATTORNEY GENERAL McGRATH TO FBI DIRECTOR HOOVER</u>, December 1, 1949

Source: J. Howard McGrath Papers, The President, Harry S. Truman Library.

This will acknowledge your memorandum of November 29, entitled "National Lawyers Guild, Internal Security".

I am forwarding a copy to the President, for his information.

(171) <u>LETTER, PRESIDENT TRUMAN TO ATTORNEY GENERAL McGRATH</u>, December 6, 1949

Source: J. Howard McGrath Papers, The President, Harry S. Truman Library.

Thanks a lot for your note about the National Lawyers Guild, and the enclosure of the memorandum from the F.B.I.

I read it with a lot of interest.

(172) <u>LETTER, ATTORNEY GENERAL McGRATH TO PRESIDENT TRUMAN</u>, December 7, 1949 [Extract]

Source: J. Howard McGrath Papers, The President, Harry S. Truman Library.

It has come to my attention that the National Lawyers Guild is preparing a report attacking the Administration, and the Department of Justice in particular, on the basis of the reports of

the Federal Bureau of Investigation made public at the espionage
trial of Judith Coplon in Washington, D.C., in May and June of
1949.

The proposed report will attack certain alleged practices of
the Federal Bureau of Investigation and will recommend that you
issue immediately a directive ordering the Federal Bureau of Investigation to cease wiretapping, mail opening, and illegal
searches in which, according to the report, the Bureau engages.
The proposed directive would limit the jurisdiction of the FBI in
internal security cases and will request that you direct a thorough investigation of the programs, practices, policies and personnel of the FBI. The report will suggest that this investigation be conducted by a group of disinterested private citizens
having by executive authority full access to the files of the
Federal Bureau of Investigation and plenary powers of interroga-
tion.

It has been learned that the National Lawyers Guild contem-
plates a national publicity campaign in behalf of the report. It
has been suggested that the release of the report should follow
its delivery to you and to me and that an attempt will be made to
arrange a conference with both of us. The National Lawyers Guild
will seek the cooperation of other bar groups and will attempt to
enlist the support of several well-known names in the legal field.
A recommendation has also been made within the National Lawyers
Guild to consider the possibility of judicial proceedings to stop
the alleged illegal and improper practices of the Federal Bureau
of Investigation.

In connection with this proposal of the National Lawyers
Guild, you will recall that on May 21, 1940, President Roosevelt
directed the Attorney General to authorize agents of the Federal
Bureau of Investigation to secure information by means of wire-
tapping in limited types of cases relating to the national defense. . . .

. . . while it is no secret that the Bureau does tap tele-
phones in a limited type of case, this is done only with the express approval in each instance of the Attorney General and only
in cases involving espionage, sabotage, grave risks to the internal security of the nation, or cases in which human lives are in
jeopardy. In the few cases which have arisen in these categories
my predecessors have from time to time authorized the installation
of technical interception devices. This fact has been freely
acknowledged by the several Attorneys General and by the Director
of the Federal Bureau of Investigation. It is the invariable
practice, of course, in accordance with Section 605 of the Communications Act to make no prohibited disclosure of such intercepted
information.

The report of the National Lawyers Guild will purportedly
criticize the practice of the Federal Bureau of Investigation in
opening mail. It has been the long standing practice of investigative agencies to utilize mail covers. This is entirely authorized by law. Regarding the criticism of the Bureau in respect
to the alleged illegal searches, it is the practice of the FBI,
whenever possible, to procure warrants in advance of arrest. It
is only in the unusual cases, such as the Coplon case, that an

individual is apprehended and searched in advance of procuring a warrant. This power is granted by statute.

In view of the fact that representatives of the National Lawyers Guild or certain persons speaking in their behalf will undoubtedly attempt to confer with you in the near future in regard to the proposed investigation of the practices of the Federal Bureau of Investigation, I thought you should have the benefit of the facts set forth in this letter.

(173) LETTER, PRESIDENT TRUMAN TO ATTORNEY GENERAL McGRATH, December 17, 1949

Source: J. Howard McGrath Papers, The President, Harry S. Truman Library.

Your letter of the 7th, regarding the report of the National Lawyers Guild was received and read with a lot of interest. There are a number of crackpots in that organization who like very much to stir up trouble.

I don't think there is any way to stop the report, and I would suggest that you handle it in the best manner possible when it comes out.

(174) MEMO, FBI DIRECTOR TO ATTORNEY GENERAL, December 22, 1949

Source: J. Howard McGrath Papers, The President, Harry S. Truman Library.

There is enclosed herewith a memorandum concerning the National Lawyers Guild.

This memorandum contains a summary of all pertinent information appearing in the files of this Bureau concerning the Guild. It will be noted that much of these data were obtained either from public sources or incidental to other investigations conducted by the Bureau.

Because of the Guild's current attacks upon the Department of Justice and particularly upon the FBI, I felt you should have the benefit of this information. It is requested that the enclosed memorandum be treated in strict confidence and further that it not be disseminated outside the Department of Justice.

Although FBI Director Hoover might have succeeded in dissuading President Truman from appointing a presidential commission to investigate the FBI, the cumulative impact of the Coplon trial disclosures of the Bureau's abuses of power alarmed the liberal community. Seeking to undercut questions about the authority for FBI wiretapping, raised notably by the Washington Post *and prominent ADA officials like Joseph Rauh, in January 1950 Justice Department officials urged the President to release publicly President Roosevelt's 1940 directive. Ironically, this request resulted in Truman's learning of the process by which Attorney General Clark had secured, in 1946, his approval to extend FBI wiretapping authority. (Truman did not then learn, how-*

*ever, that the initiative for this letter came from Hoover.) Al-
though the President's immediate reaction was to rescind his 1946
authorization, he eventually decided otherwise. Accordingly,
Truman's 1946 directive remained the basis for the FBI's wiretapping authority until the enactment of Title III of the Omnibus
Crime Control and Safe Streets Act of 1968.*

(175) <u>MEMO, GEORGE ELSEY TO PRESIDENT TRUMAN</u>, February 2, 1950

Source: Stephen Spingarn Papers, National Defense-Internal Security, Harry S. Truman Library.

The Department of Justice has requested permission to make
available to the press the text of President Roosevelt's memorandum to the Attorney General, dated May 21, 1940, authorizing the
Attorney General to permit agents of the F.B.I. to "wire-tap" in
certain types of investigations. A copy of this memorandum is
attached.

It appears to me that this request for permission to make
public a "confidential" White House directive raises the whole
question of "wire-tapping" and leads us to consider the President's position with respect to this subject.

The factual background is as follows:

President Roosevelt directed Attorney-General Jackson on May
21, 1940 to "wire-tap" in cases including "persons suspected of
subversive activities", but he also stated, "You are requested
furthermore to limit these investigations so conducted to a minimum and to limit them insofar as possible to aliens."

On July 17, 1946, Attorney General Clark informed President
Truman in writing of Mr. Roosevelt's 1940 directive, but he failed
to quote the above sentence. Not only did Clark fail to inform
the President that Mr. Roosevelt had directed the F.B.I. to hold
its wire-tapping to a minimum, and to limit it insofar as possible
to aliens, he requested the President to approve very broad language which would permit wire-tapping in any case "vitally affecting the domestic security, or where human life is in jeopardy."
This language is obviously a very far cry from the 1940 directive.
At Attorney General Clark's request, the President approved this
new and broader language. A copy of Clark's letter, with the
President's concurrence, is attached.

Now, for reasons not clearly understood at the White House,
Justice wishes to release the 1940 directive for publication. [Assistant Attorney General] Peyton Ford says its publication will be useful in answering current critics who say the
F.B.I. is wire-tapping without proper authority. Ford advances
as his main argument for the release of the Roosevelt directive
the fact that it will "protect" President Truman, and President
Truman's directive need not become public knowledge.

I believe this is fallacious reasoning.

Although there have been public controversies before such as
the present one about wire-tapping, Justice never before has felt
impelled to release the text of the Roosevelt memorandum. It is
not necessary that it be released at this time.

In point of fact, the 1940 directive is <u>not</u> the basis
for the present F.B.I. policy of wire-tapping , and this fact
will be apparent to critics of F.B.I. activities. The release of
the Roosevelt memorandum would result in additional criticism of
the F.B.I. on the grounds that it is exceeding the authority
granted to it by President Roosevelt. This would lead inevitably,
I believe, to public reference to President Truman's much broader
directive.

Thus, instead of protecting the President, the release of the
Roosevelt memorandum would only involve the President in a manner
in which he has not heretofore been involved.

I therefore recommend:

(a) that the Justice request for permission to release the
    Roosevelt memorandum be denied,

(b) that the President refuse to comment on wire-tapping
    at any press conference, but refer all questions to the
    Attorney General, and

(c) that the President consider rescinding his 1946 direc-
    tive.

(176) <u>MEMO, GEORGE ELSEY TO STEPHEN SPINGARN</u>, February 2, 1950

Source: Stephen Spingarn Papers, National Defense-Internal Security, Harry S. Truman Library.

The President this morning directed Mr. Murphy and me to prepare for his signature a directive to the Attorney General which
would cancel the current authorization for wire-tapping by the
F.B.I. and would return to the authorization granted by President
Roosevelt in May, 1940.

Mr. Murphy asked that you and I recommend to him the manner
in which we should carry out the President's request. . . .

(177) <u>DRAFT MEMO, PRESIDENT TRUMAN TO ATTORNEY GENERAL</u>, February
7, 1950 [Not issued]

Source: Stephen Spingarn Papers, National Defense-Internal Security, Harry S. Truman Library.

It is my desire that the following policy apply in the future
with respect to the interception, listening in on, or recording
of telephone communications by investigative personnel of your Department.

You are authorized, in such cases as you may expressly approve
in writing after you have investigated and determined in each
case that it is necessary in the interests of the national security, to authorize investigative personnel of your Department to
intercept, listen in, or record telephone communication in the
investigation of the following categories of cases only: cases
involving the investigation of persons suspected of treason,
espionage, sabotage, or subversive activities directed against
the United States.

I desire that the foregoing authority be exercised only in those cases where the national security requires it, and that you establish appropriate measures of control to assure this result.

The Coplon trial had further policy consequences in that, because of the illegality of FBI wiretapping and the fact that FBI officials had ordered the destruction of the tapes produced through the taps, Ms. Coplon's conviction was reversed on appeal. Partially influenced by this development, on October 6, 1951, the FBI Director solicited the views of the Attorney General, J. Howard McGrath, as to Justice Department's electronic surveillance policy. In a memorandum of that date, Hoover wrote: "As you are aware, this Bureau has employed the use of microphone installations on a highly restrictive basis, chiefly to obtain intelligence information. The information obtained from microphones, as in the case of wiretaps, is not admissible in evidence. In certain instances it has been possible to install microphones without trespass, as reflected by opinions rendered in the past [in 1944] by the Department on this subject matter. In these instances the information obtained, of course, is treated as evidence and therefore is not regarded as purely intelligence information." McGrath, in his response of February 26, 1952, did not formally acknowledge knowing about this practice and went on record affirming his inability to authorize such installations. Significantly, the Attorney General did not specifically prohibit utilization of this technique for "intelligence" purposes and the FBI continued to install microphones illegally and on its own authority until Hoover secured Attorney General Herbert Brownell's formal authorization in May, 1954.

(178) MEMO, ATTORNEY GENERAL McGRATH TO FBI DIRECTOR HOOVER, February 26, 1952 [Extract]

Source: U.S. Senate, Committee on the Judiciary, Subcommittee on Constitutional Rights, *Report on Surveillance Technology - 1976*, 94th Congress, 2d session, p. 414.

Reference is made to your memoranda relative to wire tapping surveillances.

There is pending, as you know, before the Congress legislation that I have recommended which would permit wire tapping under appropriate safeguards and make evidence thus obtained admissible. As you state, the use of wire tapping is indispensible in intelligence coverage of matters relating to espionage, sabotage, and related security fields. Consequently, I do not intend to alter the existing policy that wire tapping surveillance should be used under the present highly restrictive basis and when specifically authorized by me.

The use of microphone surveillance which does not involve a trespass would seem to be permissible under the present state of the law, . . . Such surveillances as involve trespass are in the area of the Fourth Amendment, and evidence so obtained and from leads so obtained is inadmissible.

The records do not indicate that this question dealing with microphones has ever been presented before; therefore, please be

advised that I cannot authorize the installation of a microphone
involving a trespass under existing law.   .

It is requested when any case is referred to the Department
in which telephone, microphone or other technical surveillances
have been employed by the Bureau or other Federal Agencies (when
known) that the Department be advised of the facts at the time the
matter is first submitted.

4.   The FBI's Emergency Detention Program

   With the enactment of Title II of the (McCarran)
Internal Security Act of 1950, the Congress formally
authorized the apprehension and detention during a declared state of "Internal Security Emergency" of those
Americans who endangered the internal security. Although
proponents of the legislation might have thought that
they were finally providing authorization for a needed
emergency detention program, and thus were assisting the
FBI, in point of fact an emergency detention program had
been initiated by the FBI in 1939. FBI Director Hoover
briefed Attorney General Robert Jackson about this program in 1940. In 1943, however, Francis Biddle,
Jackson's successor, ordered that this "custodial detention" program be terminated. Technically complying with
Biddle's order to terminate a "custodial detention" program, Hoover simply changed the name to "security index"
and advised FBI officials to ensure that the Attorney
General not learn of this renamed program. With a more
sympathetic Administration and Attorney General, in the
person of Tom Clark, FBI officials in 1946 sought authorization for a "security index" program. Protracted
discussions ensued and Clark formally authorized the
program in August 1948. When Congress enacted the
McCarran Act in 1950 it had not merely provided
needed statutory authority for an ongoing program,
but because the standards for apprehension and detention under the McCarran Act were more restrictive than
those approved by Clark in 1948, the FBI immediately
sought and eventually secured Attorneys General J.
Howard McGrath's and James McGranery's authorization to
ignore these congressional standards. We do not know
whether President Truman was briefed about these decisions. His veto message of September 22, 1950, suggests that he might have been, given his critical comments on the bill's sections 100-117. In addition, in
September-November 1950 the Administration seriously
considered (see King legislation to amend the McCarran
Act) including helping to draft a bill introduced by
Congressman Clarence Cannon which comported with the
"security index" program Clark had authorized in 1948.

(179) MEMO, ATTORNEY GENERAL FRANCIS BIDDLE TO ASSISTANT ATTOR-
NEY GENERAL HUGH COX AND FBI DIRECTOR HOOVER, July 16, 1943

Source: U.S. Senate, Select Committee to Study Governmental Operations with respect to Intelligence Activities, *Hearings on Intelligence Activites*, Vol. 6 Federal Bureau of Investigation, 94th
Congress, 1st session, pp. 412-413.

I refer to Mr. [*officially deleted*] memornadum to me dated June
28, 1943, which reviews the history, development, and meaning of
the Special Case work [the FBI's Custodial Detention program] and
of the danger classifications that were made as a part of that
work.

After full re-consideration of these individual danger classifications, I am satisfied that they serve no useful purpose. The
detention of alien enemies is being dealt with under the procedures established by the Alien Enemy Control Unit. The Special
Case procedure has been found to be valueless and is not used in
that connection. There is no statutory authorization or other
present justification for keeping a "custodial detention" list of
citizens. The Department fulfills its proper functions by investigating the activities of persons who may have violated the law.
It is not aided in this work by classifying persons as to dangerousness.

Apart from these general considerations, it is now clear to
me that this classification system is inherently unreliable. The
evidence used for the purpose of making the classifications was
inadequate; the standards applied to the evidence for the purpose
of making the classifications were defective; and finally, the
notion that it is possible to make a valid determination as to
how dangerous a person is in the abstract and without reference
to time, environment, and other relevant circumstances, is impractical, unwise, and dangerous.

For the foregoing reasons I am satisfied that the adoption of
this classification system was a mistake that should be rectified
for the future. Accordingly, I direct that the classifications
heretofore made should not be regarded as classifications of dangerousness or as a determination of fact in any sense. In the
future, they should not be used for any purpose whatsoever. Questions raised as to the status or activities of a particular person should be disposed of by consideration of all available infor-

mation, but without reference to any classification heretofore made.

A copy of this memorandum should be placed in the file of each person who has hitherto been given a classification. In addition, each card upon which a classification appears should be stamped with the following language:

> "THIS CLASSIFICATION IS UNRELIABLE. IT IS
> HEREBY CANCELLED, AND SHOULD NOT BE USED
> AS A DETERMINATION OF DANGEROUSNESS OR OF
> ANY OTHER FACT. (SEE MEMORANDUM OF JULY 16,
> 1943 FROM THE ATTORNEY GENERAL TO HUGH B.
> COX AND J. EDGAR HOOVER)."

(180) <u>LETTER, FBI DIRECTOR HOOVER TO ALL SACS (SPECIAL AGENTS IN CHARGE</u>), August 14, 1943

Source: U.S. Senate, Select Committee to Study Governmental Operations with respect to Intelligence Activities, *Hearings on Intelligence Activities*, Vol. 6 Federal Bureau of Investigation, 94th Congress, 1st session, pp. 414-415.

Effective immediately, the character of investigations of individuals (other than alien enemies) who may be dangerous or potentially dangerous to the public safety or internal security of the United States shall be "Security Matter" and not "Custodial Detention." The phraseology, "Custodial Detention," shall no longer be used to designate the character of any investigation, nor shall it be used for any purpose in reports or other communications. Investigations involving organizations or "key figures" in the Communist Party will continue to bear the character, "Internal Security," as in the past, but the dual character of "Custodial Detention" will be eliminated.

Henceforth, the cards previously known as Custodial Detention Cards will be known and referred to as Security Index Cards, and the list composed of such cards will be known as the Security Index.

For your information, the Attorney General, on July 16, 1943, ordered that the dangerousness classifications previously made by the Special Defense Unit and its successor, the Special War Policies Unit, be not used in the future for any purpose whatsoever.

The Bureau will continue to investigate dangerous and potentially dangerous individuals other than alien enemies under the characters of Security Matter and Internal Security. It will also continue to prepare and maintain Security Index Cards. The fact that the Security Index and Security Index Cards are prepared and maintained should be considered as strictly confidential, and should at no time be mentioned or alluded to in investigative reports or discussed with agencies or individuals outside the Bureau other than duly qualified representatives of the Office of Naval Intelligence and the Military Intelligence Service, and then only on a strictly confidential basis. . . .

(181) MEMO, FBI ASSISTANT DIRECTOR D. M. LADD TO FBI DIRECTOR
HOOVER, November 13, 1952 [Extract]

Source: U.S. Senate, Select Committee to Study Governmental Operations with respect to Intelligence Activities, *Hearings on Intelligence Activities*, Vol. 6 Federal Bureau of Investigation, 94th
Congress, 1st session, pp. 416–426.

At a staff meeting on November 6, 1952, Deputy Attorney General [Ross] Malone brought up a memorandum from the Bureau which
inquired as to whether the "Security Portfolio still controls our
activities in the event of a national emergency." . . .

Our entire Security Index program and our plans for the detention of dangerous individuals in the time of an emergency have
been set up in compliance with instructions furnished to the
Bureau in a plan drawn up by the Department and furnished to the
Bureau on August 3, 1948. After the passage of the Internal Security Act of 1950 on September 23, 1950, the Bureau felt that the
Department would have to make a decision as to whether we should
continue our plans to operate under the Department's Portfolio or
to change our plans in order to meet the provisions of the Internal Security Act of 1950. . . .

The Bureau can discharge its responsibilities more effectively
under our present plan than under the Internal Security Act. In
view of the differences it is imperative that we have a definite
commitment from the Department as to whether the Department will
follow its own Portfolio or the provisions of the Internal Security Act. Since the passage of the Internal Security Act, the
Department has consistently hedged on whether the Act can be ignored completely and the Bureau can proceed under the plans set
forth in the Department's Portfolio.

The memorandum brought to your attention by Mr. Malone was our
memorandum to the Attorney General dated October 15, 1952, which
requested advice in this matter. It is not deemed advisable that
the Bureau make recommendations to the Department concerning this
matter inasmuch as the highly controversial question involving
the suspension of the Writ of Habeas Corpus is included in the
Department's Portfolio. Also, in the event the Department elects
to proceed under the Internal Security Act in addition to revising all of our plans many people who we feel constitute a danger
to the internal security of the country will be dropped from our
Security Index in view of the more limited provisions for apprehension set forth in the Internal Security Act of 1950.

Nonetheless in view of the questions which will be raised as
to the necessity of the Department proceeding under a plan of its
own device contrary to the existing law, it is not felt we should
make any recommendations to the Department with respect to this
matter since the decision is one which is solely the responsibility of the Department to make. There is attached a letter to
Deputy Attorney General Malone requesting an early decision in
view of the urgency of this matter. . . .

As early as March 8, 1946, you suggested to the Attorney
General that he might desire to initiate a study to determine
what legislation was available or what should be sought to authorize effective action of a general and precautionary nature in the
event of a serious emergency. . . .

After a number of conferences held between Bureau representatives with Department attorneys they drew up a plan with complete instructions from the Attorney General to the Bureau, a proposed Presidential Proclamation and a proposed Joint Resolution to be passed by Congress in support of the President's Proclamation. This plan is generally referred to as the Department's Portfolio. . . . The Portfolio was submitted to the Bureau by the Department on August 3, 1948. Since that time our entire planning and operational procedure to apprehend individuals contained in our Security Index has been based on the Department's Portfolio and not upon the detention provisions of Title II of the Internal Security Act of 1950, which became law on September 23, 1950.

At the time the Department's Portfolio was furnished to the Bureau on August 3, 1948, there was no law in existence which provided for the detention of dangerous individuals at the time of an emergency. After the passage of the Internal Security Act of 1950, which did provide for such action, the Bureau felt the Department would have to make a decision as to whether we should continue our plans to operate under the Department's Portfolio or to change our plans in order to meet the provisions of the Internal Security Act of 1950. . . .

The reason that it is imperative that the Department make this decision is because of the differences between the Department's Portfolio under which we are now operating and the provisions of Title II of the Internal Security Act of 1950. Some of the major points of difference are:

(1) Under the Department's Portfolio the Writ of Habeas Corpus will be suspended. The Internal Security Act of 1950 does not provide for the suspension of the Writ of Habeas Corpus.

(2) The current standards we use in determining the names of individuals to be placed in the Security Index are based on the provisions for apprehension in time of an emergency as set forth in the Department's Portfolio. The provisions set forth in the Internal Security Act of 1950 for the detention of dangerous individuals in time of an emergency are more restricted than those contained in the Department's Portfolio. Basically, the Internal Security Act of 1950 provides for the detention of Individuals who have been active in subversive organizations since January 1, 1949. Under the provisions contained in the Department's Portfolio we have included in our Security Index individuals who have not been known to be actively engaged in any subversive activities subsequent to January 1, 1949 but were active previous to that date.

(3) The Portfolio provides for apprehension of dangerous individuals at a time of threatened invasion. The Internal Security Act of 1950 restricts this to actual invasion, insurrection or declaration of war.

(4) The Portfolio provides for the apprehension of all subjects in the Security Index at the time of an emergency under one master warrant of arrest executed by the Attorney General. Under the Act apprehension of subjects will be effected by individual warrants obtained only upon probable cause supported by oath of affirmation.

(5) The Portfolio provides for searches and confiscation of contraband, whereas, the Act apparently does not contain such provisions.

(6) The Portfolio provides that hearings are to be held within 45 days after the apprehension of the subjects, whereas, the Act provides that preliminary hearings will be held within 48 hours or as soon thereafter as provision for such hearings may be made.

(7) Under the Portfolio the Boards of Review to be set up to hear the cases shall not be bound by the rules of evidence. It appears that the rules of evidence shall apply under the Internal Security Act.

(8) Under the Portfolio persons apprehended will have the right of appeal only to the President. Under the Act they shall be entitled to judicial review in any U.S. Court of Appeals.

There is no question but that the Bureau could discharge its responsibilities much more effectively under the Department's Portfolio than under the Internal Security Act of 1950. . . . it is imperative that we know as soon as possible in the event the Department decides that it will be necessary to follow the provisions of the Internal Security Act. Our entire planning and procedure relative to preparation for an emergency has been directed by the instructions contained in the Department's Portfolio. . . . We cannot afford to wait until an emergency is upon us and then have the Department decide that we would have to move against dangerous subversives under the Internal Security Act of 1950 rather than under the Department's Portfolio. Should this occur our entire operation would break down inasmuch as it would mean that our entire procedure would have to be altered. . . .

It was with these facts in mind that we called this matter to the Department's attention at the time of the passage of the Internal Security Act of 1950. On September 25, 1950, we directed a memorandum to the Attorney General requesting to be advised whether the detention provisions of Title II of the Internal Security Act of 1950 would affect the detention plans previously prepared by the Department. We also requested that the Attorney General advise whether he contemplated making any changes in the program as previously planned by the Department.

At a conference between yourself and former Attorney General J. Howard McGrath on the morning of September 27, 1950, he informed you that he had received a memorandum from the Bureau inquiring as to whether the Internal Security Act of 1950 affected in any way the Department's detention program under which the Bureau had been working in conjunction with the Department. Mr. McGrath advised you that he did not believe that the passage of the bill should in any way interfere with the Department's detention program and that he desired the Bureau to proceed with the program as outlined in the Department's Portfolio. By memorandum dated October 9, 1950, Mr. James M. McInerney, former Assistant Attorney General in charge of the Criminal Division, . . . stated that Title II of the Internal Security Act of 1950 undoubtedly is in conflict with the Department's proposed detention program. He said that if Title II remains in effect at such time as initiation of the program becomes necessary, appropriate provisions for its repeal will be introduced in Congress along with the proposed joint resolution inasmuch as the Internal Security Act of 1950 as enacted contains many provisions which would be unworkable in the event of an emergency or outbreak of hostilities and that it was not anticipated that Title II will permanently supersede the Department's Portfolio. . . .

At the concluding session of the U.S. Attorneys' Conference on May 25, 1951, which was attended by [FBI official Alan] Belmont, [Assistant Attorney General] Raymond P. Whearty [head, Criminal Division] of the Department outlined the detention provisions of the Internal Security Act of 1950. At that time he pointed out that the Act is unwieldly and unworkable.

On May 31, 1951, Mr. Whearty, in conference with Mr. Belmont and [FBI] Section Chief [Frederick] Baumgardner, orally advised that the standards being drawn up by the Department at that time for persons to be apprehended in an emergency were to be based principally on the Internal Security Act of 1950 but that leeway had been added to the standards specified by the Act to include persons we have on our Security Index who will not meet the requirements of the Act. He stated that the Department does not consider the detention provisions of the Internal Security Act of 1950 as workable and will continue to operate under the Emergency Detention Program as drawn up by the Department.

On March 14, 1952, Mr. Whearty was informed in conference with Mr. Belmont and Mr. Baumgardner that it was apparent that the Department was attempting to interpret the provisions of the Internal Security Act of 1950 through the drawing up of the Department's proposed standards for individuals to be included in the Security Index to bring them within the provisions of the Internal Security Act. Mr. Whearty was informed that from the Bureau's standpoint it would appear that the Department is hedging on its previous stand that apprehensions would be made under the Emergency Detention Program of the Department rather than the Internal Security Act of 1950 and any attempt to bring the Department's program within the provisions of the Internal Security Act would require extremely broad interpretation of the Act. He was advised that our position is that we must be ready from an operative standpoint to implement the apprehension program under clear authority from the Attorney General and there can be no question of doubt as to whether we are operating under standards specifically authorized by the Attorney General. It was pointed out that the broad interpretation by the Department of the provisions of the Act may not stand up in the event the apprehension program is launched under the Act and that the Department's interpretation of the Act is a matter of opinion and not of fact. At this conference Mr. Whearty stated that it is the definite intent of the Department to proceed under its program rather than under the Internal Security Act 1950. He said that if an emergency occurs, the Presidential Proclamation [drafted under the Portfolio as part of strategy to secure *ex post facto* congressional authorization] will be issued and brought immmediately before Congress for ratification. He said that at that time, if it has not been accomplished before that time, repeal of the Act will be sought in order that the Department's program can be instituted. He stated that at that time the unworkability of the Act will again be brought to the attention of Congress.

On July 9, 1952, at which time Mr. Belmont and [FBI official C. E.] Hennrich were in conference with [Assistant Attorney General James] McInerney of the Department regarding getting approval by the Department of the standards used by us for placing persons in the Security Index and having them review our Security Index cases, Mr. McInerney stated that the Department had already given the Bureau written authority to apprehend anyone on the Security Index pending the Department's decision with regard to the standards. The Bureau representatives insisted on the Attorney General's specific approval of the standards under which we are operating, inasmuch as we are an investigative agency, and the policy as to whom should be apprehended under any detention program must rest with the Attorney General.

From time to time the Department while maintaining that the plan as set forth in the Department's Portfolio will be used in the event of an emergency, has intimated that the Internal Security Act of 1950 cannot be ignored. The Department last brought this fact to the Bureau's attention in a memorandum dated October 8, 1952, which stated in part that while it is contemplated that in the event of war other legislation relating to the apprehension and detention of potentially dangerous persons will be speedily sought, nonetheless so long as the standard provided in the Internal Security Act of 1950 remains the guiding legislative principle for apprehension and detention of potentially dangerous individuals, the Department must consider this standard in reviewing the files of individuals who may be subject to apprehension and detention.

We replied to this memorandum in a letter to the Attorney General dated October 15, 1952, and pointed out . . . that all authority for our Security Index program including all preparations and plans made by the Bureau to effect the apprehensions are based solely upon the planning and instructions contained in the Department's Portfolio. We requested, . . . that the Attorney General give us his assurance at this time that he intends to proceed in an emergency under the program as outlined in the Department's Portfolio and that the standards to be used are those we are now using. We requested advice of the Attorney General as to whether he is in agreement with the Bureau's concepts of the detention program and Security Index standards as outlined in our memorandum to Mr. Peyton Ford dated June 28, 1951. . . .

All of our plans for an emergency, which are extensive, in connection with the detention of dangerous individuals in time of an emergency are based upon instructions contained in the Department's Portfolio. There are contained among the 19,577 individuals listed in our Security Index the names of many persons whom we consider dangerous but who do not fall within the standards set forth in the Internal Security Act of 1950. If the Department should elect to proceed under this Act it would mean that in revising our plans many people who are now included in our Security Index as potentially dangerous to the internal security would necessarily have to be excluded therefrom.

The fact that the Internal Security Act of 1950 does not provide for suspension of the Writ of Habeas Corpus would prove a definite hindrance to the execution of necessary measures to be taken in the event of an emergency because of lengthy litigation which would no doubt result and presents the possibility that

dangerous individuals might obtain release from confinement pending hearings in their cases. The Department's Portfolio provides
that these persons shall be continued in detention until their
cases are decided by the Boards of Review.

The lack of provision in the Act for measures to be taken in
the event of threatened invasion precludes the President from
taking action against potentially dangerous persons prior to an
actual invasion, insurrection or declaration of war.

The provision in the Act for apprehension of subjects by individual warrants is a factor which would be a detrimental, time-
consuming procedure as compared to the use of one master warrant
of arrest for all subjects apprehended as provided in the Department's Portfolio.

The apparent lack of provision in the Act for searches and
for confiscation of contraband would be a definite deterrent to
our operations in that we would be unable to search the headquarters of subversive organizations as well as premises of dangerous
individuals for contraband. Such contraband would, under the Act,
apparently be left in the control and custody of persons who
could use it against the interests of the Government.

The provision in the Act that preliminary hearings are to be
held within 48 hours after the subjects' apprehension or as soon
thereafter as provisions for such hearings may be made could
place a restrictive time element upon the Government which would
interfere with our apprehension efforts.

The fact that subjects apprehended under the Act would have
the right to appeal to the courts and since it appears that the
rules of evidence would apply creates another obstacle in the
Government's way in that in order to obtain continued detention
of persons considered dangerous we may, in many instances, have
to disclose the identities of our informants and confidential
techniques. This, of course, would be a fatal blow to our subsequent efforts to maintain coverage of subversive activities during
the emergency.

While . . . I firmly believe that the internal security of
the country could best be protected in the time of an emergency if
we proceed under the plans set forth in the Department's Portfolio, I do not believe that it is desirable that the Bureau go
on record with recommendations to the Department concerning this
matter. The Department's Portfolio contains a plan for the suspension of the Writ of Habeas Corpus which without question will
be a highly controversial subject and will undoubtedly cause considerable debate in the event it is ever openly proposed. Other
questions will be raised as to why it is necessary to proceed
under a plan devised by the Department of Justice when there is a
law on the statute books which ostensibly covers the purpose for
which the Department's plan was set up to handle. A decision as
to procedure in the event of an emergency is clearly the responsibility of the Department. The Department's Portfolio has been
devised by the Department and we have operated under those instructions to date. Any decision as to a method of operation
whether it be under the Department's Portfolio or under the Internal Security Act of 1950 is clearly a matter to be decided by the
Attorney General because it is concerned with high Government
policy.

Obviously the Department does not want to be placed in a position of having stated that it is not going to pay attention to the Internal Security Act of 1950. They have hedged in this matter in the past and it is to our interest that we receive from them a positive expression of approval of our concepts of the Emergency Detention Program and our concepts of the standards for including individuals in the Security Index which is tantamount to scheduling these persons for apprehension. I believe that we should continue to call for a positive statement from the Department and that we should under no circumstances make any commitments regarding the desirability of proceeding under the Emergency Detention Program or under the Internal Security Act of 1950.

ACTION:

If you agree, there is attached hereto a memorandum to Deputy Attorney General Ross L. Malone, Jr., stating our position and requesting that the Bureau be advised of the Department's decision in this matter.

[Handwritten notation of Hoover, November 14, 1952]

"While I have sent memo forward I do think we are hedging in not at least being on record as to what is best for the internal security of the country & then leaving it to Dept. to decide whether to adopt."

(182) MEMO, ATTORNEY GENERAL McGRANERY TO FBI DIRECTOR HOOVER, November 25, 1952

Source: U.S. Senate, Select Committee to Study Governmental Operations with respect to Intelligence Activities, *Hearings on Intelligence Activities*, Vol. 6 Federal Bureau of Investigation, 94th Congress, 1st session, p. 427.

Reference is made to my memorandum of October 8, 1952, approving the standards used by your Bureau for the listing of names of individuals in the Security Index, and to your subsequent memorandum of October 15.

Pursuant to the questions which you have raised in the latter memorandum, I wish to assure you that it is the Department's intention in the event of emergency to proceed under the program as outlined in the Department's Portfolio invoking the standards now used. This approval, of course, indicates agreement with your Bureau's concepts of the Detention Program and the Security Index standards as outlined in your memorandum of June 28, 1951, to former Deputy Attorney General [Peyton Ford].

(183) MEMO, STEPHEN SPINGARN TO PRESIDENT TRUMAN, July 14, 1950 [Extract]

Source: Stephen Spingarn Papers, Internal Security, Harry S. Truman Library.

On July 13, 1950 you asked me to analyze [H.R. 4703, a Justice-sponsored internal security] bill and give you a memorandum indicating my opinion as to whether it represents a proper balance between your two objectives - to protect the internal security of the United States and to protect the individual rights of citizens. . . .

This legislation was originally prepared in 1947 by the Interdepartmental Intelligence Committee which is composed of the Director of the Federal Bureau of Investigation and the heads of the military intelligence services. In its original form . . . it was a very drastic bill indeed. [The Bureau of the] Budget sent the bill to the interested agencies, almost all of whom had serious criticisms to make of it. The Treasury's comments and criticisms on the bill were the most extensive. In a letter of March 23, 1948, to the Budget, Secretary [of the Treasury John] Snyder pointed out that several provisions of the draft bill would not "provide safeguards for adequate protection of civil rights of the people of the United States from infringement or abuse in the name of security". . . . [and] that changes could be made to obviate such objections "without injury to the vitality of the security measure".

The Secretary of Defense (then [James] Forrestal), the State Department, the Federal Communications Commission, and the Secretary of Interior agreed with some, and in most cases with all of the recommendations made by the Treasury to correct the bill. In April 1948 [White House aide Charles] Murphy gave you the file on the matter . . . and [you later] told him that the Justice Department should be required to amend its draft bill in accordance with the suggestions made by the Treasury Department.

On April 16, 1948, Budget wrote the Attorney General that if the draft bill were amended in the respects suggested by the Treasury "there would be no objection by this office to the presentation of the proposal so modified to the Congress for its consideration".

In the original drastic bill . . . there were three particularly objectionable provisions:

1. It would have brought within the penalties of the Espionage Act of 1917, the transmission (in writing or orally) of any "information relating to the national defense", to a person not entitled to receive it. It would have made no difference as far as the offense was concerned that the person transmitting the information had no intention of committing espionage and had no reason to believe that his transmission of the information would do any injury to the United States. . . .

The Treasury position was that this new criminal offense was so broadly defined that it would cover innocent transmission of information, as well as transmission dangerous to the national security, and thus could be regarded as a serious and unjustified infringement upon free speech and a free press. The Treasury felt also that it had dangerous potentialities for abuse as a convenient governmental excuse for withholding or suppressing information, thus offering protective insulation from unfavorable and possibly salutary publicity with respect to embarrassing facts involving a modicum of national defense information.

Treasury, therefore, suggested that the provision be amended to require intent or reason to believe that the information transmitted would be used to the injury of the United States. . . . [that] separate provisions be made for the various possible degrees of offenses ranging from the relatively minor to the genuine act of espionage. . . . [and] that no person should be prosecuted under it for any violation except on the express direction of the Attorney General of the United States.

2. The bill would have authorized the FBI and the military services to engage in wire tapping and would have made evidence thus obtained admissible in court proceedings in which the United States was a party. Under its terms, the investigative or intelligence agency involved was the sole judge of when and where wire tapping should be conducted.

Treasury indicated that it appreciated the need for wire tapping in major cases involving important aspects of national security and law enforcement. It, therefore, favored a limited authorization of wire tapping but under proper safeguards. Specifically, it suggested (a) that the head of the department involved (and not the head of the investigative agency) should certify in each individual case in writing his belief that the case was of major importance and that wire tapping was necessary to its successful investigation before the investigative agency could engage in that practice; and (b) that the investigative agency after obtaining authority from its department head must also secure from an appropriate Federal judge the equivalent of a search warrant before engaging in wire tapping. . . .

The Department of Justice was not satisfied with the Presidentially-approved Budget direction of April 16, 1948, as to the form in which the internal security bill should be submitted to Congress. Justice, therefore, first came to the Treasury and attempted to persuade that Department to withdraw completely all of its recommendations for changes in the Justice bill. Treasury said that it could not withdraw its views. In the first place they were a matter of conviction and in the second place they had been approved by the Budget and the President. However, Treasury told Justice that it would be happy to discuss the whole bill and see if the two departments could compromise their views in any respects with the Budget sitting in as an arbitrator. The Justice representative told the Treasury that he had no authority to negotiate any compromise, that what Justice desired was a complete withdrawal of the Treasury views. This naturally ended the discussion.

Subsequently, Justice went to Budget and discussed the matter further. As a result there was a certain relaxing of the previous Budget position that the Justice bill should be revised in all the respects recommended by the Treasury. . . .

In this revised form, Justice submitted the bill to Congress in January 1949. It is my understanding that they were informally advised at the time that they were to treat it as a departmental bill and not as a Presidentially-recommended bill.

After the bill was sent to the Hill, considerable controversy arose over the wire tapping provisions. These were, therefore, dropped from the bill entirely and, with some relatively minor changes in the rest of the bill, it has now passed the House and the companion bill (S. 595) has been reported in the Senate. . . .

Summarizing as to the bill in its present form, it is clear that in most respects the Treasury recommendations for changes

(as originally approved by the Budget and the President) have
been adopted. . . .

There would be certain distinct advantages in the enactment of
this Justice-sponsored bill. The current version of the Mundt-
Nixon bill [introduced in 1948 by Republican Congressmen Karl
Mundt and Richard Nixon] (which was reported several months ago
by the Senate Judiciary Committee by a 12 to 1 vote) is gaining
strength as a result of the tensions created by the Korean situation. Only a couple of weeks ago the Republican Policy Committee
voted to put that bill on its "Must List" and has been seeking
to get the Democratic leadership to do the same thing. Since it
is usually difficult to lick something with nothing, it is suggested that enactment of the internal security legislation described in this memorandum might be the answer to the Mundt-Nixon
bill (now known as the Mundt-Johnston-Ferguson bill) [revised to
incorporate provisions advocated by Democratic Senator Olin
Johnston and Republican Senator Homer Ferguson].

Summing up the situation, it is my conclusion that the enactment of this internal security bill would be desirable from the
overall standpoint and, therefore, suggest that you so advise
Senator [Scott] Lucas [Senate majority leader] and Represenative
[John] McCormack [House majority leader].

(184) SPECIAL MESSAGE TO CONGRESS, PRESIDENT TRUMAN, August 8,
1950 [Extract]

Source: *Public Papers of the Presidents: Harry S. Truman, 1950.*
Washington: U.S. Government Printing Office, 1965, pp. 571-576.

I am presenting to the Congress certain considerations concerning the steps we need to take to preserve our basic liberties
and to protect the internal security of the United States in this
period of increasing international difficulty and danger. We
face today . . . the question of how to keep our freedom secure
against internal as well as external attack, without at the same
time unduly limiting individual rights and liberties. . . .

It has always been difficult to draw the line between restrictions which are proper because they are necessary for internal
security, and restrictions which are improper because they violate
the spirit or the letter of the Constitution. It is clear that
on certain occasions, that line has been over-stepped. . . .

Since the time of the Alien and Sedition Laws, there have
been recurrent periods - especially in wartime - when the safety
of our Nation has been in danger. Each of these occasions has
confronted us with a new set of conditions, to which we have had
to adjust our internal security laws and procedures.

At the same time, each of these periods of danger has been
seized on by those who, in good faith or bad, would severely limit
the freedom of our people in a misguided attempt to gain greater
security. . . . there have been certain times when we have, to
some extent, repudiated our own ideals of freedom in an excess of
zeal for our safety. Nevertheless, it is a tribute to the strong
faith and common sense of our people that we have never for long

been misled by the hysterical cries of those who would suppress our Constitutional freedoms.

The present period is one of the times in which it has been necessary to adjust our security measures to new circumstances. The particular danger which we have had to meet has been created by the rise of totalitarianism. . . .

Today, we face most acutely the threat of the communist movement, international in scope, directed from a central source, and committed to the overthrow of democratic institutions throughout the world. . . .

Through their own political parties, and by trying to make alliances with non-communist political groups, the communists attempt to gain political power. The best defense against this aspect of the communist threat is a vigorous, functioning democracy which succeeds in meeting the needs of its people. . . .

If the communists confined their activities in this country to the open and public channels of the democratic process, we would have little concern about them. But they do not so limit their activities. Instead, to serve the ends of a foreign power, they engage in espionage, sabotage, and other acts subversive of our national safety.

To protect us against activities such as these, we must rely primarily upon Government action. We must have effective internal security measures to prevent acts which threaten our national safety.

These measures must be accurately devised to meet real dangers. They must not be so broad as to restrict our liberty unnecessarily, for that would defeat our own ends. Unwise or excessive security measures can strike at the freedom and dignity of the individual which are the very foundation of our society - and the defense of which is the whole purpose of our security measures.

In considering the laws that are needed to protect our internal security against communist activities, we should remember that we already have tested legal defenses against treason, espionage, sabotage, and other acts looking toward the overthrow of our Government by force or violence. Strong laws exist on the statute books - a number of them enacted or strengthened in recent years - under which we have proceeded and are proceeding vigorously against such crimes. . . .

More than three years ago, the Executive Branch revised and improved its procedures for dealing with questions of employee loyalty and security. These new procedures have proved effective in protecting the Government against disloyal persons and persons whose employment constitutes a security risk.

The various laws and procedures I have outlined make up a strong set of legal safeguards against acts by individuals and groups which strike at the internal security of the United States.

Over the last few years, we have successfully prosecuted several hundred cases in the courts under existing internal security laws. In this process we have obtained a great deal of experience in the application of these laws. We have discovered a few defects, some of them minor and others of greater importance, in some of the existing statutes. In view of the situation which confronts us, it is important that these defects be remedied. At this time, therefore, I wish to recommend that the Congress enact certain legislation before the close of the present session.

First, I recommend that the Congress remedy certain defects in the present laws concerning espionage, the registration of foreign agents, and the security of national defense installations, by clarifying and making more definite certain language in the espionage laws, by providing an extended statute of limitations . . . for peacetime espionage, by requiring persons who have received instruction from a foreign government or political party in espionage or subversive tactics to register under the Foreign Agents Registration Act, and by giving broader authority than now exists for the President to establish security regulations concerning the protection of military bases and other national defense installations.

Second, I recommend that the Congress enact legislation permitting the Attorney General to exercise supervision over aliens subject to deportation and to require them, under the sanction of criminal penalties, to report their whereabouts and activities at regular intervals. . . .

Under the leadership of the National Security Council, the agencies of the Government which administer our internal security laws are keeping these laws under constant study to determine whether further changes are required to provide adequate protection. If it does appear that further improvements in these laws are needed, I shall recommend them to the Congress.

By building upon the framework now provided by our basic laws against subversive activities, we can provide effective protection against acts which threaten violence to our Government or to our institutions, and we can do this without violating the fundamental principles of our Constitution.

Nevertheless, there are some people who wish us to enact laws which would seriously damage the right of free speech and which could be used not only against subversive groups but against other groups engaged in political or other activities which were not generally popular. . . .

Laws forbidding dissent do not prevent subversive activities; they merely drive them into more secret and more dangerous channels. Police states are not secure; their history is marked by successive purges, and growing concentration camps, as their governments strike out blindly in fear of violent revolt. Once a government is committed to the principle of silencing the voice of opposition, it has only one way to go, and that is down the path of increasingly repressive measures, until it becomes a source of terror to all its citizens and creates a country where everyone lives in fear.

We must, therefore, be on our guard against extremists who urge us to adopt police state measures. Such persons advocate breaking down the guarantees of the Bill of Rights in order to get at the communists. They forget that if the Bill of Rights were to be broken down, all groups, even the most conservative, would be in danger from the arbitrary power of government.

Legislation is now pending before the Congress which is so broad and vague in its terms as to endanger the freedoms of speech, press, and assembly protected by the First Amendment. Some of the proposed measures would, in effect, impose severe penalties for normal political activities on the part of certain groups, including communists and communist party-line followers. This kind of legislation is unnecessary, ineffective, and dangerous.

It is unnecessary because groups such as the communists cannot accomplish their evil purposes in this country through normal political activity. . . .

It is ineffective because it does not get at the real dangers from the communists in this country. These dangers come, not from normal political activity, but from espionage, sabotage, and the building up of an organization dedicated to the destruction of our Government by violent means - against all of which we already have laws.

This kind of proposed legislation is dangerous because, in attempting to proscribe, for groups such as the communists, certain activities that are perfectly proper for everyone else, such legislation would spread a legal dragnet sufficiently broad to permit the prosecution of people who are entirely innocent or merely misguided. As far as the real conspirators against our institutions are concerned, such legislation would merely have the effect of driving them further underground and making it more difficult to reach them. Furthermore, if such legislation were held unconstitutional, as it well might be, it would make martyrs out of our worst enemies and create public sympathy for them.

Extreme proposals of this type reflect the widespread public concern about communism which most of our people feel today. In some communities, this concern has resulted in the enactment of unnecessary or unconstitutional laws or ordinances designed to suppress subversive activity.

We must not be swept away by a wave of hysteria.

It is natural, perhaps, to think that we can wipe out the dangers which confront us by passing a law. But we cannot get rid of communism just by passing a law. We must, of course, have effective legal defenses, but the principal protection of a free society against subversion is an alert and responsible citizenry dedicated to the advancement of freedom through democratic means. . . .

(185) <u>VETO MESSAGE, PRESIDENT TRUMAN</u>, September 22, 1950 [Extract]

Source: *Public Papers of the Presidents: Harry S. Truman, 1950*. Washington: U.S. Government Printing Office, 1965, pp. 645-653.

I return herewith, without my approval, H.R. 9490, the proposed "Internal Security Act of 1950."

I am taking this action only after the most serious study and reflection and after consultation with the security and intelligence agencies of the Government. The Department of Justice, the Department of Defense, the Central Intelligence Agency, and the

Department of State have all advised me that the bill would seriously damage the security and the intelligence operations for which they are responsible. They have strongly expressed the hope that the bill would not become law.

This is an omnibus bill containing many different legislative proposals with only one thing in common: they are all represented to be "anti-communist." But when the many complicated pieces of the bill are analyzed in detail, a startling result appears.

H.R. 9490 would not hurt the communists. Instead, it would help them.

It has been claimed over and over again that this is an "anti-communist" bill - a "communist control" bill. But in actual operation the bill . . . would actually weaken our existing internal security measures and would seriously hamper the Federal Bureau of Investigation and our other security agencies.

It would help the communists in their efforts to create dissension and confusion within our borders. . . .

1. [The bill] would aid potential enemies by requiring the publication of a complete list of vital defense plants, laboratories, and other installations.

2. It would require the Department of Justice and its Federal Bureau of Investigation to waste immense amounts of time and energy attempting to carry out its unworkable registration provisions.

3. It would deprive us of the great assistance of many aliens in intelligence matters. . . .

5. It would put the Government of the United States in the thought control business.

6. It would make it easier for subversive aliens to become naturalized as United States citizens.

7. It would give Governmental officials vast powers to harass all of our citizens in the exercise of their right of free speech

Legislation with these consequences is not necessary to meet the real dangers which communism presents to our free society. Those dangers are serious, . . . But this bill would hinder us, not help us, in meeting them. Fortunately, we already have on the books strong laws which give us most of the protection we need from the real dangers of treason, espionage, sabotage, and actions looking to the overthrow of our Government by force and violence. Most of the provisions of this bill have no relation to those real dangers.

One provision alone of this bill is enough to demonstrate how far it misses the real target. Section 5 would require the Secretary of Defense to "proclaim" and "have published in the Federal Register" a public catalogue of defense plants, laboratories, and all other facilities vital to our national defense - no matter how secret. I cannot imagine any document a hostile foreign government would desire more. . . .

I know that the Congress had no intention of [working to the detriment of our national security] when it passed this bill. I know that the vast majority of the members of Congress who voted for the bill sincerely intended to strike a blow at the communists.

It is true that certain provisions of this bill would improve the laws protecting us against espionage and sabotage. But these provisions are greatly outweighed by others which would actually impair our security.

I repeat, the net result of this bill would be to help the communists, not to hurt them.

I therefore most earnestly request the Congress to reconsider its action. . . .

H.R. 9490 is made up of a number of different parts. . . .

Sections 1 through 17 . . . are intended [first] to force communist organizations to register and to divulge certain information about . . . their officers, their finances, and, in some cases, their membership. These provisions would in practice be ineffective, and would result in obtaining no information about communists that the FBI and our other security agencies do not already have. But in trying to enforce these sections, we would have to spend a great deal of time, effort, and money - all to no good purpose.

Second, those provisions are intended to impose various penalties on communists and others covered by the terms of the bill. So far as communists are concerned, all these penalties which can be practically enforced are already in effect under existing laws and procedures. But the language of the bill is so broad and vague that it might well result in penalizing the legitimate activities of people who are not communists at all, but loyal citizens. . . .

Sections 18 through 21 and section 23 of the bill constitute, in large measure, the improvements in our internal security laws which I recommended some time ago. Although the language of these sections is in some respects weaker than is desirable, I should be glad to approve these provisions if they were enacted separately, since they are improvements developed by the FBI and other Government security agencies to meet certain clear deficiencies of the present law. . . .

Sections 22 and 25 of this bill would make sweeping changes in our laws governing the admission of aliens to the United States and their naturalization as citizens.

The ostensible purpose of these provisions is to prevent persons who would be dangerous to our national security from entering the country or becoming citizens. In fact, present law already achieves that objective.

What these provisions would actually do is to prevent us from admitting to our country, or to citizenship, many people who could make real contributions to our national strength. The bill would deprive our Government and our intelligence agencies of the valuable services of aliens in security operations. It would require us to exclude and to deport the citizens of some friendly non-communist countries. Furthermore, it would actually make it easier for subversive aliens to become United States citizens. . . .

Section 24 and sections 26 through 30 of this bill make a number of minor changes in the naturalization laws. . . . These

provisions, for the most part, have received little or no attention in the legislative process. I believe that several of them
would not be approved by the Congress if they were considered on
their merits, rather than as parts of an omnibus bill.

Section 31 of this bill makes it a crime to attempt to influence a judge or jury by public demonstration, such as picketing.
While the courts already have considerable power to punish such
actions under existing law, I have no objection to this section.

Sections 100 through 117 of this bill (Title II) are intended
to give the Government power, in the event of invasion, war, or
insurrection in the United States in aid of a foreign enemy, to
seize and hold persons who could be expected to attempt acts of
espionage or sabotage, even though they had as yet committed no
crime. It may be that legislation of this type should be on the
statute books. But the provisions in H.R. 9490 would very probably prove ineffective to achieve the objective sought, since
they would not suspend the writ of habeas corpus, and under our
legal system to detain a man not charged with a crime would raise
serious constitutional questions unless the writ of habeas corpus
were suspended. Furthermore, it may well be that other persons
than those covered by these provisions would be more important to
detain in the event of emergency. This whole problem, therefore,
should clearly be studied more thoroughly before further legislative action along these lines is considered.

In brief, when all the provisions of H.R. 9490 are considered
together, it is evident that the great bulk of them are not directed toward the real and present dangers that exist from communism. Instead of striking blows at communism, they would strike
blows at our own liberties and at our position in the forefront
of those working for freedom in the world. At a time when our
young men are fighting for freedom in Korea, it would be tragic
to advance the objectives of communism in this country, as this
bill would do. . . .

Most of the first seventeen sections of H.R. 9490 are concerned with requiring registration and annual reports, by what the
bill calls "communist-action organizations" and "communist-front
organizations," of names of officers, sources and uses of funds,
and, in the case of "communist-action organizations," names of
members. . . .

Under the provisions of the bill, if an organization which
the Attorney General believes should register does not do so, he
must request a five-man "Subversive Activities Control Board" to
order the organization to register. The Attorney General would
have to produce proof that the organization in question was in
fact a "communist-action" or a "communist-front organization."
To do this he would have to offer evidence relating to every aspect of the organization's activities. The organization could
present opposing evidence. Prolonged hearings would be required
to allow both sides to present proof and to cross-examine opposing witnesses.

To estimate the duration of such a proceeding involving the
Communist Party we need only recall that on much narrower issues
the trial of the eleven communist leaders under the Smith Act
consumed nine months. In a hearing under this bill, the diffi-

culties of proof would be much greater and would take a much longer time.

The bill lists a number of criteria for the Board to consider in deciding whether or not an organization is a "communist-action" or "communist-front" organization. Many of these deal with the attitudes or states of mind of the organization's leaders. It is frequently difficult in legal proceedings to establish whether or not a man has committed an overt act, such as theft or perjury. But under this bill, the Attorney General would have to attempt the immensely more difficult task of producing concrete legal opinions. This would inevitably require the disclosure of many of the FBI's confidential sources of information and thus would damage our national security.

If, eventually, the Attorney General should overcome these difficulties and get a favorable decision from the Board, the Board's decision could be appealed to the Courts. The Courts would review any questions of law involved, and whether the Board's findings of fact were supported by the "preponderance" of the evidence.

All these proceedings would require great effort and much time. . . .

The simple fact is that when the Courts at long last found that a particular organization was required to register, all the leaders of the organization would have to do to frustrate the law would be to dissolve the organization and establish a new one with a different name and a new roster of nominal officers. . . . And nothing could be done about it except to begin all over again the long dreary process of investigative, administrative, and judicial proceedings to require registration.

Thus the net result of the registration provisions of this bill would probably be an endless chasing of one organization after another, with the communists always able to frustrate the law enforcement agencies and prevent any final result from being achieved. It could only result in wasting the energies of the Department of Justice and in destroying the sources of information of its FBI: To impose these fruitless burdens upon the FBI would divert it from its vital security duties and thus give aid and comfort to the very communists whom the bill is supposed to control. . . .

In so far as the bill would require registration by the Communist Party itself, it does not endanger our traditional liberties. However, the application of the registration requirements to so-called communist-front organizations can be the greatest danger to freedom of speech, press and assembly, since the Alien and Sedition Laws of 1798. This danger arises out of the criteria of standards to be applied in determining whether an organization is a communist-front organization.

There would be no serious problem if the bill required proof that an organization was controlled and financed by the Communist Party before it could be classified as a communist-front organization. However, recognizing the difficulty of proving those matters, the bill would permit such a determination to be based solely upon "the extent to which the positions taken or advanced by it from time to time on matters of policy do not deviate from those of the communist movement."

This provision could easily be used to classify as a communist-front organization any organization which is advocating a single policy or objective which is also being urged by the Communist Party or by a communist foreign government. . . . Thus, an organization which advocates low-cost housing for sincere humanitarian reasons might be classified as a communist-front organization because the communists regularly exploit slum conditions as one of their fifth-column techniques. . . .

The basic error of these sections is that they move in the direction of suppressing opinion and belief. This would be a very dangerous course to take, . . . because any governmental stifling of the free expression of opinion is a long step toward totalitarianism. . . .

We can and we will prevent espionage, sabotage, and other actions endangering our national security. But we would betray our finest traditions if we attempted, as this bill would attempt, to curb the simple expression of opinion. This we should never do, no matter how distasteful the opinion may be to the vast majority of our people. . . .

And what kind of effect would these provisions have on the normal expression of political views? Obviously, if this law were on the statute books, the part of prudence would be to avoid saying anything that might be construed by someone as not deviating sufficiently from the current communist propaganda line. And since no one could be sure in advance what views were safe to express, the inevitable tendency would be to express no views on controversial subjects.

The result could only be to reduce the vigor and strength of our political life . . .

Our position in the vanguard of freedom rests largely on our demonstration that the free expression of opinion, coupled with government by popular consent, leads to national strength and human advancement. Let us not, in cowering and foolish fear, throw away the ideals which are the fundamental basis of our free society.

Not only are the registration provisions of the bill unworkable and dangerous, they are also grossly misleading in that all but one of the objectives which are claimed for them are already being accomplished by other and superior methods - and the one objective which is not now being accomplished would not in fact be accomplished under this bill either.

It is claimed that the bill would provide information about the communist party and its members. The fact is, the FBI already possesses very complete sources of information concerning the communist movement in this country. If the FBI must disclose its sources of information in public hearing to require registration under this bill, its present sources of information, and its ability to acquire new information, will be largely destroyed.

It is claimed that this bill would deny income tax exemptions to communist organizations. The fact is that the Bureau of Internal Revenue already denies income tax exemptions to such organizations.

It is claimed that this bill would deny passports to communists. The fact is that the Government can and does deny passports to communists under existing law.

It is claimed that this bill would prohibit the employment of communists by the Federal Government. The fact is that the employment of communists by the Federal Government is already prohibited and, at least in the Executive Branch, there is an effective program to see that they are not employed.

It is claimed that this bill would prohibit the employment of communists in defense plants. The fact is that it would be years before this bill would have any effect of this nature - if it ever would. Fortunately, this objective is already being substantially achieved under the present procedures of the Department of Defense, and if the Congress would enact one of the provisions I have recommended - which it did not include in this bill - the situation would be entirely taken care of, promptly and effectively.

It is also claimed . . . that it would require communist organizations to label all their publications and radio and television broadcasters as emanating from a communist source. The fact is that this requirement, even if constitutional could be easily and permanently evaded, simply by the continuous creation of new organizations to distribute communist information.

Section 4(a) of the bill . . . would make unlawful any agreement "to perform any act which would substantially contribute to the establishment within the United States" of a foreign-controlled dictatorship. Of course, this provision would be unconstitutional if it infringed upon the fundamental right of the American people to establish for themselves by constitutional methods any form of government they choose. To avoid this, it is provided that this section "shall not apply to the proposal of a constitutional amendment." If this language limits the prohibition of the section to the use of unlawful methods, then it adds nothing to the Smith Act . . . and would be more difficult to enforce. . . . Moreover, the bill does not even purport to define the phrase, unique in a criminal statute, "substantially contribute." A phrase so vague raises a serious constitutional question.

Sections 22 and 25 of this bill are directed toward the specific questions of who should be admitted to our country, and who should be permitted to become a United States citizen. I believe there is general agreement that . . . We should admit to our country, within the available quotas, anyone with a legitimate purpose who would not endanger our security, and we should admit to citizenship, any immigrant who will be a loyal and constructive member of the community. Those are essentially the standards set by existing law. . . .

The changes which would be made in the present law by sections 22 and 25 would not reinforce those sensible standards. Instead, they would add a number of new standards, which, for no good and sufficient reason, would interfere with our relations with other countries and seriously damage our national security.

Section 22 would, for example, exclude from our country anyone who advocates any form of totalitarian or one-party government. We of course believe in the democratic system of competing political parties, offering a choice of candidates and policies. But a number of countries with which we maintain friendly relations have a different form of government.

Until now, no one has suggested that we should abandon cultural and commercial relations with a country merely because it has a form of government different from ours. Yet section 22 would require that. . . . under the definitions of the bill the present government of Spain, among others, would be classified as "totalitarian." As a result, the Attorney General would be required to exclude from the United States all Spanish businessmen, students, and other non-official travellers who support the present government of their country. . . .

Moreover, the provisions of section 22 of this bill would strike a serious blow to our national security by taking away from the government the power to grant asylum in this country to foreign diplomats who repudiate communist imperialism and wish to escape its reprisals. . . . it is in our national interest to persuade people to renounce communism, and to encourage their defection from communist forces. Many of these people are extremely valuable to our intelligence operations. Yet under this bill the Government would lose the limited authority it now has to offer asylum in our country as the great incentive for such defection.

In addition, the provisions of section 22 would sharply limit the authority of the Government to admit foreign diplomatic representatives and their families on official business. Under existing law, we already have the authority to send out of the country any person who abuses diplomatic privileges by working against the interests of the United States. But under this bill a whole series of unnecessary restrictions would be placed on the admission of diplomatic personnel. This is not ungenerous for a country which eagerly sought and proudly holds the honor of being the seat of the United Nations, it is also very unwise, because it makes our country appear to be fearful of "foreigners," . . .

Section 22 . . . would actually put the Government into the business of thought control by requiring the deportation of any alien who distributes or publishes, or who is affiliated with an organization which distributes or publishes, any written or printed matter advocating (or merely expressing belief in) the economic and governmental doctrines of any form of totalitarianism. This provision does not require an evil intent or purpose on the part of the alien, as does a similar provision in the Smith Act. Thus, the Attorney General would be required to deport any alien operating or connected with a well-stocked bookshop containing books on economics or politics written by supporters of the present government of Spain, of Yugoslavia, or any one of a number of other countries. Section 25 would make the same aliens ineligible for citizenship. . . .

This illustrates the fundamental error of these immigration and naturalization provisions. . . . Instead of trying to encourage the free movement of people, subject only to the real requirements of national security, these provisions attempt to bar move-

ment to anyone who is, or once was, associated with ideas we dislike, and in the process, they would succeed in barring many
people whom it would be to our advantage to admit. . . .

Another provision of the bill which would greatly weaken our
national security is Section 25, which would make subversive
aliens eligible for naturalization as soon as they withdraw from
organizations required to register under this bill, whereas under
existing law they must wait for a period of ten years after such
withdrawal before becoming eligible for citizenship. This proposal is clearly contrary to the national interest, and clearly
gives to the communists an advantage they do not have under existing law.

I have discussed the provisions of this bill at some length
in order to explain why I am convinced that it would be harmful
to our security and damaging to the individual rights of our
people if it were enacted. . . .

This is a time when we must marshall all our resources and
all the moral strength of our free system in self-defense against
the threat of communist aggression. We will fail in this, and we
will destroy all that we seek to preserve, if we sacrifice the
liberties of our citizens in a misguided attempt to achieve national security. . . .

(186) MEMO, STEPHEN SPINGARN TO ROGER JONES (BUREAU OF THE BUDGET
STAFF), September 29, 1950 [Extract]

Source: Stephen Spingarn Papers, National Defense, Harry S.
Truman Library.

On Wednesday, September 27, Chairman [Clarence] Cannon of the
House Appropriations Committee saw the President and requested
that I come up to the Capitol to work with [staff counsel] George
Harvey and the staff of the Appropriations Committee on the preparation of a sensible internal security bill which Mr. Cannon
could introduce. Mr. Cannon had voted to sustain the President's
veto on the Wood-McCarran bill and had persuaded virtually all
the other members of the Missouri House delegation to do the same
thing. At that time, Mr. Cannon had announced that he was going
to introduce a real internal security bill and he was anxious to
get it in shape just as soon as possible.

I went up to the Capitol about 10:30 a.m., Wednesday morning,
and spent almost three hours with Mr. Harvey, Mr. Hobbs and another member of the House Appropriations Committee staff [on
September 27] going over with them the possibilities and particularly commending for their consideration the President's internal
security recommendations. I made it clear that my assistance was
merely technical and involved no commitment whatever on the part
of the White House or the Executive Branch on any bill that Mr.
Cannon chose to introduce. . . . I then made arrangements with
the Department of Justice, through Peter Brown (Peyton Ford being
out of town), for a Justice lawyer to come up that afternoon to
assist Mr. Harvey and his group in the actual drafting. In the
absence of Bob Ginnane on leave, Peter Brown sent Mike Horan, the
Justice lawyer who did most of the work on the original Justice
internal security recommendations. . . .

Basically the Cannon draft bill takes the Presidential recommendations . . . with some changes, notably the complete elimination of the statute of limitation in espionage cases rather than its extension from three to ten years. It adds to this a short provision authorizing the President to suspend the writ of habeas corpus under the circumstances in which the Constitution authorizes this action to be taken and for him to authorize the Attorney General to arrest and detain persons as to whom there is reasonable ground to believe that they will engage in, or conspire with others to engage in, acts of espionage, sabotage or other activity inimical to the public's safety. There are no review or screening provisions actually written into this detention section but the President is authorized to prescribe such regulations as he shall deem necessary to carry out his purposes. . . .

Finally, the draft bill repeals the Internal Security Act of 1950, . . . the Wood-McCarran Act which was passed over the President's veto.

I talked with Mr. Harvey today. He seemed very pleased with the bill which had been formulated in the manner described above. He said that the bill could not actually be introduced until Congress returns in November. However, he asked me to set in motion an Executive Branch analysis of the bill so that we would be in a position to furnish Mr. Cannon with at least technical comments on it. He understands, of course, that only the President could make a commitment on the general policy involved in the bill.

I think . . . we should collect the agencies' views so that Budget and the White House staff will be ready to advise the President on this bill when Congress reconvenes.

From a quick examination of the bill, it does not seem to me that it is too far out of line with something which the President could approve if it attracted any real support as a substitute for and repealer of the Wood-McCarran Act. One thought that occurs to me is that perhaps there should be written into the detention provision some assurance that the President's regulations must include fair administrative screening and review provisions for persons detained under that authority.

Will you, therefore, be good enough to start the ball rolling on collection of agencies' views on the Cannon draft bill, with the objective of a Budget report to the White House on this before Congress gets back here in November?

(187) LETTER, DEPUTY ATTORNEY GENERAL PEYTON FORD TO FREDERICK LAWTON (BUREAU OF THE BUDGET DIRECTOR), November 22, 1950 [Extract]

Source: Bureau of the Budget Bill Files, Harry S. Truman Library.

This is in response to your letter of October 5, 1950, asking for this Department's views with regard to the bill entitled "A bill to protect the security of the United States, and for other purposes" proposed by Representative Clarence Cannon . . .

As you remember, the President, on August 8, 1950, submitted to the Congress his program for strengthening the internal security of the United States, which included specific legislative recommendations . . . This Department helped formulate the recommendations and, of course, entirely concurred in the President's message.

The Congress, in enacting the Internal Security Act of 1950, added much more than was recommended by the President, and much that was regarded by him and this Department as detrimental to the protection of internal security . . . Nevertheless, the President's veto was overridden by the Congress and the Internal Security Act of 1950 became law on September 23, 1950.

It was against this background that Representative Cannon made his proposal, which essentially would repeal the Internal Security Act of 1950 and re-enact those few of its provisions which were generally in conformity with the President's program for strengthening the heretofore existing protections against sabotage and espionage.

While we would heartily agree with this general aim of the bill, the existence of the Internal Security Act, and the process through which it went in becoming law, raise questions as to whether the bill is now the appropriate vehicle for obtaining the President's program without the objectionable features of the present law. However, rather than discussing the general problem at this time, this letter is devoted simply to an examination of the provisions of Congressman Cannon's bill.

Sections 2, 4, 5 and 6 of the Cannon bill are, with certain additions and subtractions, the same as sections 18, 20, 21, and 23 of the Internal Security Act of 1950. These sections, plus section 19 of the Internal Security Act, substantially embodied the President's program. In some instances, the additions to these four sections, which the Cannon bill would effect are desirable. . . . Still another example is proposed section 5(c) of the Cannon bill, which would authorize the President in time of war or national emergency, to extend the anti-sabotage provisions of the whole section to any property or places designated by the President in the interest of national security. This was a provision strongly recommended by the Attorney General in his letter to Senator Lucas, dated August 26, 1950, commenting on S. 4037 (McCarran bill).

Section 7 of the Cannon bill would, in effect, substitute suspension of the writ of habeas corpus in time of rebellion or invasion for the emergency detention provisions of Title II of the Internal Security Act. . . .

Section 9 of the Cannon bill would authorize the head of every federal agency, in his absolute discretion, to dismiss any employee whenever the head of the agency "shall deem such termination necessary or advisable in the interests of the United States." It may be that this provision is not necessary in view of P.L. 733 (81st Congress), approved August 26, 1950, which authorizes a summary suspension procedure in national security cases by named agencies of the Government, plus such other agencies as the President may designate. Section 9 of the Cannon bill contains no safeguards against mistakes or injustice, whereas P.L. 733, while it authorizes immediate suspension to be followed by termination of employment if deemed necessary, also provides for subsequent review procedures. . . .

Section 12 specifically repeals the Internal Security Act of 1950. Without more, this would create difficulties. In the first place, since the Internal Security Act of 1950 has amended many of the basic provisions of the immigration and nationality laws, precaution is desirable in providing clearly for the reinstatement of sound earlier provisions which have been repealed by the Internal Security Act and which might not necessarily be revived by the new repealer. Secondly, there are some useful changes, not already touched upon, made by the Internal Security Act in some pre-existing laws, which the Cannon bill does not reenact or save from repeal. For example, section 24 of the Internal Security Act, amending the Alien Registration Act of 1940 (8 U.S.C. 456, 457), contains provision for periodic notification to the Immigration and Naturalization Service of aliens' addresses, a provision which this Department sought to obtain for several years. Accordingly, a blanket repeal of the Internal Security Act, without certain savings clauses, would not be desirable.

(188) MEMO, ROGER JONES (BUREAU OF THE BUDGET ASSISTANT DIRECTOR) TO MR. PERLMETER, April 2, 1952 [Extract]

Source: Harry S. Truman Papers, Official File, Harry S. Truman Library.

In reference to Senator Magnuson's letter of March 17, 1952, regarding the construction of camps for detention of "persons allegedly violating the McCarran Act," the following information appears pertinent.

The "Internal Security Act of 1950" . . . provides . . . that in the event of an invasion of the United States or its possessions, declaration of war by Congress, or insurrection within the United States in aid of a foreign enemy, the President may proclaim an "Internal Security Emergency."

The Act further provides . . . that "Whenever there shall be in existence such an emergency, the President, acting through the Attorney General, is hereby authorized to apprehend and by order detain, pursuant to the provisions of this title, each person as to whom there is reasonable ground to believe that such person probably will engage in, or probably will conspire with others to engage in, acts of espionage or of sabotage."

. . . the Attorney General is given authority to prescribe places of detention for persons apprehended [and] to prescribe necessary regulations, but states that "No such regulation shall require or permit persons detained under the provisions of this title to perform forced labor or any tasks not reasonably associated with their own comfort and well-being, or to be confined in company with persons who are confined pursuant to the criminal laws of the United States or of any State."

In order to be able to immediately carry out responsibilities under the "Internal Security Act of 1950," camps at Avon Park, Florida; Allenwood, Pennsylvania; El Reno, Oklahoma; Wickenburg, Arizona; Florence, Arizona; and Tule Lake, California, are being placed in stand-by status. . . . A sum of $775,000 was appropriated in 1952 to take over and operate the six stand-by camps, and $811,500 has been requested for 1953.

5. *The Truman Presidency and the Department of Justice*

In its long-term consequences, the most far-reaching development of Truman's presidency involved the breakdown of presidential control of and supervision over the Department of Justice, and thereby the FBI. Thus, by misinforming Truman about President Roosevelt's 1940 wiretapping directive and 1939 investigative authorization directive, FBI and Justice Department officials thereby secured his approval for a radical expansion of FBI authority. The Truman White House, moreover, failed to determine even the Justice Department's legislative strategy. Desirous of far-reaching legislative changes, including measures which would have negated constitutional and legal safeguards against abuses of power, Justice Department officials were generally successful in defining the Truman Administration's "internal security" legislative policy. Justice Department legislative recommendations might have been consistently opposed by White House aides and other Administration officials on civil liberties and constitutional grounds; nonetheless, even requirements that the Department revise its legislative proposals or cease lobbying for particular measures were circumvented. The culmination of this ineffectual oversight ironically occurred after White House officials convinced President Truman in May 1950 to require that the Justice Department review its legislative recommendations in the light of their impact on civil liberties. This effort was almost immediately aborted by the outbreak and impact of the Korean War - to the extent wherein by July of that year White House officials hesitated to consult the Department of Justice concerning "additions to the urgent [legislative] list by virtue of The Korean Crisis" for fear of the Justice Department's possible recommendations. As a consequence, by 1951 the Department obtained virtual immunity both when drafting internal security legislation and when seeking to create a more alarmist public opinion essential to effecting its internal security goals.

(189) LETTER, BUREAU OF THE BUDGET ASSISTANT DIRECTOR FRANK PACE
TO ATTORNEY GENERAL CLARK, April 16, 1948

Source: John Snyder Papers, Bureau of Budget Files, Harry S.
Truman Library.

This is in reference to [Assistant Attorney General Douglas]
McGregor's letter of June 23, 1947, transmitting a draft bill entitled "Relating to the internal security of the United States",
and requesting advice as to the relationship of the proposed
recommendation to the program of the President.

The views of the Federal Communications Commission and the
Department of State upon this proposal were transmitted by the
Bureau of the Budget to the Department of Justice on November 12,
1947. Following the receipt of [Assistant to the Attorney General
Peyton] Ford's letter of January 28, 1948, commenting on the views
of those agencies, the Bureau obtained the views of the Treasury
Department with respect to this draft bill. That Department,
. . . expresses the view that the bill in its present form might
result in impairing fundamental civil rights, and suggests a number of safeguarding and other amendments to the bill which it
feels can be accomplished without sacrifice to the desirable objectives of your proposal.

You are advised that, if the draft bill were appropriately
amended in the respects suggested by the Treasury Department,
there would be no objection by this office to the presentation of
the proposal so modified to the Congress for its consideration.

(190) LETTER, SECRETARY OF THE TREASURY JOHN SNYDER TO BUREAU OF
BUDGET DIRECTOR, March 23, 1948 [Extract]

Source: John Snyder Papers, Bureau of Budget Files, Harry S.
Truman Library.

Reference is made to your letter of February 17, 1948, requesting this Department's views on a proposed recommendation of
the Attorney General transmitting a draft bill relating to the
internal security of the United States.

Legislation of this nature has a dual responsibility: to
provide for adequate protection of the security of the United
States, and, at the same time, to provide safeguards for adequate

protection of civil rights of the people of the United States
from infringement or abuse in the name of security. Several provisions of the draft bill fall seriously short of the latter goal,
and should be corrected. . . .

I. The first section of the draft bill would, among other
things, amend . . . the Espionage Act of 1917 . . . by adding the
phrase "or information" to the specifically named items relating
to the national defense which, under the subsection, it is a crime
to communicate or transmit. This amendment would make it a crime
for any individual to "willfully give or attempt to give any information relating to the national defense to any person not entitled to receive it. The stated purpose for this amendment is
to "render the law more effective against unauthorized transmissions and retentions which may not come within the specific references but are considered none the less dangerous to the national
security".

This proposed new criminal offense is so broadly defined that
it would cover innocuous transmissions as well as transmissions
dangerous to the national security. Any statement, oral or written, is within the definition of the offense if it relates to the
national defense and if it is given to a person not entitled to
receive it. The implications are most sweeping. . . . The provision as drafted can, in short, be regarded as a serious and unjustified infringement upon free speech and a free press. It also
has dangerous potentialities for abuse as a convenient governmental excuse for withholding or suppressing information, offering
protective insulation from unfavorable (and possibly salutary)
publicity with respect to embarrassing facts involving a modicum
of national defense information. . . .

In the light of the above considerations, the following recommendations are made:

(1) It is strongly recommended that the definition of the
proposed criminal offense of transmitting information relating to
the national defense be revised to include, in lieu of the word
"willfully", a requirement of intent or reason to believe that the
information will be used to injure the United States. . . .

(2) It is suggested that instead of one inflexible provision
with a uniform severe penalty, separate provision be made for
various degrees of offenses. . . . A graduated classification of
offenses should aid in an effective and just application of this
security measure.

(3) To provide for a uniform and reasonable policy of enforcement, it is recommended that there be added a provision similar
to that in . . . the Atomic Energy Act, that no person shall be
prosecuted for any violation except upon the express direction of
the Attorney General of the United States.

(4) With specific reference to leaks of information by government employees, in cases not serious enough to merit criminal
prosecution, it should be noted that a remedy of removal from
employment, without hearing, is available under existing general
law (5 U.S.C. 652). It is suggested that a specific provision,
buttressing the very general language of the present removal
statute, would be desirable, providing for removal from government

employment of persons unauthorizedly disclosing non-public or confidential information relating to national defense. . . .

(5) As a corollary to the above recommendations, it would seem that provisions for the control of information relating to the national defense cannot easily be woven into section 1 of the Espionage Act, but should more appropriately be written as independent provisions of law in the draft bill.

II. Section 5 of the draft bill would, among other things, authorize the Federal Bureau of Investigation and the intelligence branches of the Army, Navy, and Air Force to intercept telephone communications in the conduct of investigations to ascertain, prevent or frustrate any interference with the national security and defense, and makes evidence thus obtained admissible in court proceedings in which the United States is a party.

This Department appreciates the need for telephone interception in major cases which involve important aspects of national security and law enforcement, and favors a limited authorization of these practices, under careful and proper safeguards. . . .

With respect to the equally important need for control of the dangers of abuse, however, section 5 provides no effective safeguards. The investigative or intelligence agency involved is the sole judge of when or where wire-tapping should be conducted, under section 5 in its present form. This places in the hands of the investigative personnel great power which by its nature is highly susceptible of perversion. There is opportunity for wire-tapping for political or personal motives, under this provision. Excessively widespread wire-tapping for legitimate motives is also dangerous, if not adequately controlled. Unless the power is very carefully and sparingly employed, a mass of extraneous information of a highly personal nature will be developed which can be used oppressively or for personal advantage. The penalty provided for unauthorized disclosure or use of information obtained is not, by itself, an effective safeguard. . . .

To provide essential protection with respect to telephone interceptions, it is recommended that the following safeguards be inserted in section 5 of the draft bill:

(1) A requirement that the head of the department involved in each individual case certify in writing his belief that the case is of major importance and that telephone interception is necessary to its successful investigation, before the investigative agency be permitted to make arrangements for the interception. The authorization should specify the names and addresses of the persons involved, the phone lines involved, and the purpose of the interception in each case. . . .

(2) An additional requirement that the investigative agency (after obtaining authority from its department head) must secure from an appropriate Federal magistrate the equivalent of a search warrant (which would be issued only upon a showing by a sworn statement that there was reasonable ground to believe that evidence of a specific Federal crime might thus be obtained and which would describe the person whose telephone communications were to be intercepted, the phone lines involved, and the purpose). . . .

In addition to authorizing telephone interceptions, section 5 of the draft bill would authorize the head of the investigative agency involved to require that telegrams, cablegrams, radiograms, and similar communications, and copies of records thereof, be disclosed and delivered, and would authorize interception thereof. The evils of abuse of such a power are markedly less than in the case of obtaining information by listening in on, recording, or otherwise intercepting telephone communications, which, by their nature, are peculiarly and essentially private. Accordingly, the attendant safeguards need not be as stringent.

It is recommended, with respect to telegraph, cable, and radio communications, that section 5 of the draft bill be revised to include:

(a) A requirement that the power to obtain disclosure and delivery of such communications be exercised under rules and regulations to be prescribed by the head of the department involved (rather than the head of the investigative agency) stating limitations and conditions upon the exercise of the power. . . .

(191) MEMO, STEPHEN SPINGARN (TREASURY DEPARTMENT COUNSEL) TO THOMAS LYNCH (TREASURY DEPARTMENT COUNSEL), January 26, 1949 [Extract]

Source: Stephen Spingarn Papers, Internal Security, Harry S. Truman Library.

Attached is a copy of this [Justice Department-sponsored internal security] bill and the Attorney General's recent letter of transmittal to Congress, which I obtained from the Bureau of the Budget.

There is also attached an analysis of the bill . . . comparing the version submitted to Congress by the Attorney General with the recommendations made by the Secretary [of the Treasury John Snyder] to Budget last March on the previous version of this bill.

Several of our recommendations have been adopted in full or in substantial part, . . . The new Justice version has been modified slightly in our direction, but very slightly. . . .

It is my understanding that this bill is being sponsored by the Department of Justice individually, but not as an Administration measure, and that Justice was authorized to go ahead on this basis but did not receive formal clearance on the bill from Budget. However, there is considerable mystery as to just what did happen to reverse the previous Budget (and Presidential) position on this bill - that it would be okay if amended to conform with the Treasury recommendations - without any consultation with the Treasury. I might be able to find out the story by talking to [White House aide] Charlie Murphy, but I have not done so since I thought it best to check with you first.

(192)   MEMO, CHARLES MURPHY (SPECIAL COUNSEL TO THE PRESIDENT) TO
ATTORNEY GENERAL TOM CLARK, February 4, 1949

Source: Charles Murphy Files, Internal Security, Harry S. Truman
Library.

With further reference to our conversations concerning
testimony by the Department of Justice on the Internal Security
Bill, I respectfully suggest the following course of action:

1.   That you designate the lowest ranking man
within the Department that you think appropriate to testify before the sub-committee.

2.   That, to the extent possible, his testimony be
directed toward an explanation of the bill rather than
toward advocating its passage.

3.   That the bill be approached as a matter presented
for the consideration of the Congress in response to a
number of indications from that body that it would like
to have proposals along this line and that, if the Congress wishes to reject portions of it or provide additional safeguards for civil liberties, amendments along
that line will not be resisted by the Department.

4.   If the question should be raised by members of
the committee as to clearance with the President or as
to the President's views on the subject, it should be
stated that the bill is presented as a departmental
proposal and that it was not cleared with the President.

5.   If the question of Budget clearance is raised,
it should be stated that the Budget authorized its submission by the Department of Justice for consideration by
the Congress but with the understanding that it was not
to be presented as part of the program of the President.

(193)   MEMO, STEPHEN SPINGARN (WHITE HOUSE AIDE) TO CHARLES
MURPHY (SPECIAL COUNSEL TO THE PRESIDENT), February 1, 1950

Source: Philleo Nash Files, Harry S. Truman Library.

This will serve as a reminder to you, as requested, on this
bill [H.R. 10, an alien deportation bill] which you and I discussed with the President on January 30.   At that time he approved the proposal that you call Attorney General [J. Howard]
McGrath and ask him to do what he can to stop the progress of
this bill and specifically to call off Representative [Francis]
Walter (who reported the bill from the Judiciary Committee last
August) and who, according to advice from [White House aide]
Charlie Maylon, says he is going to press forward vigorously on
the bill, which is still in the Rules Committee.   My suggestion
would be that the Attorney General tell Mr. Walter that he wishes
to reconsider the bill with the idea of submitting a substitute
version, but that in the meanwhile he hopes no further action will
be taken on H.R. 10 which is no longer regarded as acceptable.

I understand from Charlie Maylon that [Presidential press sec-
rectary] Matt Connelly talked to [Assistant Attorney General] Peyton
Ford about this matter last week after Peyton had sent a letter to the

Hill reiterating the Department of Justice's previous favorable recommendation on the bill. It seems to me important that the Attorney General personally participate in reconsideration of the matter not only on its individual merits, but from the standpoint of considering ways and means of improving Department of Justice formulation of legislation in the internal security field.

This type of legislation normally originates in the security branches of the Department, the FBI and the Immigration Service. These branches are staffed by sincere and honest men, but their outlook is naturally and properly limited to the security field in which they work. They are inclined to resolve all doubts in favor of security. Looking at it from their standpoint this is as it should be. But every security bill encroaches to a greater or lesser extent on individual rights and liberties. Before the Department of Justice and the Administration stamp of approval is placed on such a bill, it should be carefully weighed to determine whether the best possible balance has been struck between the protection of national security and the protection of individual rights. The Department of Justice, after all, has responsibility for civil liberties as well as internal security. It has a Civil Rights Section, the enlargement of which the Attorney General has just recommended. The Department, therefore, should be peculiarly qualified to make a fair appraisal of proposed security legislation on the two basic standpoints I have described.

However, the Justice sponsorship of H.R. 10 and its original drastic 1948 version of the omnibus internal security bill (which was developed by an Interdepartmental Intelligence Committee, headed by the FBI) suggests that its consideration of security legislation may be one-sided rather than balanced.

This may or may not be the appropriate occasion to discuss the general picture with the Attorney General in addition to H.R. 10, but it is somthing which I think should be discussed with him at an early date. The Alger Hiss conviction will certainly give impetus to the passage of increasingly more repressive internal security legislation, such as the Mundt-Nixon-Ferguson bill, for example. The green light on the construction of the hydrogen bomb is also likely to have that effect. I am not suggesting that no further internal security legislation is necessary or desirable, but I am suggesting that internal security considerations are not the only ones which should be considered in connection with such legislation.

(194) MEMORANDUM, STEPHEN SPINGARN FOR THE FILE, August 12, 1949 [Extract]

Source: Stephen Spingarn Papers, Internal Security, Harry S. Truman Library.

****

On August 19, I discussed [S. 2311, an internal security bill by Senators Karl Mundt, Homer Ferguson, and Olin Johnston] with [White House aide] Charlie Murphy. It was agreed that I should advise Budget as follows:

(1) that Justice should be encouraged to include in its report on the bill a less ambiguous statement on its position,

that is to say that it should state it was opposed and not
include the meaningless statement that it was a question of
legislative policy whether or not the bill should be enacted.

(2) that Justice should be urged to make it clear in its report that the same constitutional doubts attached to S. 2311
as would to the [original] Mundt-Nixon bill [of 1948], and

(3) that Budget in finally clearing the Justice report should
state only that there was no objection to the submission of
this report, and should not indicate the relationship of the
bill to the President's program. . . .

(195) <u>MEMO, CHARLES MURPHY AND STEPHEN SPINGARN TO THE PRESIDENT</u>,
May 16, 1950 [Extract]

Source: Stephen Spingarn Papers, Internal Security, Harry S.
Truman Library.

The cold war has naturally resulted in increased attention to
internal security legislation. The Departments of Justice and
Defense have recommended some tightening in existing internal
security laws. In addition, there has been a rash of internal
security bills from non-Administration sources - some of them
very drastic measures indeed (the present version of the 80th
Congress Mundt-Nixon bill for example). The prevailing impetus
is toward ever increasingly stiffer internal security measures.
The tendency also is to draft these measures in very broad, loose
terms - to paint the whole barn in order to cover the knothole.

Our internal security laws must, of course, be adequate. To
the extent that they are not adequate now, they should be strengthened. Excessive security, however, can be as dangerous as inadequate security. . . .

There have been indications over the past two years or so that
the Department of Justice has sometimes been somewhat one-sided
in its consideration of internal security proposals, both those
it sponsors and those it merely reports on to Congress. . . .

Justice policy on internal security legislation normally originates in the security branches of the Department, the FBI and
the Immigration Service. These branches . . . are inclined to resolve all doubts in favor of security. . . . But every security
bill encroaches to a greater or lesser extent on individuals rights
and liberties. Before the Department of Justice and the Administration stamp of approval is placed on such a bill, it should be
carefully weighed to determine whether the best possible balance
has been struck between the protection of national security and
the protection of individual rights. The Department of Justice,
after all, has responsibility for civil liberties as well as internal security. As you know, Justice has a Civil Rights Section
and you have recommended the enlargement of that Section to division size with an Assistant Attorney General heading it up. Justice, therefore, should be peculiarly qualified to make a fair
appraisal of proposed internal security legislation from the
standpoint of both internal security and individual rights.

B. <u>Recommendation</u>

In the light of the above considerations, we suggest that you
call in the Attorney General and Peyton Ford and tell them:

1) Your desire that our internal security legislation be fully adequate to protect national security.

2) Your equal desire that excesses in this field be avoided and that a balance be struck between internal security and individual rights.

3) Your wish that all internal security proposals be carefully scrutinized by the civil rights branch of Justice (or other appropriate Justice personnel) as well as by the security branches, and that the Attorney General satisfy himself that a proper balance has been struck between internal security and individual rights before Justice sponsors or approves any internal security measures.

(196) MEMO, PRESIDENT TRUMAN TO ATTORNEY GENERAL McGRATH, May 19, 1950

Source: Stephen Spingarn Papers, Internal Security, Harry S. Truman Library.

I have asked Steve Spingarn to talk to you about ways and means of improving Executive Branch policy formulation in the field of internal security legislation. He knows my views, and I shall be glad if you will discuss the matter fully with him.

In summary, this is my thinking on this matter. Our internal security laws must be adequate. To the extent that they are not adequate now, they should be strengthened. Excessive security, however, can be as dangerous as inadequate security. Excessive security brings normal administrative operations to a stand-still, prevents the interchange of ideas necessary to scientific progress, and - most important of all - encroaches on the individual rights and freedoms which distinguish a democracy from a totalitarian country.

Every proposal for new internal security laws, therefore, should be carefully scrutinized not only from the standpoint of how much it will add to national security but also from the standpoint of the other considerations noted above, and particularly the last.

(197) MEMO, STEPHEN SPINGARN FOR THE FILES, May 20, 1950 [Extract]

Source: Stephen Spingarn Papers, Internal Security, Harry S. Truman Library.

On May 18, Mr. Murphy and I presented the President with our joint memorandum of May 16 on [Justice Department internal security legislation] . . .

The President directed me to go down to Justice and see the Attorney General and discuss the whole subject matter with him along the lines of the Murphy-Spingarn May 16 memorandum. [Presidential Secretary Matthew] Connelly made the appointment for me for the afternoon of May 19 and I took with me a brief memorandum from the President to the Attorney General, . . .

I spent the better part of an hour with the Attorney General discussing the matter. I told him about the President's desire for adequate internal security legislation and at the same time his concern that considerations of individual rights should be properly balanced against considerations of internal security, and his feeling that the present procedure for formulating internal security legislation did not involve sufficient consideration from the standpoint of individual rights. . . .

I told Mr. McGrath that I understood the new head of his Civil Rights Section . . . was his personal selection . . . and an excellent man although I did not know him personally, and the Attorney General might care to have an inventory made of pending internal security legislative proposals and let [the Civil Rights Section] go over them with the Attorney General making the final decision as to whether the proper balance had been struck between security and individual rights. I told the Attorney General that the White House staff was small and over-worked and that we simply had to depend on them to a large extent on this kind of thing. I also mentioned the fact that it was not the White House staff which had first called the President's attention to the drastic character of H.R. 10 but outside persons in whom he had confidence.

The Attorney General was most receptive on the whole matter. He said that he knew the President's deep convictions of the need for protecting individual rights because the President had frequently spoken to him about it. As for H.R. 10, it was a bill that Tom Clark had initiated two years ago when he was Attorney General. McGrath had not heard about the President's recent position of opposition to it and no doubt therefore his people were still pressing it. He said that he had not given the bill a fresh look but had assumed that it was o.k. because Clark had sponsored it and it had originally been cleared by Budget on behalf of the President. He indicated that he would take prompt action to correct this situation not only on H.R. 10 but across the boards. He also told me that if we had any further problems in this field at any time I should call him direct. . . .

(198) MEMO, RICHARD NEUSTADT (WHITE HOUSE AIDE) TO STEPHEN SPINGARN, July 3, 1950 [Extract]

Source: Stephen Spingarn Papers, Internal Security, Harry S. Truman Library.

Ben Brown at State and John Adams at Defense have called . . . to say that they have no suggested changes for the urgent list at this time. [David] Kendall at NSRB [National Security Resources Board] says they have nothing to place in the urgent category. . . . [Roger] Jones at Budget says there is nothing to add from their point of view. Tom Lynch at Treasury says they've got authority for foreign funds control and wouldn't want to call for more until time to call for everything.

I would let it rest here for the time being. I have not checked Justice for fear they would want to up-grade the priority on one or another of the internal security bills. (Congress will do enough of that on Justice's urging, if any, without White House intervention). . . .

(199) <u>MEMO, STEPHEN SPINGARN FOR THE FILES</u>, August 11, 1950 [Extract]

Source: Stephen Spingarn Papers, Internal Security, Harry S. Truman Library.

At the staff meeting yesterday, Mr. Murphy and I discussed with the President the handling of the legislation to carry out the recommendations in the President's August 8 internal security message to Congress. Mr. Murphy said that [Democratic Senate Majority Leader Scott] Lucas had called him to ask whom he was to deal with at the White House on this matter . . .

The President told Mr. Murphy that he was his Special Counsel and that he was the man to deal with Senator Lucas, . . . Following the staff meeting, Mr. Murphy talked to Senator Lucas and told him the situation and that I would be working with him and his staff on the matter. Mr. Murphy also passed this information on to [Assistant Attorney General] Peyton Ford. . . .

I talked to Peyton Ford this morning and told him about the President's views, that there should be no new legislation in this field other than that which he recommended in his August 8 message. Peyton said that that did not seem to be consistent with what the President had told the Attorney General at Cabinet today - that the President had no objection to Justice drafting for Lucas a registration type bill. I said that there was no inconsistency. Of course, there was no objection to Justice furnishing Lucas any technical drafting service he desired, but that it was to be clearly understood that this was only a drafting service and that no such bill had any Administration backing or approval. Peyton said that was understood and had been explained to Lucas. . . .

[Addendum] This morning [August 12] I told the President about my talk with Peyton Ford yesterday. The President explicitly confirmed that my reporting to Ford of the President's views was correct - namely that he does <u>not</u> believe that any new legislation in the internal security <u>field</u> is either necessary or desirable except for the legislative recommendations in his August 8 message to Congress. The President told me to hold the line on this matter. The President added that this was what he had told the Attorney General at Cabinet yesterday and he was sure the Attorney General understood his views.

I called Peyton Ford later in the morning and told him that to be on the safe side I had checked with the President again and told him of my conversation with Ford, and that the President had again confirmed his views as I had reported them to Ford.

(200) <u>LETTER, DEPUTY ATTORNEY GENERAL PEYTON FORD TO CHARLES MURPHY</u>, September 12, 1950 [Extract]

Source: Charles Murphy Files, Harry S. Truman Library.

I am transmitting herewith a draft of a proposed bill to amend Section 3141, Title 18, United States Code (relating to the granting of bail in criminal cases) by providing the courts with the same powers in that regard with respect to peacetime espionage, sabotage and sedition cases, and certain other like security cases in time of war or emergency, as they now possess with respect to treason and other capital cases. The Department considers it highly important that such a measure be enacted, particularly in view of the current and immediately foreseeable international situation, in order to strengthen control over persons arrested for offenses involving threats to the national security pending disposition of the charges against them. . . .

. . . as to capital cases only the courts, as distinguished from commissioners and like committing magistrates, have the power to admit to bail and that latitude for the exercise of discretion in granting or refusing bail is at all times present. In all cases not punishable by death, however, the obligation to admit to bail is mandatory and, whatever the nature or seriousness of the offense, whatever its relation to the national situation and security, the court or commiting magistrate is required to fix an amount, the furnishing of which will result in the immediate release of the alleged offender. Sabotage, sedition and the several security violations to which the proposed amendment is directed under existing law are at no time punishable by death and espionage is a capital offense only when committed in time of war and an actual or attempted foreign transmission is involved.

It is quite true that in either type of case, capital or non-capital, the issue to be determined is the probable amenability of the defendant to the process of the court and that, as a matter of practice, in passing on that question the courts take into consideration the nature of the charge as well as the background, present circumstances and record, if any, of the defendant but, notwithstanding the conclusion reached, in non-capital cases the obligation to fix bail remains and if, in weighing all the circumstances, the court feels the defendant's bail should not be enlarged, it is without statutory authority to exercise any discretion in the matter. Nor can the court insure confinement by fixing any amount greater than the ability of the defendant to provide, since excessive bail is constitutionally prohibited by the 8th Amendment. The offender, directly or through the resources of his principal or others, is thus the master of his own liberty. . . .

It is the Department's position that this situation presents a distinct weakness in our existing system which considerations of national security alone, if no others, should not permit to continue. In view of the developing international situation, the Department anticipates the volume of cases in these categories to rise sharply. It also anticipates a substantial increase in a number of other types of offenses, generally violating the safety and security of military and war installations and materials and the integrity of government and the armed forces, and therefore recommends a like extension with respect to such offenses in time of emergency proclaimed by the President, as well as in time of war. . . .

(201) <u>MEMO, BUREAU OF THE BUDGET ASSISTANT DIRECTOR ROGER JONES
TO CHARLES MURPHY</u>, October 13, 1950 [Extract]

Source: Bureau of the Budget Bill Files, Harry S. Truman Library.

On September 28, you sent me a copy of Peyton Ford's letter
to you of September 12 to which there was attached a proposed
amendment . . . which would permit judges of United States courts
to deny bail in cases of alleged offenses involving peacetime
espionage, sabotage and sedition, and other security cases in time
of war or emergency.

. . . Instinctively, we all recoil from the proposal as being
inconsistent with our traditions and heritage. At the same time,
no one quite wants to take the responsibility of challenging the
judgment of the Department of Justice as to the possible need for
such legislation in certain kinds of cases. . . .

It seems to us that this proposed statute can be construed to
have only two effects: (1) to get around the constitutional provision that excessive bail shall not be required, and (2) to permit prosecuting authorities, by requesting that bail be denied, to
suggest to the courts a considerable degree of impotence both in
our police system and in our court system. We feel it is quite
a different thing to deny bail in capital cases, where there is
at least a presumption that physical harm to others might occur
if an alleged murderer or rapist is left at large. So far as
treason is concerned, it should certainly stand alone. A spy or
a stupid, misguided zealot, once arraigned, has little capacity
to hurt the country further even if admitted to bail.

It seems to us that it would be far better to press for immediate trial in cases in which the Government felt the issue
should be decided at once. Presumably in such cases the Government does not make an arrest until it is reasonably sure of its
case, and we find it difficult to believe that the courts need to
give so much time to the defense to prepare its case as to make
the fears expressed by Justice a real factor.

In summary, we are very apprehensive about any statutory provision which would permit denial of bail in non-capital cases,
particularly when they get watered down to something like alleged
sedition conspiracy. The problem cannot be considered in the Federal context alone. The precedent which is set for the States,
to my mind, is nothing short of shocking. With every passing
month, I become more and more convinced that we are going through
a period of hysteria, of fear, and that we cannot protect liberty
by denying or circumscribing its normal processes and privileges
and institutions. . . .

We earnestly recommend that you reconsider this proposal and
urge the Department of Justice to reconsider.

(202) <u>LETTER, ATTORNEY GENERAL J. HOWARD McGRATH TO PRESIDENT
TRUMAN</u>, November 19, 1951

Source: Philleo Nash Files, Harry S. Truman Library.

Pursuant to the request contained in your memorandum of
October 5, 1951, I have the honor to forward herewith the final

legislative program of the Department of Justice for the Second Session of the Eighty-second Congress.

(203) JUSTICE DEPARTMENT RECOMMENDATIONS FOR THE PRESIDENT'S STATE OF THE UNION ADDRESS [Extract]
Source: Philleo Nash Files, Harry S. Truman Library.

****

I wish to invite the attention of the Congress to a provision of law through which persons who may be guilty of criminal subversive conduct - or, indeed, of other crimes - have sometimes been able to frustrate our law enforcement officials and our courts, and remain at large with impunity to constitute an ever-present danger to society. This loophole is the deliberate and malevolent abuse of the right to refuse to testify, on the grounds of self-incrimination, before a grand jury or court, or before an investigative body of the Congress.

Certainly the right to protection against self-incrimination is fundamental with us, and none of us would wish to see its self-protective features diminished in scope or in strength. Nevertheless, federal criminal law enforcement would be greatly facilitated, without any depreciation of the great value of this right, if the Attorney General were granted the power, in proper cases and under appropriate safeguards, to require the giving of testimony by an offer of a grant of immunity from criminal prosecution to a witness who refuses to testify on the ground of his right against self-incrimination. If any witness, assured of the grant of immunity, refused to testify, he could then be punished for contempt; or if he committed perjury in his testimony he could be convicted and punished. The right against self-incrimination would be maintained in its full vigor, but it could no longer be utilized to thwart the disclosure of conspiracies and group efforts to violate the law.

Legislation to vest the Attorney General with such power in proceedings before courts and grand juries was proposed to the last session of Congress in S. 1747. I recommend that this bill be enacted.

There is also before the Congress another bill, S. 1570, which would provide that a witness might be compelled to testify before investigative committees of the Congress if immunity from criminal prosecution were granted him by certain Congressional officials without reference to the Attorney General. If it be considered desirable to extend immunity to witnesses before committees of the Congress, I recommend that this end be achieved by centralizing authority either in the Attorney General, as the chief law enforcement officer of the Government, or in appropriate Congressional officials acting with the concurrence of the Attorney General. If this central authority is not maintained, there would be an undesirable risk of unnecessarily impeding or even completely blocking prosecutions contemplated by the Department of Justice on matters touched upon in its criminal investigations, without the control of our law enforcement agencies over the extent of the immunity afforded, and perhaps often without their knowledge. . . .

(204) SPECIFIC JUSTICE DEPARTMENT LEGISLATIVE RECOMMENDATIONS
[Extract]

Source: Philleo Nash Files, Harry S. Truman Library.

Criminal Law

(1) To amend title 18, United States Code, chapter 79, by
    adding a new section to extend the law relating to perjury
    to the willful giving of contradictory statements under
    oath. The purpose of this bill is to eliminate the need
    for proving which of inconsistent statements made under
    oath is false. . . .

Criminal Law

(1) To permit the compelling of testimony under certain con-
    ditions and to grant immunity from prosecution in connec-
    tion therewith. The purpose of this proposal is to give
    to the Attorney General the authority to grant immunity
    from prosecution to witnesses whose testimony may be es-
    sential to an inquiry conducted by a grand jury, or in
    the course of a trial, or in the course of a congressional
    investigation. . . .

Internal Security

(1) To amend section 2151 of title 18, United States Code re-
    lating to sabotage. The objective of this measure is to
    strengthen the sabotage chapter of the criminal laws of
    the United States by redefining "war premises" and
    "national-defense premises" as used therein. . . .

Internal Security

(1) To transfer responsibility for certain investigations from
    the Federal Bureau of Investigation to the Civil Service
    Commission. The objective of this bill is to relieve the
    Federal Bureau of Investigation of the responsibility of
    conducting personnel investigations so that its efforts
    may be wholly devoted to the pursuit of its primary re-
    sponsibilities of detecting and apprehending violators of
    federal laws, discharging its assignments with respect
    to espionage, sabotage, and subversive activities, and
    rendering such other vital services as may be required of
    it by congressional and executive directives. . . .

Internal Security

(1) Proposed amendments to the Internal Security Act of 1950.
    The objective of this legislation is to improve the ad-
    ministrative provisions of the Act and to afford some
    latitude of discretion with respect to certain classes of
    aliens now barred from admission to the United States.
    . . .

Internal Security

(1) To regulate the interception of communications in the in-
    terest of national security and the safety of human life.
    The purpose of this legislation is to provide for the
    interception of certain communications upon the express
    authorization of the Attorney General, to make information

so obtained admissible in evidence in United States courts
in criminal prosecutions arising out of security investigations, and to provide a severe penalty for the unauthorized interception of communications. . . .

6. *FBI Political Activities*

*Given the White House's ineffectual oversight over
the Department of Justice and the FBI, not surprisingly
FBI officials no longer were as constrained to abuse
power to further conservative political goals. Already
indifferent to constitutional or legal restrictions on
the Bureau's investigative authority, and no longer
subject to intensive executive scrutiny, FBI officials
acted purposefully to undermine radical and left-liberal
dissent. On the one hand, FBI Director Hoover regularly
forwarded to the Truman White House reports on dissident
political activities, some of which furthered the Administration's partisan interests. On the other hand, FBI
officials leaked derogatory information about individuals or organizations to "friendly" reporters and congressmen in an effort to discredit those individuals
and organizations whom conservative FBI bureaucrats believed to be "subversive." Congressman Richard Nixon
was a favored recipient of these leaks - Nixon's January
26, 1950 speech most dramatically illustrates this, the
speech being based on privileged access to FBI reports
and memoranda.*

(205) LETTER, FBI DIRECTOR HOOVER TO HARRY VAUGHAN (MILITARY AIDE
TO PRESIDENT TRUMAN), January 11, 1946 [Extract]

Source: Harry S. Truman Papers, President's Secretary's Files
Personal-FBI, Harry S. Truman Library.

I wanted to inform the President and you of a report that the
United People's Action Committee of Philadelphia, Pennsylvania,
has agreed with two other organizations in Philadelphia to "march
on" the Capitol in Washington, D.C., and to take part in a mass
demonstration in Washington on January 17, 1946. The purpose of
these activities is to agitate for the passage of a bill establishing a permanent Fair Employment Practice Committee.

. . . It might be noted that the United People's Action Committee is reported to have Communist influence in it.

With regard to the agitation for the passage of a bill establishing a permanent Fair Employment Practice Committee, information has been received from various parts of the country where
the Communist Party is active, that Communist elements are actively engaged in agitating pressure campaigns to have such a
bill enacted.

In the event additional pertinent details are received in
this regard, they will be brought to the President's and your
attention.

(206) LETTER, FBI DIRECTOR HOOVER TO HARRY VAUGHAN, December 6,
1946

Source: Harry S. Truman Papers, President's Secretary's Files
FBI I, Harry S. Truman Library.

Reference is made to your telephonic request of December 4,
1946, asking whether any information is available in the files
of this Bureau with respect to a possible connection between Mr.
Harold L. Ickes former Secretary of the Interior, and any gas
company interested in acquiring the Big Inch Pipe Line.

A search of the files of this Bureau has failed to disclose
any information relative to an affiliation of Mr. Ickes with any
gas company. However, it is to be observed that on the basis of
information furnished by a confidential source [a wiretap of

Corcoran] Mr. Ickes has been very friendly with [former Roosevelt aide] Thomas C. Corcoran who reportedly is in the process of organizing a gas company for the purpose of submitting bids for the procurement of the Big Inch Pipe Line. The name of the gas company in which Mr. Corcoran is interested is not known although, according to the source, during the initial stages of this company's formation, Mr. Ickes was proposed for consideration as a director.

(207) <u>LETTER, FBI DIRECTOR HOOVER TO HARRY VAUGHAN</u>, June 25, 1947

Source: Harry S. Truman Papers, President's Secretary's Files, FBI S, Harry S. Truman Library.

As of possible interest to the President and you, information has come to the attention of this Bureau from a confidential source, indicating that a scandal pertaining to sugar is brewing and undoubtedly will become public in the near future. Our informant expressed the opinion that this scandal will be very embarrassing to the Democratic Administration.

(208) <u>LETTER, FBI DIRECTOR HOOVER TO HARRY VAUGHAN</u>, June 25, 1947

Source: Harry S. Truman Papers, President's Secretary's Files FBI W, Harry S. Truman Library.

I thought that the President and you would be interested in the following information concerning the Progressive Citizens of America and [former Vice President] Henry A. Wallace which has been brought to this Bureau's attention by a confidential source reported to be reliable.

According to the report received, Mr. C. B. Baldwin, a prominent national officer of the Progressive Citizens of America and former secretary to Mr. Henry A. Wallace, appeared at a luncheon held . . . on June 18, 1947, under the auspices of the Progressive Citizens of America.

. . . Baldwin is said to have referred to the talk of a third Party in 1948, with Mr. Wallace as a Presidential candidate, as offensive propaganda. [In fact, Wallace did agree in December 1947 to become the Presidential candidate of the newly-formed Progressive Party] . . . the Wallace forces whose center point appears to be the Progressive Citizens of America, have had their strength in the Democratic Party surveyed by a public opinion institute. This survey reflected that at the present time the "left-wing" Democrats control about 22% of the Democratic vote which can be relied upon in a primary election. Baldwin is reported to have stated that he believed the left-wing forces with an expenditure of money and some diligent work in the field, would be able to make it possible for the Progressive Citizens of America and affiliated organizations to increase their proportion of the Democratic Party's regular vote to approximately 40% by the time the next National Democratic Convention is held. It was felt that with such a large minority present it would be impossible for the Democratic Party to conduct a harmonious convention and to nominate candidates for the Presidency of the United States without making concessions to the Wallace forces.

. . . the Progressive Citizens of America had been making money and that Mr. Wallace had been heard by many people. Mr. Baldwin related that with continued demonstrations of strength of this type he was hopeful that shortly after the first of next January he would be able to sit down with the Democratic National Committee and work out "a deal". He further related that the Progressive Citizens of America and those forces supporting Wallace should be willing to accept a compromise whereby Wallace is made the Democratic nominee for the Vice Presidency of the United States. Baldwin asserted that there is no question but what the Democratic National Committee has already decided to nominate President Truman for the Presidency at the next National Democratic Convention. He is also reported to have asserted that there was no possibility of securing another nominee from the Democratic National Committee, even though one is desired by the Progressive Citizens of America and its affiliates.

Baldwin is also said to have asserted that Wallace as Vice President could act as a restraining influence upon the "reactionary Harry Truman" and would, of course, be in a position to succeed him in the event Mr. Truman came to "an untimely end". Baldwin admitted it might be that Mr. Wallace might have to be content with a lesser position than the Vice Presidency, that is, a Cabinet position. He assured his listeners, however, that Wallace would not accept less and that if the regular Democratic forces failed to reach some compromise, then the anticipated 40% of the Democratic delegates at the National Convention would walk out and set up a third Party, which group would undertake a campaign to elect Wallace to the Presidency of the United States.

By way of background concerning the Progressive Citizens of America, I desire to point out that this organization was formed on December 28 and 29, 1946, in New York City out of the now defunct Independent Citizens Committee of the Arts, Sciences and Professions and the National Citizens Political Action Committee, together with other progressive groups. . . . Communists were active in the formation and guidance of the Independent Citizens Committee of the Arts, Sciences and Professions. Also, many individuals identified with the National Citizens Political Action Committee were active in Communist front groups. The program of the Progressive Citizens of America since its inception has closely paralleled that of the Communist Party. Among its recent activities has been the vigorous fight against the President's proposal for aid to Greece and Turkey.

Should additional information concerning this matter be brought to this Bureau's attention, it will be immediately furnished to you.

(209) LETTER, FBI DIRECTOR HOOVER TO HARRY VAUGHAN, January 27, 1948 [Extract]

Source: Harry S. Truman Papers, President's Secretary's File FBI Communist-Data, Harry S. Truman Library.

I thought the President and you would be interested in the following information. . . .

. . . the National Secretariat of the [Communist] Party held a special meeting the day after Henry Wallace announced that he would run for President of the United States on a Third Party Ticket. . . . the Secretariat decided to take immediate steps to organize national groups in the United States behind the Wallace movement. . . . the Nationality Groups Commission of the Communist Party was asked to contact the leaders of organizations with whom the Commission is in contact for the purpose of "starting the ball rolling." Every District Organizer of the Communist Party throughout the United States was reportedly informed of this decision and asked to contact national group organizers for the same purpose.

. . . the American-Slav Congress, which controls some one million Slavs in the United States, has already started its activities and has lined up all of its organizations throughout the country behind the Wallace movement. The Jewish Commission of the Communist Party is likewise reported to be organizing Jewish national organizations throughout the country. . . .

. . . every Communist in the Trade Union Movement [has been ordered] to become active in behalf of [the Wallace] movement. [A] member of the National Committee reportedly stated, "We believe that if we succeed in organizing in a big way, the national minority groups in the country, we have no doubt that we will succeed in doing it and by constantly propagandizing the workers in the Trade Unions, we will roll up between seven million and nine million votes for Wallace. This will be just enough votes to defeat Truman and prepare the way for the election of a progressive president in 1952.

Any further information concerning the above which comes to the attention of this Bureau will be made promptly available to you.

(210) LETTER, FBI DIRECTOR HOOVER TO HARRY VAUGHAN, March 31, 1948 [Extract]

Source: Harry S. Truman Papers, President's Secretary's Files FBI T, Harry S. Truman Library.

****

Tilford Dudley, Assistant Director of the Political Action Committee, Washington, D.C., was recently discussing the coming elections with [former OPA Director] Chester Bowles of Essex, Connecticut. Dudley . . . stated he had discussed the elections with [CIO President] Philip Murray who is interested in having the ADA (Americans for Democratic Action) group take an active part in this program. The informant was of the opinion that Dudley had in mind a delegation to be sent to draft Dwight Eisenhower for the Presidency. Bowles reportedly stated that this was fine because if "we're going to try to remove him (the informant stated that Bowles referred to President Truman), we'd better get all the help we can."

In discussing labor's position, Murray, according to Dudley, thought that the CIO should not become too involved because they did not want to be branded but should get people like Bowles and

Dudley to start things with labor helping out later. Bowles reportedly agreed with Murray's views, but commented that people like Murray and Walter Reuther (United Automobile Workers - CIO President) should speak out as individuals. It was further pointed out by Bowles that if Philip Murray, Walter Reuther and Jack Kroll (National PAC Director) would come out against President Truman, stating that it was impossible to get support for him but that they desired to stick with the Democratic Party, this alone would almost be enough to kill President Truman's chances.

In the event further information is received in this regard, you will be promptly advised.

(211) <u>MEMO, GEORGE ELSEY TO CLARK CLIFFORD</u>, August 25, 1948

Source: George Elsey Papers, General File 1948, Harry S. Truman Library.

[Assistant Attorney General] Peyton Ford states that, so far he has been able to ascertain, the Department of Justice has never been requested by the White House to ascertain the validity of the alleged exchange of correspondence between Henry Wallace and ex-President [Lazaro] Cardenas of Mexico.

Even if such a request is now made, Ford doubts that Justice will be able to supply any useful information. He points out that the FBI does not operate in Mexico, and that it would be highly hazardous for numerous obvious political reasons for the FBI to attempt to ascertain from Mr. Wallace's intimate associates whether he wrote a letter printed over his name.

The Central Intelligence Agency is understood to have agencies in Mexico, but I doubt the wisdom of requesting that organization to ascertain the validity of these letters.

(212) <u>LETTER FBI DIRECTOR HOOVER TO PRESIDENTIAL APPOINTMENTS SECRETARY MATTHEW CONNELLY</u>, January 27, 1950 [Extract]

Source: Harry S. Truman Papers, President's Secretary's File FBI N, Harry S. Truman Library.

I thought you would like to have the following information received by this Bureau from a very confidential source regarding a recent meeting of newspaper representatives at Chicago, Illinois, held [several days ago] to formulate plans for a publicity campaign against organized gambling.

. . . at the meeting plans were reportedly made to publish a series of copyrighted stories pertaining to organized gambling and other racketeering activities. . . . Strong emphasis was placed on the importance of developing information showing the connection of racketeers with corrupt politicians in each of the cities to be treated in this series of stories.

The first of these stories is reported to be scheduled for release February 12 or 13, 1950. It will deal with organized gambling and its connection with corrupt politicians and, . . . will be critical of the Attorney General [Tom Clark] and will in-

clude information relating to his supposed association and contacts with members of the underworld, particularly in Kansas City,
Missouri, and with the President's supposed association with
these individuals and their contributions to the Presidential
campaign.

. . . the newspaper representatives who attended the above
meeting had information that the American Municipal Association
had exerted pressure on the Attorney General to bring about the
issuance of invitations to its representatives to attend the
Attorney General's conference in Washington next month and that
the American Municipal Association intends to give publicity to
the former associates of the President and of the Attorney General
and to publicize the supposed foothold or organized crime in national politics.

This information is being made available to you as a matter
of interest. It is also being furnished to the Attorney General.

(213) LETTER, FBI DIRECTOR HOOVER TO SIDNEY SOUERS (SPECIAL CON-
SULTANT TO THE PRESIDENT), February 20, 1951 [Extract]

Source: Harry S. Truman Papers, President's Secretary's File FBI
I, Harry S. Truman Library.

In view of the recent public pronouncements pertaining to the
files of the Institute of Pacific Relations, which were subpoenaed
by the Subcommittee on Internal Security of the Senate Committee
on the Judiciary, I thought you would be interested in knowing
that in March, 1950 a confidential informant [a break-in] of this
Bureau made available to the Federal Brueau of Investigation
copies of approximately 3600 documents from the files of the
Institute of Pacific Relations . . .

[In addition] The following information was furnished by a
confidential source of this Bureau. This information, the accuracy for which this Bureau cannot vouch, is being furnished you
for your information.

The source of this Bureau advised that the son of the care-
taker employed on [Institute of Pacific Relations official Edward]
Carter's farm at Lee, Massachusetts, had contacted the "New York
Journal American," a Hearst daily newspaper, and after accepting
a sum of money, had allowed representatives of that newspaper to
review the documents located on this farm. . . . these Hearst
newspaper representatives photostated certain of these documents
but, realizing they had not been acquired in a legal manner, contacted Senator Joseph McCarthy and turned these photostatic
documents over to him. Senator McCarthy, . . . in order to obtain
legal possession of these documents, caused the Senate Subcommittee to issue a subpoena. . . . while this matter was handled
through the aforementioned Subcommittee, it was actually "master-
minded" by Senator McCarthy and his investigators.

. . . the Senate Subcommittee and Senator McCarthy feel that
nothing of real importance is contained in these documents. . . .
Senator McCarthy, [McCarthy aide] Dr. J. B. Matthews, [Hearst
columnist] George Sokolsky and, apparently, [Hearst columnist]
Westbrook Pegler have started a move to try to get a joint commit-

tee comprised of the House Committee on Un-American Activities
and the Senate Subcommittee [on Internal Security] in order that
the Senate Subcommittee can have access to the files of the House
Committee on Un-American Activities and its personnel. The reason for this maneuver . . . is . . . that the Senate Subcommittee
does not have enough background or personnel to adequately investigate this matter. . . . Senator McCarthy and the Subcommittee
feel that they actually have nothing of any real importance in
the Institute of Pacific Relations' documents and they further
feel that this attempt to form a joint committee will fail.
Senator McCarthy will then be able to claim that the fact that
nothing has come of this matter was due to the insufficient background and personnel of the Senate Subcommittee.

The confidential source of this Bureau further advised that
apparently the primary aim of the Senate Subcommittee is to reopen
the "Amerasia" case. [The Subcommittee did hold intensive hearings later in 1951 based on the IPR files in which it sought to
establish that IPR members had unduly influenced U.S.-China policy
and, in the process, had ensured the communization of China.]

(214) MEMO, FBI DIRECTOR HOOVER TO FBI OFFICIALS CLYDE TOLSON,
QUINN TAMM, D. MILTON LADD, AND (FIRST NAME UNKNOWN) CLEGG, March
19, 1946

Source: FBI Files, Alger Hiss, Harvard University Library.

While discussing other matters with the Attorney General [Tom
Clark] he said that Senator James O. Eastland (D-Mississippi) had
called him and said he understood that the FBI had a file on
Alger Hiss (State Department, Director of the Office of Special
Political Affairs); that the Senator said he understood Hiss was
involved in the Canadian Case [Soviet defector Igor Gouzanko's
charges of Soviet espionage activities in Canada], and that he
wanted to see the file. He also stated that he saw Secretary [of
State James] Byrnes this afternoon, and Byrnes said his relations
with Senator Eastland were very friendly. I told the Attorney
General that the Senator had called me and made the same request;
that I had sent Mr. Clegg to see him, and Mr. Clegg had explained
to the Senator that the files were confidential and could not be
shown without the authority of the Attorney General. I told the
Attorney General that the Senator further stated at this time that
he knew him well and would try to convince him he should see the
files privately. The Attorney General said he would not do this.
I told him that I felt this was a thing for the State Department
to work out with Senator Eastland; that we have given the State
Dept. all we have on Hiss and they should work out something with
the Senator so he would not press an investigation.

The Attorney General further stated that Secretary Byrnes
wants to dismiss Hiss but had been told he cannot do this without
giving him a hearing as he is a Civil Service employee. I told
him I did not think a hearing would be wise as the material is
confidential and if it were not used there would not be enough
evidence against him; that I thought the best thing the Secretary
could do would be to move Hiss to an innocuous position where he
would understand the situation and resign. I also told him that
the Secretary should take Senator [Tom] Connally and [Arthur]

Vandenberg into his confidence as they are friends of Hiss, then they will understand the situation. The Attorney General said he would call the Secretary and tell him this.

[Typed at bottom of this memorandum: "This memorandum is for administrative purposes to be destroyed after action is taken and not sent to files." The memorandum was not destroyed because on January 5, 1949 Hoover ordered that it be transferred to Bureau File 62, Hoover's "Official and Confidential Files."]

(215) MEMO, FBI DIRECTOR HOOVER TO FBI OFFICIALS, TOLSON, TAMM AND LADD, March 20, 1946

Source: FBI Files, Alger Hiss, Harvard University Library.

While talking with the Attorney General on another matter I mentioned that I had a call from Secretary Byrnes asking me to call him. The Attorney General said he thought the Secretary would discuss Alger Hiss. He said that Byrnes wanted to isolate Hiss but in view of the 3 or 4 congressional committees that were probing around the State Department, he would suffer because of Hiss's presence in the Department, as he (Byrnes) would be charged with sending Hiss to "the attic" and wasting government money on him.

The Attorney General said that Byrnes proposed, if the Justice Department agreed, to call Hiss in and inform him that complaints against him had been received but not disclose the source to him. I told the Attorney General that it seemed to me that as soon as you begin to question Hiss, the very questions will alert him as to the nature of the information we have about him. I indicated the possibility that Secretary Byrnes may use the Department of Justice as an alibi saying that he had called upon the Department to investigate Hiss and that following these investigations the Justice Department had found nothing to warrant the dismissal of Hiss. I pointed out that this would put the Justice Department in an awkward position and would subject us to possible future criticism.

I suggested that Byrnes take into his confidence men like Tom Connally, [Democratic Congressman] John McCormack, and Arthur Vandenberg, point out to them frankly the position he is in, telling them that Hiss will be put in a place where he can do no harm, and by this means avoid any criticism from "the hill." The Attorney General asked me to advise him about my conversation with Secretary Byrnes. I told him I would do this.

[Addendum to memorandum, 5:24 PM] I returned the call of Secretary Byrnes and told him that I understood the position he was in, but because of the fact that any interview with Hiss at this time would alert him and ruin an important espionage investigation; as an alternative I would suggest that he contact several key men in the House and the Senate like Tom Connally, Arthur Vandenberg, John McCormack or [Democratic House Speaker] Sam Rayburn, and explain his predicament to them, pointing out that he wanted their help in avoiding any criticism from "the hill."

Secretary Byrnes indicated that he thought this might be a solution to the problem and said he would call some of these men.

[Addendum, 5:42 PM] I called the Attorney General and told him what I had suggested to Secretary Byrnes. I said that he thought this was a good idea and that it was apparently was what he was going to do.

[As in the preceding memorandum, this memorandum contained the same separate filing notation and later was transferred to the 62 file on January 5, 1949.]

(216) MEMO, FBI DIRECTOR HOOVER TO FBI OFFICIALS TOLSON, TAMM, AND LADD, March 21, 1946, 5:35 PM

Source: FBI Files, Alger Hiss, Harvard University Library.

Secretary Byrnes telephoned and explained that after talking with me yesterday, he determined that he had better talk with Alger Hiss, as he was going to attend the meeting of the [UN] Security Council in New York next week, and would not have the time to contact anyone on the hill as I had suggested. He said that he had talked with Sam Rayburn who advised him that he could do nothing with [Conservative Democratic Congressman John] Rankin. [Rankin had charged that Communists had infiltrated the State Department and stated his intention to initiate hearings on this matter.]

Secretary Byrnes stated that he called Hiss in and asked him if he was ever a member of any organization with subversive tendencies. Hiss swore that he had never been a member of any such organization. He said that his name might be on the mailing list of such an organization, but that was all. Byrnes said that he did not tell Hiss much about the background, but asked him if his association with [former Agriculture Department counsel Lee] Pressman meant anything. Hiss replied that he had been associated with him in the early part of the Roosevelt administration, but since then there had been no close association. Byrnes advised that Hiss asked him what he could do about this matter to which the Secretary replied that he did not know, that it bothered him, and that he had been having requests from [conservative Democratic Congressman Louis] Rabaut about it mentioning Hiss's name with one or two others, and consequently the matter would come up, and before he went to New York for the Security Council meeting, he should come and see me [Hoover], and present to me what he says is the truth about the situation. Hiss replied that he would like to do this, and would like to invite me to cross-examine him, and then check upon his statements.

I told Byrnes that Hiss had called this afternoon and talked with [FBI Assistant Director D. M.] Ladd in my absence. I said that I told Mr. Ladd that if Hiss wanted to come over and talk to us it would be perfectly agreeable, but, of course, there were some things that we could not ask him, because certain questions would dislcose information on current cases. I told the Secretary that if Hiss wanted to make any statement, or related anything about his association that he might surmise would place him under suspicion, we would be very glad to listen to him. The Secretary stated that he wished we would do this. Byrnes said again, that Hiss swears he would gladly welcome an investigation of any kind.

The Secretary advised that the part of the report on Hiss that impressed him was the statement of [Whittaker] Chambers. He

asked me what kind of a man Chambers was. I told him that he was
a very good man, explaining that he was Senior Editor of Time
magazine.

I again told the Secretary that I would arrange for Mr. Ladd
to talk with Hiss and see what he had to say, pointing out again
to Mr. Byrnes that there were matters that we could not mention,
because to do so would disclose the source of our information. I
told him that he would be advised after Hiss had talked with Mr.
Ladd.

ADDENDUM, 6:15 PM

I telephoned the Attorney General and he stated that he had
just talked to Secretary Byrnes. The Attorney General said that
Byrnes had told him what he had done, and termed the Secretary's
action "an outrage".

I generally outlined my conversation with Secretary Byrnes,
pointing out that when Hiss came down to the Bureau, he was going
to do the talking and we would do the listening.

[The same filing notation yet later decision to transfer to File
62 was contained on the bottom of this memorandum.]

(217)   FBI ASSISTANT DIRECTOR LOUIS NICHOLS TO FBI ASSOCIATE
CLYDE TOLSON, December 2, 1948

Source: FBI Files, Alger Hiss, Harvard University Library.

[Following a visit to Whittaker Chambers's farm that night,
HUAC member Richard Nixon immediately contacted FBI officials to
brief them of the result of the meetings.] Congressman Richard
Nixon called Nichols at home late last night on a strictly personal
and highly confidential basis to inform that he was going to
Panama where he would be at the Tivoli Hotel and that he would
return to Washington on December 15, that on December 18 he plans
to reopen the Alger Hiss-Whittaker Chambers matter [by convening
HUAC hearings]. Nixon stated he understood that the Department
of Justice told the FBI that there was no violation involved [the
matter had been presented to a federal grand jury in November] and
that consequently no further action was to be undertaken by the
FBI. However, it is Nixon's understanding that Chambers recently
let go and turned in some highly incriminating documentary evidence [to Hiss's attorneys on November 17, 1948] which consisted
of State Department information typed by Mrs. Hiss, turned over
by Hiss to Chambers, and by Chambers ultimately to the Russians.
Nixon understands that [Assistant Attorney General] Alexander
Campbell in the Department [who was presenting the case to the
grand jury] has some of these documents and he also understands
that Chambers did not tell the FBI everything he knew and as a
matter of fact still has other documents and material that sub-
stantiate and vindicate his position which have up to this time
not become publicly known.

Nixon stated it was his intention to subpoena these documents
at the [HUAC] hearings on December 18 and the purpose of his call,
which he reiterated was strictly personal and highly confidential,
was merely to apprise the Bureau so that the FBI would not be
caught off base. He stated they were handling the matter so that

there will be no criticism to the FBI and he particularly urged that we [FBI officials] do nothing about the information which he has just furnished as he feels the statute of limitations has run.

Nixon specifically urged that we not tell the Attorney General that we were told of this information as the Attorney General undoubtedly would try to make it impossible for the Committee to get at the documents. He also asked that the Bureau not look for the documents themselves.

It looks like the only thing we could do would possibly be to inquire of Alexander Campbell if he has any documentary evidence without revealing the reason for our inquiry or our source.

[Handwritten notation by Tolson, This is being done by Dept order]

> [Handwritten notation by Hoover,
> Do so & let me know result]

(218) MEMO, FBI ASSISTANT DIRECTOR L. B. NICHOLS TO FBI ASSOCIATE DIRECTOR CLYDE TOLSON, December 3, 1948, 1:15 PM
Source: FBI Files, Alger Hiss, Harvard University Library.

[Robert] Stripling [chief counsel of the House] Un-American Activities Committee called and left word for me to get in touch with him. I have just talked to him. He says, in connection with the Hiss-Chambers case, that he wanted us to know for our confidential information - and he specifically asked that the information not go out of the Bureau - that at 1 o'clock this morning he secured a series of microfilm containing reproductions of confidential documents from the State Department, which Alger Hiss allegedly gave to Whittaker Chambers. While Stripling would not say, it was quite obvious that Chambers has turned the material over to him. This, of course, is my own conclusion and impression from my conversation with Stripling.

Stripling is now having the microfilm reviewed and typed up. He does not know exactly what to do but states that he will keep in close touch with me, and as soon as he gets a copy typed up he will try to get some authorization from somebody on the Committee to furnish us with a copy. He stated that the last document is dated in 1939 [the documents released publicly by the Committee during its public hearings contained no 1939 document, the last date being January 13, 1938 - since Chambers broke from the Communist Party in 1937 or 1938 his possession of a 1939 document raises certain irresolvable questions], and proves the case conclusively that Whittaker Chambers was telling the truth and that Hiss was not. He stated that Hiss certainly is guilty now in the face of this evidence, that of course the question comes up about Chambers withholding information.

He is cabling Congressman Nixon, who is presently en route to Panama, urging him to return immediately as he does not feel that they can sit on this until December 18.

I will keep in touch with him from time to time although I do not feel that we should make any formal request for the material because obviously it would be difficult to take prosecutive actions that occurred in 1938. [Despite this conviction, the decision was soon made to seek a perjury indictment of Hiss for denying under oath to the grand jury that he had given State Department documents to Chambers in 1938.]

(219) MEMO, ASSISTANT FBI DIRECTOR L. B. NICHOLS TO ASSOCIATE FBI DIRECTOR CLYDE TOLSON, December 9, 1948 [Extract]

Source: FBI Files, Alger Hiss, Harvard University Library.

[Conservative Republican] Congressman [Karl] Mundt called. He apologized for his delay in returning my call yesterday and for what occurred in the Committee yesterday afternoon. . . .

I pointed out to him that of course the recent developments merely confirmed what the Bureau had reported to appropriate authorities years ago and that this might be a good point for him to get across. He stated that he would certainly try to keep this in mind.

(220) MEMO, FBI ASSISTANT DIRECTOR D. M. LADD TO FBI DIRECTOR J. EDGAR HOOVER, December 9, 1948 [Extract]

Source: FBI Files, Alger Hiss, Harvard University Library.

Former [FBI] Special Agent Patrick Coyne advised me that he was with former [FBI] Special Agent Bob King last night, that King is a good friend of Congressman Nixon, that they visited Congressman Nixon at his hotel room and Nixon exhibited to them copies of the documents in the Chambers-Hiss matter. . . .

Mr. Coyne stated that Nixon is extremely mad at the Attorney General and at [Assistant Attorney General] Alex Campbell for not having more vigorously prosecuted this whole matter, but Mr. Coyne stated that Congressman Nixon had nothing but praise for the Director and the Bureau. He voluntarily stated during the course of the evening that he had worked very close with the Bureau and with Mr. Nichols during the past year on this matter. . . .

(221) MEMO, (FBI AGENT) L. WHITSON TO (FBI AGENT) H. B. FLETCHER, December 9, 1948 [Extract]

Source: FBI Files, Alger Hiss, Harvard University Library.

On this date, former [FBI Special Agent] Robert L. King personally contacted [FBI] Supervisor William A. Branigan and furnished the following information: . . .

. . . King stated that Congressman Nixon had exhibited to him on a personal and confidential basis the documents which the House Committee had obtained from Chambers. King informed that Nixon said that if the matter were not properly handled the House Committee [on Un-American Activities] intended to blast their disclosures in the public press because they felt that without a doubt those who were responsible for stealing the government's secrets should be held accountable. King stated that Nixon had informed him that the House Committee had succeeded in identifying

certain written notations on the documents as being in the handwriting of Alger Hiss. Throughout the conversation King stressed
the fact that Congressman Nixon personally felt that the Bureau
was the only agency capable of handling this matter and stressed
that Nixon had indicated his personal belief that the case should
be turned over the the Bureau exclusively. . . .

(222) MEMO, FBI ASSISTANT DIRECTOR D. M. LADD TO FBI DIRECTOR
HOOVER, December 17, 1948 [Extract]

Source: FBI Files, Alger Hiss, Harvard University Library.

At 7:20 PM on December 16, the Attorney General [Tom Clark]
called and stated that he had heard Fulton Lewis on the radio
making a statement attributed to a high Justice official who was
unnamed, accusing the House Investigator of having turned his
flash light on some of the film in this case and therefore having
fogged it. I told the Attorney General that I knew nothing about
any flash light . . .

The Attorney General asked if the Bureau could have developed
[the microfilm HUAC obtained from Chambers] clearer had they received it originally. I advised him it could not be so stated,
that it would be impossible after the films were developed to
determine whether it could have been developed clearer had the
Bureau had it originally.

The Attorney General inquired if I knew of anything the Committee [HUAC] had done that had caused a delay or hurt our investigation. I told him I knew of no such action on the part of the
House Committee. He asked me to think the matter over and he
would call me on the morning of December 17. . . .

While the Attorney General was talking to me he stated that
he has taken the position that the Committee's questioning of
[Franklin Vincent] Reno , etc. [identified by Chambers as having
been a member of the Communist underground in Washington] flushes
other possible witnesses and is therefore harmful to the Department's investigation. I very carefully made no commitment or
acknowledgement to this so that this statement could not be attributed to me or the Bureau as being critical of the Committee.

The Attorney General then asked "Have you received instructions not to cooperate with the Committee". I advised the Attorney General that I had [neither] seen nor received . . . such instructions, that our policy in connection with this entire matter
has been to refer any inquiries from the committee to the Attorney
General as is our policy in connection with all congressional
committees.

The Attorney General then referred to the newspaper article
in the "Washington Post" for December 17 which quotes Congressman
[Richard] Nixon as having said that he had called the FBI and had
been advised by the FBI that they had no documents. I made no
comment on this and the Attorney General did not follow this matter up.

I have checked with [FBI Assistant Director Louis] Nichols
who states that the night prior to Congressman Nixon's leaving
for Panama the Congressman had called him but that he, Nichols,

had not made any such comment. He advised that there is a memorandum in the file reflecting his conversation with Nixon.

(223) MEMO, FBI ASSISTANT DIRECTOR LOUIS NICHOLS TO FBI ASSOCIATE
DIRECTOR CLYDE TOLSON, December 10, 1948 [Extract]

Source: FBI Files, Alger Hiss, Harvard University Library.

I talked to Russell Turner in [Hearst columnist and radio
commentator] Fulton Lewis' office. Fulton seldom comes to the
office anymore and makes his broadcast from a studio in his home
in Maryland. . . .

In the course of the conversation the Hiss-Chambers case came
up. [Turner] was wondering if there were any angles on it. I
told him that, of course, speaking strictly for his own information and guidance and not for quotation, as both he and Fulton
[Lewis] very well knew, the Bureau had been investigating this entire matter over a period of years and that we did not have the
authority or power to take action; that we should not have this
authority or power, but that our reports had been communicated to
higher authorities and, of course, it was up to them to take the
action; that everything we had secured on Hiss had been communicated to the State Department as well as other individuals in the
Washington Communist underground, but this had been going on for
a period of years. He wanted to know if we were doing anything
special at the moment and I told him that since the most recent
developments with the production of the microfilm by Chambers, the
Grand Jury in New York had intensified its activities and we were
running out a lot of leads and the like; that so far as we were
concerned the microfilm merely tended to corroborate what he
[Chambers] had told us years ago and what we had reported [to
Administration officials] years ago; that we had endeavored to
secure corroboration from Chambers when he was first interviewed
several years ago [in 1942] and on subsequent occasions; that he
had never told us about the microfilm and in fact had stated he
did not have any of the documents. I further told Turner that in
connection with the Washington underground that we, of course,
were fully cognizant of the deficiencies of the law, the difficulties of presenting evidence and corroborating information which
we had and which we believed to be true; that the [FBI] Director's
position had been that it was inadvisable to go to the Grand Jury
until we knew we had a case; however, notwithstanding this, the
case was presented to a Grand Jury; and that from that time on
the Director has advocated that if the Grand Jury were unable to
secure corroboration, they should issue a report on their findings
so that the American public would know what has been going on and
would know what the FBI has been doing, because we ourselves
could not make our reports known to the public. I told him this
might be an excellent idea for Fulton to undertake. Turner got
very much excited about this and stated he was sure Fulton would
like nothing better than to undertake a campaign such as this to
bring our full disclosures of what the FBI has done.

I further told him we are in a very awkward and difficult position; that obviously we could not talk about the case or about
what we had done because the action to be taken was not within
our province. He said he thoroughly understood this. I empha-

sized this is the point Fulton should endeavor to get across as
much as he can. He said Fulton has already commented along these
lines but that it would not be amiss to do it again which he will
do.

(224) SPEECH, CONGRESSMAN RICHARD NIXON, January 26, 1950
[Extract]

Source: U.S. Congress, *Congressional Record*, 81st Cong., 2d
session, pp. 999-1000, 1002-1006.

[Following Hiss's conviction of perjury on January 21, 1950
and sentencing by Judge Henry Goddard on January 25, 1950, Nixon
delivered a lengthy speech in the House assessing the significance
of the case and Hiss's conviction.] . . . I feel that I have a
solemn responsibility, both as a member of the Committee on Un-
American Activities and as a Member of this House to [publicize]
. . . certain facts concerning the case which led to the trial
and conviction of Alger Hiss for perjury . . .

This case and the implications which arise from it involve
considerations which affect the very security of this Republic.
This Nation cannot afford another Hiss case. . . . we [must] recognize the seriousness of the crime involved, the extent and
scope of the conspiracy of which Mr. Hiss was a member, the reasons for failure to bring that conspiracy to light until it was
too late to prosecute those involved for the crime they had committed, and the positive steps which we can and must take now to
guard against such a situation in the future. . . .

On November 17, 1948, Mr. Hiss' attorneys took Mr. Chambers'
deposition in Baltimore, and in that deposition Mr. Hiss' attorneys were to make their greatest mistake.

They asked Mr. Chambers to produce any documentary evidence
that he might have which would establish that Mr. Hiss and he
were Communists together. Mr. Chambers produced a thick envelope
containing four pages in Mr. Hiss' handwriting and a great number
of typewritten documents which he said had been typed on Hiss'
typewriter. These documents contained excerpts and summaries of
scores of confidential and secret State Department messages.

. . . That very same day, Mr. Alexander Campbell, the Assistant Attorney General in charge of the Criminal Division, was
called by counsel for both sides to come to Baltimore to pick up
the documents. Two weeks later on the 1st day of December, a
very interesting United Press dispatch appeared in the *Washington
Daily News*. This article said in effect that the Justice Department was going to drop the Hiss-Chambers case for lack of evidence
and that unless some new evidence was presented the Department
would not be able to determine which man was lying.

Now, understand, the dispatch quoted Justice Department
sources. And the Department at that time had had in its possession for 2 weeks what Mr. Murphy, the prosecutor in the Hiss
trial, had so well called the immutable proof of espionage. . . .

It was at this point that the Committee on Un-American Activities came back into the picture. [HUAC counsel Robert] Stripling
and I went to Westminster, Md. [on December 1, 1948]. We ques-

tioned Mr. Chambers; we asked him if it were possible that he
might have some additional evidence which might bear upon this
case in view of the fact that the Justice Department was going to
drop it. He was shocked when he learned of this proposed action.
He told us that he had been told not to talk about what had happened at the deposition hearing [involving Hiss's libel suit] in
Baltimore on November 17, but we were able to gather from the
conversation with him that some new development in the case had
occurred on that date, so when we returned to Washington, D.C., I
ordered that a subpena be served upon Mr. Chambers for any other
documents that he might have.

As a result of that subpena being served upon him, we obtained
the so-called pumpkin papers, 5 rolls of microfilm, containing
photostatic copies of literally scores of confidential and secret
documents from the State Department and the Bureau of Standards.
With this evidence in our possession, we were able to force the
matter into the open by convincing the Justice Department that
unless it did proceed with its investigation the Committee on Un-
American Activities would have to conduct its own investigation
of the case. . . .

Among the other individuals that Mr. Chambers testified [before
HUAC in August 1948] were members of his Communist apparatus was
Harry Dexter White, former Assistant Secretary of the Treasury.
You will recall that shortly after Mr. White's appearance before
the Committee on Un-American Activities in 1948, he passed away.
Immediately the critics of the investigations charged that the
Committee on Un-American Activities was responsible for his death
because we had given credence to the completely unfounded and,
note this, undocumented charges that had been made against him by
Whittaker Chambers and Elizabeth Bentley [in July 1948 before a
Senate Subcommittee]. . . .

When Mr. Chambers testified before the committee, in 1948, he
stated that Mr. White was not a member of the Communist Party but
that he was ideologically in sympathy with the party's objectives.
In the second trial, which has just been concluded in New York,
Mr. Chambers was questioned further about Mr. White and declared
in open court that Mr. White was a source of information for the
Soviet espionage ring and that he, Chambers, had received various
documents from White which he turned over to Soviet espionage
agents.

Since December of 1948, I have had in my possession photostatic copies of eight pages of documents in the handwriting of
Mr. White which Mr. Chambers turned over to the Justice Department on November 17, 1948 [sic, the White documents were not
turned over on this date, although the FBI received them from
Chambers on November 26, 1948]. I had intended to say nothing
about these documents, but since Mr. Chambers testified that he
did receive documents from Mr. White, I think the public is entitled to see and consider the evidence. . . .

The full text of the papers which were in Mr. White's handwriting follows:

****

The third point we should bear in mind is that the conspiracy
was so effective, so well-entrenched and so well-defended by

apologists in high places that it was not discovered and apprehended until it was too late to prosecute those who were involved
in it for the crimes they had committed. There were several occasions during the past 10 years on which, if vigorous action had
been taken, the conspiracy could have been exposed and its effectiveness destroyed. . . .

I am sure that some Members of the House are wondering why
the FBI which received information concerning the various charges
in 1943 [sic, 1942] was unable to take any direct action leading
toward prosecution and exposure of the individuals involved.

At this point, I think it would be well to outline the duties
of the FBI as distinguished from the Enforcement Division of the
Department of Justice. The FBI is solely an investigatory body.
It has no power to subpena witnesses, to bring them together for
purposes of confrontation against their will, or to prosecute
individuals that the Bureau may feel deserve prosecution.

It is a fact-gathering agency and once the facts are laid before the Enforcement Division of the Justice Department, its
responsibility is ended. Consequently, no blame can attach to the
FBI for failure to expose the facts of this case. The FBI has no
power to make public the findings of its investigations except
when called upon to do so in a court of law. Responsibility,
however, does lie with those officials of the Government who had
access to the FBI reports, and who failed or refused to institute
an investigation which would lead to prosecution and conviction of
those involved.

In answer to the charge that they were lax in investigating
and prosecuting the members of the conspiracy, some administration
officials have stated that the Chambers' charges were completely
unsubstantiated and that there was no reason to take his word
against that of the individuals he had named. I have information
which bears on that point which I would like to present to the
House at this time.

You will recall the Canadian Atomic Espionage case [of 1945-
1946] which resulted in the trial and conviction of nine members
of the Soviet espionage ring in that country in less than 1 year's
time after the charges had been made against them. Incidentally,
the prompt action on the part of our neighbor to the north is in
sharp contrast to the humiliating failure of our Government to
take any action whatever in this country against the individuals
involved in wartime espionage for the Soviet Union until it was
too late to prosecute them for the crimes they had committed. . . .

. . . statements have been made, but until now not confirmed,
that at the time of the Canadian exposé of Igor Guzenko, the Soviet
code clerk, who turned over information to the Canadian Government which resulted in the trials and convictions had been questioned by intelligence agents of the United States and had furnished information dealing with espionage activities in this country.

I can now confirm that statement. Shortly before the first
trial of Mr. Hiss, I learned that a secret memorandum, dated
November 25, 1945, dealing with Soviet espionage in the United
States and prepared by an intelligence agency of this Government
[the FBI], was circulated among several key Government departments

and was made available to the President. I said nothing at that
time about the information which was contained in the memorandum
because I did not want to take action which might influence the
trial one way or the other. Now that the trial is over, I believe
that the country is entitled to the information.

I quote directly from that memorandum:

> Igor Guzenko, former code clerk in the office of
> Col. Nicholi Zabotin, Soviet military attaché, Ottawa,
> Canada, when interviewed by a representative of this
> Bureau and officers of the Royal Canadian Mounted Police,
> stated that he had been informed by Lieutenant Kulakov in
> the office of the Soviet military attaché that the
> Soviets had an agent in the United States in May 1945
> who was an assistant to the then Secretary of State,
> Edward R. Stettinius.

Note the date of this memorandum, November 1945. Note the
position held by the individual alleged to be the Soviet espionage
agent - assistant to the Secretary of State, Mr. Stettinius. Mr.
Hiss was an assistant to Mr. Stettinius at the Yalta Conference
in February of 1945.

What was done when this shocking information came to the attention of the officials of our State Department, and the President of the United States? You would think now that Mr. Hiss
would be confronted with Mr. Chambers and that the mystery would
be cleared up, but instead Mr. Hiss continued to serve in high
positions in the State Department until he resigned in January
1947 to take a position as head of the Carnegie Foundation for
International Peace. . . .

To complete this story of inexcusable inaction upon the part
of administration officials to attack and destroy this conspiracy,
let me review briefly the conduct of the President and the Department of Justice during the investigation of this case by the
Committee on Un-American Activities. On August 5, [1948] the day
Mr. Hiss first appeared before the committee and denied the
charges which had been made against him, the President threw the
great power and prestige of his office against the investigation
by the committee and for Mr. Hiss by declaring that the hearings
of the committee were simply a "red herring." . . .

That same day, [Truman] issued a Presidential directive [sic,
actually on March 14, 1948] which ordered all administrative agencies of the Government to refuse to turn over any information relating to the loyalty of any Government employee to a congressional committee. This meant that the committee had to conduct its
investigation with no assistance whatever from the administrative
branch of the Government. Included in this order was, of course,
the FBI, who, by reason of that fact, was unable to lend assistance to the committee. [In his memoirs, however, Nixon wrote:
"Because of Truman's executive order we [HUAC] were not able to
get any direct help from J. Edgar Hoover or the FBI. However, we
had some informal contacts with a lower-level agent that proved
helpful in our investigations."]

The most flagrant action, however, was yet to come. As I
have already stated, the day Mr. Chambers turned over documentary
evidence in the handwriting of Mr. Hiss, together with typewritten

documents which were later established to be written on his typewriter, the Justice Department was immediately notified and the
material was on that day, November 17, turned over to Alexander
Campbell, head of the Criminal Division of that Department. The
various participants in the deposition were directed in the interests of national security to keep silent on the whole matter. I
[shall now read the] . . . United Press dispatch which appeared
on December 1 in the *Washington Daily News*. . . .

HISS AND CHAMBERS PERJURY PROBE HITS DEAD END

The Justice Department is about ready to drop its
investigation of the celebrated Alger Hiss-Whittaker
Chambers controversy, it was learned today.

Department officials still have under study the
question of a possible perjury prosecution. But officials said privately that unless additional evidence is
forthcoming, they are inclined to forget the whole
thing.

One Department source said that on the basis of
available evidence, officials in charge of the case believe it would be unwise to take it before a grand jury.

What happened during that critical 2-week period between
November 17 [1948] when the papers [produced by Chambers] were
turned over to the Justice Department and December 1 [1948] when
this article appeared?

I have learned from personal investigation [either access to
FBI files or from FBI officials] that no agents of the Department
of Justice even approached Mr. Chambers during that period let
alone questioned him about the highly important evidence which he
had turned over to the Justice Department. In view of the story
which appeared on December 1, stating that the Justice Department
was ready to drop the investigation for lack of new evidence, the
only conclusion which can be drawn when this fact is coupled with
the Department's failure to conduct an investigation during that
2-week period is that it was the intention of the Department not
to make an investigation unless they were forced to do so.

As a result of having in its possession the microfilm documents, which we obtained on December 2, the committee was able to
force the Department to institute an investigation and the result
was the eventual indictment of Mr. Hiss by the Federal grand jury.
It is significant to note that even as late as December 5, members of the committee learned from an unimpeachable source [the
FBI] that Justice Department officials before proceeding with
further investigation of Mr. Hiss were considering the possibility
of indicting Mr. Chambers for technical perjury due to this failure to tell the whole story when he first appeared before the
committee and the grand jury. For that reason, I publicly stated
on that same day that if the Department should proceed in that
manner, it would in effect mean that Mr. Hiss and the others
named by Mr. Chambers as being members of an espionage group
could not possibly be proceeded against due to the fact that the
principal witness against them would be an indicted perjurer.
. . .

It is essential that we learn the tragic lessons which the Hiss case has so vividly portrayed, and develop a policy which will reduce the possibility for the existence and successful oper- ation of such a conspiracy in the future. . . .

First. Above all, we must give complete and unqualified sup- port to the FBI and to J. Edgar Hoover, its chief. Mr. Hoover recognized the Communist threat long before other top officials recognized its existence. The FBI in this trial did an amazingly effective job of running down trails over 10 years old and in developing the evidence which made the prosecution successful.

I note in the papers this morning that the National Lawyers Guild has again launched an all-out attack against the FBI. [Hereafter Nixon was citing information from the derogatory re- port on the Guild which Hoover had sent in December 1949 to the Attorney General and then to the White House.] The character of the guild is well illustrated by the fact that 5 of the lawyers for the 11 convicted Communists in New York City, who were cited by Judge Medina for contempt of court because of their disgraceful conduct, are prominent members of the Lawyers Guild. Let me say just this: That when the National Lawyers Guild or any similar organization is successful in obtaining an investigation of the FBI and access to its records, a fatal blow will have been struck against the protective security forces of this Nation. I am sure that the Members of the House will join with me in resisting such an attack. . . .

(225) MEMO, FBI ASSISTANT DIRECTOR NICHOLS TO FBI ASSOCIATE DIRECTOR TOLSON, July 18, 1950

Source: FBI Files, National Lawyers Guild, J. Edgar Hoover Build- ing.

Congressman [Richard] Nixon advised me today that he has now learned the reason for the delay in [HUAC's] issuing the report [on] the National Lawyers Guild. [The released HUAC report in- cluded sentences lifted verbatim from the FBI's report on the Guild.] [HUAC member] Congressman [Francis] Walters was a member of the Guild in 1939. [HUAC member] Congressman [William] Harrison of Virginia is slowly burning on the subject of the Lawyers Guild and approximately one month ago wrote the Attorney General [J. Howard McGrath] a letter requesting the list of the names of Departmental attorneys who are members of the Lawyers Guild. To date he has not had a reply.

[HUAC chairman] Congressman [John] Wood told Nixon today that he is ready to release the report and that the matter will be finally passed on at the next meeting of the Un-American Activi- ties Committee, which should be late this week or early next week.

Congressman Harrison would like to get a list of the names of all members of the Lawyers Guild released with the report. I told Nixon that I did not know where an accurate up-to-date list could be secured and as to whether or not the Lawyers Guild had a roster. He stated that he would continue to push this matter.

(226) MEMO, FBI ASSISTANT DIRECTOR NICHOLS TO FBI ASSOCIATE
DIRECTOR CLYDE TOLSON, June 28, 1949

Source: FBI Files, National Lawyers Guild, J. Edgar Hoover Building.

[UPI Washington bureau chief] Lyle Wilson called. Charlie
Ross [Presidential press secretary] at his press conference this
morning was asked the question as to what the President intended
to do about the [National Lawyers Guild] request for an investigation of the Bureau. Ross stated that there was no such request
in the White House. He was then told that it was understood the
[National] Lawyer's Guild had called for a citizens' investigation
of the Bureau. He said that he did recall there was such a request but that the President had no intention of investigating
the Bureau.

Ross asked that the statement not be attributed to him but
that the statement for publication be attributed to a White House
staff member. He stated it was a new policy he was adopting as he
was allergic to having his name used as an authority in answering
questions which bear upon the future, the correct answer to which
he gives at the moment, but future events might change the situation. This, of course, had nothing to do with us.

He reiterated that President Truman has no present intention
of investigating the FBI; that no such plan was under consideration and he knew of no prospects for such a plan.

It seems to me that Lyle [Wilson] and Merriman Smith [of the AP's
Washington Bureau] got together and really pinned this thing down.
I am dictating a note to Wilson which will come through shortly.

[Handwritten notation by Tolson: Have checked with Rex C. &
Frank to see it is given coverage.]

[This memorandum contained the typed notation at the bottom: "This
memorandum is for administrative purposes to be destroyed after
action is taken and not sent to files." Yet the memo was not
destroyed pursuant to an August 9, 1958 request to send it to the
files section under File category 51.]

(227) LETTER, FBI DIRECTOR HOOVER TO LYLE WILSON, June 28, 1949

Source: FBI Files, National Lawyers Guild, J. Edgar Hoover Building.

I wanted you to know how deeply I appreciated your most recent assistance. Over the years, I have come to look upon you
as a real friend, and I did want you to know of my deep appreciation for your interest in the current situation.

7.   Conservatives and Internal Security

Until the Cold War years, conservative politicians and jurists were committed to reining in executive power, fearing that otherwise power would be abused in the absence of effective constraints. After 1945, conservatives continued to rail in libertarian terms against presidential or federal powers pertaining to the economic and social areas. Sharing in the Cold War consensus, and holding alarmist views about subversive threats to the internal security, however, conservatives enthusiastically advocated far-reaching restrictions on civil liberties. This revised conservative position is aptly captured in the majority opinion of the U.S. Supreme Court when upholding the conviction of the U.S. Communist Party leadership under the Smith Act on June 4, 1951 and former Republican President Herbert Hoover's rejection of Truman's invitation to head a special presidential commission created for the purpose of restoring public confidence in the Administration's handling of internal security matters.

(228) *DENNIS ET AL. V. UNITED STATES*, June 4, 1951 (Majority
Opinion, Chief Justice Fred Vinson) [Extract]

Source: 341 U.S. 494 (1951).

****

The obvious purpose of the statute [Smith Act of 1940] is to
protect existing Government, not from change by peaceable, lawful
and constitutional means, but from change by violence, revolution
and terrorism.   That it is within the power of the Congress to
protect the Government of the United States from armed rebellion
is a proposition which requires little discussion.   Whatever
theoretical merit there may be to the argument that there is a
"right" to rebellion against dictatorial governments is without
force where the existing structure of the government provides for
peaceful and orderly change.   We reject any principle of governmental helplessness in the face of preparation for revolution,
which principle, carried to its logical conclusion, must lead to
anarchy.   No one could conceive that it is not within the power
of Congress to prohibit acts intended to overthrow the Government
by force and violence.   The question with which we are concerned
here is not whether Congress has such power, but whether the means
which it has employed conflict with the First and Fifth Amendments
to the Constitution. . . .

The very language of the Smith Act negates the interpretation
which petitioners [the eleven indicted leaders of the U.S. Communist Party] would have us impose on that Act.   It is directed at
advocacy, not discussion.   Thus, the trial judge properly charged
the jury that they could not convict if they found that petitioners did "no more than pursue peaceful studies and discussions or
teaching and advocacy in the realm of ideas." . . . Such a charge
is in strict accord with the statutory language, and illustrates
the meaning to be placed on those words.   Congress did not intend
to eradicate the free discussion of political theories, to destroy
the traditional rights of Americans to discuss and evaluate ideas
without fear of governmental sanction.   Rather Congress was concerned with the very kind of activity in which the evidence
showed these petitioners engaged.

But although the statute is not directed at the hypothetical
cases which petitioners have conjured, its application in this
case has resulted in convictions for the teaching and advocacy of

the overthrow of the Government by force and violence, which, even though coupled with the intent to accomplish that overthrow, contains an element of speech. For this reason, we must pay special heed to the demands of the First Amendment marking out the boundaries of speech.

. . . the basis of the First Amendment is the hypothesis that speech can rebut speech, propaganda will answer propaganda, free debate of ideas will result in the wisest governmental policies. . . . An analysis of the leading cases in this Court which have involved direct limitations on speech, however, will demonstrate that both the majority of the Court and the dissenters in particular cases have recognized that this is not an unlimited, unqualified right, but that the societal value of speech must, on occasion, be subordinated to other values and considerations. . . .

In this case we are squarely presented with the application of the "clear and present danger" test [of *Schenck v. U.S.* 1919] and must decide what that phrase imports. We first note that many of the cases in which this Court has reversed convictions by use of this or similar tests have been based on the fact that the interest which the State was attempting to protect was itself too insubstantial to warrant restriction of speech. . . . Overthrow of the Government by force and violence is certainly a substantial enough interest for the Government to limit speech. Indeed, this is the ultimate value of any society, for if a society cannot protect its very structure from armed internal attack, it must follow that no subordinate value can be protected. If, then, this interest may be protected, the literal problem which is presented is what has been meant by the use of the phrase "clear and present danger" of the utterances bringing about the evil within the power of Congress to punish.

Obviously, the words cannot mean that before the Government may act, it must wait until the *putsch* is about to be executed, the plans have been laid and the signal is awaited. If Government is aware that a group aiming at its overthrow is attempting to indoctrinate its members and to commit them to a course whereby they will strike when the leaders feel the circumstances permit, action by the Government is required. The argument that there is no need for Government to concern itself, for Government is strong, it possesses ample powers to put down a rebellion, it may defeat the revolution with ease needs no answer. . . . Certainly an attempt to overthrow the Government by force, even though doomed from the outset because of inadequate numbers or power of the revolutionists, is a sufficient evil for Congress to prevent. The damage which such attempts create both physically and politically to a nation makes it impossible to measure the validity in terms of the probability of success, or the immediacy of a successful attempt. . . . We must therefore reject the contention that success or probability of success is the criterion.

Likewise, we are in accord with . . . the trial court's finding that the requisite danger existed. The mere fact that from the period 1945 to 1948 petitioners' activities did not result in an attempt to overthrow the Government by force and violence is of course no answer to the fact that there was a group that was ready to make the attempt. The formation by petitioners of such a highly organized conspiracy, with rigidly disciplined members subject to call when the leaders, these petitioners, felt that the time had come for action, coupled with the inflammable nature of our relations with countries with whom petitioners were in the very least ideologically attuned, convince us that their convictions were justified on this score. And this analysis disposes of the contention that a conspiracy to advocate as distinguished from the advocacy itself, cannot be constitutionally restrained, because it comprises only the preparation. It is the existence of the conspiracy which creates the danger. . . . If the ingredients of the reaction are present, we cannot bind the Government to wait until the catalyst is added. . . .

There remains to be discussed the question . . . whether the statute as we have interpreted it is too vague, nor sufficiently advising those who would speak of the limitations upon their activity. It is urged that such vagueness contravenes the First and Fifth Amendments. This argument is particularly nonpersuasive when presented by petitioners, who, the jury found, intended to overthrow the Government as speedily as circumstances would permit. . . .

We agree that the standard as defined is not a neat, mathematical formula. . . . But petitioners themselves contend that the verbalization "clear and present danger" is the proper standard. We see no difference, from the standpoint of vagueness, whether the standard of "clear and present danger" is one contained *in haec verba* within the statute, or whether it is the judicial measure of constitutional applicability. . . . We do not think we have rendered that standard any more indefinite by our attempt to sum up the factors which are included within its scope. We think it well serves to indicate to those who would advocate constitutionally prohibited conduct that there is a line beyond which they may not go - a line which they, in full knowledge of what they intend and the circumstances in which their activity takes place, will well appreciate and understand. . . . Where there is doubt as to the intent of the defendants, the nature of their activities, or their power to bring about the evil, this Court will review the convictions with the scrupulous care demanded by our Constitution. But we are not convinced that because there may be borderline cases at some time in the future, these convictions should be reversed because of the argument that these petitioners could not know that their activities were constitutionally proscribed by the statute.

We hold that the Smith Act [does] not inherently, or as construed or applied in the instant case, violate the First Amendment and other provisions of the Bill of Rights, or the First and Fifth Amendments because of indefiniteness. Petitioners intended to overthrow the Government of the United States as speedily as the circumstances would permit. Their conspiracy to organize the Communist Party and to teach and advocate the overthrow of the Government of the United States by force and violence created a "clear and present danger" of an attempt to overthrow the Government by force and violence. They were properly and constitutionally convicted for violation of the Smith Act. . . .

(229) *DENNIS ET AL. V. UNITED STATES*, June 4, 1951 (Dissent,
Justice William Douglas) [Extract]

Source: 341 U.S. 581 (1951).

If this were a case where those who claimed protection under
the First Amendment were teaching the techniques of sabotage, the
assassination of the President, the filching of documents from
public files, the planting of bombs, the art of street warfare,
and the like, I would have no doubts. The freedom to speak is not
absolute; the teaching of methods of terror and other seditious
conduct should be beyond the pale along with obscenity and im-
morality. This case was argued as if those were the facts. The
argument imported much seditious conduct into the record. That
is easy and it has popular appeal, for the activities of Communists in plotting and scheming against the free world are common
knowledge. But the fact is that no such evidence was introduced
at the trial. . . . Petitioners, however, were not charged with a
"conspiracy to overthrow" the Government. They were charged with
a conspiracy to form a party and groups and assemblies of people
who teach and advocate the overthrow of our Government by force
or violence and with a conspiracy to advocate and teach its overthrow by force and violence. It may well be that indoctrination
in the techniques of terror to destroy the Government would be
indictable . . . But the teaching which is condemned here is of a
different character.

So far as the present record is concerned, what petitioners
did was to organize people to teach and themselves teach the
Marxist-Leninist doctrine contained in four books: . . .

Those books are to Soviet Communism what *Mein Kampf* was to
Nazism. If they are understood, the ugliness of Communism is revealed, its deceit and cunning are exposed, the nature of its
activities becomes apparent, and the chances of its success less
likely. That is not, of course, the reason why petitioners chose
these books for their classrooms. They are fervent Communists to
whom these volumes are gospel. They preached the creed with the
hope that some day it would be acted upon.

The opinion of the Court does not outlaw these texts nor condemn them to the fire, as the Communists do literature offensive
to their creed. But if the books themselves are not outlawed, if
they can lawfully remain on library shelves, by what reasoning
does their use in a classroom become a crime? It would not be a
crime under the Act to introduce these books to a class, though
that would be teaching what the creed of violent overthrow of the
Government is. The Act, as construed, requires the element of
intent - that those who teach the creed believe in it. The crime
then depends not on what is taught but on who the teacher is.
That is to make freedom of speech turn not on <u>what is said</u>, but
on the <u>intent</u> with which it is said. Once we <u>start down</u> that road
we enter territory dangerous to the liberties of every citizen.
. . .

Intent, of course, often makes the difference in the law. An
act otherwise excusable or carrying minor penalties may grow to
an abhorrent thing if the evil intent is present. We deal here,
however, not with ordinary acts but with speech, to which the
Constitution has given a special sanction. . . .

Free speech has occupied an exalted position because of the high service it has given our society. Its protection is essential to the very existence of a democracy. The airing of ideas releases pressures which otherwise might become destructive. When ideas compete in the market for acceptance, full and free discussion exposes the false and they gain few adherents. Full and free discussion even of ideas we hate encourages the testing of our own prejudices and preconceptions. Full and free discussion keeps a society from becoming stagnant and unprepared for the stresses and strains that work to tear all civilizations apart.

Full and free discussion has indeed been the first article of our faith. We have founded our political system on it. It has been the safeguard of every religious, political, philosophical, economic, and racial group amongst us. We have counted on it to keep us from embracing what is cheap and false; we have trusted the common sense of our people to choose the doctrine true to our genius and to reject the rest. . . . We have deemed it more costly to liberty to suppress a despised minority than to let them vent their spleen. We have above all else feared the political censor. We have wanted a land where our people can be exposed to all the diverse creeds and cultures of the world.

There comes a time when even speech loses its constitutional immunity. Speech innocuous one year may at another time fan such destructive flames that it must be halted in the interests of the safety of the Republic. That is the meaning of the clear and present danger test. When conditions are so critical that there will be no time to avoid the evil that the speech threatens, it is time to call a halt. Otherwise, free speech which is the strength of the Nation will be the cause of its destruction.

Yet free speech is the rule, not the exception. The restraint to be constitutional must be based on more than fear, on more than passionate opposition against the speech, on more than a revolted dislike for its contents. There must be some immediate injury to society that is likely if speech is allowed. . . .

The nature of Communism as a force on the world scene would, of course, be relevant to the issue of clear and present danger of petitioners' advocacy within the United States. But the primary consideration is the strength and tactical position of petitioners and their converts in this country. On that there is no evidence in the record. If we are to take judicial notice of the threat of Communists within the nation, it should not be difficult to conclude that as a political party they are of little consequence. Communists in this country have never made a respectable or serious showing in any election. I would doubt that there is a village, let alone a city or county or state, which the Communists could carry. Communism in the world scene is no bogeyman; but Communism as a political faction or party in this country plainly is. Communism has been so thoroughly exposed in this country that it has been crippled as a political force. Free speech has destroyed it as an effective political party. It is inconceivable that those who went up and down this country preaching the doctrine of revolution which petitioners espouse would have any success. In days of trouble and confusion, when bread lines were long, when the unemployed walked the streets, when people were starving, the advocates of a short-cut by revolution might have had a chance to gain adherents. But today there are no such conditions. . . .

How can it be said that there is a clear and present danger that this advocacy will succeed is, therefore, a mystery. Some nations less resilient than the United States, where illiteracy is high and where democratic traditions are only budding, might have to take drastic steps and jail these men for merely speaking their creed. But in America they are miserable merchants of unwanted ideas; their wares remain unsold. The fact that their ideas are abhorrent does not make them powerful.

The political impotence of the Communists in this country does not, of course, dispose of the problem. Their numbers; their positions in industry and government; the extent to which they have in fact infiltrated the police, the armed services, transportation, stevedoring, power plants, munitions works, and other critical places - these facts all bear on the likelihood that their advocacy of the Soviet theory of revolution will endanger the Republic. But the record is silent on these facts. If we are to proceed on the basis of judicial notice, it is impossible for me to say that the Communists in this country are so potent or so strategically deployed that they must be suppressed for their speech. . . . To believe that petitioners and their following are placed in such critical positions as to endanger the Nation is to believe the incredible. It is safe to say that the followers of the creed of Soviet Communism are known to the F.B.I.; that in case of war with Russia they will be picked up overnight as were all prospective saboteurs at the commencement of World War II; that the invisible army of petitioners is the best known, the most beset, and the least thriving of any fifth column in history. Only those held by fear and panic could think otherwise.

(230) <u>LETTER, HERBERT HOOVER TO PRESIDENT TRUMAN</u>, November 26, 1950.

Source: Harry S. Truman Papers, Official Files 2750-A, Harry S. Truman Library.

I have your letter suggesting that I should take the Chairmanship of a Presidentially appointed bi-partisan Commission to report on the question of the "infiltration of communists in the Government."

Despite the encroachments of advancing age, I do not wish to ever refuse service to the country. There are some phases of the matter, however, which greatly trouble me and which I should like frankly to lay before you.

First. I doubt if there are any consequential card-carrying communists in the Government, or if there are, they should be known to the F.B.I.

Second. Your admirable purpose is "to restore the confidence of the people in the organization of the Government" and thereby "help the Foreign Policy situation." I suggest that the current lack of confidence arises from the belief that there are men in Government (not Communists) whose attitudes are such that they have disastrously advised on policies in relation to Communist

Russia.   The suspicion is abroad that they continue in the Government.

Third.   Without a wide-spread inquiry into the past and present of such men and the facts, the answer to this problem could not be determined.   It would require the authority to examine on oath, together with large expenditure for investigation staff, and to include access to all files of all officials and departments over the years.   Such powers could come jointly from yourself and a Congressional Act.   The personnel of such a Commission would need be approved by the leaders of both parties in that body if it were to carry conviction to them.

Fourth.   The Congress itself is likely to be engaged in such investigations anyway.

Therefore it seems to me that any inquiry as to "Communists in the Government" by an informal Commission would not be likely to satisfy the public or to restore confidence.

I dislike indeed to respond in terms of declination to any request of yours as I would like greatly to be helpful to you in these troublous times.

In that direction may I suggest that a statement might be issued by you that you would be glad if the Congress would either create such a Commission or would itself make an inquiry on the broadest basis, such as I have outlined, both as to the past and the present.   That very statement by you would greatly restore confidence in the Administration's Foreign Policy makers.

8. Official Secrets

Conservative politicians and intelligence agency bureaucrats became alarmed during the 1970s over the actions of former intelligence agents in leaking classified documents to the public. Unable to prosecute these former agents (whether Victor Marchetti or Frank Snepp) under the Espionage Act, intelligence officials looked with envy at the British Official Secrets Act of 1911 which made it an offense merely to publish or communicate classified information. Traditional principles and the contrary conceptions of sovereignty of the American political system (residing in the people and not the Crown) made the possibility of enactment of an American version of the Official Secrets Act unlikely. Nonetheless, the closest approximation of the British Official Secrets Act enacted into law in the United States occurred during the Truman years - section 783 of title 50 of the U.S. Code and section 798 of title 18 of the U.S. Code.

Alarmed by the revelations with Whittaker Chambers' production of the so-called Pumpkin Papers and the existing legal situation which did not criminalize the transmission of classified information by federal employees to foreign agents, Senator Karl Mundt introduced legislation on March 8, 1949 to criminalize such activities. Section 4(b) of Mundt's bill. S. 1194, was eventually incorporated in the omnibus internal security bill, the McCarran Internal Security Act of September 1950. Under this section, as clarified in an exchange between Senators Mundt and Homer Ferguson, the mere classification of information (and not whether the information was properly classified) provided the basis to prohibit its being transmitted. During Senate debate, Senator Ferguson directly defined the purpose of this section: "Then this goes so far as to allow an administrative officer to classify anything, and the transfer that would be criminal under your [Mundt's] act." A subsequent case brought under this provision, Scarbeck v. U.S., in 1962 upheld this new criminal test.

(231) INTERNAL SECURITY ACT, 1950 [Extract]

Source: 50 U.S. Code 783, §783; 64 Statute 991 (1950)

§. Offenses

****

(b) Communication of classified information by Government officer or employee.

It shall be unlawful for any officer or employee of the United States or of any department or agency thereof, or of any corporation the stock of which is owned in whole or in major part by the United States or any department or agency thereof, to communicate in any manner or by any means, to any other person whom such officer or employee knows or has reason to believe to be an agent or representative of any foreign government or an officer or member of any Communist organization defined in paragraph (5) of section 782 of this title, any information of a kind which shall have been classified by the President (or by the head of any such department, agency, or corporation with the approval of the President) as affecting the security of the United States, knowing or having reason to know that such information has been so classified unless such officer or employee shall have been specifically authorized by the President, or by the head of the department, agency, or corporation by which this officer or employee is employed, to make such disclosure of such information. . . .

(e) Limitation period.

Any person may be prosecuted, tried, and punished for any violation of this section at any time within ten years after the commission of such offense, notwithstanding the provisions of any other statute of limitations: Provided, That if at the time of the commission of the offense such person is an officer or employee of the United States or of any department or agency thereof, or of any corporation the stock of which is owned in whole or in major part by the United States or any department or agency thereof, such person may be prosecuted, tried, and punished for any violation of this section at any time within ten years after such person has ceased to be employed as such officer or employee.

Concurrent with its efforts to secure enactment of legislation to authorize the interception of international communications, the so-called Operation SHAMROCK, the Truman Administration
drafted and in 1948 introduced a provision which would also criminalize the mere disclosure of information pertaining to communications intelligence (as opposed to having to prosecute offenders
under the Espionage Act). A few of the technical changes proposed
under this standard were enacted into law by the Congress on
October 31, 1951. The Department of Defense and the intelligence
community remained dissatisfied with this limited legislative
measure and in 1952 Secretary of Defense Robert Lovett proposed
to the President that the Administration seek legislation similar
to the British Official Secrets Act. The Justice Department prepared such legislation but it did not reach the floor of either
house of Congress.

(232) H.R. 3899, AMENDING CERTAIN TITLES OF THE U.S. CODE, 1951
[Extract]

Source: 18 U.S. Code 798; 65 Statute 719 (1951).

§798. Disclosure of classified information.

(a) Whoever knowingly and willfully communicates, furnishes,
transmits, or otherwise makes available to an unauthorized person,
or publishes, or uses in any manner prejudicial to the safety or
interest of the United States or for the benefit of any foreign
government to the detriment of the United States any classified
information –

(1) concerning the nature, preparation, or use of any
code, cipher, or cryptographic system of the United States or
any foreign government; or

(2) concerning the design, construction, use maintenance,
or repair of any device, apparatus, or appliance used or prepared or planned for use by the United States or any foreign
government for cryptographic or communication intelligence
purposes; or

(3) concerning the communication intelligence activities
of the United States or any foreign government; or

(4) obtained by the process of communication intelligence
from the communications of any foreign government, knowing the
same to have been obtained by such processes –

Shall be fined not more than $10,000 or imprisoned not more
than ten years, or both.

(b) As used in subsection (a) of this section –

The term "classified information" means information which, at
the time of a violation of this section, is, for reasons of national security, specifically designated by a United States Government Agency for limited or restricted dissemination or distribution;

The terms "code," "cipher," and "cryptographic system" include
in their meanings, in addition to their usual meanings, any method
of secret writing and any mechanical or electrical device or

method used for the purpose of disguising or concealing the contents, significance, or meanings of communications;

The term "foreign government" includes in its meaning any person or persons acting or purporting to act for or on behalf of any faction, party, department, agency, bureau, or military force of or within a foreign country, or for or on behalf of any government or any person or persons purporting to act as a government within a foreign country, whether or not such government is recognized by the United States;

The term "communication intelligence" means all procedures and methods used in the interception of communications and the obtaining of information from such communications by other than the intended recipients;

The term "unauthorized person" means any person who, or agency which, is not authorized to receive information of the categories set forth in subsection (a) of this section, by the President, or by the head of a department or agency of the United States Government which is expressly designated by the President to engage in communication intelligence activities for the United States.

(c) Nothing in this section shall prohibit the furnishing, upon lawful demand, of information to any regularly constituted committee of the Senate or House of Representatives of the United States, or joint committee thereof.

APPENDIX

LIST OF DOCUMENTS BY TITLE

Title	Document Number
Letter, President Truman to Chairmen Congressional Committees on Military and Naval Affairs, June 15, 1946	11
Memo, Clark Clifford (Special Counsel to the President) to General Hoyt Vandenberg (Director, Central Intelligence Group), July 12, 1946	12
Memo, George Elsey for the File, July 17, 1946	13
Memo, Walter Pforzheimer (Chief, Legislative Liaison Branch, Central Intelligence Group) to Director of Central Intelligence Hoyt Vandenberg, November 26, 1946	14
National Security Act of 1947	15
Final Report, Senate Select Committee on Intelligence Activities, the CIA, 1945-1953	16
Special Message to Congress, President Truman, March 5, 1949	17
Statement, President Truman, August 10, 1949	18
Message to Congress, President Truman, June 20, 1949	19
Record, Under Secretary of State's Staff Meeting, April 15, 1949	20
Memorandum, Under Secretary of State James Webb, May 4, 1949	21
Memorandum, Acting Secretary of State James Webb to Sidney Souers (Executive Secretary, National Security Council), May 24, 1949	22
Letter, President Truman to Sidney Souers (Executive Secretary NSC), July 26, 1949	23
Memorandum, Deputy Under Secretary of State for Administration, John Peurifoy, November 17, 1949	24
Memorandum, Acting Secretary of State James Webb, October 1, 1949	25
Letter, President Truman to Sidney Souers (Executive Secretary, NSC), November 19, 1949	26
Memorandum, Sidney Souers (Executive Secretary, NSC) to National Security Council, December 20, 1949	27
Letter, President Truman to NSC Executive Secretary James Lay, April 12, 1950	28
Letter, President Truman to Secretary of State Acheson, July 19, 1950	29

Title	Document Number
Radio and TV Address, President Truman, April 8, 1952	71
Executive Order 10340, April 8, 1952	72
Youngstown Sheet & Tube Company et al. v. Charles Sawyer, June 2, 1952	73

III. NATIONAL SECURITY

    A. International Security

        1. Evolution of Foreign Policy Decisions

Radio Address, President Truman to San Francisco (United Nations) Conference, April 25, 1945	74
Memo, Secretary of War Henry Stimson to President Truman, July 19, 1945	75
Statement, Joint Declaration of Atomic Energy (United States, Great Britain, Canada), November 15, 1945	76
Protocol of the Proceedings of the Berlin (or Potsdam) Conference, August 1, 1945	77
Statement, President Truman, December 15, 1945	78
Speech, Secretary of State James Byrnes, February 28, 1946	79
Statement, Acting Secretary of State Dean Acheson, October 11, 1946	80
Address to Congress, President Truman, October 23, 1945	81
Address, President Truman, March 17, 1948	82
Special Message to Congress, President Truman, May 6, 1946	83
Statement, President Truman, October 17, 1946	84
Cable, George Kennan, February 22, 1946	85
Memo, Joseph Jones (State Department Official) to Assistant Secretary of State William Benton, February 26, 1947	86
Speech to Joint Session of Congress, President Truman, March 12, 1947	87
Special Message to Congress, President Truman, February 16, 1948	88
Memo, Joseph Jones (State Department Aide) to Mssrs. Harlik, Cleveland, Stokes, Stinebower, Ness, and Russell (State Department Officials), May 20, 1947	89

Title	Document Number
Commencement Address, Harvard University, Secretary of State George Marshall, June 5, 1947	90
Letter, President Truman to Chairmen of Congressional Committees, October 1, 1947	91
The Marshall Plan, April 2, 1948	92
FACC D-3, Policy Paper Approved by the Foreign Assistance Correlation Committee (Composed of Representatives from Department of State, the Department of Defense, and the Economic Cooperation Administration), February 7, 1949	93
PPS/50, Report by the Policy Planning Staff, Department of State, March 22, 1949	94
Draft Report, National Security Council Staff, March 30, 1949	95
Statement, Secretary of State Dean Acheson, March 18, 1949	96
North Atlantic Treaty (NATO), April 4, 1949	97
Special Message to Senate, President Truman, April 12, 1949	98
SANACC 360/11, Report by State-Navy-Air Force Coordinating Committee, August 18, 1948	99
Report to President, Special Committee of the National Security Council, March 2, 1949	100
Minutes, Policy Planning Staff, Department of State, October 12, 1949	101
Press Conference, President Truman, October 19, 1949	102
Memorandum, Carlton Savage (Policy Planning Staff, Dept. of State) and Robert Hooker (Associate Chief, Division of Eastern European Affairs, Dept. of State) to George Kennan (Director of Policy Planning Staff), November 14, 1949	103
Memorandum, Omar Bradley (Chairman, Joint Chiefs of Staff) to Secretary of Defense Louis Johnson, November 23, 1949	104
Report to the President, Special Committee of the National Security Council, January 31, 1950	105

Title	Document Number
Press Conference, President Truman, September 20, 1951	125

2. Expansion of the Power of the Intelligence Agencies

Staff Report, Senate Select Committee on Intelligence Activities, CIA Covert Action Authority, 1976	126
NSC Actions 7-12, November 14, 1947	127
Note, NSC Executive Secretary Sidney Souers to National Security Council, November 14, 1947	128
Memorandum, Secretary of State Dean Acheson to James Lay (Executive Secretary, NSC), October 26, 1950	129
Annexes to NSC 68/3, Report to the National Security Council by NSC Executive Secretary James Lay, December 8, 1950	130
Final Report, Senate Select Committee on Intelligence Activities, Program Branch 7, 1976	131
Press Conference, President Truman, July 26, 1951	132
Memo, CIA Director Walter B. Smith to the President, March 21, 1952	133
CIA Inspector General's Survey of the Office of Security CIA, Annex II, undated but written during the early 1960s	134
Statement and Report, Senator Frank Church, Chairman Senate Select Committee on Intelligence Activities, November 6, 1975	135
Final Report, Senate Select Committee on Intelligence Activities. Operation SHAMROCK, 1976	136
Letter, Secretary of the Treasury John Snyder to Bureau of Budget Director, June 8, 1948	137

B. Internal Security

1. The Federal Employee Loyalty/Security Program

Memo, FBI Director J. Edgar Hoover to Attorney General Tom Clark, July 25, 1946	138
Memo, Attorney General to FBI Director, July 31, 1946	139

Title	Document Number
Letter, Thomas Inglis (Office of Naval Intelligence) to A. Devitt Vanech (Chairman, the President's Temporary Commission on Employee Loyalty), January 8, 1947	140
Minutes, Temporary Commission, January 17, 1947	141
Memo, Attorney General Clark to Vanech, February 14, 1947	142
Memo for the Files, Stephen Spingarn (Treasury Department Representative on Temporary Loyalty Commission), February 20, 1947	143
Executive Order 9835, March 21, 1947	144
Letter, Harry Mitchell (President, U.S. Civil Service Commission) and Frances Perkins (Commissioner) to President Truman, April 25, 1947	145
Memo, Clark Clifford (Special Counsel to the President) to the President, May 7, 1947	146
Memo, Clark Clifford to President Truman May 9, 1947	147
Memo, David Edelstein and Joseph Duggan (Special Assistants to the Attorney General) to Assistant to the Attorney General Douglas McGregor, July 24, 1947	148
Letter, Attorney General J. Howard McGrath to Donald Dawson (Administrative Assistant to President Truman), December 23, 1949	149
Statement, President Truman, January 23, 1951	150
Memorandum, President Truman to Secretary of State Dean Acheson, January 3, 1953	151
Memorandum Secretary of State Acheson to President Truman, January 3, 1953	152
Letter, Donald MacPhail (Bureau of the Budget Assistant Director) to William Hopkins (White House Aide), August 25, 1950	153
Letter, President Truman to Robert Ramspeck (Chairman, Civil Service Commission), August 8, 1952	154

	Title	Document Number

INDEX